WHAT THE IRS DOESN'T WANT
YOU TO KNOW

WHAT THE
IRS
DOESN'T WANT YOU
TO KNOW

A CPA Reveals the Tricks of the Trade

Revised for 1997

MARTIN KAPLAN, CPA,
AND NAOMI WEISS

VILLARD · NEW YORK

Copyright © 1996, 1995, 1994 by Martin Kaplan, CPA, and Naomi Weiss

All rights reserved under International and Pan-American Copyright Conventions. Published in the United States by Villard Books, a division of Random House, Inc., New York, and simultaneously in Canada by Random House of Canada Limited, Toronto.

VILLARD BOOKS is a registered trademark of Random House, Inc.

This work was originally published as a trade paperback by Villard Books, a division of Random House, Inc., in 1994. A revised edition was published in 1995 by Villard Books, a division of Random House, Inc.

Library of Congress Cataloging-in-Publication Data

Kaplan, Martin.
What the IRS doesn't want you to know:
a CPA reveals the tricks of the trade / Martin Kaplan
and Naomi Weiss.—Rev. ed.
p.   cm.
Includes bibliographical references and index.
ISBN 0-679-77371-1
1. Tax administration and procedure—United States—Popular works.
2. Tax auditing—United States—Popular works. 3. Income tax—Law and legislation—United States—Popular works I. Weiss, Naomi. II. Title.
KF6300.Z9K37   1996
343.7305′2—dc20
[347.30352]   94-41874

Random House website address: http://www.randomhouse.com

Printed in the United States of America on acid-free paper

2 4 6 8 9 7 5 3
Second Revised and Updated Edition

I would like to dedicate this book to Harriet, my wife and best friend, for her love and unselfish support of all my endeavors, and for always being there for me. Also to Sharon, Jason, Hillary, and Bruce, children that any parent would be proud of. A special note to my new granddaughter, Lindsay: It's never too early to begin tax planning.

—MARTIN KAPLAN

During the time it took to write this book, one person consistently expanded my range of resources by tracking down information, photocopying, reading and rereading, double-checking calculations, performing financial analyses, and allowing me the privilege to work as I needed to. That person is my husband, William Halpern, and I dedicate this book to him.

—NAOMI WEISS

ACKNOWLEDGMENTS

I would like to thank Georgine Sargent, a CPA with quality skills and a sense of humor, for her patient copy editing in the book's early stages. Thank you also to George K. Greene, CLU, for being such a good sounding board, and Shelley Davis, IRS historian, for helping us get organized in the early stages of research.

The authors wish to acknowledge the publicity department at Villard Books for spreading the word about our unique message and how important this material is for every taxpayer.

—MARTIN KAPLAN

I wish to thank all the staff at the IRS who promptly answered my calls, mailed me information, and remained consistently courteous and patient, especially Sandy Byberg in the Statistics of Income office and those in the departments of Media Relations, Public Affairs, and Communications and Campaign Development. I especially want to thank David Burnham and Susan Long, cofounders of the Transactional Records Access Clearinghouse (TRAC) at Syracuse University, which gathers, disseminates, and makes available to the public detailed information about the enforcement and regulatory activities of federal agencies such as the IRS, the Department of Justice, the Environmental Protection Agency, and the Nuclear Regulatory Commission.

I also want to thank Chuck Rappaport for introducing us to Alan Weiner, CPA, and the crew at Holtz Rubenstein & Co., who gave us a wonderful head start.

ACKNOWLEDGMENTS

I also acknowledge my friend and neighbor Sondra Gregory for her ability to zoom in on all the minute details when proofreading the bibliography, footnotes, index, and galleys; and Dottie Hook for always being there despite being an ocean away.

Finally, I want to thank my daughter, Micayla, for her steadfast support, respect, and love, and for filling in where I couldn't be.

—NAOMI WEISS

CONTENTS

CONTENTS

CLOSE TO HOME

How the IRS really decides
whose return gets audited.

WHAT THE IRS DOESN'T WANT
YOU TO KNOW

1

Why Every Taxpayer Must Read This Book

Each year hundreds of reputable books are written about taxes, audits, and the Internal Revenue Service (IRS). No-nonsense, definitive, and powerful, the titles literally scream out ways that we can deal with the IRS: Fight, Win, Battle, Negotiate. Words such as *The Only* or *The Best* followed by *Audit, Tax Forms, Small Business*, or *Corporate Tax Guide Book You'll Ever Need* appear more than enough to guarantee results. Worried about the IRS, or in doubt about your personal tax situation? The confidence and warm cozy feelings titles such as these bring give a clear and unmistakable message to the taxpaying public: "Buy me," these books say, "and all of your tax problems will be resolved." So each year thousands of curious taxpayers buy these books, or select them off library shelves, hoping to discover the secret to keeping their tax payments low and their returns away from the scrutiny of the IRS.

Unfortunately, the information taxpayers really need to satisfy these goals rarely, if ever, surfaces. No matter how much information taxpayers read, hear, or research on the subject, they still remain easy targets for the IRS.

Isn't anyone aware of the self-generating scam that keeps taxpayers in semidarkness and the IRS ecstatic? There is a very specific group of people who are aware. They just aren't talking.

The time has come to deal with some clear-cut, shocking truths about what's behind the unsettling phenomenon that perpetually keeps blinders on the taxpaying public. This requires exploring the overall phenomenon, and then examining why those in the know have remained silent.

First the scam. Let's face facts: The IRS has a reputation for being big, tough (many would say vicious), and all-powerful. It is seen to have extensive manpower and technological resources, and the law is on its side. Taxpayers have never had a problem with being openly critical or highly vociferous about how they believe the IRS operates. Without the public's actually knowing what the IRS is and how the organization really works—or, perhaps more important, how it *doesn't* work—the IRS's reputation as the Big Bad Wolf continues to have a no-holds-barred grip on the public.

Millions of taxpayers live with the fear that one day an IRS agent will single out an item from their tax return, decide an audit is in order, and come after them. Fingering alleged cheaters and applying retribution is, after all, the acknowledgment IRS agents crave. In fact, the IRS is often referred to as an agency out of control—and with good reason. Once it selects its culprits, it chooses the punishment and proceeds to administer it with very little containment from any other governmental or nongovernmental agencies. So it's really not surprising that most taxpayers envision the IRS as harassing and abusing them, using its power in an uncaring and even brutal way to possibly destroy their careers and families.

Taxpayers' paranoid fears represent how enormously successful the IRS has been in creating its all-powerful-and-untouchable image. Furthermore, by sustaining these fears, the IRS maintains a status quo that actually prevents taxpayers from

- Questioning how much of the IRS's reputation is actually true.
- Considering why a never-ending body of information, designed by well-meaning authors and "tax experts" to help them pay less taxes and better manage the demands of the IRS, never genuinely helps them accomplish those goals.

Now let's talk about those who know exactly what is going on and find out why they aren't talking. Any good Certified Public Accountant (CPA) or tax professional knows how to beat the IRS at its own game. **But an unwritten law among tax professionals has traditionally prevented this vital information from being revealed publicly.** What is this law based on? It's based on tax professionals' healthy fear that the IRS will turn against them.

In practice, tax professionals, when filling out their clients' tax returns, use information they have gained as experts in their field. **But** these very same professionals do not traditionally disclose, in anything resembling a public forum, information in three crucial areas that can make a huge difference in the lives of the millions of taxpayers who aren't their clients:

1. What the IRS really is and how it operates, or, more precisely, *doesn't* operate.
2. Endless loopholes in our tax laws that can be used in the preparation of an individual tax return.
3. How *both* of these can be used consistently to benefit taxpayers.

Tax professionals have made it a practice NOT to reveal such information to the media—and with good reason: They've seen firsthand how people can be destroyed by both warranted and unwarranted IRS attacks. Why would CPA's, or any professionals in the tax field, put their lives, families, careers, and futures on the line? The answer to this question has traditionally prevented tax professionals from publicly explaining why the right kind of information never gets to the taxpaying public. It also keeps them from revealing that information on a broad scale.

So, to prevent an all-out personal conflagration and probably endless repercussions, tax professionals continue to offer whitewashed material that tells taxpayers how they can disappear from the IRS's view. In fact, much of this information is correct and does work. **But it is not the whole story. Too much information is left out for these guides to be helpful, and no one knows this better than the authors themselves.**

After almost 30 years as a CPA, I have consistently watched how the IRS can financially ruin all kinds of people: rich, middle-class, the average working family—people exactly like you.

In one horrendous case that attracted national attention, a middle-aged couple were undergoing a routine audit of a $70,000 art-lithograph tax shelter. The husband, an accountant by training, was a small real estate developer in Winston-Salem, North Carolina. The IRS examiner who audited the couple's return in 1979 said she would disallow the tax shelter. Three years later, the couple received a tax due notice from the IRS in the amount of $183,021. Although the notice arrived five months after the three-year statute of limitations on tax assessments had expired, the IRS insisted they had sent two earlier letters, including a notice of deficiency 20 days before the deadline.

For the next eight years, as their case was passed from one IRS officer to another, the couple exhausted their savings trying to prove that they owed nothing. Finally, in 1987, with a tax bill nearing $300,000, the case reached the

U.S. District Court. At the hearing, the judge granted the IRS a further delay to gather more evidence!

In June 1988, with a court date still months away, with no more money to pay for lawyers, and facing a loss of both his home and business, the husband walked behind his house, put a .38-caliber pistol in his mouth, and pulled the trigger.

Following the instructions that he left, the wife used the $250,000 she collected in life insurance to finance a lawsuit against the IRS. Finally, in court, the IRS revealed its certified mailing list, something the couple had fought for years to bring to someone's attention. Guess what? Some IRS clerical person, back in April 1983, had mistyped the couple's address. IRS notices that they were supposed to receive had been sent to the wrong place. A man's life was lost because of a typo!

The judge canceled the entire $289,282 tax deficiency and revoked the lien against the home. The family no longer owed the IRS anything. The IRS, however, owed the wife something, according to the judge—$27,971, the maximum allowed for legal fees at that time when a taxpayer sues the IRS.

So there you have it. The loss of a life over a clerical mistake. But this mistake was made by the IRS, an agency that knows no bounds, that functions without having to answer to anyone, and whose bureaucratic incompetence has no match.

Here's another case that demonstrates the blatant and unmitigated arrogance of the IRS.

A high-level executive in a nationally known insurance company was the subject of an extensive IRS investigation. Allegedly he owed $3,500. The taxpayer agreed to admit to tax evasion, and the IRS promised, in a written agreement, to keep the matter out of the public eye. When the executive informed his employer of his tax problem, he was told that the one thing he must avoid was a public scandal. Since the agreement with the IRS seemed to preclude this, the matter should have ended there. But it didn't. About three months into the investigation, the IRS issued to more than 21 sources news releases that included the taxpayer's name, his address, and the name of his employer. The taxpayer promptly lost his job, had to move out of town, and never again regained his prominent position.

Why was the IRS so interested in pursuing a case in which the tax liability was less than $3,500? The answer was revealed about two years later at a trial where the executive brought suit against the IRS. Here's what really happened:

Initially, when the taxpayer found out that the IRS was investigating him, he asked the agent assigned to the case what he had done wrong. He was told that his wife had made some bookkeeping errors in managing his records, resulting in the amount owed. However, according to a transcript from the trial, the real reason for the extensive investigation was that the IRS needed publicity. "The only publicity that is good for the IRS is when it brings a big one down," were the agent's words at the trial. Since the taxpayer was a prominent figure in his area, he satisfied that need. The agent admitted that he didn't think there was any real proof that the taxpayer even owed money to the IRS, but the kind of publicity that would be generated was exactly what the IRS was looking for.

In short, the entire investigation, which effectively destroyed the taxpayer's career and reputation, was actually a publicity stunt engineered by some IRS personnel!

I know many cases like these, but I have also come to learn and fully understand which words, style, techniques, and knowledge can effectively make the IRS come to an abrupt standstill.

In 1992 I took on a new corporate client, the president of a firm in the medical field, who began to receive incessant correspondence from the Social Security Administration saying that it had not received Wage and Tax Statements (W-2's) from his organization for 1989 and 1990. After going through the client's files, I found that the original W-2's for those years had, in fact, never been filed by the company's former accountant. It appeared that employees received their W-2 copies for those years, but the accompanying forms were never sent to the Social Security Administration.

On further exploration, I also discovered that the same accountant had not filled out or sent in to the IRS the Employer's Quarterly Federal Tax Returns (Form 941) with the payroll taxes, which include the withheld federal income tax and Social Security payments for those years. To bring this rather hard-to-believe and baffling mess to some kind of solution, I spent an entire day recreating the firm's liability and ended up with a shortfall of approximately $85,000. When I contacted the former accountant, he told me that he had prepared the quarterly forms and he sent them to me a month later.

At this point, I recommended the following course of action for my client: To file all the missing forms with the IRS and the Social Security Administration. To enclose a cover letter explaining that my client had, in fact, followed the directions of his former accountant and had no idea that the payroll tax payments were delinquent (which was true). To state in the letter that my client would pay any taxes and interest owed as soon as he could but that we would appreciate the abatement of penalties incurred.

Two issues are key here. First, failure to remit withheld taxes is a breach of fiduciary responsibility for which my client could have been held personally liable. Second, failure to file payroll taxes is one area that the IRS is very firm on; they want immediate payment, or else.

The IRS responded several weeks later, notifying my client that he owed over $100,000 in back payroll taxes and accumulated interest, and over $20,000 in penalties.

Now I had to negotiate a payment schedule with the IRS in an area where they traditionally refuse to negotiate. I filled out IRS Form 433-A (Collection Information Statement for Individuals) and Form 433-B (Collection Information Statement for Businesses), which detail personal and business assets and liabilities, and income and expenses. These forms are used by the IRS to determine a taxpayer's ability to make monthly payments of balances owed. Because my client's corporation was a service organization that represented manufacturers on a commission basis, the corporation had no inventory or accounts receivable on which the IRS could file a lien.

The revenue officer first insisted that my client sell his house, but the house already had an IRS lien against it owing to an ongoing four-year audit battle over a tax shelter presented on his 1984 personal return (another case of bad judgment by the former accountant). Next she insisted that my client immediately pay the $100,000 owed in back payroll taxes. She wanted him to sell his car, which would bring in only a few thousand dollars, and his second home in North Carolina, even though she knew that would bring barely enough to pay off the existing mortgage.

I knew my only chance was to put an offer on the table that she could not refuse. So I did. The taxpayer had just received a $35,000 payment from a customer, which gave me the leeway I needed. We would give the IRS $25,000 immediately and the balance of $75,000 payable in equal installments over a five-month period. In return, she promised to abate most of the $20,000 in penalties as being attributable to the negligence of the former accountant.

What had I gained for my client? I was able to prove conclusively that the nonpayment of payroll taxes was due to the incompetence and poor judgment of the company's former accountant, thereby freeing my client from any fiduciary responsibility. Concurrent with this explanation of "reasonable cause," the revenue officer agreed to waive the penalties for failure to file the payroll taxes in a timely manner. She also waived the negligence penalty equal to 100 percent of the tax. We negotiated a payment schedule that fully satisfied my client's time and monetary restraints, allowing him use of his bank accounts and ensuring no interruption in the flow of his business. Furthermore, my client's customers and staff never knew he was in trouble with the IRS. It was business as usual.

Over the years, as I continued to witness the seemingly uncontrollable behavior of the IRS juxtaposed against taxpayer successes such as the one I just described (and there are lots more of them), I realized that I could no longer keep silent.

I have been collecting the information contained in this book for years. Am I afraid of repercussions from the IRS? Yes. But this information is too important *not* to be told. The value of the assistance it can bring to every U.S. taxpayer will, I hope, minimize my risk.

In *What the IRS Doesn't Want You to Know* I will

- Tell taxpayers why they have been kept in the dark for so many years.
- Present a point of view that can make taxpayers more powerful than they ever thought possible.
- Give the taxpaying public new information, legal and legitimate, that is traditionally only presented by CPA's to clients in low voices and behind closed doors.
- Let taxpayers know *in advance* what they need to watch out for and how to protect themselves from new IRS onslaughts.

This information will allow taxpayers to

- View the IRS from an entirely new and realistic perspective.
- Learn how to use glitches, crevices, and loopholes in our tax laws to their benefit.
- Recognize the shortfalls of the IRS so that the scales of justice are tipped in the taxpayers' favor.

I have decided to make this information available so that you, the average taxpayer, can be armed with the same tools of the trade that I use every day. Don't you think it's about time? Through step-by-step explanations, never-before-told facts, and case studies, you will learn how to use these tools to

- Avoid an audit.
- Minimize your tax assessment.
- Dramatically improve your business and tax situation, especially if you are self-employed, a service provider, or an independent contractor.
- Increase your tax-deductible expenses without drawing attention to your return.
- Dramatically reduce your personal tax liabilities by learning little-known techniques used in the tax trade.
- Make the IRS consistently work for you, once and for all reversing a long-standing trend.

These commonsense tools, rarely divulged to the average taxpayer, represent specific legal steps you can take to shield yourself from the far-reaching clutches of the IRS.
It's rare to find this information anywhere else, even if the titles of a bevy of books suggest that they contain it. They don't.

Furthermore, the attitude that only wealthy individuals, those who hire expensive tax attorneys or those in the know, can avail themselves of aggressive tax information is false. Anyone has the right to receive the same kind of information and advice on how to best handle the demands of the IRS, particularly the average taxpayer. **No one is too small to DEAL SUCCESSFULLY with the long, powerful, and often ruthless and arbitrary arm of the IRS.**

I intend to set taxpayers free by offering them a brand-new foundation from which they can deal with the IRS, one based on expert knowledge never before revealed publicly. For example, did you know the following?

- Despite spending billions of dollars, most of the technological advances the IRS predicted for the year 2000 will not happen.
- In 1994 the IRS restated its statistical tables back to 1988, in effect raising the percentage of audited returns higher than it actually is.
- Each year the IRS loses files on which audits have commenced; the audit is then abruptly terminated.
- Travel and entertainment are still the first areas that are examined by an IRS auditor, because a partial disallowance of deductions is virtually certain.
- The IRS has a tough time locating original tax returns within its system.
- You should never represent yourself at an IRS audit. Such an ego trip usually ends up costing taxpayers dearly.

With this information, and a great deal more like it, taxpayers will not only have a fighting chance in dealing with the IRS but can actually come out winners.

Now, let's enter a CPA's inner sanctum, a place most taxpayers are not privy to.

Over time it has become customary for tax professionals to "grade" their clients. Clients who have made the grade from the tax professional's view pay less taxes, are rarely audited, and have more money in their pockets. I would venture to say that in our profession we deal with three types of clients. Let's call them Type A, Type B, and Type C. Here's how this works.

Type A are the "good" clients. A good client is a person who heeds the professional's advice most of the time, but especially when the professional presents the advice in the form of a strong recommendation. The ideas presented in this book are strong recommendations and nothing irks a tax professional more than when a client doesn't follow strong recommendations and ends up paying higher taxes or, worse, is audited.

Let's skip Type B clients for a moment and discuss Type C. Type C clients, because of their difficult behavior and negative attitudes, are at the bottom of the totem pole. The fee that they are charged is never commensurate with the time that is spent with them, both at face-to-face meetings or on the telephone. They are usually terrible listeners who refuse to hear much-needed information, which must therefore be continually repeated. Type C's often argue against the recommended course of action because they usually have a know-it-all mentality. Type C's also receive the greatest number of notices from the IRS, simply because they do not follow the tax professional's instructions. In short, a Type C client causes the professional the greatest amount of aggravation, the professional earns the lowest hourly rate, and, as you would expect, Type C's are usually the first to complain that the bill is too high.

Type B represents all the other clients who don't fit into Type A or C categories. As you might suspect, the majority of people are Type B's. Although Type B's aggravate you once in a while, they may overcome this by paying bills promptly. They may complain a lot, but they may also be a source of client referrals.

The dilemma faced by tax professionals concerning their client base should be becoming clear to you: Wouldn't it be great if we could drop Type C's from our client roll, and have Type B's gradually mend their ways and work themselves up to Type A's? But, alas, this is a tax professional's fantasy. In reality, clients do drop down from Type A or B to become a Type C, but a Type B or C rarely moves up to become a Type A.

Now that you are aware of this aspect of the tax business, I'd like you to benefit as fully as possible from it by incorporating what you have just discovered into your own thinking and behavior from this moment on, **while you are reading this book.** Here's how.

Most of the advice, recommendations, and tips contained in *What the IRS Doesn't Want You to Know* have not been made available to the average taxpayer before. Therefore, to receive the full value of what I am revealing, you need to respond like a Type A client. In fact, I'd like each of you to become a Type A client by the time you have completed this book. The closer you come to being a Type A client, the easier it will be for you to understand how your own thinking and behavior can positively or negatively affect how your return will ultimately be handled by the IRS. **Behaving like a Type A or B instead of a Type C client can actually make the difference between an unnoticed return or an audit.** Here's what I mean:

A Type C client, Mr. Richards, came to me with a problem. He had received a fee of $35,000, for which the payer issued a 1099-Misc form (Miscellaneous Income) listing him as the recipient. Mr. Richards claimed that the fee was actually earned by his son. I suggested that he contact the payer of the fee and obtain a revised 1099 in his son's name. Without any further explanation, Mr. Richards said that wasn't the solution. Instead, he asked me if he should prepare a 1099 in his son's name showing that he paid the $35,000 to his son, acting as the boy's agent. I strongly advised against this course of action. If this were noticed and subsequently questioned, the IRS would ask for full documentation, including a contractual agreement and canceled checks. But Mr. Richards, acting like the perfect Type C, insisted that he knew better and refused to heed my advice. I knew it would be useless to argue further. He prepared the 1099 form showing the $35,000 payment to his son.

Six months later, when the IRS detected the existence of two apparently related 1099 forms, both belonging to Mr. Richards, they contacted him and, not satisfied with his explanation, proceeded with a full-scale audit. The audit encompassed all of Mr. Richards's personal and corporate activities, which were substantial, since he was a highly paid executive. An audit lasting more than three years culminated with Mr. Richards's paying the IRS $140,000 in tax, interest, and penalties, plus $25,000 in accounting and legal fees. To this day, Mr. Richards still insists that he knows best, and his behavior has not changed one iota, despite the fact that if he had listened to me in the first place, I could have made his life a lot easier and saved him thousands of dollars.

Finally, there is one ability that average taxpayers cannot acquire on their own, but is crucial for them to have: **the ability to understand how the IRS thinks, operates, and responds.** This is definitely something you as a taxpayer want to learn about and put into practice, yet it is rarely, if ever, made available.

In my interactions with countless clients and the IRS, a great deal of unofficial information surfaces that is often more important than a specific tax law. **In fact, quite often what is most important is not what a tax law says, but how the IRS interprets and acts on it.** This knowledge, which tax pros gain from years of working in the field and interacting at all levels with the IRS, is what enables them to complete your return and know how the IRS will respond to each individual item recorded. This is the kind of information I will be revealing in this book. Here is a typical case:

Early in 1991, a Mr. Gruen, who owned an exporting business, came to me for the preparation of his 1990 tax return. In reviewing his file, I saw that both his 1988 and 1989 returns had been audited. On the basis of what I knew about how the IRS thinks, it seemed to me that the audits were triggered by two items: First, Mr. Gruen's gross income for each year was over $100,000, which in itself increases the chances of an audit. Second, in both years Mr. Gruen claimed about 30 percent of his gross income, an unusually large amount, for entertainment, auto expenses, and travel, as reported on his Schedule C, Profit or Loss from Business (Sole Proprietorship). IRS regulations require anyone who is an unincorporated sole proprietor to file this schedule.

I knew that my approach would have to be based on presenting Mr. Gruen's expenses from one perspective: in case he were audited. Any good CPA employs this kind of thinking automatically, but in this case it was more crucial because of the two previous audits. In addition, I had to eliminate, or reframe, whatever I could that had been previously questioned.

When my client and I set to work examining his business diary for 1990, one thing consistently kept showing up: Meal expenses on most days were for breakfast, lunch, and dinner. There is a rather obscure IRS regulation that some meals must be considered personal in nature. In other words, the IRS does not take kindly to three meals a day taken as a business expense. Mr. Gruen was operating under the illusion that because these meals were business expenses, he would be able to reduce his overall tax bill by listing them that way. But he did *not* know that he was treading upon a favorite IRS attention getter: entertainment expenses.

I told my client about this regulation and promptly reduced Mr. Gruen's business-related meals to two a day. To offset this loss, I also told him of another IRS regulation that would allow him to expense meals *under* $25 *without a receipt* if his business diary noted the person, place, and date of the meal, along with a brief description of what was discussed. With these additional diary entries, entertainment expense was back to its previous total, but because of the way it was presented on his return (and in backup material), I knew he would be safe if he were audited. I also insisted that my client substantiate every entertainment item *above* $25 with a receipt or canceled check, a practice he had previously been lax about.

Next Mr. Gruen's business diary showed $10,000 for out-of-pocket expenses but only $6,000 worth of checks made payable to himself. With his history, I knew the IRS would grab this in a flash. With a little investigation, I uncovered the source of the missing $4,000—cash gifts from his parents made during the year. In this case I used as documentation a section from the *Internal Revenue Code (IR Code)* that allows each taxpayer to personally give $10,000 annually to any other person without filing a gift tax return. Now we could prove the source of the $4,000, and best of all, gifts of this nature are *nontaxable*. However, to clear him even further, I advised my client to have his parents write and sign a one-sentence letter that documented the fact that they had given him the money during the year as a gift.

Finally, to save Mr. Gruen from ever having to file a Schedule C again, where his entertainment, automobile, and travel expenses would be placed under continued scrutiny, I strongly recommended that he change his business from a sole proprietorship to a new small business corporation, an S corporation. By doing this, Mr. Gruen accomplished the following: He substantially reduced his chances of being audited (i.e., his $100,000 in personal income would not light up the IRS computers). As an S corporation, he had available to him new techniques for reducing Social Security costs that he didn't have as a sole proprietor. And he had all the other advantages of being incorporated (e.g., limited liability to creditors). The end result was exactly what I had hoped for: Mr. Gruen's personal and business tax returns since 1990 have not been selected for audit by the IRS.

YOUR TAX-SAVING STRATEGY.

As of September 30, 1995, the IRS no longer requires receipts for business travel and entertainment unless the expense exceeds $75.

Now, I have two requests of all taxpayers who read this book. First, I would like you to extract from the material all the points that have some relevance to your own situation. Then bring these points to the attention of your tax professional and ask for comments. If your tax professional says, for example, that you are too small to become an S corporation, ask for specific reasons to support that conclusion. If you are not satisfied with the response, find another pro for a second opinion.

My second request can be applied only after you have finished reading. When that time arrives, go back to your tax professional and ask what it will take to make you a Type A client. Encourage your tax pro to let you know how successful you have been in following his or her advice. I'm sure he or she can pull some specific examples out of the files. Walk through one or two together to assess how your behavior held up. Were you cooperative? Did you listen carefully? Follow instructions? As a result of your way of responding to your tax professional's advice, did you gain a stronger tax position, or end up with a loss that could have been avoided?

If your tax professional claims that he or she doesn't know what a Type A client is, tell that person to read this book.

A note on IRS statistics: As we went to press, the most recent source of IRS statistics was the advance draft of the *IRS 1995 Data Book*, which the IRS publishes later and later each year.

2

The IRS Personality:
Playing It to Your Advantage

Each of us who pays taxes to the U.S. government is involved in a relationship with the IRS. The good news is that we have choices for influencing how that relationship will turn out. We can behave like sheep, following IRS dictates and threats as if they were gospel. We can take a middle-of-the-road approach and, amidst our complaints, begin to ask why and how the IRS does what it does. Or we can choose to work with and beat the IRS from a sound foundation built upon experience, knowledge, and an understanding of who the IRS is and how it operates.

Imagine that you've just met someone new and that you're very interested in finding out what that person is like. Naturally, you're curious about family history, aspirations, career, and key incidents that have shaped that person's life. You can use the same principle of learning what you can about someone to become familiar with the IRS.

EVENTS THAT SHAPED THE IRS PERSONALITY

I believe it is time for taxpayers to recognize that the IRS is an entity with a distinct personality that affects you each time you fill out your tax return.

The significant events that make the IRS what it is today are clear-cut and straightforward. Through these the IRS personality unfolds.

THE EVENT: Establishing the Right to Collect Taxes
THE PERSONALITY: Stubborn. Tenacious. Undaunted.

Significance to Taxpayers

The U.S. government's privilege to levy taxes was incorporated into the Constitution in 1787. The responsibility for creating the machinery for collecting taxes was given to the Treasury Department (where it has remained ever since), under the supervision of the assistant to the secretary of the Treasury. In 1792 that position was replaced with the Office of the Commissioner of Revenue.

By 1817 the issue of taxes was abandoned because the government's revenue needs were met by customs duties (taxes on imports). The outbreak of the Civil War forty-five years later and the government's need for massive financing led to President Lincoln's signing the Revenue Act of July 1, 1862, establishing (actually re-establishing) the Office of the Commissioner of Internal Revenue via a legislative act in which the commissioner was to be nominated by the president and approved by the Senate. The IRS was officially born.

The following table charts the tax revenues in key years, starting with the first year tax was collected on a formal basis until the present time. This two-century span shows a great deal more than numbers on a page. Stretches of stability and the depths of a country's economic depression are reflected here. So, too, are the strife and nationalistic fervor of war years, the growing pangs of a new nation, and periodic transitions as the U.S. moved from an agriculture-based economy to an industrial one. When the government's need for more income suddenly escalated, usually as a result of a war, taxes on products and/or income were imposed. Probably most impressive are the enormous sums the IRS has collected during our lifetimes.

Fiscal Year	Revenue Collected
1792	$208,943
1814	$3,882,482
1863	$41,003,192
1866	$310,120,448
1900	$295,316,108
1917	$809,393,640
1918	$3,698,955,821
1932	$1,557,729,043
1941	$7,370,108,378
1944	$40,121,760,232
1965	$114,434,633,721

Fiscal Year	Revenue Collected
1970	$195,722,096,497
1980	$519,375,273,361
1991	$1,086,851,401,000
1992	$1,120,799,588,000
1993	$1,176,685,625,000
1994	$1,276,466,776,000
1995	$1,375,731,835,000

Source: Shelley L. Davis, *IRA Historical Fact Book: A Chronology, 1646–1992* (Washington, D.C.: U.S. Government Printing Office, 1992), Appendix 3, pp. 245–47. The figures from 1992 on are from the *IRS 1992 Annual Report*, p. 25, and the advance drafts of the *IRS 1993–94 Data Book* and the *IRS 1995 Data Book*, Table 1.

How Taxes Are Raised Without Taxpayers' Noticing

Tax Bracket Creep

Congress, together with the IRS, continues to introduce new taxation policies to keep up with changing times.

One phenomenon that increases taxes without a change in tax law is tax bracket creep.

Until 1986, there were 15 tax brackets into which taxpayers could fall on the basis of taxable income. The lowest bracket started at $2,390 and the highest was $85,130 and over. Each year, owing to inflation, our taxable income typically increases. This increase eventually puts us into a new, higher tax bracket, forcing us to pay higher taxes. Voilà! This takes place without any change whatsoever in the tax law. Although currently there are only five tax brackets instead of 15, the principles of bracket creep remain the same.

Softening the blow of tax bracket creep are cost-of-living increases in the bracket ranges, designed to prevent you from creeping upward into the next-higher bracket. For example, a married person with taxable income of $38,000 was in the 15 percent tax bracket in 1995. His taxable income increased to $40,000 in 1996, but he remained in the 15 percent bracket because the top of the 15 percent range was raised from $39,000 in 1995 to $40,100 in 1996.

Isolated Ploys Raise Taxes

A strong focus of the 1990 tax bill, referred to as OBRA '90 (Omnibus Budget Reconciliation Act), enacted under President George Bush's administration, was to reduce the budget deficit. Accordingly, it contained a strict requirement that any money going out of the Treasury (for new spending programs, weapons, foreign aid, research) be replaced by money coming in, from new sources of revenue or revenue gained from cuts in existing programs. Now, you know that in an election year, the party in power will do all it can *not* to raise taxes and not to cut programs. So the question was where to get the new sources of revenue, or how to cut existing programs without too much resistance from voters.

The answer, which Congress and the IRS know only too well, is to create new ways of raising funds that actually go *unnoticed* by the taxpaying public. Here is an example. When the Bush administration extended unemployment benefits—a laudable measure—where was the money, about $2 billion, supposed to come from? From pension fund distributions. Beginning on January 1, 1993, anyone taking a lump-sum distribution from his or her corporate pension was subject to a 20 percent withholding tax. Many people who leave companies before 59½ years of age prefer to take their corporate pension, on which taxes aren't paid, in a lump sum rather than keep it with their company until they retire. By taking it this way they keep the money under their control—they determine the monthly payout, they're certain that they will receive it, and they don't have to worry about companies going bankrupt or investing their money unwisely.

Let's assume that your distribution entitled you to $100,000, which you took in 1996 (you actually held the check *payable to you* for the full or partial amount in your hands). Twenty percent, or $20,000, was withheld and you received only $80,000.

Now, the $100,000 had to be rolled over into *another tax-exempt qualified plan*, such as an IRA, within 60 days if you wanted to avoid paying tax. But since you did not have the $20,000 that was withheld, that shortfall is considered taxable income. **You may also be subject to a 10 percent early-withdrawal penalty.** (As most taxpayers know, the actual penalty amount is based on age restrictions. With a pension plan or an IRA, a penalty is usually incurred if you withdraw money before the age of 59½. Anytime between 59½ and 70½, you may start drawing out your pension dollars without penalty. At 70½ you *must* begin taking some benefits.) (For an update, see New Tax Legislation for 1996, page 275.)

How many taxpayers do you suppose know that this 20 percent tinkering around was earmarked to fund the unemployment extension? How many also realize that all Congress did in this case was create an illusion that it was paying for unemployment benefits without increasing the deficit? In fact, the $2.1 billion expected for 1993 never fully materialized. It all boiled down to an accounting gimmick that simultaneously produced several loopholes for avoiding the tax altogether.[1]

Taxation Through Lifetime Exclusions

Here's another situation being studied by President Clinton; the aim is to manipulate a tax entitlement called "lifetime exclusion" so that more assets of a person's estate are taxable.

Each U.S. citizen is entitled to a $600,000 lifetime exclusion for taxable gifts made or for assets left in an estate, which means that the first $600,000 of assets in an estate are free from being taxed. As for gifts made during your lifetime, if you give $50,000 to each of your four children above the annual exclusion of $10,000 per person, you deplete $200,000 of your lifetime exclusion, which leaves only a $400,000 exclusion for the assets of your estate. Of course, the gift and estate tax laws that contain lifetime exclusion provisions are voluminous, and there are countless loopholes. Working out the best deal is a job for a good estate planner, but for our purposes, I have given a simple example.

Tax experts thought that part of President Clinton's 1993 tax legislation would include a reduction in the lifetime estate and gift tax exclusion, from $600,000 down to possibly $300,000. Other possible changes could have been made in the gift tax provision by reducing the annual exclusion of $10,000 per person or by limiting the amount one may give. None of these was included in RRA 1993, but in 1994 they resurfaced as part of President Clinton's effort to provide funding for U.S. health care legislation. Like many other proposals, no changes will come in this area until the next big wave of tax reform arrives sometime in 1997.

Phasing Out Itemized Deductions and Personal Exemptions

Itemized deductions, listed on Schedule A, Form 1040, are a group of expenditures you are entitled to deduct from your adjusted gross income that reduce your taxable income. Some examples are home mortgage interest, real estate taxes, state and local taxes, and charitable contributions.

An exemption is not an expenditure but an amount of your income not subject to taxation at all, for example, a certain amount of income for each dependent. The effect of exemptions is also to reduce taxable income.

Beginning January 1, 1991, in a nifty new way to pick taxpayers' pockets, itemized deductions started to be phased out. (Excluded are medical expenses, investment interest, and casualty and theft losses, which each have their own unique limitations.)

It begins with your Adjusted Gross Income (AGI), which is a collection of all income items less a small number of adjustments to income, such as the deductions for self-employed pension deductions (Keogh plans) and alimony. AGI is typically the last line of page 1 of Form 1040 (U.S. Individual Income Tax Return).

If your AGI is more than $117,950 (married, filing jointly, or single), the IRS can disallow, or increase your taxable income by, as much as 80 percent of your total itemized deductions, at the worst leaving you just 20 percent. Working in real numbers, things might look like this. For the year 1996, Jay and Sharon Jennings have these itemized deductions:

Real estate and state income taxes	$15,000
Contributions to charities	2,000
Mortgage interest on their home	15,000
Total	$32,000

If their combined AGI for 1996 is $167,950, it means that $1,500 of their deductions is lost ($167,950 − $117,950 × .03), leaving net deductions on Schedule A of $30,500.

If they had a combined AGI of $267,950 and the same starting deductions, then they would lose $4,500 of their deductions ($267,950 − $117,950 × .03), leaving net deductions on Schedule A of $27,500.

In short, the more you earn, the more you lose in itemized deductions. Where does the money from this loss on itemized deductions go? It goes out of the taxpayers' pockets into the government's hands. Or, to phrase it positively, out of the goodness of Congress's heart, no matter how high your AGI is, you can keep 20 percent of your itemized deductions.

At the same time the phaseouts for itemized deductions were initiated, a new barrage of phaseouts involving personal exemptions was introduced.

A personal exemption is a deduction determined by law annually that reduces your taxable income. Personal exemptions are taken on Form 1040 and usually include the taxpayer, the taxpayer's spouse, and anyone else who meets the *Internal Revenue Code* dependency and support requirements. These phaseouts start at $176,950 for married couples filing jointly and $117,950 for singles. When the AGI exceeds the threshold level, the taxpayer loses 2 percent of the total exemption amount for every $2,550 or fraction thereof for AGI that exceeds the threshold.

Thus, for example, when your AGI reaches $124,951 more than your AGI threshold of $176,950 (or $117,950), you lose 100 percent of your personal exemptions.

Mathematically it works like this: $124,950 ÷ $2,550 = 49. 49 × 2 percent = 98 percent. The extra $1 over $124,950 causes 49 to become 50.

This multiplied by 2 percent equals 100 percent of lost exemptions. This is clearly a three-Excedrin explanation, so let's look at it again.

Carl and Judy Jimson file jointly and their AGI for 1996 is $240,700. They have three children and claim five exemptions, each one worth $2,550. Subtracting the $176,950 threshold from the $240,700 leaves $63,750. Dividing $63,750 by $2,550 equals 25. Multiplying 25 by 2 percent gives a 50 percent loss of exemptions. Because of the phaseout, the Jimsons' deduction for their five exemptions will be slashed in half—from $12,750 to $6,375.

But wait. It could be worse. Suppose the Jimsons had $5 more added on to their AGI. Under the phaseouts, they would lose another 2 percent of their total exemptions, or an extra $255 in deductions down the drain. The temporary phaseouts of both personal exemptions and itemized deductions were made a permanent part of our tax law with RRA '93.

So be prepared. Taxation policy is going to get more intricate, more sly, and more creative as it subtly reduces the income it lets you keep.

THE EVENT: Income Tax Becomes a Favorite Child
THE PERSONALITY: As stubborn, tenacious, and unmoving as the government's right to levy and collect taxes. Also highly effective. You'll find it shifty, unfair, and subject to changing times. But be aware that it is flexible and workable as well.

Significance to Taxpayers
The Sixteenth Amendment, which was passed on February 3, 1913, states:

> The Congress shall have the power to lay and collect taxes on incomes, from whatever source derived, without apportionment among the several states, and without regard to any census or enumeration.

This amendment made it legal for Congress to impose a direct tax on the net incomes of both individuals and corporations, overruling an 1895 Supreme Court ruling that asserted that the income tax was unconstitutional because it was a direct tax rather than one apportioned among the states on the basis of population.

The right of Congress to levy an income tax, and the right of the IRS, as part of the U.S. Treasury Department, to collect taxes, periodically comes under fire from people who believe, mistakenly, that these functions are illegal or who fall prey to tax evasion schemes.

Do not be fooled by the latest: a variety of "tax kits," costing anywhere from $900 to $2,000, that promote the bogus philosophy that individuals are not part of the United States or aren't taxpayers, as defined by the federal tax code, but sovereign entities.[2] A sovereign entity is someone who exercises supreme authority within a limited sphere. Have no doubt, no matter how many dependents these kits recommend you take (often up to 98), or how many W-4 forms (Withholding Exemption Certificate), W-8 forms (Certificate of Foreign Status), "Affidavits of Citizenship and Domicile," or "Affidavits of Claims for Exemption and Exclusion from Gross Income of Remuneration, Wages, and Withholding" they include, any sucker who tries will eventually discover that the IRS is much more sovereign than you or I. A U.S. citizen is subject to U.S. law, and that includes paying taxes.

Following its passage, the income tax very quickly became the favorite of the federal government, producing more revenue than anyone could ever have thought possible. One writer observes, "during World War II . . . the individual income tax, in one of the most significant developments in American fiscal history, surpassed all other sources of revenue of the federal government."[3]

Despite its past and current inequalities, the goal of the income tax is to establish a close connection between a person's income and his or her ability to pay taxes. In theory, a progressive income tax aims to ensure that those with a greater ability pay more taxes than those who earn less. In reality, things don't work that way. The rich hire the best tax lawyers and accountants, which works to shift the taxpaying burden downward. Since the poor have little ability to pay any taxes at all, the tax burden tends to fall on the middle class, thus undermining the theory.

As Americans, we are allowed to express opinions about the income tax. Once we express them, however, the numbers speak for themselves. In 1980, out of a total of over $519 billion in federal revenues collected (gross dollars), 55.4 percent, or over $287 billion, came from individual income taxes.[4] By 1993, that figure rose to almost $586 billion, and in 1995 it was almost $676 billion.[5] Income tax dollars continue to represent over 50 percent of federal revenues collected—the largest piece of the pie.

But don't give up completely on finding a way to use the income tax to your advantage. Because income tax continues to be a function of who you are and how you earn your money, there is room within its bounds to determine how you report that income.

In 1994 (the latest calendar year for which the following figures are available), the IRS Statistics of Income Office reported that out of approximately 116.1 million individual tax returns, 99.8 million indicated salaries or wages earned. Taxpayers in this group are typically more limited in how they report income than the 15.8 million who filed as sole proprietorships and the 1.5 million who filed as partnerships during the same year. (Choices regarding income tax reporting for straight wage earners do exist, and will be discussed further on.)

The basis of our system of taxation lies in something the IRS likes to call compliance. I'd like you to view compliance as having two components: **Part of compliance relies on the honor system and the other part relies on knowing how to report what you earn so that your return goes unnoticed by the IRS.** Accomplishing this goal will render your return audit-proof, and that's the goal you want to achieve. You'll learn how as you read on.

THE EVENT: Rise of Lobbying and Special Interest Groups
THE PERSONALITY: Highly focused, egotistical, selfish, forceful, frenzied, calculating, and determined to the point of being obnoxious. Can also be extremely vociferous, well connected, and generally very organized.

Significance to Taxpayers

Politics and tax-making policy were intricately and inseparably intertwined when reviving the income tax became a cause célèbre at the turn of the century. Immediately after the income tax law became official in 1913, affecting both individuals and corporations, the IRS scurried to organize a Personal Income Tax Division and create a structure to handle the instant rush of telephone calls and correspondence.

Simultaneously, virtually every business trade association set up a tax committee or hired a full-time person to keep abreast of tax changes.[6]

So what was intended to be a discreet, rather insular process performed by the House and Senate was gradually transformed into a kind of free-for-all through which politicians, political parties, businesses, and private interest groups exerted their own brand of influence.

Once begun, these influences quickly became so widely accepted as part of tax-making policy that whenever a tax bill was in the process of becoming a law, widespread lobbying efforts were a given. Though they probably never realize it, millions of taxpayers are affected.

Although one likes to believe that there are some principles left in the tax-making process, there is no doubt that organized interests are at the origin of most tax provisions. There is some pluralism here, some interest group bargaining there, some special versus general interest over here, some politics of principle over there, some sacred cow pleading its cause to attentive ears in that corner, some politics of indignation in another one, some strange bedfellows over there, someone tuning his political antenna over here, and so on.[7]

Today it is the norm for Congress to be consistently bombarded with hordes of lobbyists representing individuals, corporations, foreign governments, and trade associations representing diverse industries (agriculture, oil, banking, real estate, dairy), all demonstrating why tax laws should be structured to accommodate their special needs.

Although this might sound like a more modern, democratic way of having the American people influence the voting, unfortunately it usually isn't. What happens is that the groups with the greatest financial resources, who are well connected, have greater access to the media, are savvy in the communications process, are the more powerful, and they win out over the rest. The end result doesn't usually benefit most taxpayers. Here's an example:

Remember that old thing called the lemon law? That was the one under which millions of used-car buyers would be protected by a Federal Trade Commission (FTC) ruling developed in the late 1970's in case the used car he or she purchased turned out to have defects. Guess which lobby group was vehemently opposed to that law? That's right, used-car dealers who had to make known to their customers any defects they knew of in the cars they offered for sale. In 1980, Congress passed a law permitting Congress to veto FTC rules like the lemon law, and so the used-car dealers went to work. Their principal instrument was the political action committee (PAC) formed in 1972 by the National Automobile Dealers Association (NADA). A PAC is one of the organized routes through which interest groups collect money, which is then contributed to targeted politicians. After a slow start, the NADA PAC grew explosively. By 1976 its collections had swelled to over $368,000, which it distributed in gifts of memorable size among 270 candidates—half the entire Congress.

Four years later, after Congress acquired veto power over FTC rules, the NADA PAC's 1980 contributions virtually tripled, breaking the million-dollar mark. Throughout 1981 and 1982 as Congress readied itself to vote on the lemon-rule veto, the NADA PAC continued to pour forth further campaign contributions.

Here is a typical sequence of events, involving Republican Congressman Mickey Edwards of Oklahoma City:
- August 19, 1981—Congressman Edwards receives a $2,500 campaign contribution from the NADA PAC, even though it's not an election year.
- September 22, 1981—Congressman Edwards signs up as cosponsor of the resolution killing the FTC used-car lemon law, in keeping with NADA's strong wishes.
- October 19, 1981—Congressman Edwards receives an additional $200 campaign contribution from the NADA PAC.
- May 26, 1982—Congressman Edwards votes for a resolution killing the FTC used-car rule.
- September 30, 1982—Congressman Edwards receives an added $2,000

contribution from the NADA PAC, bringing the total he had received from that PAC since 1979 to $8,100.[8]

THE EVENT: Tax-Making Policy Permanently Changed

THE PERSONALITY: Capricious and easily swayed, leading to favoritism and inequities. Grows increasingly more complex each year but offers substantial rewards to those who can decipher and manipulate the ins and outs.

Significance to Taxpayers

The Constitution states that a tax or revenue bill must be introduced in the House of Representatives. In making this determination, our Founding Fathers created a direct link between the creation of tax laws and the American people who directly elect members of the House. The actual step-by-step process was a clear-cut, sound model. But the rise of interest groups, which created a new set of linkages between government and its citizens, altered that model by opening up and actually distorting the process. As concessions or exceptions became introduced into our tax law because of pressure from a special interest group, innocent taxpayers got caught in the cross fire. Now we are forced to reckon with three types of tax traps:

- Tax laws that favor one segment of the population over another.
- An increase in the complexity of our tax laws.
- A rapidly expanding number of loopholes for avoiding or manipulating tax laws.

Each of these has a tremendous impact on taxpayers and their pocketbooks.

Tax Laws Play Favorites

A recent case of unmistakable favoritism is connected with the Tax Reform Act of 1986 (TRA '86), which in over 500 pages tried to ensure that tax shelters were on their way to extinction. Why is this issue so important to Congress and the IRS?

In the early seventies, tax shelters began to become a favored device of many to pay less taxes. A tax shelter is a way to protect your money from being touched by the IRS. (The politically correct manner to refer to this is "reducing your tax liability.")

Essentially the tax shelter generated tax benefits in the form of investment tax credits, depreciation, and business losses, which allowed taxpayers to save more in taxes than they had invested in the shelter. The person investing in the tax shelter became a *passive investor*—he or she had no say in the management of the actual operation of the investment; the investments became known as *passive investments;* and losses were referred to as *passive losses.*

Once they caught on, tax shelters couldn't be stopped, and through the 1970's and into the '80's they grew geometrically, from $5 billion to $10 billion to $25 billion in write-offs.

Eventually the IRS was successful in pressuring Congress to include in the TRA '86 a series of new tax laws that eventually outlawed most tax shelters (passive investments)—with one exception: **Taxpayers could continue to direct their money into tax shelters involving oil and gas investments.**

By now you can most likely figure out who and what was behind this exception—that's right, a well-organized, well-connected, and especially strong oil and gas lobby.

Although some sound reasons for allowing the exception were put forth—such as, if people stopped investing in this field, it would drastically reduce oil and gas exploration—the bottom line was indisputable: The two groups that made out well were the IRS, and oil and gas interests.

One of the largest groups to take advantage of tax shelters over the years was the real estate industry. That group got its comeuppance in TRA '86, which included the following: If a taxpayer was a participant or owner in an active business, losses were legitimately allowed, *except in the field of real estate.* No investments in real estate that threw off losses could be used to offset other income by passive investors, or even owners or others who were *legitimately* in the real estate business. (This does look like a clear-cut case of the IRS getting even.)

But the real estate lobby fought hard, eventually gaining an amendment to this tax law before its effective date that allows active owners in the real estate business to take the first $25,000 of operating losses as a deduction against other income if their Adjusted Gross Income is less than $100,000.*

Yes, this was a minor compromise, considering the thousands of people legitimately engaged in the real estate business who did not fit into the under-$100,000 category. But look at what happened to this group in RRA '93. Instead of giving the real estate advantage back to everyone,

---

*This advantage is phased out as AGI exceeds $100,000. When AGI reaches $150,000, the benefit disappears entirely.

it gave the tax breaks back to the real estate professionals who should not have been excluded to begin with. Beginning in 1994, taxpayers engaged full-time in real estate activities (according to the new law, those who spend more than 750 hours per year in the activity) were once again able to use real estate losses to offset other sources of income, but passive, inactive investors were still excluded. With the help of this one stroke, rentals and new construction are on the rise, and unemployment just hit a seven-year low, as I predicted. (Because of a loose definition of who qualifies as a real estate professional, the loopholes on this new law are already beginning to surface.)

Another group that benefits through favoritism is the very wealthy. They have money to spend, political connections, influence, and bargaining power. Working to reduce their share of the tax burden is part of their life.

Through a lengthy and intricate series of events that took place between 1972 and 1974, four well-to-do California business executives were successful in having special provisions written into the tax law that would apparently benefit no one but them.

They retained a Los Angeles lawyer, John H. Hall, who as deputy assistant secretary of the Treasury for tax policy from 1972 to 1974 had worked closely with Congress in drafting tax measures.

Using the Washington connections he had made as a government official, Mr. Hall went to Senator Carl T. Curtis of Nebraska, the ranking Republican of the Senate Finance Committee, which has jurisdiction over tax legislation in the Senate.

Senator Curtis arranged for the preferential language the businessmen wanted to be written into the tax bill that was pending before the Senate.

Although the entire Finance Committee adopted the Curtis amendment, no other senator knew the identities of the beneficiaries or understood the details of the amendment.

The special provisions the four business executives wanted had to do with establishing foreign trusts for their children, which would save them lots of tax dollars. How do we know this provision benefited only them? Because when the provision was initially tacked on to the pending tax bill, the House Ways and Means Committee plugged or voted down that loophole with the proviso that any such trusts had to be established by May 21, the day the voting took place. In essence, this meant that *no one* would be able to fulfill the requirements unless they knew about it beforehand.

That tax bill never was passed, but it resurfaced the following year, when, as it turned out, the four business executives completed their paperwork for the trusts on May 29. This meant they would not be eligible for the tax break.

After several conversations between their lawyer and key connections, Senator Curtis arranged for the deadline date to be changed to May 29 in the Finance Committee bill. No one on the committee asked Mr. Curtis who the beneficiaries were or why he wanted the change.[9] The four businessmen had won.

Tax Laws Become Increasingly Complex

Creating exceptions for special groups has resulted in a steady stream of new and revised tax laws, which have lengthened the *Internal Revenue Code* to over 4,500 pages and rendered it virtually unreadable. Often one section can run up to several hundred pages. A special tax service used by tax professionals (there are many), which explains the meaning and application of each part of the code, is contained in another 12 volumes!

The end result is an increasingly complex tax code that tries to please everyone but pleases no one. It is barely understandable to even the most experienced tax professionals. The harder Congress tries to simplify it, the more complex it becomes.

What does all this mean for you, the taxpayer? Preparing your tax return, delving into a tax law, if you need to, and strategizing how to keep more of your hard-earned dollars in your pocket becomes increasingly difficult with each passing year.

Even tax professionals with years of experience—trained and steeped in tax preparation—must religiously attend tax seminars and read myriad journals, magazines, and monthly tax tips, among other things, to correctly interpret the tax code and gain the advantage over the IRS.

Finding and Using Tax Loopholes: An Industry in Itself

Exemptions created in the tax-making process have led to the birth of an entire industry dedicated to searching out tax loopholes and using them to the searchers' advantage. **One of the most effective ways you can get the IRS before it gets you is to learn how to find and manipulate to your advantage loopholes in the tax law—before the IRS uses those same loopholes against you.**

Loopholes in the Lump-Sum Distribution Laws

A short while ago we discussed how President Bush tried to pay for the extension of unemployment benefits by instituting a 20 percent withholding tax on lump-sum distributions from corporate pension plans. Let's just take a few minutes to examine the loopholes that were created as a result of that seemingly insignificant gesture.

One loophole that lets you out of paying the 20 percent is to arrange to have your distribution transferred from the financial institution that currently has your pension money directly to another financial institution (such as your own IRA). This procedure, known as a trustee-to-trustee transfer, in which you do not touch the money in any way, absolves you of paying the withholding tax.

Here's a loophole within a loophole for a taxpayer who wants to keep the distribution but does not want any money to be withheld. If you want to take the distribution early in, say, 1997, and use the proceeds—*not* roll it over—you can be adequately covered by following these steps:

- First transfer the lump sum from your pension plan to your IRA via the trustee-to-trustee transfer.
- After the transfer is complete, you can make a cash withdrawal from your IRA, which will not be subject to a 20 percent withholding.

There are a few trade-offs: Although you have avoided withholding, you cannot avoid the fact that any proceeds you take from an IRA or retirement plan distribution are fully taxable, just like any other income. You are also subject to an additional 10 percent penalty if you take money out prematurely from an IRA (before you reach the age of 59½). (For an update, see New Tax Legislation for 1996, page 275.)

Let's examine this situation one step at a time.

In 1996 you are eligible to receive a $9,000 distribution from your employer's pension plan and you need $7,500 to buy a new car. You arrange to have the $9,000 transferred directly to your IRA account. You then withdraw the $7,500 you need for the purchase of the car. (Note: You can transfer an unlimited amount of money into your IRA from another qualified plan, such as a pension. This is not to be confused with the $2,000 limit on new IRA contributions.)

YOUR TAX-SAVING STRATEGY.

- Since the distribution was taken from your IRA, there is no 20 percent withholding tax requirement.
- If you change your mind and decide not to buy the car, you have 60 days to put the money back into the IRA (to roll it over).
- In April 1997, you can withdraw the final $1,500 from your IRA and use it to help pay the extra income tax and the 10 percent penalty for the earlier withdrawal. You'll now be responsible for the income tax and penalty on the last $1,500 withdrawal, but this is a small amount and you should be able to handle it. You have a whole year to plan for it.

If you choose this ploy, you have gained an extra 12 months—from April 1996 to April 15, 1997—to utilize your money and to pay any possible additional tax caused by the inclusion of the pension distribution in your 1996 income.

If there is a balance due when you file your return, you *might* be charged a penalty. Even if no balance is due, you could still incur a penalty if you did not pay estimated taxes in four equal installments. In other words, you cannot arbitrarily wait until you send in your return to pay a large balance due. The IRS wants the money throughout the year. **The bottom line is, you can take your distribution, but you must be aware of some of the pitfalls, which actually aren't that terrible.** Sound advice from a good tax professional will usually see you through them legally.

Of course, it is impossible to define and report on all the loopholes that occur in our tax laws, although many will be explored in this book. So my advice is: Be aggressive. Ask your tax professional to advise you of any loopholes you can take advantage of to make your burden easier. If you do not assert yourself, your tax pro could mistakenly conclude that you don't know loopholes exist, or that you are too conservative in your thinking to use them to your advantage.

If you don't have a tax professional (or even if you do), it's a good idea to contact a local CPA firm, one that issues a monthly or quarterly tax newsletter and perhaps even a year-end tax tips letter. Ask to be added to the firm's mailing list; usually you'll find a great deal of valuable tax help here. You don't have to feel as if you're using the information without giving something back. Most firms expect that one day you'll become a client, or that at the very least you will give them free publicity by circulating their newsletters and telling others what you have learned.

THE EVENT: The IRS as a Criminal Watchdog
THE PERSONALITY: Macho, showy, tough. Glib yet dangerous.

Significance to Taxpayers

In 1919 the commissioner of internal revenue was given official responsibility for investigating and enforcing infringements relating to the National Prohibition Enforcement Act, which rendered illegal literally any activity connected with intoxicating beverages: manufacturing, selling, buying, or transporting. To best get the job done, a group was created in the bureau that was first labeled the Intelligence Unit, then in 1954 the Intelligence Division, and ultimately, in 1978, the Criminal Investigation Division (CID). (Sounds like an out-and-out rival to the FBI!)

Back when the Intelligence Unit was created, it was the Roaring Twenties, a scene densely packed with notorious gangsters, mob violence, and organized crime. Just imagine it! The Office of the Commissioner of Internal Revenue, established by our Founding Fathers as a revenue producer to meet federal needs, had grown into a full-fledged criminal investigation arm of the government characterized by tough guys, shootings, and all the regalia associated with any police narcotics unit. Correspondingly, the IRS Intelligence Unit began its own private war against organized crime. With the expansion of its duties into criminal law enforcement, the IRS's bad-guy image was born.

Very few would question the fact that investigating and bringing to light people who commit tax fraud or engage in criminal activities that affect our country's revenue is work that needs to be done. Furthermore, there is no doubt that the Criminal Investigation Division was and still is made up of dedicated people, some of whom lost their lives during those early Prohibition years.

But the contrast between what the agency set out to do and what it ended up doing shows us an agency that is certainly out of bounds, if not out of control.

This part of the IRS personality hits taxpayers hard. First there is the initial training IRS personnel receive, which brands taxpayers as criminals and cheats. This "us against them philosophy," reported on by IRS personnel who work there today and by those who worked there over 20 years ago, allows the IRS to do their jobs with the requisite aggressive mind-set: If you're dealing each day with taxpayers labeled as lying, dishonest cheats, you need to be suspicious, unemotional, inflexible, ruthless, and determined.

THE EVENT: Tax Payment Act of 1943—Withholding and the W-2 Form
THE PERSONALITY: Efficient, slick, savvy, and extraordinarily dependable. It is also highly inflexible, unless you know the key.

Significance to Taxpayers

The next milestone to impact the personality of the IRS was the Tax Payment Act of 1943, which made the withholding of taxes from wages and salaries a permanent feature of our tax system. It also introduced the W-2 form (Wage and Tax Statement). Under this system, the employee files a W-4 form (Employee's Withholding Allowance Certificate) with his or her employer that indicates name, address, Social Security number, marital status, and the number of exemptions claimed. By law, the employer then withholds specified amounts from each employees' salary, correlated to an income rate scale, and periodically remits these amounts to the IRS. Annually, employers must also report to the Social Security Administration the total annual amount withheld on a W-2 form (Wage and Tax Statement) and provide their employees with this information. Taxpayers fulfill their reporting obligations by attaching the W-2 to their 1040 (U.S. Individual Income Tax Return) and mailing both to the IRS, hopefully before April 15. This information reflects income for the preceding year.

People who are subject to withholding taxes work for a company or an organization and are paid a salary by that entity. According to the IRS Statistics of Income office, for tax year 1994, 99.8 million tax returns indicated salaries or wages earned, meaning that almost 86 percent of those who mailed in a 1040 form received a salary from a given employer. That's a lot of W-2's. (Taxpayers who work at more than one job receive multiple W-2's.)

Today, withholding continues to be lucrative for the IRS. In 1995, 38.8 percent of gross tax dollars collected by the IRS represented withholding by employers. The actual dollar amount collected was over $533 billion, up from almost $460 billion in 1994.[10]

The collection process flows relatively easily; money comes into the government's coffers automatically from over 6 million employers across the U.S. With this device, the IRS learns exactly how much employees are paid and how much is withheld from their earned income for federal, state, and Social Security taxes. Getting employers to do the dirty work was not only smart, it was also a real plus because it makes the IRS look terribly efficient. With good reason, withholding has been called the backbone of the individual income tax.

The attitude of taxpayers toward withholding is predictable: You never see it; it is a chunk that is taken out of each paycheck; there is nothing one can do about it. Most employees just accept it and forget it.

With the W-4's basic information from the employee and the W-2's wage and salary information submitted directly from the employer, the IRS figured that the government couldn't lose. But loopholes in tax laws weakened that position providing opportunities for taxpayers to rescue tax dollars in the area of withholding.

Loopholes in the Withholding Law and How to Benefit

There is one important loophole in the withholding law available to many taxpayers; unfortunately, many are not versed in how to manage it to their benefit.

An employee's paycheck reflects the amount of withholding taken out. However, if your deductions are high, and you know they will remain so—for example, if you just filed your 1996 tax return and received a ridiculously high refund—it makes sound tax sense to reduce the amount of your income withheld.

To accomplish this, you need to engage in a balancing act between your deductions and exemptions. If you know that your itemized deductions (deductions that are allowable on a 1040 form) are going to be high for a given year, you should submit a revised W-4 form to your employer. The revised form should indicate a higher number of exemptions than you would ordinarily be entitled to. More exemptions will reduce your withholding, which in turn will result in your taking home more money each payday.

If, when you file your W-4, it turns out to be overly optimistic (for example, you closed on your new house six months later than anticipated and therefore estimated your itemized deductions too high), you can recoup. Just submit a revised W-4 to your employer requesting larger withholding payments from your paychecks in the last few months of the year. The amount will be sent to the IRS with the fourth-quarter 941 form (Employer's Quarterly Federal Tax Return, the form used by companies to pay withholding), and will increase your "federal income tax withheld," box 2 on your W-2. The end result is that the W-2 system will record your withholding tax as being paid evenly throughout the year. In fact it wasn't, but you've made the system work for you.

(By the way, you do not want to overwithhold early in the year, because in effect you would be lending money to the IRS without collecting interest from them. This is a real no-no!)

How to Put More Money Back into Your Pocket Throughout the Year

A first-time homeowner exemplifies what happens when it's time to use this loophole to put more money back into your pocket. For the most part, first-time homeowners, who have never before had very high deductions, suddenly have enormous deductions for mortgage interest and real estate taxes. All new homeowners who are wage earners (both partners in a couple) should revise their W-4's immediately by balancing their exemptions to reduce their withholdings.

When you use this approach you may end up owing a few dollars, but don't worry. No penalties are involved as long as your total payment for the current year (withholding and estimated taxes) comes to at least 100 percent of the total tax liability for the previous year, 110 percent if your AGI is more than $150,000 higher than the previous year, or 90 percent of the current year's tax. Here's how this one works:

Amy and Charles Lynfield had a joint 1990 income of $80,000 per year, $50,000 for Amy and $30,000 for Charles, and lived with their one child in an apartment that they purchased in January for $80,000. The purchase was financed with a $70,000 mortgage.

I determined their deductions to be $5,600 (8 percent mortgage interest), $5,500 real estate taxes, $5,900 state income tax, and $3,000 in contributions—a total of $20,000. Before they bought the house, the Lynfields were taking three exemptions (the husband one, and the wife two). After revising both W-4's, Amy could take six exemptions, and Charles could take four, a total of 10. This change reduced Amy's withholding and put $37 more per week in her paycheck, an increase of $1,924 for the year. And Charles saw a paycheck increase of $1,092 for the year, or $21 more per week.

As a result of rising real estate prices, the apartment doubled in value after four years, to $160,000, so the couple decided to buy a home. The new home cost $150,000, with a mortgage of $100,000. Based on the new itemized deductions (see the chart below), the Lynfields legitimately increased the number of their exemptions from 10 to 12. Their deductions now equaled $23,600, and they gained two extra exemptions. Since they bought their first home, the added exemptions provided Amy with $44 per week, or an extra $2,288 for the year, and Charles with an increase to $28 a week, or another $1,456 per year.

	First House	Second House
Mortgage interest	$ 5,600	$ 8,000
Real estate tax	5,500	6,700
State taxes	5,900	5,900
Contributions	3,000	3,000
	$20,000	$23,600

Total increase in itemized deductions: $3,600

Computing the formula to fit individual needs should be performed on the worksheet on the back of the W-4 form. This advises taxpayers how many exemptions they are entitled to on the basis of their dollar level of itemized deductions. Additional help can be found in IRS publication 919, *Is My Withholding Correct?*

How to Use the Withholding Loophole
If You Pay Estimated Taxes

Determining the correct amount of estimated tax and working through whatever overruns or underruns result at year end is a complex process. This is because anyone who uses the estimated tax method must generally calculate and pay the amounts in four equal installments to avoid penalties. However, this is only a general statement, a ground rule. In practice, often a taxpayer's itemized deductions and income will, like the Lynfields', vary during the year. When this occurs, although the required amount of estimated taxes will also vary, the taxpayers must still try to pay the four installments in equal amounts.

To do this successfully, you must determine how many changes in itemized deductions or income reductions affect your total estimated tax for the entire year. Then you simply reduce the second, or third, or fourth, or any combination of estimates, to achieve the same goal—to avoid overpaying income taxes. This is an area best handled by a tax pro. The worksheet contained in the Form 1040-ES (Estimated Tax for Individuals) booklet also provides assistance.

YOUR TAX-SAVING STRATEGY.
When applying part of this year's refund to next year's estimated taxes, try not to overestimate. If you are having a bad year and need the money from your applied estimates back quickly, you will have to wait until you file your next year's return.

Furthermore, though most people realize that estimated taxes are paid by self-employed taxpayers who don't receive a W-2 and therefore can't use withholding to control their tax payments, many people are unaware that estimated taxes must also be paid by taxpayers who earn the majority of their money from W-2's, but also receive extra income *not* covered by withholding. This includes a mélange of miscellaneous money earned on anything from interest and dividend income to serving as a member of a board of directors to prize and award money to royalties or gambling winnings. In cases such as these, and there are many more, if federal tax on any one item amounts to more than $400 a year, quarterly estimated taxes must be filed.

Estimated payments are made by people who fall into this category for two reasons:

1. So you're not stuck with an unusually large amount of taxes to pay all at once with your return.
2. To avoid penalties for failure to pay at least 100 percent of the previous year's total tax liability.

How to Use the Withholding Loophole If You Earn W-2 Income and Have Extra Income

A client of mine filing as single who earned an annual salary of $64,000 recently inherited $150,000, which produced $9,000 a year in interest. To cover the extra tax liability of $2,500 on the interest income, I instructed my client to prepare and submit to her employer a revised W-4 that reduced her exemptions from three to zero. The result produced an additional $2,500 being withheld from her paycheck. Simply by increasing her withholding, she extinguished the possibility of incurring a new tax burden on April 15, avoided any underpayment penalties, and eliminated any nasty surprises—at least in this area—that the IRS could hit her with at tax time.

How to Manage Withholding If You're an Employer

The concept of managing withholding also applies to small, closely held businesses that can massage withholding laws to their benefit. Here's how.

Small business owners often wait until the end of the year to take a bonus, since up until that point they're not certain about how much profit they'll have. As a small business owner, you can rely on your accountant to come in toward the end of the business year to determine your profit, which will in turn dictate how much of a bonus you will take in the last month of the year.

True, this is manipulation of the withholding law because this same owner/taxpayer may have been taking loans from the business throughout the year in lieu of salary and paying no withholding to the IRS. (The payments are considered loans, not salary.)

If you continue to take these loans in the place of salary, the IRS will interpret this as a mechanism to avoid paying taxes. On an audit the IRS can easily see through this. However, during the year you *can* treat the money as a loan. When you, the owner/taxpayer, know the amount of salary you can take as a bonus at the end of the year, you convert the loans into "salary"—and "salary" is how it will be reported on your books. This technique is allowable as long as it is temporary.

One cannot continue to operate this way on a permanent basis, because in practice loans have to bear rates of interest and from there the situation gets rather complicated. But the loan-to-salary conversion process is perfectly acceptable if performed within a time frame of one year.

In fact, the IRS does not normally question why withholding was or wasn't paid out during the year. To be sure, employers are required to report to the IRS any W-4's indicating more than 10 withholding allowances and when any employee claims that he is exempt from withholding on wages that exceed $200 per week. The IRS always has the right to request W-4's. But the fact is, they don't.

This brief withholding exposé can offer some real, albeit temporary, benefits to taxpayers. For example, if you can increase your monthly take-home pay by as little as $300 a month, you can afford to move up to a larger apartment, or pay the interest on an equity loan that you use to buy a new, medium-priced car, or add a room to your home.

If you choose to use this device, you must find out how quickly your employer can process the necessary paperwork. When you fill out the W-4 form and indicate the amended number of exemptions, it should be recorded on a company's payroll system almost immediately, but some organizations don't work quite that fast. Obviously the element of timing is key if everything is to run smoothly.

Earned Income Credit

The Earned Income Credit is a refundable credit for low-income working families. To qualify, a taxpayer must

- Have a job.
- Earn less than $24,396 if there is one qualifying child (essentially the child must live with you for more than six months of the year in a U.S. home).
- Earn less than $26,673 if there are two or more qualifying children.
- Earn less than $9,230 if no children, with an adjusted gross income of less than $9,230, and you or your spouse must be between 25 and 65 years old.

In a one-time occurrence in 1992 the IRS actually reached out to more than 300,000 taxpayers, notifying them that they had not taken the EIC and suggesting that they review their returns to include it. This seemed to make some difference, since the number of individual returns on which the credit was claimed rose from 12.5 million in 1991 to 14 million in 1993.[11]

The best thing about the EIC is that it's the only credit the IRS makes available even if a taxpayer doesn't pay in any tax. Moreover, *if taxpayers have zero taxable income, they are still eligible to receive part or all of the EIC credit, which is granted as a refund.* The requirements for the EIC credit are not impacted by itemized deductions.

In an interesting aside, the General Accounting Office (GAO) reported in November 1992 that the IRS, in its desire to ensure that all taxpayers who were entitled to the EIC would receive it, sent out 1991 refunds on the basis of its assumption that some categories of low-income families were entitled to the EIC even though they had not filed a claim for it. In fact, a majority of these taxpayers did not even qualify. This error allowed 270,000 nonqualified filers to get the EIC credit, and it cost the government $175 million in erroneous refunds, an average of $650 per return.

At a Senate Governmental Affairs Committee hearing in April 1994, IRS commissioner Margaret Milner Richardson reported that an IRS study of 1,000 returns with the EIC filed electronically through January 28, 1994, showed that 35 to 45 percent of the returns contained errors. Fifty percent of these errors are suspected to be intentional.[12]

Most CPAs know that poor EIC compliance is the result of involved paperwork, confusing definitions, and the fact that EIC rules have been changed ten times since 1976.

Staunch as you know them to be, however, as of August 1995 the IRS nevertheless projected that EIC claims from taxpayers with children would fall by up to 200,000 as a result of the IRS's refund protection efforts.[13] These efforts began to materialize in a big way throughout 1995 when the number of service center or correspondent audits leaped from 405,475 in 1994 to over one million in 1995.[14] The reason, according to IRS Media Relations, was an enormous increase in EIC audits.

Nevertheless, the number of taxpayers who take the EIC has continued to rise, from 14.8 million in 1994 to 18.8 million in 1995.[15] This increase was probably due to extending the credit to taxpayers without children.

What conclusions can the average taxpayer draw? Despite a recent tightening of EIC qualifications (see update, page 277), take the time to find out whether you do qualify. You might be surprised by an unexpected windfall.

THE EVENT: The IRS Meets Corruption Head-on
THE PERSONALITY: Ever-present and inescapable. From its darkest self, the IRS can be sneaky, defiant, and too smart for its own good. But eventually everyone learns what's going on.

Significance to Taxpayers

The Founding Fathers were quite savvy in recognizing the potential for corruption in the tax collection process. Section 39 of the *Public Statutes at Large* for March 3, 1791, lists penalties for crimes that duplicate almost down to the letter those indulged in periodically since the inception of the IRS by its employees, public officials, and business people. Although many IRS publications downplay or eliminate them altogether, scandal built to volcanic proportions during the early 1950s. Unfortunately, the IRS was ripe for corruption.

Since its inception, the IRS had grown geometrically. Existing tax rates went up, new taxes were added, and the force of employees required to keep up with the workload jumped from 4,000 to 58,000 in the same period.[16] A low point in the history of American tax collection came in the post–World War II period, when collections soared by 700 percent as the number of taxpayers rose from 8 million to 52 million.[17] By the early 1950s, the IRS was plagued with deplorable processing operations and a corrupt patronage system stemming from the presidential appointment of all 64 collectors of internal revenue. The system became so inbred that favor after favor was passed up and down the line, and bribe taking, influence peddling, and widespread defrauding of the government through payoffs, extortion, and embezzlement of government funds were endemic. Settling a large tax bill of $636,000 with a payment of $4,500 was commonplace.[18] So was having a case worth $2 million in tax claims somehow mysteriously disappear, preventing the government from collecting on it.[19]

After a three-year housecleaning, initiated in 1949, hundreds were let go at all levels, resulting in a major reorganization of the bureau in 1952 as recommended by President Harry Truman and incorporated into legislation passed by Congress.

In an effort to reduce the possibility of misconduct and corruption exerted through political influence, all employees except the commissioner of internal revenue would henceforth be under the civil service.

The bureau became a strongly decentralized organization in which a district office and its local branch offices were set up as self-contained operating units. Here taxpayers filed their returns, paid their taxes or got their refunds, and discussed and hopefully settled their tax problems. In short, the district offices became the focus in the organization where the primary work of the service was carried out. (Years later much of this work was taken over by IRS service centers.)

This new arrangement successfully reduced the power of IRS personnel in Washington, but it left regional commissioners and district staff, from directors to auditors and collections people, with considerable discretion to wield their powers. The situation eventually produced a new slew of problems. Instead of corruption being removed from the top and eliminated completely, it resurfaced at a new level. "While the data appears [*sic*] to indicate an increasing effectiveness and control of the integrity problem," writes one historian of the IRS, "IRS officials are the first to admit that internal criminal activity has by no means been wiped out."[20]

Despite the vigilance of an internal inspection service independent of the rest of the bureau, the IRS is periodically consumed with corruption and scandals.

The task of keeping on top of the integrity problem in the IRS is compounded not only by the magnitude of its fiscal operations, but also by the fact that the daily work of employees consists of their making constant value judgments that can expose them to opportunities for graft. There is no easy way for someone reviewing a revenue agent's work to determine whether a monetary favor from a taxpayer influenced the agent's determination on certain issues.

The IRS's Internal Security Program typically initiates about 3,000 cases a year involving theft, bribery, fraud, embezzlement, and more. These resulted in 180 convictions in 1995, up from 159 in 1994, and over 500 lesser punishments such as reprimands, suspensions, and terminations.[21] One wonders how many other cases were soft-pedaled or overlooked altogether.

THE EVENT: Information Gathering and the Matching Program
THE PERSONALITY: A technological whiz-bang that excels in some areas but fails in others. Shows unpredictable future potential because it is dependent on budget dollars and strong management skills.

Significance to Taxpayers
The final event to impact the personality of the IRS probably had its antecedents in that seemingly innocent W-2 form, a by-product of the withholding process, initiated in 1943.

The W-2 provided the IRS with a new source of information on how much money employers paid to employees. Comparing information submitted by the taxpayer with information reported by outside sources would put the IRS in a strong position to

1. Catch taxpayers who have underreported or failed to report an amount.
2. Catch nonfilers, taxpayers who have submitted no return.

The possibility of catching underreporters or nonfilers by matching information on individual tax returns to information received from a wide range of outside sources soon whet the IRS's appetite for more of the same. Propelled by the information age and the introduction of new technologies, the IRS went full steam ahead to create a situation whereby increasing amounts of information must, by law, be reported to the IRS from an expanding range of sources for the sole purpose of verifying if taxpayers, and those who should be taxpayers, are playing by its rules (see also chapter 5, pages 101–104). For tax year 1995, employers, banks, mortgage companies, and other financial institutions filed an estimated one billion information documents, or third-party reports, with the IRS.[22] Through the magic of IRS technology, these were matched to the over 100 million individual income tax returns filed.

Through its document-matching program, for the last three years the IRS contacted an average of 4.4 million taxpayers per year because of underreporting of income or nonfiling. This generates an average of $3.75 billion per year in additional taxes and penalties.[23]

But not all of the IRS's technology efforts are aimed at matching items of income. Because computers are an increasingly visible part of IRS operations, a separate chapter explores the subject. In that chapter you will discover what very few will tell you about what the IRS *can* do and, much more important, what it *can't* do with its current technological capabilities.

NEVER FORGET!

Throughout this book I will be hitting on several themes. It is to your benefit to absorb these points until they become second nature:

- Don't be scared by the IRS image. Learn what's really behind it.
- You *can* become audit-proof. Managing and reporting income so that you reduce or eliminate your chances of being audited is a function of knowing certain tax information and techniques. These will be explained throughout this book.
- Our tax laws are enormously complex, with loopholes large and numerous enough so that taxpayers can understand and use them to their advantage.
- There are many reasons why the IRS may be unable to verify certain aspects of your income. It has operated and will continue to operate under budget and to be understaffed, disorganized, and mismanaged.
- Despite its technological successes, the IRS is still overburdened with paper and not technologically up to speed.

ACKNOWLEDGING DEDICATED IRS PERSONNEL

Many people working for the IRS are committed and hardworking and are concerned with doing their jobs properly, improving taxpayer service, and making the agency's operations more effective and responsive.

But no matter how much we may want to view the agency employees as nice guys, inevitably the IRS can be counted on to go so far off course in the process of collecting the ubiquitous tax bill that lives and families have been and continue to be severely disrupted, even destroyed in the process.

Peeking behind the scenes of the IRS and describing what really goes on there is my attempt to tip the scales in the taxpayers' favor.

3

Who Runs the Show:
What You're Up Against

THE IMAGE

How the IRS Gets You Where It Wants You

How much of the IRS's all-powerful and heartless reputation is truth and how much is fiction? The IRS expends a great deal of effort to ensure that it comes across as a Big Bad Wolf to the general public. Image creation is how chic Madison Avenue advertising firms make their money. But do taxpayers know that the IRS secures the image it wants without incurring expensive advertising fees?

The IRS counts on taxpayers to spread the word about its image by telling their friends, neighbors, and business associates how an ordinary audit over something as simple as a padded expense account was turned into a horror story by the machinations of the IRS. An expensive public relations firm couldn't do nearly as good a job of getting the message out as taxpayers themselves.

As tax season approaches, stories that define and hone the IRS image begin to appear on the evening news and in the daily papers in a way they never do during the rest of the year. Now, I won't say that each criminal tax fraud or tax evasion case that breaks into the news is carefully timed and placed there by the IRS. Nevertheless, it is true that the IRS's Public Affairs Department at the National Office and IRS public affairs officers at local levels work hard to establish good relationships with print and broadcast media. Even state tax departments get into the act. **It is no coincidence that a rash of articles publicizing IRS** enforcement activities, investigations, and convictions typically begins to appear in January and February (to set the correct tone for the new year), and again in early April, before D Day for taxes.

These cases tend to involve high-profile taxpayers: entertainment and sports figures like Willie Nelson, Pete Rose, and Darryl Strawberry; or attorneys, accountants, and political and religious figures like Lyndon LaRouche, Jr., and Jerry Falwell; and even John Gotti and Harry and Leona Helmsley, whose tax evasion charges hit newspapers just before April 15.

Then, as tax time approaches, in addition to the scare stories, there's another new twist: The IRS becomes Mr. Nice Guy. We've all seen Sunday tax supplements that appear in national newspapers during early March just as taxpayers are beginning to deal with the fact that tax season, like it or not, is upon them. These supplements usually contain valuable information about recent tax news, tax tips, and even human interest stories about how the nice, hardworking people at the IRS are ready to help you. This is positive propaganda.

WHAT IT LOOKS LIKE FROM THE INSIDE OUT

Taxpayers need to recognize that the IRS cares a great deal about how it is perceived by its own employees. To the contrary, how many taxpayers do you think ever give a thought to what IRS employees think of U.S. taxpayers? I promise you that they don't see us as hardworking, compliant citizens who are trying to scrape together annual tax dollars from a salary that never seems to be enough. In fact, they see us as exactly the opposite.

If IRS employees are to do their jobs correctly, they must buy into the IRS credo that taxpayers are cheaters and that they themselves are getting the government its due.

To the IRS employee, the image of us, the taxpayers, as the bad guys and them as the tough but strong and righteous good guys becomes a motivational tool, a positive role model. And they love it. They get to play the role of the hero (from their perspective) and get paid for it.

A former attorney who worked for the IRS for over 10 years recently said to me, "During an audit we used to watch taxpayers squirm, and the more they squirmed and dug themselves into a deeper hole, the more we'd laugh at them later on."

THE ORGANIZATION

From its inception the IRS has operated under the U.S. Treasury Department (see IRS organization chart, page 75). Currently with 106,350 employees, the IRS is the largest law-enforcement agency in the U.S. Taken together, the police departments in New York City, Los Angeles, Chicago, Detroit, and Philadelphia don't even come close to the number of those working for the IRS. The IRS has more employees than each of these major corporations: Xerox, Chrysler, American Express, and Mobil Oil.

The IRS has approximately six hundred offices across the U.S., and branches in 14 countries enforce an entirely different set of rules and regulations for hundreds of thousands of U.S. citizens living abroad. Talk about the long arm of the law!

IRS headquarters, in its National Office in Washington, D.C., has almost 7,150 administrators, the latest figures according to the IRS's Statistics of Information office. (For future changes, see IRS Downsizing, page 281.) From this base the organization reaches across the nation through its regional and district offices and service centers. In an effort to streamline operations, on October 1, 1995, the regional offices fell from 7 to 4, and district offices were cut from 63 to 33. According to IRS published reports, smaller districts were merged with neighboring ones to form larger, more uniform districts. The 14 largest districts stayed the same. The downsizing breaks an IRS tradition of having at least one IRS district office in each state. (See IRS Regional and District Management Consolidation, pages 72–73.)

Regional offices execute policies handed down by the National Office, tailor specific procedures to fit local needs, evaluate the effectiveness of current policies, programs, and procedures, and make suggestions to headquarters on how to improve operations. Each regional office also oversees a number of district offices and service centers.

Each district office, which is a self-contained unit that serves specific geographic areas, is responsible for four distinct operations: examination, collection, criminal investigation (tax fraud), and taxpayer services.

This organizational setup allows IRS employees to wield extraordinary power in these functions that deal intimately with taxpayers.

In keeping with the term *service* in its name, the IRS has 10 service centers across the country and plans to have up to 23 so-called customer service centers (see chapter 11 and map on page 74, Customer

Service Centers). Service centers process individual and business re-turns and serve as the local data-processing arm of the IRS. These of-fices are where the bulk of the work associated with the IRS occurs. Additional technological support is provided by the IRS's National Computer Center in Martinsburg, West Virginia, and another data cen-ter in Detroit, Michigan.

Service centers across the U.S. receive returns, process them (open, sort, record the data, check the arithmetic, credit accounts), match re-turns with third-party reports, mail out refunds, and communicate with taxpayers regarding their tax situation by fax, letter, and/or telephone. Because of the range of work they do, service centers have areas or divisions (depending on their size) devoted to examination, collection, and criminal investigation.

One of the largest service centers is the Brookhaven Service Center (BSC) located in Holtsville, New York, which processes tax returns for the five boroughs of New York City and nearby counties. Brookhaven employs over 4,700 people during peak filing season, April and May, and maintains a permanent workforce of 2,700, including data transcri-bers, tax examiners, computer operators, technicians, and clerical workers. For the 1995 filing season, Brookhaven received and pro-cessed 7.2 million tax returns.[1]

If the organizational structure I've laid out looks a bit too clean and simple, it is. If you dig deeper, you'll become significantly confused with the chiefs and deputy chiefs, assistants layered upon assistants, and countless lengthy titles. Furthermore, the decentralization makes it almost impossible to understand the real parameters of specific jobs. The IRS wants it this way. Confusion is one of the strategies the IRS uses to keep us, the taxpayers, at a distance.

Where the Taxpayer Fits In
Taxpayer involvement begins and usually ends at the district level, where all of the four major IRS functions (examination, collection, criminal investigation, taxpayer services) are carried out. If you're going to stand your ground and deal with the IRS face-to-face, after becoming familiar with the IRS personality, the next skill you want to add to your repertoire is to know where your district office is and learn about its main functions. Knowing what each function entails will give you a running start on when to call "Halt" if somebody gets out of line.

What You Need to Know About the Examination Division

What They Say They Do
In 1995 the Examination Division had over 29,500 employees, up from 27,800 in 1994. Although the assistant commissioner for examination, operating out of the National Office in Washington, D.C., administers the nationwide program, the actual responsibility and authority for examining specific returns is in the hands of IRS employees in the district offices in each state.

DIF Scores
The majority of returns are selected for audit by a computer program that uses mathematical parameters to identify returns that are most likely to generate additional revenue. The method of scoring, called the Discriminate Information Function (DIF), is kept top secret by the IRS. No one outside the IRS and few insiders know how it really works.

We do know that every return filed receives a score in which a number of DIF points are assigned to key items included on or omitted from the return. The higher the DIF score, the greater the likelihood of an audit.

The DIF process that examines data from your tax returns is carried out at the Martinsburg Computing Center. Once selected, the "score cards" (cards representing tax returns whose scores fall into the audit range for one or more of the categories) are returned to the service center, where they are matched with the actual tax returns (hard copy). DIF selection represents the start of the audit selection process. (The actual step-by-step procedures of the audit selection process are discussed in chapter 6.) In the final analysis, only 1 to 1.5 percent of all individual tax returns filed, or about 1 to 1.5 million, are actually audited.

What's Behind the IRS Audit Strategy
Another very different type of audit is the Taxpayer Compliance Measurement Program (TCMP). Unlike the DIF system, TCMP chooses only about 50,000 returns for each audit year chosen. Although this is a comparatively small number for the IRS, the data collected is crucial. Here's why.

The TCMP has one major objective: to measure the effectiveness of the tax collection system by evaluating if taxpayers are voluntarily complying with the law. To make this kind of determination, detailed data must be developed on selected groups of taxpayers, on the basis of which norms of all kinds are established. That's what the TCMP audits accomplish. TCMP information is gathered directly from one-on-one sessions with taxpayers whose responses are then compared to established national or regional norms or averages. As a result, the TCMP effectively shows the IRS where people are cheating and telling the truth on their tax returns. It also tells where voluntary compliance is at its highest and lowest levels in terms of income groups and other categories.

Gathering raw data from taxpayers across the nation through the TCMP is a crucial device used by the IRS to update the DIF scores.

Although we know that DIF and TCMP data are highly confidential, by comparing tax returns that have been audited, we *can* surmise that some of the items within the DIF database that can trigger IRS computers to raise an audit flag probably include:

- Expenses that are inconsistently large when compared to income, e.g., if a taxpayer shows $25,000 of expenses and only $15,000 of income on the Schedule C (Profit or Loss from Business). Other triggers could include itemized deductions (interest, taxes, contributions) that are much higher than "average" returns with the same level of income.
- Required schedules or forms that are missing.
- Reporting installment property sales (sales in which the seller receives the proceeds over more than one year, and interest for the unpaid balance accrues to the seller) but failing to report related interest income.
- Reporting the sale of a stock but failing to report dividend income from that stock.
- Married couples filing separate returns that contain large itemized deductions, perhaps with one or more duplications.

A TCMP audit is an all-encompassing, excruciatingly long (at least four times longer than an office audit), intense examination of your tax return where every dollar and deduction must be documented. If you receive an audit notice with the letters TCMP somewhere, you had better go directly to a tax professional for guidance.

Since I began to do research for this book, the IRS's position on TCMP audits has changed repeatedly. In 1992 the IRS said it intended to redesign the audits to make them less burdensome for taxpayers. But by 1994, to feed its Market Segment Specialization Program (see pages 53–54 and 171–174), in which specially trained auditors investigate taxpayers in specific industries, the IRS decided it needed more TCMP information than ever. So it went on record to expand the audits with the focus on Schedule C sole proprietorships, partnerships, S corporations, and companies with less than $10 million in assets. Then, in late 1995, Congress reduced the IRS's manpower budget for 1996, indefinitely postponing the planned TCMP audits of 153,000 taxpayers. The General Accounting Office (GAO) responded by suggesting a trimmed-down TCMP of 34,000 taxpayers conducted over a number of years, rather than in one shot. The basis for this would be a trade-off of quantity and quality for an update of audit selection criteria. This, it seems, is where TCMP audits currently stand.

The IRS also uses supplemental systems to identify tax returns for audit. These systems address specific noncompliance areas such as tax shelters, tax protesters, returns containing deductions for unallowable items, and returns in which certain income amounts do not match with amounts reported by third parties.[2]

What IRS Auditors Really Do

If you receive official notice that you are to appear for a formal audit, you need to know that examinations or tax audits are conducted on one of three levels:

- Office
- Field
- Correspondence

Recent auditing initiatives include economic reality or financial status audits and the new Market Segment Specialization Program (see pages 52–54 and 168–174).

A nonbusiness audit is generally conducted as an *office audit* by a *tax auditor* in an IRS district office. In addition, some small-business audits are done as office audits, but generally these contain few complex accounting or tax issues.

Tax auditors are generally trained by the IRS and have no other special qualifications in tax law or accounting. As a result, they handle the less-complicated types of audits, which tend to be office audits.

Some tax auditors are pretty good at what they do. The nature of their work is highly repetitive and the auditing routine is second nature to them. The items they audit are very specific, and often the same, whereas in a field audit, *any* line of income and expense is open for exploration.

After a while, tax auditors have seen and have asked questions about every possibility for the items they are continually auditing. The IRS recognizes that this process of assigning tax auditors to repeatedly audit the same issues increases the effectiveness of the audit process. To ensure that this remains the case, the IRS has devised a series of kits on different aspects of conducting an office audit, which are presented in "Pro-Forma Audit Kits—Office Examination," in the *Internal Revenue Manual*—the IRS's "bible"—page 4231-11. Specific audit kits instruct the auditors on what to look for, what questions to ask, and how to proceed regarding the following examination items:

Miscellaneous
Taxes
Medical
Interest
Casualty Loss
Moving Expense
Contributions
Rental Income and Expenses
Employee Business Expense

Although the use of the pro-forma aids is mandatory for all office examinations, the *Internal Revenue Manual* does remind the auditors that the kits suggest the *minimum* amount of work to be completed and are *not* designed to include all possible audit procedures. Accordingly, the auditor is encouraged to use his or her judgment in deciding what extra steps should be taken in each case.

Now, while the repetitiveness of an office audit can make tax auditors more efficient, it can also make them unreasonably shortsighted by encouraging them to stick too closely to the rules while ignoring the bigger picture. Obviously efficiency benefits the IRS, while shortsightedness benefits the taxpayer.

The *field audit*, or on-site examination, generally occurs at the taxpayer's place of business, where the books and records pertinent to the examination are kept. It involves the examination of individual, partnership, and corporate tax returns. Corporate or partnership returns are audited *only* in the field. In addition, some individual returns are field-audited, especially those thought to contain complex accounting or tax issues.

In my experience the *only* individuals who are field-audited are:

- Self-employed people who fill out a Schedule C and have significant income. Even a corporate wage earner who earns between

$100,000 and $200,000 is not as great an attraction to the IRS as a self-employed person who earns over $100,000.

- Those with multiple rental properties, especially properties that throw off net losses. With the deductibility of rental losses severely limited by TRA '86, there has been a reduction in audits of rental properties. However, beginning January 1, 1994, rental losses can again be deducted in full by taxpayers who are involved full-time in real estate.
- People who are self-employed in a service business (no product/ inventory) can be assigned to *either* an office or field audit. If a service business has a large gross income, over $100,000 annually, it will probably end up field-audited. However, sometimes the IRS makes mistakes in assignments and a case that should have been audited in the field may be assigned to an office audit or vice versa.

An often overlooked benefit to having an IRS agent conduct an audit at your office is that you have the psychological advantage. Although agents are used to going to all sorts of locations to dig into all sorts of returns, as the business owner you will feel more comfortable in your own territory. A request for an on-site examination is often granted by the IRS if it is too difficult to bring the books, records, and other materials needed for the audit to the IRS district office. Also, the IRS usually considers a field audit if a taxpayer has other valid circumstances, such as someone being a "one-man" operation or being physically handicapped, that necessitate conducting the audit on-site.

Field audits are typically conducted by a *revenue agent*, also referred to as a *field auditor*. These are the most experienced of all audit personnel. The revenue agent will usually have a minimum of 24 credits of college-level accounting courses, and will have received advanced audit training by the IRS.

With the downturn in the economy in the early 1990's, the IRS was able to attract people to accept jobs as revenue agents who have college degrees in accounting *and* prior work experience in private industry. Many of these newly hired revenue agents are quite familiar with the methods used to present data on tax returns in such a way as to avoid the scrutiny of the IRS, specifically revenue agents. This has introduced a new phenomenon into the examination function; if you are assigned an agent with this background, be prepared for the worst.

In a case I handled recently, the revenue agent was a 54-year-old man who had worked for a large corporation for 25 years and then was fired when the corporation downsized. My client, Mr. Haley, was a dealer in original art, mostly oil paintings, in the $25,000 to $100,000 price range. For the year being audited, Mr. Haley's corporate tax data showed the following:

Net sales income	$950,000
Cost of goods sold	836,000
Gross profit	114,000
Expenses	113,000
Net taxable income	$ 1,000

Now, if this were the late 1980's, the pattern for the "typical" revenue agent would have been to spend Day 1 verifying that my client's bank deposits reconciled with the reported sales. Day 2 the agent would have checked paid bills for two or three random months. Day 3 he would have scrutinized auto, travel, and entertainment expenses, which would finally result in some disallowed expenses that he and I could agree upon.

The "new breed" of revenue agent, in this case Mr. Arthur, performs differently. He spent the first two days working conscientiously so that by the start of the third day he was ready to discuss how we had priced the artwork for sale, and how cost prices were determined. Then, he wanted me to trace the disposition of all items that were included in the closing inventory at the end of the year. With his corporate experience, Mr. Arthur knew two things that most revenue agents generally ignore:

1. Downward adjustments of closing inventory is a common and easy way to lower the gross profit, and
2. The gross profit percentage of 12 percent for the art industry (which was indicated on my client's corporate tax return) is unrealistic. Thirty percent is more the norm.

After a full day of discussions, the agent and I settled the case with an adjustment of $50,000 added to the closing inventory, which resulted in a $7,500 tax assessment.

I try to learn early on whether or not the person assigned to a case of mine has had prior corporate or public accounting experience. I no longer assume these people are lifetime civil service employees.

Correspondence audits are conducted primarily through the mail between taxpayers and the Correspondence Audit section of their service center. Although not technically audits, these are an attempt to resolve certain issues, or complete areas of your tax return, simply by having you mail specific information or documents requested. This type of audit is a recent attempt by the IRS to allow taxpayers to bypass the bureaucracy.

Often a correspondence audit is generated through the Automated Correspondence Procedure, the most common one resulting from a mismatch between your W-2 or 1099 or on a third-party report with what appears on your tax return. For example, if a third-party report indicates you received a stock dividend of $1,000 and that amount did not appear on your return, you will receive a CP-2000, Notice of Proposed Changes to Your Tax Return. The taxpayer's reply may clear up the situation, or a bill may be sent for the amount due. The CP-2000 letter, often referred to as a "matching letter," is *not* a bill. It is a request for information that, hopefully for the taxpayer, will resolve the mismatch. At this point, a taxpayer has the right to request an office audit, to be conducted at his or her local district office.

CP-2000 letters are used when a tax return cannot alone be used to make a determination of the tax due. CP-2000's are spit out by computers and sent to literally millions of taxpayers annually.

For the 1995 filing season, 24 percent of all audits were done at the IRS district offices, 18 percent were conducted in the field—usually at a taxpayer's business or a tax professional's office—and 58 percent were done through correspondence audits at the service centers. These figures are significantly skewed over last year's figures of 37, 30, and 33 percent, respectively. What the statistics reveal is that the IRS has placed a tremendous emphasis on the service centers examining returns, a more judicious use of manpower and technology.

Here's what the dollar amounts show:

Tax Dollars Collected by Type of Audit of Individual Returns, 1995

- Office audits, conducted by tax auditors, averaged $3,497 per taxpayer in taxes and penalties.
- Field audits, conducted by revenue agents, resulted in additional tax and penalties, averaging over $13,403 per taxpayer.
- Correspondence audits generated on average additional monies of $1,404 per taxpayer.[3]

Most recently, economic reality audits and the Market Segment Specialization Program have been used by the IRS to carve out more auditing dollars from its favorite place, the underground economy.

FINANCIAL STATUS AUDITING

"Taxpayers, beware! Economic reality audits are here," began an article in *J. K. Lasser's Monthly Tax Letter*. Financial status auditing, formerly known as economic reality or cost of living audits, is a new name for an old technique.

Whereas the standard method of uncovering unreported income and other possible taxpayer irregularities focused on verifying information on the tax return, the IRS's current training modules emphasize investigating the "whole taxpayer." This approach is supposed to provide revenue agents and tax auditors with an economic profile that will help them to reach certain assumptions regarding the reasonableness of what is reflected on the return versus the taxpayer's actual lifestyle. In our increasingly consumer-oriented society, how a taxpayer spends money can be a better indication of income than the tax return itself. "Does the level of income reported on the return support the lifestyle being led?" is how tax examiners are being instructed to approach audit examinations.

The program allows agents to use aggressive interviewing techniques that could include such questions as: Do you own any large assets (over $10,000) besides autos and real estate? What is it and where is it kept? Is it paid for, and if not, what is the payment? Do you ever take cash advances from credit cards or lines of credit? How much and how often? What cash did you have on hand last year, personally or for business, not in a bank—at your home, safe-deposit box, hidden somewhere, etc.?

While in the past these and similar questions might have been routinely asked in audits where fraud was suspected, taxpayers are now facing barrages of this nature at the onset of an ordinary audit examination. Taxpayers are caught unawares and unprepared. For further pitfalls and ways to protect yourself from this dangerous situation, read the in-depth discussion in chapter 7.

MARKET SEGMENT SPECIALIZATION PROGRAM

Sometime in mid-1995, IRS district offices began to instruct their revenue agents in gaining in-depth market knowledge of certain industries. The Market Segment Specialization Program (MSSP) is replacing auditing techniques that examined compliance problems within a particular geographic region or ones that looked at income ranges for individuals or asset ranges for corporations.

Using this method, instead of focusing on a single doctor, gas station, attorney, or grocery store, agents now focus on tax returns by industry.

With this initiative, the IRS believes it can significantly strengthen its audit capability as more of its examiners become trained industry experts able to uncover as yet undreamed-of sources of income. To make this a reality, the IRS has isolated over 100 such industries and has kept quite busy developing and publishing a series of industry-specific guidebooks that address key issues and concerns, set guidelines for audits, and provide concrete, in-depth background information such as balance sheet accounting, components of sales and other income sources, costs of goods sold, and typical expenses. (For a more complete discussion of the industries targeted and what to do if you are in the line of fire, see chapter 7.)

An Examiner's Personality

In general, the procedures that revenue agents and tax auditors are supposed to go through appear logical and well ordered when one reads them in the *Internal Revenue Manual.*

Under the heading "Research of Unfamiliar Items," the *Manual* (page 4231-10) advises revenue agents that "an examiner cannot perform adequately unless he is familiar with the issues on the return which scrutiny raises. . . . The tax law, regulations, Treasury decisions, rulings, court cases, the published services, and a myriad of other sources of information are the tools of the trade. No one can work without tools, and no one can improvise substitutes for such tools."

What really happens, however, is that this IRS "bible" can become virtually irrelevant as an agent's personality supersedes, modifies, and seems to rewrite any procedures that should have been followed.

Often, I've walked into an audit genuinely concerned for my client, only to find that because of the personality of the agent assigned, not only does the audit go smoothly, but most of the information I was concerned about was never even touched upon. (Of course the reverse can also happen, as you will see in chapter 4, when Mr. Fields, the IRS revenue agent, audited my client, an exporting agency.) Here's an example of how the revenue agent assigned to your case affects the course of the audit process.

Mrs. Price was the president of a closely held corporation dealing in wholesale medical supplies. After she received notice that her company's return would be audited, she called me to handle the audit and to review the tax work done by the company's corporate controller. I immediately saw several major audit issues that required more research. I secured additional backup data and prepared myself for some difficult negotiations. But I knew the final determining factor, the IRS revenue agent, could turn the whole thing around. In this case, he did.

The agent, Mr. Stores, was a pleasant young man who did not have much experience handling complicated audits. I determined this early on by his manner and the questions he began with.

On Day 1, Mr. Stores routinely inquired about how my client's corporation conducted business: Who its customers and suppliers were, and the names and addresses of the banks the business used. He also went through the standard routine of examining paid bills for two random months and verifying them to cash disbursements journals. Then he verified two random months of sales invoices and traced them to cash receipts journals.

He worked so slowly that he didn't complete his work on a reconciliation of bank deposits until the close of Day 3.

At this point, I was waiting for him to raise a few of the larger issues that were part and parcel of this corporation's return, issues that would be quite evident to any trained professional, such as:

Officers' loans. A balance of $400,000 was owed to the corporation by Mrs. Price. Although the money had been advanced over a six-year period, interest had only been accrued on the books; Mrs. Price had never actually paid any interest or principal. Moreover, the corporation's earnings were sufficient to pay Mrs. Price dividends, but she had never been paid any. Clearly, the IRS would strongly argue that some of the loans be reclassified as dividends, which are not deductible by the corporation. Therefore, they would be considered taxable income for Mrs. Price.

Officers' salaries. In the corporation's year-end accounting journal entry, the corporate controller recorded $50,000 of officers' salaries, which was paid to Mrs. Price 45 days after the close of the corporate year. In a closely held corporation, salaries are deductible *only* in the year paid, not in the year they are accrued or recorded on the books.

Officers' life insurance. During the year, $30,000 of officers' life insurance was paid and was deducted as an expense on the corporate tax return. However, it was not listed as a separate item; it was buried in the category of "General Insurance." The problem with this is that officers' life insurance is *not ever* deductible.

Instead of stopping to discuss even one of these issues, the revenue agent made additional requests for more information to support bills paid for entertainment, travel, auto expense, and commissions. These areas are old standbys that revenue agents seem to fall back on especially when they have decided not to delve into other issues that are more complex. At the next meeting, Mr. Stores wasted half the day verifying the expense information he previously requested. He also verified a schedule of bank interest that was nothing more than a reprise of two items per month that represented interest for two corporate bank loans. He pulled all 12 bank statements to verify that the interest was listed on our schedule accurately.

Why did Mr. Stores choose to engage in this painstakingly slow and practically redundant exercise? In my opinion, he was padding his work papers by including a schedule of bank interest to let his group chief know he hadn't omitted anything.

Toward the end of Day 4, he finally got around to insurance. I submitted paid bills for all ordinary insurance such as auto, worker's compensation, and health insurance, plus the bills for officers' life insurance totaling $30,000.

Finally he asked for promissory notes covering the officers' loans, which I gave him. He dropped the matter entirely without ever asking why interest had never been paid on the loans.

The audit was concluded with the agent disallowing the $30,000 in officers' life insurance. He also disallowed approximately $15,000 of travel and entertainment.

The issue of the officers' salaries paid in the wrong year was never discussed. This alone could have meant an additional tax liability of $25,000. Since the agent had my client's 1040's for several years, he could have traced the salaries if he had chosen to. He didn't.

If you're reading this and are awestruck, don't be. This kind of audit is not unusual. I know that Mr. Stores fully believed he was performing conscientiously. Revenue agents with more experience think and act differently (they get through the routine information more quickly), and stand a better chance of uncovering larger issues.

If you are audited, you never can predict how the process will go because so much depends on the kind of revenue agent assigned to your case. I don't believe that reading books on auditing will change that, either, although you can pick up a lot of very worthwhile and specific information. You really want to focus on preventive medicine: **Make sure you never receive that audit notice**—by following the advice in this book. If you do receive an audit notice, get the best professional you can find, one who has had plenty of experience facing IRS agents at audits, to represent you.

Note: According to the *IRS 1995 Data Book*, there were almost 670 more revenue agents and 244 more tax auditors in 1995 than in 1994 in the Examination Division.

Have no delusions: the IRS is making the most of its funds by fortifying its examination resourcs.

What You Need to Know About the Collection Division

What They Say They Do
In 1995, the Collection Division had over 19,360 employees. As with the Examination Division, policies and procedural guidelines for collecting delinquent taxes and securing delinquent tax returns are established in the Office of the Assistant Commissioner of Collection in Washington, D.C. Carrying out those policies and guidelines becomes an enormous decentralized operation managed at the district level.

Collection deals with people who owe tax who say they cannot pay, those who never filed, and the innocent, victimized taxpayer who unfortunately falls into the IRS's "I made a mistake" category.

IRS personnel from Collection are the ones who can wipe out your possessions and often do so with great gusto.

Collection has three major components: the service center, the Automated Collection System, and the district office.

What Collection Really Does

Since all tax returns are mailed to a taxpayer's appropriate service center, the actual collection process begins in the collection areas in each of the 10 service centers across the country.

To resolve balance due or delinquent tax matters, the service center routinely sends up to four "balance due" or "return delinquency" notices. Because these are currently numbered from 501 to 504, they are often referred to as "500 notices."

501 is Reminder of Unpaid Tax
502 is Overdue Tax
503 is Urgent—Payment Required
504 is Final Notice

If you receive a 504 letter, this is really not the "final" notice, just the final notice from the service center. If you don't pay in full within 30 days of receiving this notice, the IRS can begin the enforced collection process. After this, the process can take on a life of its own.

In 1983, the amount collected from taxpayers on the first notice was close to $2 billion. In 1993, the average first notice from the IRS claiming money due brought in over $7.4 billion from taxpayers who were probably relieved to get the IRS off their backs simply by writing one check. By 1995, the figure rose to almost $7.7 billion. You can see the IRS's progress in this area alone.

The initial mailings of notices for tax due should include certain publications. *Your Rights as a Taxpayer*, IRS Publication 1, commonly referred to as the "Taxpayer Bill of Rights," is usually mailed with the first notice, and *Understanding the Collection Process*, IRS Publication 594, is mailed prior to enforced-collection action. The latter will answer many of your questions and explain clearly and objectively what's in store if you don't pay your bill. (It's not a pretty picture, and certainly one you want to avoid.) Although the value of these kinds of IRS publications may seem to be questionable—because you are up against the IRS and are thinking that no matter what they print, the IRS still does as it pleases—you should keep and read these publications. They tell you what *should* take place and what to expect next. If you don't receive the publications call the taxpayer assistance telephone numbers in your state and ask to have them sent. (See Appendix B.)

If a taxpayer has not responded after receiving the last notice, or if the situation looks as though it may not be easily resolved, the Automated Collection System (ACS) takes over.

Automated Collection System (ACS)

ACS has offices around the country staffed with employees responsible for collecting unpaid taxes and securing tax returns from delinquent taxpayers who have not responded to previous service center notices. Their work is carried out strictly through the mail or over the telephone. Chances are, no matter how many people you speak to from ACS, you will never meet with any of them in person.

The work that goes on in the ACS offices is quite focused. Personnel trained to locate errant taxpayers are supported in their efforts by computer links to a range of information resources. These include state tax files and local offices, and other records, such as the registry of motor vehicles, voter registration office, and membership in union, trade, professional, or other organizations. They also use telephone books and post office records and can easily obtain unlisted phone numbers. ACS employees also routinely write letters of inquiry to your employees, next-door neighbors, and schools that you or your family have attended. All of this is performed as part of their vigorous attempts to locate Mr., Mrs., or Ms. taxpayer who owes the government money.

Once the contact is made, the IRS says what will happen next:

> When taxpayer contact is made, either through an outcall or in response to an ACS letter or enforcement action, the ACS employees will discuss how best to resolve the tax matter. Where there are unpaid taxes, the IRS has written guidelines for considering an installment agreement to pay the tax over a period of time, for adjusting incorrect tax bills and reducing or eliminating penalties, and for determining situations where the case should be reported currently not collectible.[4]

If and when the ACS fails to get as far as it should and/or it looks like the taxpayer is not cooperating, and/or it appears as if the situation is not easily going to be resolved, the service center sends the case to the district office for further investigation.

District Office Collection

When ACS has determined that nothing else has worked and that it's time to take enforcement action, you've reached the final step in the collection process.

What happens at the district level is the all-too-familiar nightmare of the "surprise visit" to your home or office, where the revenue officer (or officers) will ask lots of questions and arrange for a more formal interview. During the formal meeting, the officer will fill out a detailed financial report on an IRS form with the information you supply. Then the two of you will work through the methods and means you will use to pay the money you owe. These might include certain routes the revenue officer decides you must take no matter what, such as producing immediate monies to pay the bill, selling specific assets, or strongly suggesting that you pay a visit to your bank to secure a bank loan. Payment could also be made via a carefully detailed installment plan, Form 9465, which, compared to the other choices available, begins to sound good. But be wary of this. (For more information, see chapter 10, pages 228–229.)

If none of these are workable for the taxpayer, the situation literally deteriorates right before your eyes and things are, for the most part, taken out of your hands.

To fully realize the extent of authority vested in the Collection Division, each taxpayer should know the major steps Collections can take to, as the IRS says, "protect the government's interest in the tax matter, or if the taxpayer neglects or refuses to pay, or fails to help resolve a tax matter."[5]

A *summons* simply requires that you must appear at a given time and place and offer specific information as you are grilled by IRS revenue officers.

A *lien* is a much more dangerous weapon. First of all, it means that the IRS is going to publicly notify all your creditors and business associates that the IRS has a claim against your property and your rights to property, including property that you might acquire even after the lien is filed.

Second, you will, in effect, lose your credit rating because notice of a lien is filed with all the appropriate official and legislative channels, secretary of state, and county clerk. If this happens, it will take years to stabilize your financial standing, even if you have the best tax attorney on your side. IRS Publication 594, *Understanding the Collection Process*, says under the misleading heading "Automatic Release of a Federal Tax Lien": "A lien will release automatically if we have not refiled it before the time expires to legally collect the tax. This is usually a period of 10 years."

A lien is a notice to creditors that the government has a claim against your property for a tax debt. A *levy* gives the IRS *control* over your assets, so that it can literally, physically, take the property out of your possession to satisfy your debt. A levy encompasses property that you hold (home, boat, car) or property held for you by third parties (wages, savings accounts). The principle behind this is that your possessions are no longer yours but rather belong to the government.

Under the levy (and seizure), you should be aware that the IRS is required to leave something behind. This includes fuel, provisions, furniture, and personal effects for a head of household with a total value of (effective January 1, 1997) $2,500, and books and tools used in your trade, business, or profession worth up to $1,250. The full list is in *Understanding the Collection Process*.

When taxpayers fail to make arrangements to resolve their tax debts, the IRS goes a step further. After the levy and seizure, the IRS will sell any real or personal property that a taxpayer owns or has an interest in. According to the IRS, seizure of a primary residence does require approval from a district or assistant district director, with one exception. This is when the famous *jeopardy assessment* surfaces.

A jeopardy assessment is an emergency legal procedure that allows the IRS to swiftly seize, *at any time,* the assets of taxpayers if the IRS suspects that they may flee the country. People who intend to travel for a long distance usually secure plane tickets, something the IRS should have no trouble verifying. Beyond this, however, how can anyone determine with any certainty if a person is going to leave the country? No doubt, we want the IRS to enforce the jeopardy assessment when drug dealers jam $500,000 in an expensive attaché case or brown paper bag and hop on a plane to Brazil. But in and of itself, this emergency procedure is open to unverifiable assertions that could be used purely for harassment purposes and could prove especially dangerous to taxpayers in the hands of certain IRS revenue officers.

Other collection techniques involve the IRS's making a special arrangement with

- Your employer to collect money owed, by initiating payroll deductions from your wages.
- Anyone who pays you interest or dividends, to withhold income tax at the rate of 31 percent.
- The IRS's own Collection Department, to apply your annual tax refund to offset any balance due.

Let me emphasize that all of these actions, which are part of the tax collection process and which occur across our nation, are standard operating procedures. Before any other law enforcement agency so radically disturbs a citizen's peace and lifestyle, it must by law obtain a court order. The IRS Collection Division is exempt from this procedure.

When it comes to money owed to the government, getting that money takes precedence over standard due process and protecting the legal rights of U.S. citizens.

Forms and More Forms

Each of the procedures just described, and there are even more of them, consists of very specific steps that the taxpayer and the IRS are supposed to go through before an actual collection action can be made. Enter IRS forms, those things that have become second nature to the IRS since its inception: forms that tell taxpayers what is about to happen "unless"; forms that rescind the threats; forms that announce that the IRS is going to proceed with the action after all, no matter what; forms that give the taxpayer one last chance; forms that repeal or dismiss the action because the taxpayer is ready to settle the bill.

The paperwork, telephone calls, and correspondence required both to set these actions into motion and to stop them are unbelievably intricate, voluminous, even ridiculous. Add to this the tricks and techniques tax professionals extract from their "what-to-use-against-the-IRS-Collection-Division repertoire" to stall, delay, or reverse decisions already put into action via the forms, and we could go on forever. I prefer to focus first on how to deal with the human element in the IRS if you do get involved, and second, how taxpayers need not get involved in these quagmires at all.

Collection People Mean Business

IRS collection staff mean business, and they have a great deal of power and substantial leeway to exercise it. Here's what I mean:

Sebastian was a freelance interior designer who owed the IRS $12,000 in personal taxes. The statute of limitations on collecting the amount was due to expire in two weeks. Sebastian had already entered into payment agreements three times previously, but each time had failed to meet his obligations. On his last visit to the local district office, Sebastian filled out a new financial Form 433-A (Collection Information Statement for Individuals) in which he claimed he did not own an automobile.

On a hunch, Steve, the revenue officer, checked the state department of motor vehicles records and discovered a two-year-old Mercedes registered to Sebastian. Steve tried to locate the car in several parking garages near Sebastian's apartment but had no luck. Next Steve remembered that Sebastian had said he vacationed in a well-known resort area; so he checked the telephone book for the resort, found a listing for Sebastian, and called. Initially, Sebastian denied that he was the person Steve was looking for, so the officer told him that lying about who he was and what assets he owned was a crime punishable with arrest and prison. Sebastian gave in, said he was living in a rented home for the summer, and agreed to meet Steve there the following day.

Once Steve was there, Sebastian continued to deny that he owned a car. Steve drew up all his 6'2", lowered his voice, and said, "I can go through this house right now and take all your belongings; I can empty your city apartment and repossess your Mercedes. You owe the government money, and anything I can do to clear up that debt I can and will do."

Steve was so frightening that Sebastian led him straight into the garage and the Mercedes. Steve asked Sebastian to move it onto the street, figuring he was on firmer legal ground if the vehicle was on public property. Then Sebastian handed over the auto registration and Steve removed the license plates. This was on a Friday. Monday morning Sebastian showed up in Steve's city office with a $12,000 payment in full. The registration and plates were released to him.

In another collections case, the owner of a hardware store owed $22,000 in payroll taxes. Twice before he had broken agreements to pay on an installment basis. The revenue officer on the case obtained a warrant from the court, showed up in the store, seized the entire contents of the store, and sold it at an auction a short time later.

In both these cases, the taxpayer was in trouble and the revenue officers assigned were doing their jobs—brutal, but expected. **In payroll tax cases, revenue officers are instructed to be especially forceful because the IRS holds employers to a greater degree of responsibility (they must pay employees' taxes) than an individual taxpayer who owes only his or her own taxes.**

Often, in collections, the end does not so pointedly justify the means.

A new chief of collections appointed in the Manhattan district office immediately placed a great emphasis on raising the level of collection of old cases. The new chief met with the revenue officers assigned to the district and told them to go out and get the job done, no holds barred. One story came back from this group about a taxpayer who had just undergone brain surgery. He owned a dry-cleaning establishment and owed $14,000 in payroll taxes. After agreeing to an installment plan, he had paid the agreed-upon $600 per month right on time, until illness struck. The new chief approved the seizure of the man's business, which was liquidated within a few weeks while the taxpayer was in a coma and his wife and family literally stood by helplessly.

Revenue officers are out to get what they can from you because you owe the government. If they can get all you owe, that's great for them. But they will also settle on taking whatever they can get their hands on. If this sounds brutal, I advise you that they and the process are supposed to be.

What You Need to Know About the Criminal Investigation Division

What They Say They Do

If you are the subject of a criminal investigation, you'll be involved with the IRS's Criminal Investigation Division (CID). This division formerly conducted investigations in five areas: abusive compliance (investigations involving violations in commodity futures, options, government securities transactions, excise taxes, illegal tax protesting, fraud schemes, or abusive/illegal tax shelters), narcotics crimes, organized crime, public corruption (investigations involving violations of public trust of or by government officials and employees), and white-collar crime. Of these, abusive compliance and narcotics accounted for more than 80 percent of the cases initiated. Accordingly, in 1995 the program was restructured into only two areas, fraud and narcotics, which contain data from the former categories though not labeled as such, says the IRS. In 1995, this division had 3,363 special agents, out of over 5,000 employees.

Although very powerful in its own right, CID does *not* have the power to determine tax liability. It does have the responsibility of scaring taxpayers into compliance with the tax laws, stopping criminal acts involving tax violations, and punishing violators.

The heaviest caseloads for CID vary between organized crime and illegal activities involving narcotics and money laundering, and white-collar crime committed by stockbrokers, investment bankers, money managers, and the like. As a general rule, the average amount of taxes owed by a taxpayer when the IRS files criminal charges is over $70,000. Because of the nature of their job and whom they deal with—organized-crime figures, very wealthy individuals, drug dealers, executives, professionals—special agents have a certain untouchable aura about them that goes back to CID's establishment in the 1920's.

Where CID Receives Its Leads

Cases in which criminal activity is indicated or suspected are sent to CID from various sources:

- Within the IRS—Revenue agents and other auditors; CID employees who search through newspapers, articles, broadcast media, and other public sources for circumstances that could interest CID, such as lifestyles that might indicate fraud, items reported stolen (to see if they match up to a taxpayer's reported income); other branches within the IRS.

- The Justice Department—Refers primarily narcotics and organized-crime cases. The number of special agents who work on organized crime and narcotics cases is not publicized because it represents a very high percentage of the total cases handled by CID.
- Law enforcement agencies—FBI, DEA (Drug Enforcement Agency).
- Regulatory agencies—the Department of Consumer Affairs, Securities and Exchange Commission, Food and Drug Administration, Federal Communications Commission.
- Banks and other financial institutions—All are required to report a cash transaction of $10,000 or more, as well as any other "suspicious" transactions on Form 8300 (Report of Cash Payments over $10,000 Received in a Trade or Business).
- Undercover agents—CID has its own staff who nab unsuspecting taxpayers.
- Independent CID leads from paid informants—*The Internal Revenue Code* has a provision for paying informants 10 percent of tax that is recovered as a result of a tip (see page 160); CID also has people on its payroll who regularly provide tips about criminal activities.
- Voluntary informers—Lovers left in the lurch, vindictive ex-wives or ex-husbands, former employees, and more are very willing to "tell all" to the IRS. (If CID doesn't think a case will end up with a conviction, it will turn it back to the referring IRS party.)

Special agents operate in the big time of vice and criminal activity. They don't waste time, they are diligent, focused, and well-trained, and they perform meticulous, detailed investigations.

A criminal investigation can be initiated by either the IRS, known as an administrative investigation, or by a grand jury. In an administrative investigation, a summons issued by the IRS is the vehicle that gets the taxpayer and any other witnesses to the investigation. Enforcement in this instance tends to be more difficult, and long delays are common. In a grand jury investigation, which employs the subpoena, witnesses show up faster and the U.S. attorney immediately enters the picture. Subpoenas are easier to obtain, and the process is quicker and more effective compared to an administrative investigation.

Another difference is that in an administrative investigation CID is in charge, but with a grand jury, the U.S. attorney, who works for the Justice Department, is in charge and the IRS plays second fiddle. So although a grand jury investigation is quicker and more efficient and thus an easier task for CID and its agents, it is common knowledge that the IRS doesn't like taking orders from anyone. But since a large percentage of cases are referred to CID from the Justice Department, CID doesn't have a choice. A case referred by the Justice Department automatically receives a grand jury investigation.

From a taxpayer's perspective, all I would say here is that an administrative investigation might be slightly more preferable (although being in a position of having to undergo a criminal investigation of any sort is completely *not* preferable), simply because it works much more slowly than a grand jury.

Once CID is convinced that prosecuting a citizen is in order, the case moves up through CID to the district counsel, then to the Department of Justice, Tax Division, Washington, D.C., and on to the U.S. District Court. The case must garner approval each step of the way, or it will be thrown out. This approval process normally takes two to six months.

If at the conclusion of its investigation CID decides it doesn't have a case against the taxpayer, the case will be dropped. But that's not the end of it. The case then finds its way back to an auditor, who examines it for civil penalties, which can run as high as 75 percent of what is owed. Even when a person is prosecuted and found guilty, civil penalties are likely to be imposed as well.

When CID builds a case against a suspected tax criminal, the work it performs is very thorough and precise. By the time you, your friends, family, or neighbors are contacted by a special agent, the case gathered against you will be pretty solid.

When a taxpayer falls into the criminal category, he or she stands to receive a fairer deal than a taxpayer caught up in the collections area. **That's because in the Criminal Investigation Division, the burden of proof is on the government: The taxpayer is innocent until proven guilty. For every case handled by any other division of the IRS, the reverse is true.**

In summary, putting people in jail is the job of the Justice Department. When it comes to tax violations, it's the IRS that gets them headed in the right direction.

In 1995, CID referred over 3,600 cases for prosecution, resulting in 2,800 sentences; 2,230 of these received prison terms. At that rate, 80 percent of those sentenced went to prison.[6]

What is significant in these findings is that

- The number of criminal tax cases the IRS gets involved with is relatively low, less than .003 percent of the total population of taxpayers sending in tax returns, or, for 1995, 5,000 CID investigations initiated out of almost 206 million returns filed.

- Although CID has the smallest staff of all the four major district-level operations (examination, collection, criminal investigation, and taxpayer services), it has the best reputation because of its ability to secure convictions.

You see, the decision to launch an investigation is made by CID with great care. True, CID may not always have a choice: If a person is well known and the IRS wants to make an example of him, or if the U.S. attorney insists that CID pursue a specific case in the area of organized crime, CID must follow up. But given the time and expense it takes to reach the stage where the IRS recommends a case to the Justice Department for prosecution, you can be sure that that case will stand a good chance of winning.

What CID Really Does Regarding Fraud

The *Internal Revenue Manual* clearly defines what conditions must exist for fraud, a criminal offense, to be indicated:

> Actual fraud is intentional fraud. Avoidance of tax is not a criminal offense. All taxpayers have the right to reduce, avoid, or minimize their taxes by legitimate means. The distinction between avoidance and evasion is fine, yet definite. One who avoids tax does not conceal or misrepresent, but shapes and preplans events to reduce or eliminate tax liability, then reports the transactions.
>
> Evasion, on the other hand, involves deceit, subterfuge, camouflage, concealment, some attempt to color or obscure events, or making things seem other than they are.[7]

But here's the problem: **Because the final determination is made by CID, the gap between what is criminal and what is civil allows for significant leeway, which can be and has been used against the taxpayer.**

Let's say a taxpayer files Form 4868 (Application for Automatic Extension of Time to File U.S. Individual Income Tax Return), on which he underestimates his tax liability, and then does not file the completed return. CID could hold that this seemingly innocent action involved intent to commit fraud, or criminal behavior.

In another case, suppose a taxpayer willfully lies to a special agent. This is a clear indication of intent, is it not? This makes it criminal.

Don't for one second think that criminal violations involve only organized crime, narcotics violations, and money laundering. The majority of taxpayers would never even *think* about getting involved in these kinds of vice activities. But that's all right. The IRS gives you lots of chances to be charged as a criminal violator anyway.

How to Tell If Your Behavior Borders on Criminal.

Taxpayers are at risk for criminal exposure when they

- Understate income, such as denying receipt of income and then are not able to offer a satisfactory explanation for the omission.
- Conceal accounts with a bank, brokerage firm, or other property.
- Repeatedly fail to deposit receipts to business accounts.
- Manipulate personal expenses to appear like business expenses.
- Take excessive religious and charitable contributions.
- Show substantial unexplained increases in net worth, especially over a period of years.
- Show substantial excess of personal expenditures over available resources.
- Fail to file a return, especially for a period of several years, while receiving substantial amounts of taxable income.

Are You Exhibiting "Badges" of Fraud?

If you are being examined for a civil or criminal violation, there are certain kinds of behaviors, referred to as "badges" of fraud, which according to the IRS could indicate fraud. As listed in the *Internal Revenue Manual*, some of the more common badges of fraud are as follows:

- False statements, especially if made under oath. For example, taxpayer submits an affidavit stating that a claimed dependent lived in his household when the individual did not.
- Attempts to hinder the examination. For example, failure to answer pertinent questions or repeated cancellations of appointments.
- Testimony of employees concerning irregular business practices by the taxpayer.
- Destruction of books and records, especially if it's done just after an examination was started.
- Transfer of assets for purposes of concealment.

Are You Exhibiting "Willful Intent"?

The *Internal Revenue Manual* goes on to explain that in and of themselves, these actions by the taxpayer usually are not sufficient to establish fraud. However, when these are combined with other items they may be taken to indicate a willful intent to evade tax. These other items include:

- Refusal to make specific records available.
- Diversion of a portion of business income into a personal bank account.
- Filing the return in a different district.
- Lack of cooperation by taxpayer.

These indicators are behaviors thousands of taxpayers exhibit with good reason during examination proceedings. Now that you know them, you realize that if you act in any of these ways, you could set off a lightbulb in some examiner's head that will then place you in the category of exhibiting a "badge" of fraud.

Attorneys strongly recommend that the moment taxpayers know a case is criminal they should *stop talking* and get a lawyer immediately. The lawyer should be a criminal attorney who is familiar with tax matters, and not a tax attorney who is familiar with criminal matters.

How a Tax Professional Spots an Audit Case Turned Criminal

Just as the IRS has defined certain taxpayer behaviors that indicate fraud, tax professionals have learned to stay finely tuned and spot corresponding "triggers" on the part of the IRS that could indicate that one of our audit cases is being considered as a criminal violation.

I have had several clients whose cases I suspected might be recommended to CID. As each new audit meeting arrived, I carefully watched the revenue agent to see if I could detect any change in his attitude: Was he being overly cooperative? Or, perhaps, suddenly very uncooperative by keeping a tight lid on his comments? Was he beginning to request new information unrelated to the issues we had been discussing all along? In the end, settlements were made either with the revenue agent or at an appeals conference. None of the cases in question was turned over for criminal action.

An important piece of information for taxpayers regarding the possible change in classification of a case from civil into criminal is this: During a regular audit proceeding, you can ask the revenue agent if your case is being considered as a criminal matter. The agent is required to answer truthfully. If, however, the case is *subsequently* deemed to be a criminal one, the agent is *not* obliged to voluntarily reveal this information, *even though* you previously asked that question. Of course, you are still in your rights to ask the same question again, but this could in itself be interpreted as a "badge" of fraud, especially if the agent has already decided it's criminal or has, in fact, turned your case over to CID.

A CPA colleague described the case of a taxpayer, Mr. Lockwood, with a janitorial services business whose customers were primarily large corporations. Mr. Lockwood's business was a sole proprietorship. During an audit of his tax return (Form 1040, Schedule C), the revenue agent had a problem reconciling Mr. Lockwood's books with his tax return. The agent appropriately began to request additional backup data and to ask a lot of questions.

Immediately Mr. Lockwood berated the auditor for being a clock-watcher and accused him of being "just like all the other civil servants—people without real feelings or regard for the taxpayer." At the end of the day the auditor requested a list of items, including customer invoices and vendor-paid bills for a two-month period, to be brought in to the next audit session.

My colleague told his client not to do any talking. Even though he had an appalling filing system, he was also told to show up with every item the auditor requested. The auditor was only following a set routine of selecting several test months for closer scrutiny. But my colleague had a full-fledged Type C client on his hands, as described in chapter 1. The fact that he was losing his audit seemed less important to him than being right.

Several days later, when Mr. Lockwood finally produced the information requested, almost 50 percent of the items were missing. During the session he looked the auditor straight in the eyes and told him that the other items had been misplaced.

Three weeks passed, which made my colleague uneasy. When an audit is in full swing as this one was, a sudden break without any apparent reason is cause for suspicion. The CPA telephoned the auditor to ask him if he could set up another date. It was then that the agent said he was turning the case over to CID.

Before the CID person began the investigation, she sent a letter to each of Mr. Lockwood's customers on CID letterhead. The letter stated that Mr. Lockwood was under criminal investigation for tax fraud and requested verification of payments from each customer made to the taxpayer during the year under audit. After this, the CID agent checked Mr. Lockwood's bank records, and guess what? Mr. Lockwood was able to clearly explain away all of the agent's questions. The investigation then ended—at least as far as the IRS was concerned.

Within six months of this rather minor debacle, Mr. Lockwood lost over 30 percent of his clients and half of his annual revenue. As a postscript, the IRS never did send a follow-up letter to his customers explaining that no criminal activity had occurred.

Now Mr. Lockwood decided to sue the IRS under Section 6103 of the *Internal Revenue Code*, which allows a taxpayer to bring suit if the IRS "wrongfully revealed confidential tax information," which Mr. Lockwood claimed did occur in the letter the IRS sent to his customers.

The case arrived in U.S. Tax Court where the judge agreed with the taxpayer and added that the agent should have attempted to resolve the discrepancy by examining bank and other records *before* sending out a letter to parties not directly involved in the investigation.

Not satisfied with this decision, the IRS appealed the case to the circuit court of appeals, which, unfortunately for Mr. Lockwood, overruled the lower court's decision, stating that although the agent could have used better judgment, the IRS had caused no liability to the taxpayer.

In a farcical attempt to mitigate the harshness of the decision, the circuit court added that it did not want people to think that the IRS could investigate anyone it wanted to on a whim, since this kind of investigation could devastate a small business in a local community. Well, that's exactly what it had done. Mr. Lockwood ended up devastated by the ruling, which almost cost him his business plus attorney fees.

The REAL Reason CID Contacts Third Parties

The three real reasons CID summons witnesses or third parties in an attempt to prove its case against taxpayers are

1. To obtain information that will incriminate the taxpayer.
2. To scare the very same people being contacted into never violating tax laws themselves (the deterrent mission).
3. To use the contact as an opportunity for the IRS to spread its tough-guy image.

Once CID discovers incriminating evidence, there are no statutes anywhere that forbid or prohibit this information from being used against the taxpayer. Many careers and reputations have been destroyed because some of this stuff just happened to leak out.

Unspoken Problems in the Criminal Investigation Division

Despite the positive reports reflecting the level of CID work, there are problems with CID and the entire CID process that often go unspoken.

- The cost of building a criminal case and nabbing the suspect is high. In 1991 the total amount spent for tax fraud investigations cost the IRS over $275 million. By 1993, that figure jumped to $343.5 million, and by 1995 it was $402 million.[8]
- The number of cases initiated in narcotics and organized crime is surprisingly low. In 1993 and 1994, 1,804 and 1,612 narcotics cases, and only 404 and 273 organized crime cases, were initiated.[9] (Almost 88 percent of narcotics suspects who were sentenced in 1995 were sent to prison—a sign of what CID *can* do well.)[10]
- Even though tax criminals go to prison and are assessed a given amount of tax and penalties, the IRS has *not* been successful in collecting the full amount of tax dollars owed.

For further information, see page 210 for a discussion on the major misconception taxpayers have regarding criminal cases and client-accountant confidentiality.

What You Need to Know About the Taxpayer Services Division

What They Say They Do

Taxpayer Services, with its current staff of 7,657, provides guidance and assistance to taxpayers who write, telephone, or visit an IRS district office inquiring about their federal tax obligations. It also disseminates tax information, publications, films, and other educational materials, conducts tax workshops, and generally helps people untangle IRS red tape. The programs it offers are fairly extensive, and much of the material is worthwhile and helpful.

Taxpayer Services' toll-free assistance telephone numbers consist of various toll-free answering sites in all states as well as the District of Columbia and Puerto Rico. You can call your local IRS district office for this list, or see Appendix B for state filing authority phone numbers.

There is also a "Tele-Tax" service, which provides recorded tax information tapes on over 150 topics. A complete listing of the topics available, automated refund information, and the local telephone numbers for Tele-Tax are in IRS Publication 910, *Guide to Free Tax Services*, and in the 1040, 1040A (U.S. Individual Income Tax Return), and 1040EZ (Income Tax Return for Single and Joint Filers with No Dependents) tax packages, all of which are free of charge.[11] (See also Appendix B of this book.)

Other programs provide free tax information and tax return preparation to taxpayers 60 years or older; educate high school students about their federal tax rights and responsibilities; support student tax clinics, staffed by graduate accounting students and second- and third-year law students; and assist taxpayers who would not normally obtain counsel in audit, appeals, and Tax Court cases.[12]

What Taxpayer Services Really Does

Taxpayer Services is a good place to begin with if you have a general tax question or need information that only the IRS can provide. The fact is that the Taxpayer Services Division, like the rest of the IRS, is traditionally understaffed. Getting through to them over the telephone requires time and persistence.

This division exists to service taxpayers' general tax needs and to educate people regarding U.S. taxes. These certainly are admirable goals. However, you are still essentially dealing with the IRS personality—re-

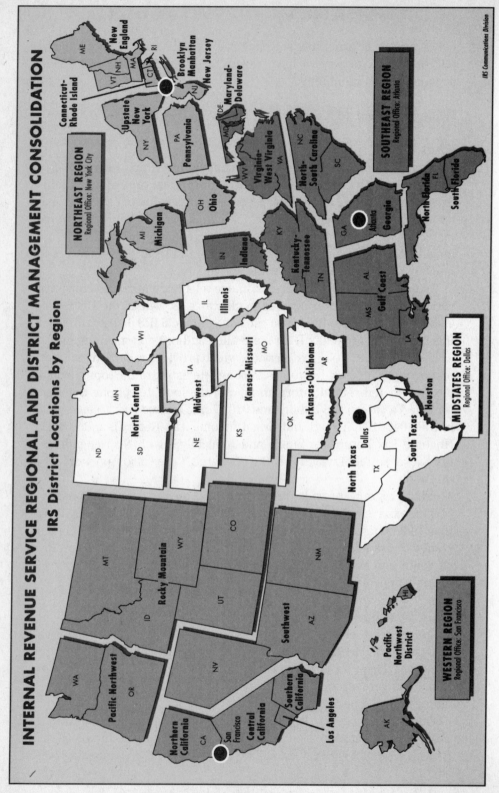

INTERNAL REVENUE SERVICE REGIONAL AND DISTRICT MANAGEMENT CONSOLIDATION

IRS District Locations by Region

NORTHEAST REGION
Regional Office: New York City

SOUTHEAST REGION
Regional Office: Atlanta

MIDSTATES REGION
Regional Office: Dallas

WESTERN REGION
Regional Office: San Francisco

New England
Connecticut-Rhode Island
Brooklyn
Manhattan
New Jersey
Upstate New York
Pennsylvania
Maryland-Delaware
Michigan
Ohio
Indiana
Virginia-West Virginia
North-South Carolina
Atlanta Georgia
North Florida
South Florida
Kentucky-Tennessee
Gulf Coast
Illinois
North Central
Midwest
Kansas-Missouri
Arkansas-Oklahoma
North Texas Dallas
South Texas
Houston
Rocky Mountain
Southwest
Pacific Northwest District
Northern California
Central California
Southern California
Los Angeles
San Francisco

ME, VT, NH, MA, CT, RI, NJ, NY, PA, MD, DE, WV, VA, NC, SC, GA, FL, KY, TN, AL, MS, LA, MI, OH, IN, IL, WI, MN, ND, SD, NE, IA, KS, MO, OK, AR, TX, MT, ID, WY, CO, UT, NV, AZ, NM, WA, OR, CA, AK, HI

IRS Communications Division

72

The following are the new districts listed under their new regions. The city names in parentheses show the new regional and district headquarters locations. The current districts are listed under the new districts.

Midstates Region (Dallas)

- Kansas-Missouri District (St. Louis)
  St. Louis
  Wichita
- Houston District
- Illinois District (Chicago)
  Chicago
  Springfield
- North Central District (St. Paul)
  Aberdeen
  Fargo
  St. Paul
- North Texas District (Dallas)
- Midwest District (Milwaukee)
  Des Moines
  Milwaukee
  Omaha
- South Texas District (Austin)
- Arkansas-Oklahoma District
  (Oklahoma City)
  Little Rock
  Oklahoma City

Southeast Region (Atlanta)

- North-South Carolina District
  (Greensboro)
  Columbia
  Greensboro
- Gulf Coast District (New Orleans)
  Birmingham
  Jackson
  New Orleans
- Kentucky-Tennessee District
  (Nashville)
  Louisville
  Nashville
- Georgia District (Atlanta)
- Indiana District (Indianapolis)
- Delaware-Maryland Dist. (Baltimore)
  Baltimore
  Washington, DC
  Wilmington
- North Florida District (Jacksonville)
- South Florida District
  (Fort Lauderdale)
- Virginia-West Virginia District
  (Richmond)
  Parkersburg
  Richmond

Northeast Region (Manhattan)

- Brooklyn District
- Manhattan District
- Michigan District (Detroit)
- New Jersey District (Newark)
- New England District (Boston)
  Augusta
  Boston
  Burlington
  Portsmouth
- Ohio District (Cincinnati)
  Cincinnati
  Cleveland
- Pennsylvania District (Philadelphia)
  Philadelphia
  Pittsburgh
- Connecticut-Rhode Island District
  (Hartford)
  Hartford
  Providence
- Upstate New York District (Buffalo)
  Albany
  Buffalo

Western Region (San Francisco)

- Central California District (San Jose)
- Los Angeles District
- Northern California District (Oakland)
  Sacramento
  San Francisco
- Pacific-Northwest District (Seattle)
  Anchorage
  Honolulu
  Portland
  Seattle
- Rocky Mountain District (Denver)
  Boise
  Cheyenne
  Denver
  Helena
  Salt Lake City
- Southern California District
  (Laguna Niguel)
- Southwest District (Phoenix)
  Albuquerque
  Las Vegas
  Phoenix

73

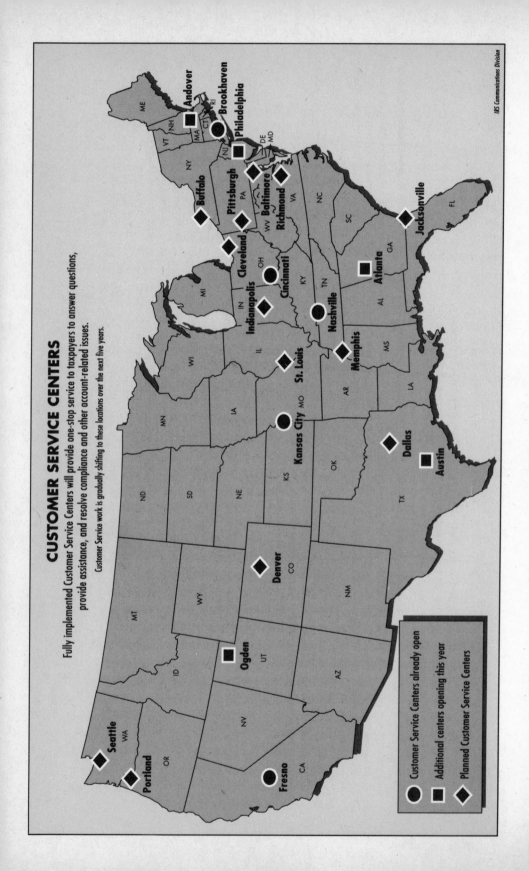

CUSTOMER SERVICE CENTERS

Fully implemented Customer Service Centers will provide one-stop service to taxpayers to answer questions, provide assistance, and resolve compliance and other account-related issues.

Customer Service work is gradually shifting to these locations over the next five years.

Customer Service Centers already open

Additional centers opening this year

Planned Customer Service Centers

Andover
Brookhaven
Philadelphia
Buffalo
Pittsburgh
Baltimore
Richmond
Jacksonville
Cleveland
Cincinnati
Atlanta
Indianapolis
Nashville
Memphis
St. Louis
Kansas City
Dallas
Austin
Denver
Ogden
Seattle
Portland
Fresno

IRS Communications Division

IRS ORGANIZATION

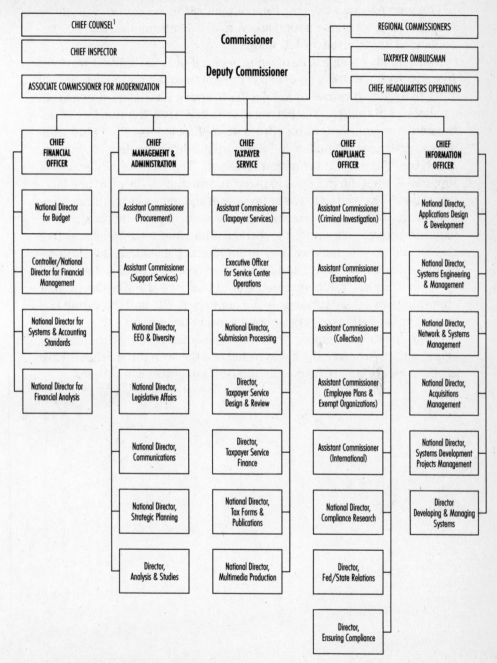

¹The Chief Counsel is part of the Legal Division of the Treasury.

member what that personality is. Many IRS employees really do care, but they simply don't have the time or inclination to show it. So don't be surprised if you receive wrong answers or misinformation and are disconnected, transferred, or left hanging.

Interestingly enough, this division secured over $57 million worth of free advertising in 1992, up over $17 million from the previous year.[13] In 1993, that figure dropped to $20.6 million, and in 1995 it was down again to almost $16 million. Yet between 1993 and 1995 the number of estimated viewers/listeners rose from 40 million to over 95.[14] One wonders where these estimates come from. This directly relates to what is called the "Taxpayer Information Program." The Taxpayer Information Program is what the IRS does to place information in the print and electronic media, as well as to assist taxpayers and increase voluntary compliance. If you were to conclude that a great deal of this material is image-sensitive, you would be correct. Thus, the news releases, fact sheets, and question-and-answer promotional pieces that the IRS prepares on diverse tax topics and offers to newspapers, local network and cable TV stations, radio stations, and others give the IRS the perfect opportunity to spread its image—the omniscient IRS and the caring IRS helping befuddled taxpayers through another tax season.

In the theater, an empty stage slowly comes to life with scenery, lights, actors. Now that the background and the structure of the IRS are in place, let's bring up the curtain on the people who work there.

4

IRS People

Whom You Need to Know
What They're Really Like
How to Work with Them
Standard Operating Procedures

THE IRS CHAIN OF COMMAND

At the top of the IRS chain of command are the commissioner and deputy counsel, both of whom are currently appointed by the president and report to the Treasury Department. The chief inspector, who is responsible for keeping the agency and its employees honest, is also at this level. As of about two years ago, constant reorganizations make it difficult to analyze or keep track of the IRS organizational structure. The chart on page 75 represents the latest one issued by the Media Relations Department.

WHO RUNS THE SHOW?

What is unique about the commissioner's job is how short-term it is. IRS commissioners reign for only brief periods of time, generally because

- A new one is appointed every four to eight years, reflecting our political process.
- Offers from law and accounting firms often seduce them away even sooner.

The author David Burnham has calculated that "since the end of World War II, the average tenure at the top position has been only 37 months."[1] Even IRS officials can deduce that given the turnover rate, taxpayers may begin to suspect that leadership at the top is somewhat negligible. After all, how much can one really learn about the workings of the largest bureaucracy in the world in three years? More important, how much can that person ever really be held accountable for the agency's failures or successes? The bottom line is, who's minding the store? As in many other cases where political tenure is short-term, entrenched bureaucrats run the show.

At the field organization level are the district directors and, on the same functional level, the service center directors, all of whom report to the regional commissioners.

Since the reorganization in 1952 and decentralization, power was handed down to the lower levels in the IRS hierarchy. According to Burnham, "The long-term effect of this sweeping reorganization has been that although the assistant commissioners who surround the commissioner in Washington are free to issue policy memos, testify before congressional committees, prepare charts, and hold meetings, they have little real authority over the tens of thousands of investigators, auditors, and clerks who actually go about the job of collecting taxes."[2]

THE EXAMINATION DIVISION

What People in the Examination Division Are Really Like
The one constant I kept hearing during my interviews for this book was "Ten years ago there were better people in the IRS," or "Things were better in the old days," or "Things have really gone downhill." All are accurate statements describing the standard IRS performance, specifically that of the Examination Division.

Tax Shelters Severely Weaken the Audit Function
In the late 1970's and throughout the 1980's, when the IRS realized the extent to which people were using tax shelters, hundreds of auditors and revenue agents were removed from their normal work assignments and assigned to ferret out and destroy tax shelters listed on individual

and corporate returns. In fiscal year 1979, tax shelter exams accounted for only 1.7 percent of a revenue agent's workload, but by fiscal 1984 this percentage had grown to 19.1 percent.[3]

The vehemence with which the IRS attacked the tax shelter was unprecedented in IRS annals and it affected an enormously broad spectrum of people and entities. The IRS declared that tax shelters were shams, concocted strictly to beat taxes and created with no intention of ever making a profit. According to tax law, if an investment is not intended to make a profit, deductions and credits and certainly the huge write-offs generated by tax shelters are not allowable.

Here's a simplified example of what used to take place with a typical tax shelter:

For $10,000 a taxpayer would purchase the rights to a well-known performer's unreleased record album that had been professionally appraised at $100,000. The balance of the acquisition costs, in this case $90,000, was regarded as a loan from the seller, to be paid down from earnings derived from sales of the record album.

As the new owner, the taxpayer got to write off as a deduction depreciation based on the appraised value, and during the early 1980's the taxpayer also received a 10 percent investment tax credit in the first year.

What is the overall effect of this simple procedure? If the taxpayer was in the 50 percent tax bracket, the $10,000 investment would have allowed him to reduce his taxes in the first year by about $15,000, including the investment tax credit. In the second year, without the taxpayer investing any additional funds, that initial $10,000 investment would still have functioned as a vehicle for a major tax write-off of about $19,000. This system of gaining substantial tax reductions annually would continue until the asset was fully depreciated—in about six years in the case of a record album. By then, the initial investment would have saved the taxpayer an estimated $58,000 in taxes.

Now you can see why the IRS was so determined to knock tax shelters off the face of the earth. They robbed the government of money and they diverted investments into frivolous assets.

Those so-called business ventures (records, tapes, movies, and others) that used artificial valuation methods cease to exist as tax shelters because of the Tax Reform Act of 1986. TRA '86 put an end to tax shelters by 1990 and made the rules retroactive as far back as 1980. To make sure the beast would never show its fangs again, TRA '86 also limited real estate write-offs so severely that it deprived legitimate real estate entrepreneurs of deductions they had always been entitled to. Fortunately, beginning January 1, 1994, because of RRA '93, taxpayers engaged full-time in real estate activities are again able to use real estate losses to fully offset other sources of income.

Many of the cases involving audits of tax shelters took years to complete and lasted into the early nineties. About 24 percent of pending Tax Court cases at one point in 1985 involved tax shelters.[4] The impact of all this on the Examination Division was practically irreparable. The shift weakened the function so severely that the percentage of taxpayer audits dropped steadily for the next 10 years from 1.77 percent in 1980 to about 1 percent in 1990. This drop translated to about 800,000 fewer individual tax returns audited each year. The current audit rate for individuals still hovers between 1 and 1.5 percent.

Outdated Management Practices Stymie Results

The turnover in entry-level positions at the IRS is quite high. The IRS hires new people into the audit function straight out of college. This group usually stays two to three years and then leaves for a private accounting firm or tax law practice, where they are likely to double their salary.

At the other end of the spectrum are the IRS career professionals, those 20-year employees who really know how to slow down the quality of work. This group represents a sizable number who are *not* interested in moving up the career ladder. They want job security (it is very difficult to get fired from the IRS), they are content to follow orders without asking questions, and they want to get through the day with minimum amounts of aggravation, mental dexterity, and energy. They think the way the IRS wants them to (middle-of-the-road), they do what they have been trained to do (not to rock the boat, conform at any cost), and try hard to maintain the status quo.

A good example of the 20-year professional is a friend of mine who was finally promoted from revenue officer to revenue agent. After four months on the job he requested a transfer back to being a revenue officer. Why? He specifically told me that the tax issues were just too complicated and he was mentally exhausted at the end of each day. As a revenue officer life was much easier. You just chased after delinquent taxpayers. No new issues were involved, and you didn't have to "tax" (pardon the pun) your brain.

Now add two more ingredients: Advancement at the IRS is almost strictly limited to people within the organization, which strips the lower ranks bare as the talented people are moved into supervisory roles; simultaneously, the overall level of supervision has dropped dramatically. According to a former IRS agent, revenue agents in the field used to review cases fairly thoroughly with their supervisors. These days if something doesn't get resolved in the time it takes to have a brief conversation, it just doesn't get resolved. (The extended four-day audit of my client Mrs. Price, the president of the wholesale medical supplies corporation discussed in chapter 3, pages 54–56, proves my point.)

IRS Auditors Always Operate Two Years Behind the Times

Unbeknownst to the majority of taxpayers, the following scenario is the norm. Tax returns are selected for audit 12 to 18 months after the filing date. By the time you, the taxpayer, have received notice of an audit appointment, it is often a year and a half after the year that your tax return under question covers. What's wrong with this picture? The revenue agent you will be working with on your old return, prepared almost two years ago, is still auditing issues using the old laws while he is simultaneously trying to learn the new laws. For example, in 1988 the Examination Division was still auditing 1986 returns, whereas on January 1, 1987, the most sweeping changes in tax history were put into effect. Or, in 1993, when the Revenue Reconciliation Act was passed, revenue agents were still examining 1991 returns.

In contrast, tax pros have already mastered the new laws. We have to because of the nature of our work. Our clients need us to advise them about how *today's* tax laws, as well as past laws, are impacting them, particularly if there's an audit.

This confusing situation translates into some important information for taxpayers:

- Given our complex tax laws, and the pressured situation of learning new tax laws while having to perform as an "expert" in past tax law, revenue agents tend to stick to the old standbys when conducting an audit. These include travel and entertainment, real estate, matching of income, and verification of cash and bank balances.
- From this we can infer that more complicated issues such as officers' loans, excessive compensation, aggressive inventory valuation methods, or accounting for the deferral of revenue from one year to another stand a good chance of not being scrutinized.

A revenue agent friend of mine admitted the following: **In a good-sized IRS district office, there are usually only one or two people who are familiar with tax laws involving capitalization of inventory costs or passive losses to an extent that they could teach it to other employees.** Now just pause for one moment and look at the significance of this. Ten years later, after they were created by TRA '86, the complex issues involved in these aspects of that tax law are still virtually undigested by the majority of IRS agents who work on the front lines with taxpayers.

There's a New Audit Mix

Today's auditors come from two very different segments of the population. The first—these are in the majority—is the younger set with three years or less of auditing experience.

The next group represents a fairly new phenomenon and is a result of the recession and loss of jobs in the private sector. Experienced people, in good positions (e.g., corporate controllers), 50 to 55 years old, who have been let go from corporations are drawn to the IRS because they want to continue working. This is the group whose corporate job probably consisted of gathering information for IRS audits and turning it over to the outside accountant who handled the company's audits.

If one of these people is subsequently hired by the IRS as a revenue agent, his or her greatest asset is knowing what deserves further scrutiny on a return. This kind of business experience, as opposed to book learning and IRS training courses, dramatically improves someone's chances of being an effective IRS auditor.

Remember the revenue agent I encountered during the audit of a client, Mr. Haley, the dealer in original art discussed in chapter 3 (pages 50–51)? An auditor from the younger set could easily have overlooked a substantial issue because he or she would have been unfamiliar with special accounting nuances in that field. But Mr. Arthur, with his corporate experience, knew enough to question the gross profit percentage listed on my client's corporate return.

But here's the rub. There aren't enough of these people to make a real difference in the quality of auditing at the IRS.

Finally, with the IRS push to educate its auditors about specific markets, an entire new group has become MSSP specialists (see pages 53–54 and 171–174).

In short, taxpayers often encounter the following when they become involved with the audit level in the Examination Division:

- IRS auditors are generally not thorough and certainly are not interested in opening a can of worms. They just want to get the job done, move caseloads off their desks, and go home.
- Some of the new IRS auditors have become experts on how to avoid answering a question.

- Some auditors have become especially efficient at shuffling taxpayers from one IRS person to another in an effort to push the work on to someone else.
- If you were to describe their work ethic, to say that auditors are clock-watchers is putting it mildly.

It will take time to ascertain how the MSSP-trained auditors will perform.

How to Work with the Examination Mentality

The auditor, therefore, has become the biggest unknown factor when a taxpayer is facing an audit. Sometimes the most difficult cases escape scrutiny because the auditor was not experienced, was not interested, or did not care enough to do a thorough investigation, like Mr. Stores in chapter 3. On the other hand, sometimes the easiest, most uncomplicated audit will turn into a nightmare.

A case I just completed involved a corporation that exports foodstuffs such as soybean oil and sugar to Central and South American countries. Although this may sound intriguing, even complicated, the guts of the audit were straightforward. The revenue agent, Mr. Fields, was a typical IRS hire with only two years' experience. After Day 3, I knew I was in for a long audit.

Obviously Mr. Fields didn't read the part of the *Internal Revenue Manual* that tells him to become familiar with the issues of his assigned audits (discussed in chapter 3) because he quickly made it clear that he knew absolutely nothing about exporting foodstuffs, freight forwarding, letters of credit, or international banking transactions.

As the audit proceeded, a number of issues required documentary proof: documents from court cases and excerpts from published tax services. Although I did all the research and had the data ready, Mr. Fields would ask whether the written material exactly covered the issue at hand or if my sources were superseded by a later ruling or law change. He was also unfamiliar with the documentation we were dealing with.

Slowly it also became apparent that this agent did not have a strong accounting background. Mr. Grant often buys goods from his customers and sells them other items. For practical reasons, my client's bookkeeper simply offsets the balances between accounts receivable and accounts payable so that only the new net balance owed to or from the person remains on the books. This simple accounting approach was completely unintelligible to Mr. Fields.

At the end of each day Mr. Fields would hand me a list of items to have on hand for the next meeting. The list contained many items I had already showed him. In my opinion the agent was either too lazy, too inexperienced, or too frightened to go to his supervisor for some direction. It was clear that he was in way over his head.

The professional fees were mounting and I saw no end in sight so I insisted that we use the next meeting to finalize things. We agreed on four routine issues—

travel and entertainment, auto expenses, insurance, and bad debts—out of a total of six. This amounted to $50,000 of disallowed expenses, which translated to a tax assessment of $17,000 plus another $7,000 in penalties and interest. As a condition of the settlement, Mr. Fields agreed to discuss the offsetting of receivables and payables with his group chief.

Six weeks later, Mr. Fields got back to me. We settled on a disallowance covering the final issue amounting to $5,000, resulting in an additional assessment of $3,000 in tax, penalties, and interest. Considering Mr. Fields's inexperience, he most likely believed that he had done a good job, and my client also was satisfied.

Handling the Auditor

Friend or Foe?

I have read accounts by professionals in the tax field who recommend making the auditor your friend. I can't say that's a reality for me; everyone involved is fully aware that an audit implicitly involves an adversarial relationship. That shouldn't mean that anger or aggression have to be a part of the audit process.

The approach I use and recommend for working with examination staff, especially auditors, is to be polite, friendly, and cooperative. You don't have to go so far as to offer information or documents unless asked, but civility is de rigueur. Be focused on reading the auditor's personality (that's usually not too difficult to do) and providing the auditor with the information requested.

Be in Control

It is also very important for you and your representative to be extremely prepared, neat, and precise. Receipts, cash register tapes, journals, bank files, and the like are better indications of integrity than dog-eared, discolored papers and containers of disorganized data. Know and look as if you are in full control. My friends in the IRS tell me this can put off the auditor, which usually works to the taxpayer's advantage. It also helps to appear relaxed.

Offer Direction

During an audit situation, things can go awry for various reasons. When an audit seems unfocused, presenting your position in a strong, clear, and affirmative way usually helps. With Mr. Fields, for example, I felt he needed a structure, since he couldn't create one for himself. Regarding the documentation that I submitted, which he kept refuting, I finally told him: "You can either accept what I am submitting or come up with new research yourself." That successfully worked to extinguish that part of his behavior. He knew that I knew I was right and he was floundering.

Handling a Clash

There may also be a clash of personalities. The auditor may become angry and challenge you. I have also known auditors to lie, bluff, and manipulate. Don't blow these things out of proportion. With all the pressure and heavy workloads that auditors face regularly, you may just be the one they've decided to take a stand against. It may pass if you stay calm.

Yes, there's a fine line between standing up for your rights and being pushed around, but it works to approach each situation individually. If you and the auditor are stuck on a few points, you can request to have the supervisor's input. I've gotten some positive responses using this method. Choices are available each step of the way, but they can and often do change at a moment's notice.

If an auditor is showing complete incompetence, the audit is getting nowhere, or the auditor is not agreeing to anything you say for reasons you may not be aware of, you have the right to request another auditor (a request not granted very often). Even if it is granted, it could all backfire, since you could end up with a competent person who may locate items that the disagreeable auditor never could have found.

If the point of disagreement is a large dollar amount and the auditor's supervisor doesn't agree with you, or if the auditor takes an entirely unreasonable position and the supervisor agrees, you can begin to move up the line to the IRS Appeals Office. (You could bring in a CPA or tax attorney at this point if you haven't already. To go it alone, see the discussion of the appeals process, pages 94–95.) The argument could end there in your favor or the case could continue to escalate, depending how far you choose to push.

Obtaining Your Tax File in a Disputed Case

Preparing an appeal takes time and can be costly if you are using a tax professional. Before you bother to take this step, be aware of the following: **There is an often overlooked IRS policy regarding protested and disputed tax cases.** Previously the IRS kept its enforcement strategies and litigation approaches secret and consistently maintained that this information should not be released to the public. As usual, the IRS didn't want to give away anything it didn't have to. In several cases, however, the federal court ordered the IRS to comply with individuals' Freedom of Information Act requests for all relevant documents in their tax files. (See Freedom of Information Act discussion on page 113.) Although the IRS does not like to admit giving way to pressure, the change in policy, as the IRS calls it, seems to have been a direct result of these cases. So a new precedent has been set: **The Examination Division must now provide taxpayers with the IRS's rebuttal position regarding issues under conflict in cases that are being forwarded to Appeals.**

The good news is, you get to see in black and white what positions the auditor has taken, and an idea of how much and what information is being sent to the appeals officer.

The bad news is the auditor's work papers are often incomplete, which could lead you to believe the auditor has a weak case. Don't assume the auditor's case is weak. He may know more than he's written down. Disregard any incompleteness. No matter what, prepare your best case for presentation at the appeals conference.

Calling a Halt to the Audit

Finally, you can terminate an audit at any time by stating that you'd rather not continue, since it appears that nothing further can be accomplished. Usually the auditor will write up the case as being "unagreed" and pass it up to the supervisor. Perhaps a new auditor or the Appellate Division will offer a solution.

THE COLLECTION DIVISION

What People in the Collection Division Are Really Like

IRS *revenue officers*, also referred to as *collections officers*, are focused, determined, and unemotional. They face taxpayers one-on-one to carry out the actual collection process and are trained to think and act quickly and efficiently. Revenue officers are pragmatists with a mission: They genuinely believe that they are paid to save our country by getting the equivalent of your house, your car, your savings, and more into the pockets of the federal government to pay your debt.

How Revenue Officers Differ from Auditors and Other IRS Employees

- First of all, revenue officers like what they do or they wouldn't be in that division.
- Second, their personalities combine with their work to make a perfect fit. If people get into collection who don't belong there because they have too much heart, they leave. The ones who remain are diehards.

- Revenue officers, at least the ones who go on-site to do the actual negotiations and confiscations, are unquestionably more ambitious than those in auditing or examination. They want to be noticed.
- The IRS highly regards a show of strength and producing the desired results and rewards such employees with plaques, honor ceremonies, and rapid promotion to higher grade levels.

How to Work with the Collection Mentality

Part of the collection mentality is formed and predicated on quotas, even though they may not be called that. This is something the IRS vehemently denies, but quotas nevertheless seem to exist, according to several former auditors and revenue officers I have spoken to. With the pressure to levy, place liens, seize property, and turn in a better weekly or monthly performance than those at desks to the left and right of them, how would you expect revenue officers to behave? They mean business and they have neither the time nor the inclination to fool around.

The best way to work with collection people is to avoid ever having to deal with them. But if you get this far down the road and end up in a tax jam in which you have to face one or more collection officers, don't mess with them. Do what they say. Follow your part in the collection process. Answer their queries. Don't ignore the letters you keep receiving. Be clear. Stick to your story.

Because there are different stages in the collection process, you are likely to encounter different personality sets common to each stage. No one tells taxpayers that. For example, quite often a lot can be cleared up at the ACS (Automated Collection System) level just by dealing with a collection representative over the telephone. Sometimes things can even be sorted out with revenue officers *before* they visit your home or office. The point is, just because you find yourself under the jurisdiction of the collection department doesn't mean you have to panic.

Here's a fairly representative case involving the beginning stages of the collection process, what you're likely to encounter, and how to deal with it.

One day, I received a call out of the blue from one of my corporate clients who told me that the securities firm he does business with had received a letter from the IRS notifying him that his brokerage account had a $2,500 levy placed on it.

Before I go further, let me give you some background. My client, a medium-sized and very successful corporation, very much in the black, was and has always been an A client. The firm's brokerage account in question did a sizable amount of securities trading and at that time contained a portfolio of stocks and bonds valued at over $600,000. A levy placed on this brokerage account was very serious. It meant the corporation was unable to engage in any securities activities; the securities firm would in turn be highly fearful of doing business with them while their account had a levy placed on it by the IRS.

I knew my client had done nothing wrong and that the IRS had messed up. The challenge was to find out where the problem was, to get the IRS to recognize what they had done wrong, and to work with them to correct it. Gearing up for the utterly outrageous and unexpected, I telephoned the revenue officer from the local district office who had signed the letter.

Within two minutes things became clearer, at least from my end. "We never received any notices," I said.

"We sent all four of them [the 500 series, remember them?]," the revenue officer replied.

"Where to?" I asked.

"To ———," he said.

"The company moved from that address almost four years ago," I answered, rather blatantly disgusted.

"Well, you should have had the mail forwarded," he said.

"We did," I replied, "but the post office only forwards mail for one year. Why didn't you look on your computer for the 1992 file, which has the new address on the corporate return?," I asked.

"No returns were showing for that year," he said. "The corporation didn't file a return."

"Of course we filed a return," I said. Now I knew that this guy was too lazy to look for it.

"Look," the revenue officer replied, totally avoiding my points because he knew that I knew that he hadn't looked for the return, "you owe us $2,500 for 1990 payroll taxes."

"If you look on your computer, you'll see you owe us a $38,000 refund due from an overpayment on corporate income tax," I replied.

"That has nothing to do with it," he said. "You still owe us $2,500."

At this point I decided to go for a compromise and fight the $2,500 later. "Since the $38,000 is due to be received by us within the next few weeks, why don't you just deduct the $2,500 from the $38,000 credit and release the levy from the stock account."

"We can't do that."

"Why not?"

"It's too much trouble. I don't have time to check into all the details. Pay us with a bank check and then we'll release the levy."

"We can't wait that long," I said. "You know that will take over a month and my client can't leave that account dormant all that time."

"Hold on a minute. I'll be right back."

"O.K. Now," I thought, "maybe something will happen because he is obviously going to speak to his group chief."

Next I hear a new voice from the other end of the phone, obviously the group chief, although he didn't introduce himself. Some IRS people don't always have the time, inclination, or awareness to recognize that it's helpful to know whom you're speaking to. They often prefer to remain anonymous, and withhold their names so they don't have to become involved or incur blame.

"We don't have the facilities to arrange for the $2,500 to be offset against the $38,000. If you want the levy released, just pay the $2,500 with a bank check."

Although I could have continued to argue that my client in no way owes $2,500, I knew I was speaking to two people who would continue to parrot each other and the only solution was to agree to do it their way, at least that time.

So we sent the bank check the second week in April and the levy was released two weeks later. The way that works is the IRS sends a release of levy form to the brokerage firm so that the firm knows everything has been cleared up and activity begins again.

A brief analysis will clue in taxpayers about the collection mentality. (Note: Any perceptible overlaps with the Examination Division are actually common threads that link all IRS divisions to the IRS personality.)

- Collection staff are inflexible.
- Collection staff generally take the easy way out.
- Lying, bluffing, and deceiving are common practices.

Another entrée into the mentality of revenue officers in Collection is this: Most whom I have met are always worried about their jobs. (This is also true for many revenue agents in the Examination Division.) If they make too many mistakes, will they be fired? Or demoted? Or put last in line for a promotion? If they disagree with the tactics that are used and do not take an aggressive line of action, which is expected, will they fall from grace? The answer is yes.

But above and beyond all of this, revenue officers have been trained to provide answers for every question, and to fill in every blank on the preprinted IRS collection procedures forms. In this division, as in Examination, it's paperwork that counts.

Sometimes when I watch revenue officers filling in line after line, page after page of IRS forms, it just seems downright stupid under the circumstances. But my conclusions fall by the wayside as they follow some IRS voice inside their head (which I certainly don't hear), which tells them to fill in the blanks, no matter what. Here's what I mean:

Similar to the tone of the last case describing the collection mentality (I know it sounds more like a bad dream), I received a notice from the IRS that a client of mine hadn't sent in the IRS federal payroll tax form for the first quarter of 1992, and that currently, with penalties and interest, the amount due had reached $30,000.

I knew this was not plausible. This client had sold her business to a big conglomerate and moved to New Mexico two years before. The revenue officer refused to hear any explanations over the telephone and insisted that I come to the district office to settle things.

At our cozy one-on-one, there sat the revenue officer with a pile of forms one inch thick on his desk. He explained that the 1992 quarterly payroll tax was missing. "But the company was sold in 1991. The last quarterly payroll tax you received was for 1990."

"It was," the revenue officer agreed, "and we've been sending notices ever since, but haven't heard anything."

Let me begin to clue you in at this point because there were obviously three irritants that prompted this situation: First, the client's bookkeeper who sent in the last form neglected my directions to properly notify the IRS that this would be the final quarterly payroll tax form.

Second, the notices were going to nowhere. Where was the post office in all of this? (Are you beginning to realize that given the nature of the tax collection process, the post office is a vital, albeit somewhat uncontrollable, link in the process?)

Finally, because the IRS did not know the company was extinguished, and because it did not receive the next quarterly payroll tax form, some clerk in the examination department checked the amount of the last payroll tax and entered a made-up figure based on the last amount entered on the quarterly form and came up with $25,000.

Once this occurs **you are face-to-face with a problem that materializes out of the vacuum created from missing information the IRS expected to receive but didn't.** Since there is no response, penalties and interest accrue, no matter what. By the time I was contacted, the amount due had reached $30,000.

Now let's return to the face-to-face meeting at the district office. I calmly told the revenue officer that my client had sold her company and had been out of business for over two years. Appearing to have heard every word, this is what happened next: The revenue officer, staring at his topmost form, pen poised for action, responded by firing a string of questions at me. "What is the new location of the business? How many employees are there? What are the taxes owed in the current year?" To jolt him out of his "fill-in-the-blank" reverie, I grabbed his arm and said rather loudly, "I already told you, my client is out of business. This is a self-generated liability. The IRS computer created it."

"No," the officer said. "It's a tax due."

"No, it's not. It's an estimate."

At that point he got up and left the room, actually another good sign, probably a trip to his group chief.

When he returned, there was good news. The group chief agreed with me. The revenue officer was told to void the liability entirely. He assured me that he'd fill out the necessary forms and send the credit. Approximately six months later, the credit was finally issued.

The fact that IRS employees are taught to leave no line blank has become a double-edged sword. Yes, there is the possibility for completeness on the one hand. But on the other, this same revenue officer, diligently performing as he was taught, becomes so focused on the line information that he fails to ask for or recognize that there are a lot of other more important things going on. It appears that group chiefs will scold someone on their staff more easily for a piece of missing information because an empty line is particularly visible.

THE CRIMINAL INVESTIGATION DIVISION

What People in the Criminal Investigation Division Are Really Like

Special agents employed in the Criminal Investigation Division are involved in the kind of investigation work and chasing down the bad guys depicted in the movies. Involvement at this level means possible criminal-level offenses levied against you, leaving you subject to a possible jury trial and imprisonment.

Special agents are formidable opponents, highly skilled in locating hidden assets and unreported sources of income and identifying false records and fraudulent tax returns. Working with a full array of the latest in police and crime detection technology, they interrogate, untangle intricate transactions, obtain corroborating statements, make third-party investigations, conduct raids, use electronic surveillance, and decide whom to summons.

The agents who work in this division are extraordinarily thorough, painstakingly patient, and tough. They have to be—it's their job to build a case against the unsuspecting taxpayer.

But they are also calm, at least initially, and have a way about them that says to the taxpayer, "You can trust me. I'm easy to talk to." Part of their job is to instill this feeling in taxpayers. But once you open up to a special agent, well, their case is made, and your fate could be sealed. That's why, if that special agent comes to your door, anything you say could be an open invitation or a recrimination. Neither does you any good. Reach for your phone and dial a good tax attorney.

While other areas of the IRS may be haphazardly run, the process involved in catching big- and small-time tax criminals is tedious and time-consuming. Completion of a good case in a year is considered a satisfactory performance for a special agent. The work may be hazardous and advancement is generally faster here than in other IRS divisions.

How to Work with the Criminal Investigation Mentality

In 1985, I was a witness before a grand jury relating to a CID investigation of one of my clients. It was there that I learned how meticulous the CID can be.

The IRS typically has a great deal of trouble locating a taxpayer's past returns, especially returns that are five years old or older. When I was on the stand, the prosecutor not only showed me the last ten 1040's filed by my client, but the original ones at that!

After that, the CID subpoenaed all my client's books and records (he owned and operated several corporations). When the records were returned to the corporation, CID inadvertently also included a large portion of the work papers it had created and assembled for the case, an obvious mistake by CID but a golden opportunity to examine their work firsthand. No, it's not illegal. Their mistake was fair game to us.

The work papers showed a complete analysis of all corporate bank accounts and the client's personal bank accounts, including every deposit slip, canceled check, and debit and credit memo. In our profession, that level of work is highly impressive. Coming from the IRS, it is astounding!

In the end, my client wound up having no charges brought against him. Ultimately the grand jury investigation was terminated and my client was not brought to trial. Therefore, I concluded that no damaging evidence had been uncovered.

When working with CID, the message is clear: CID is thorough and determined. Don't underestimate them or their abilities.

THE UPPER ECHELONS

What People in the Upper Echelons Are Really Like

A large group that stands out and apart from IRS employees is what I call the upper echelons. These are IRS attorneys, accountants, and specially trained people with advanced educational degrees. In 1995, the chief counsel's office had over 3,000 employees. The majority of them are in the upper echelons and their work exposes them to a very full range of legal matters, from appeals and criminal tax cases (including the kind that end up in the Supreme Court) to all sorts of other litigation (Freedom of Information Act opinions, unfair labor practice, bankruptcies) and international tax matters.

Never for a moment forget: **Every time you get in the sights of the IRS there is an enormous legal infrastructure ready to fire.**

What's even more interesting is that this group, which reports up through the chief counsel's office, is separate and distinct from another IRS upper-echelon function, the Legislative Affairs Division, which reports up through the deputy commissioner, directly under the IRS commissioner.

The Legislative Affairs Division is heavily focused on developing, co-ordinating, and monitoring plans to implement new or pending legislation; developing legislative proposals for the IRS; communicating legislative information to the IRS commissioner and throughout the IRS; working with Public Affairs on press releases and media strategies relating to new legislation; and coordinating IRS responses to the General Accounting Office (GAO), the investigative arm of Congress.[5]

All of these upper-echelon people are treated as a rather elite group of which the IRS is particularly proud and which it handles with kid gloves.

To keep updated on their specialties and on policy and procedural changes within the IRS, upper-echelon employees periodically attend rather high-level training courses. The nature of their work keeps them together in a sort of specialized clique. In turn, they tend to stay among themselves and are looked up to by everyone else at the IRS.

Their salary levels are fairly competitive with (but not equal to) those in the private sector, and the on-the-job experience they can gain on the basis of the volume and range of cases that they are exposed to can be truly superb. Many at this level stay an average of five to ten years before they go off to a specialized law or accounting firm, where they command larger salaries and are considered prized property, having come from the IRS.

How to Work with the Upper-Echelon Mentality

Taxpayers rarely, if ever, come in contact with this level of IRS personnel. If you do, what you'll find are highly educated professionals, many attorneys who know their stuff. They are hardworking, focused, and operate essentially like trial lawyers, doing research, interviewing, preparing legal papers, appearing in court cases.

The only time taxpayers might meet someone from the IRS upper echelon is if they go to Tax Court or the Appeals Office (formerly referred to as the Appellate Division). At both of these levels, your representative will talk to his or her person and that's where you'll get some inkling of how these people operate. The chart on page 95 gives an overview of the process described in the following pages.

You and the Appeals Process

The IRS Appeals Office has the authority to settle cases, partially or wholly, on the basis of its assessment of the IRS's chances of winning. In other words, the ultimate objective for an appeals officer (who may be a lawyer or someone trained by the IRS to handle appeals) is to prevent a case from going to Tax Court. The Tax Court calendar has a huge backlog of cases, and the process of going through it is extremely trying for both sides. **The IRS doesn't go to Tax Court unless it believes that it has a better than 50 percent chance of winning.** If the appeals officer in the Appeals Office determines that the IRS may have a tough time winning the case, he'll recommend coming to a settlement. To achieve this he will probably concede an issue to induce the taxpayer to settle without delay. Even if it looks as if the IRS will win, the appeals officer might still offer a small concession simply to avoid the time and expense of going to Tax Court.

On October 1, 1993, the IRS initiated a new program to help taxpayers prepare and file protest letters in resolving undue delays in getting a case through the appeals process. To take advantage of this service, speak to the Appeals Office representative by calling your local district office. You can also send for IRS publication 5, *Appeal Rights and Preparation of Protests for Unagreed Cases.*

OFFERING A BRIBE—WHAT ARE THE CONSEQUENCES?

Offering bribes has been against the rules of conduct for anyone working in the IRS, *at any level or division,* from its inception, as the U.S. Constitution clearly states. That doesn't mean, however, that the practice doesn't exist.

A quiet bribe between a revenue officer (or even a revenue agent or tax auditor) and a taxpayer who owes tax money (or obviously fiddled around on a tax return) is not and has never been unique. There are two primary issues to be considered here. What constitutes a bribe and did you offer one?

Generally a bribe involves an offer to an IRS employee whose purpose is to persuade or encourage that person not to take a certain action against you, the taxpayer. The bribe can be anything from a fancy lunch to a gift, a flight to Santa Fe, money, and lots more. But essentially a bribe is anything that sounds as if it is a bribe to the IRS person whose mind and actions you are trying to bend your way.

The Office of Government Ethics issues *Rules of Conduct* that apply to all governmental agencies, including the IRS. Furthermore, there is a standard procedure regarding the taking of bribes that IRS collections officers, revenue agents, and anyone else having intimate contact with a taxpayer must follow. The procedure, which is drilled into the heads of these IRS personnel, is very precise, and goes something like this:

Income Tax Appeal Procedure

Internal Revenue Service

At any stage of procedure:

You can agree and arrange to pay. You can ask the Service to issue you a notice of deficiency so you can file a petition with the Tax Court. You can pay the tax and file a claim for a refund.

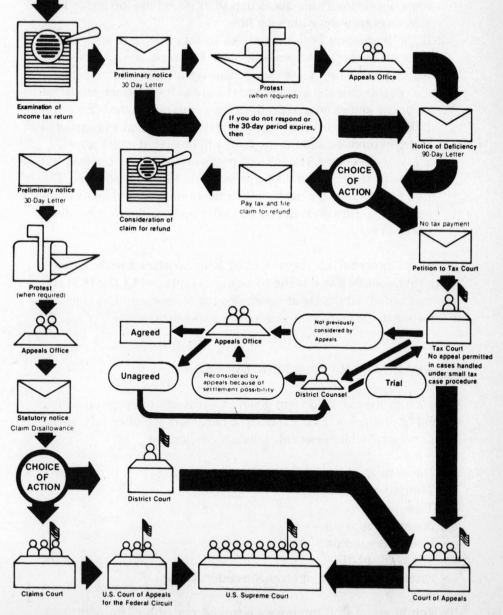

Examination of income tax return

Preliminary notice 30 Day Letter

Protest (when required)

Appeals Office

If you do not respond or the 30-day period expires, then

Notice of Deficiency 90-Day Letter

CHOICE OF ACTION

Pay tax and file claim for refund

Consideration of claim for refund

Preliminary notice 30-Day Letter

Protest (when required)

Appeals Office

Statutory notice Claim Disallowance

CHOICE OF ACTION

No tax payment

Petition to Tax Court

Tax Court No appeal permitted in cases handled under small tax case procedure

Not previously considered by Appeals

Appeals Office

Agreed

Unagreed

Reconsidered by appeals because of settlement possibility

District Counsel

Trial

District Court

Claims Court

U.S. Court of Appeals for the Federal Circuit

U.S. Supreme Court

Court of Appeals

PROCEDURE FOR REPORTING BRIBES

- If a revenue agent believes he or she has been offered a bribe, nothing is done or said at that time, while the taxpayer is present.
- As soon as the meeting with the taxpayer is over, the agent is to immediately notify the Inspection Division, whose job it is to keep tabs on corruption within the IRS.
- If the Inspection Division decides to take the next step, and in most cases it probably does because it accepts the agent's word, the taxpayer is set up with the same agent at another meeting— except this time the agent is wired and has been rehearsed so that he or she knows how to get the taxpayer to repeat the bribe offer.
- If this occurs, someone from the Inspection Division will appear at the right moment and the taxpayer will be placed under arrest.
- The worst scenario: The U.S. attorney's office will get involved and prosecute the case and the taxpayer could face a jail sentence. The best scenario for the taxpayer is if the bribe offer proves to be inconclusive. However, the items under audit will surely be disallowed in full.

I would never advise any client of mine to offer a bribe or anything that sounds like a bribe to anyone employed by the IRS. You may feel bad about paying an enormous tax assessment. But compare that feeling to the permanent scars from a stay in prison.

STANDARD OPERATING PROCEDURES

If anyone in the tax field were given two minutes to come up with a handful of epithets to characterize the behaviors we often face at the IRS, I am certain the list would include the following:

- Out-and-out lying
- Bluffing
- Threatening
- Sheer incompetence
- System breakdown
- The "IRS shuffle"
- Offering misleading or erroneous information

Watch how the first three weave in and out of a client audit that began in 1987 covering 1985 and lasted over two and a half years.

Some background: An IRS analysis of my client's 1985 checking account showed that out of a total of $500,000, only $100,000 was accounted for. My client attributed the other $400,000 to the sale of an art collection that he had accumulated over a 40-year period. The sale of the art was conducted by an auction house that had gone out of business about six months after completing the sale.

Things began to heat up as auditor number two entered the scene toward the end of 1987. (The first auditor, assigned to us by the IRS for over nine months, was in way over her head.) Her replacement was a shrewd middle-aged woman who told us she had 15 years with the IRS. She was also extremely busy with a full workload at the IRS and college teaching besides. It became common for her to cancel meetings, be out of the office for weeks at a time, and be difficult to reach.

For the final meeting she promised to bring in an IRS "expert" to refute the sales prices and/or costs we were submitting. She also said that the case would drag on unless my client accompanied me. Clearly she was hoping he would make some admission that she could use against him. How did I counter her threats? By showing her documented costs of the art, a 45-page inventory list packaged with canceled checks and receipts (vendor's bills) that were from one to 30 years old (some of the paper looked quite antique). The total came to $90,000.

Next I counseled my client so that he said nothing of use to her. I actually liked the idea of his being there because he was, in effect, the resident art expert.

Our auditor never did bring in that IRS expert (it was a big bluff) because, I believed then and still do, she was in an enormous hurry to finish with us (you'll see why), and requesting an expert can require a lot of lead time.

By the end of the day, we submitted the following data:

Total sales price	$400,000
Costs we claimed (total inventory list)	210,000
Taxable capital gain (profit)	$190,000

Since the inventory records were meticulous and authentic, the IRS auditor agreed to allow us all of the $90,000 plus half of the cost for which we had no paperwork, i.e., half of $120,000, or $60,000. (In audits of this nature, actual receipts are requested, but are not an absolute requirement to win your case.)

In summary, these were the figures:

Total gross proceeds		$400,000
Less allowable cost (justified with receipts)	$90,000	
Extra as agreed (our deal)	60,000	150,000
New capital gain		$250,000

In 1985, only 40 percent of capital gains was taxable. Hence, you can see why we argued long and hard for any unreported income to be considered from the art sale (capital gain) rather than being considered as ordinary income.

Forty percent of a capital gain of $250,000 is $100,000 of taxable income. Since my client was in the 50 percent, or highest, tax bracket, with the proposed settlement his tax liability would be $50,000 plus approximately $45,000 of penalties and interest. (This was a period of double-digit interest rates and four years had passed since the return was filed.)

We decided to accept the proposal and the auditor said she would write it up and, as is customary, submit it to her group chief for approval.

Four weeks later I called her to ask when we could expect the papers. At this point she informed me that she was allowing $90,000 for our costs (only the amount we could prove), but she did not mention the extra $60,000 she had agreed to. She insisted that she never agreed to it and as far as she was concerned, there was nothing more she could do.

I called her group chief and told him that she lied to me and my client. He took it under advisement for a couple of days and called me back to say that he believed her story and that if we were not happy, we should take the case to the Appeals Office, so we did. As was her style, she managed to drag out the meeting with the appeals officer by not forwarding her work papers until nine months later, which of course meant an additional nine months of interest tacked on to the bill.

The Appeals Office will carefully examine the merits of a case. If they don't believe there will be a clear-cut victory in Tax Court, the IRS will strike a bargain, and that's exactly what happened after a two-hour meeting.

The appeals officer allowed the original cost of $90,000 plus $50,000 of the extra $60,000. This meant that my client had "regained" $10,000 (40 percent of $50,000 equals $20,000, times the tax rate of 50 percent makes $10,000) plus accumulated penalties and interest.

P.S. Within two months after the conclusion of the audit, our shrewd auditor was promoted to the Appeals Office, a rather significant promotion for a revenue agent.

Many questions remain open: Was the revenue agent in a big rush since she expected a promotion? (In a friendlier moment, she did actually mention to me that she was expecting it.) After agreeing to allow us half of the $120,000, did she realize that she had given up too much, which was not her normal performance? Or, remembering that she was brought in as a relief quarterback, did she want to avoid showing weakness (giving a taxpayer too much), which would hurt her chances for that promotion to Appeals?

Now watch as the IRS easily and predictably produces the last few items of behavior that often show up during an audit.

In early September 1991, out of the blue I received a copy of a check that a client received from the IRS in the amount of $40,000. As I scanned it, the particulars of her case came back to me.

On her 1040 form for 1990, we requested that the IRS carry over $40,000 to her 1991 return. The money represented an overpayment that would do my client more good if carried forward to the following year. This was because by the time her 1040 was expected to be filed, June 15, 1991, she already owed $40,000 in estimated taxes for 1991, so we proceeded as if the carry-over had taken place. (As planned, her 1040 for 1990 was filed June 15, 1991.) Although we thought the IRS had honored our request, three months later, when we looked at the check in hand, we saw that obviously something had gone wrong.

The first question was "What should we do with the check?" The problem was that now my client would begin to incur penalties for not paying the April and June 1991 quarterly estimated income taxes in a timely manner.

After mailing a power of attorney to the IRS district office, I called a revenue officer at the district office (taking the number directly from the letter in hand) and asked why the IRS had sent the check. The revenue officer's response was typical: "I don't know, and I can't tell you. The 1990 return is not showing up on the computer."

"Well, what about the 1991 return? Can you locate that?" I asked.

"No, I can't. I'm too busy right now. I've got too much to get through. You'll have to call back later."

"But then I'll have to start all over again."

"Just call the same number," the revenue officer said. "You'll get someone to help you."

"Can't you just take a minute to look it up?"

"I have to go. Call back," he said and hung up.

A few hours later I called back and, surprisingly, ended up with the same revenue officer. Again I asked him to locate my client's 1991 return. Guess what? After a few minutes, he found it. "Oh, yes," he said. "Here it is. The income listed is $732,000 but no tax is due."

Now I was fully aware that my client's taxable income was $732,000. I was also aware that the tax paid on that return was $225,000. Here I was, faced with an IRS revenue officer in the Collection Division telling me that my client had no tax due. "How could there be no tax due on $732,000?" I asked, totally astonished.

"Well," the person replied, "maybe there were a lot of deductions." I actually held my breath wondering if in a few weeks my client would receive another refund, this time for $225,000. "Oh, wait a second," he said. "I've got another screen that says there is an assessment on this return of $225,000."

"That's not an assessment. That's the tax we paid on the account."

After a few more minutes of banter, the revenue officer became convinced that I was correct, and we proceeded to find an answer to the $40,000 check by going over the payments one by one. "The tax was entered in the wrong place," he said.

"That's impossible," I answered.

"Oh, not by you. On my screen." I guess an IRS entry clerk made the error.

Now a plan of action became clear. I would instruct my client to return the original $40,000 check to the IRS with a cover letter explaining that the money should have been credited to her 1991 estimated tax account.

The Secret to Finding Your Way Through the IRS

I am not interested in taxpayers understanding what each individual section of the IRS does in isolation. **You have to be able to make connections, to see literally the whole of what the IRS does, so that things take on meaning within this framework.** Those who have become experts in working with the IRS say one of the secrets to their success is the ability to grasp, even superficially, what goes on from one end of the agency to the other. Taxpayers who can afford it flock to these specialists who know how to "find their way through" the IRS because of their ability to view the agency from a larger perspective.

Above and beyond the never-ending process of collecting, enforcing, and processing billions of tax dollars, taxpayers also need to recognize where the power of the IRS comes from. Dissecting this power into its component parts, then learning how to manage it, is the next hurdle to jump.

5

Neutralizing the IRS's Power

THE IRS POWER BASE

The IRS power base comes from several sources. The IRS has unique

- Information resources
- Legal standing
- Role as a law enforcement agency
- Legislation-originating authority
- Ability to make mistakes without consequences
- Freedom to do what it wants

POWER FROM INFORMATION RESOURCES

Information gathering, with state-of-the-art equipment, has imbued the IRS with more power than any other bureaucracy in the world. This fact goes hand in hand with other more disturbing realities: IRS computer centers have questionable security; there is significant evidence of periodic leaks for political purposes; few, if any, independent private or governmental bodies review IRS operations or management processes. "Thus," comments David Burnham, "it has come to pass that the IRS has developed into the largest, most computerized, and least examined law enforcement agency in America."[1]

What Information Is Gathered About You?

Did you know that the IRS is legally entitled to collect information about you from the following sources:

- Your employer or anyone who pays you over $600 for services rendered
- Institutions that provide pensions and annuities to the elderly
- Casinos and racetracks
- Banks or corporations
- Barter deals or exchanges of property
- Real estate agents, when you buy or sell a property
- Any organization granting you a loan
- Your state unemployment office

In fact, the IRS receives information from such a wide range and number of sources that if it wanted to, it could easily discover what you earn, how you live, how many homes you own, the type of car you drive, where you spend your free time, where you go on vacation, and on and on.

Did you know that once it has the information, the IRS can do the following:

- Label you as a someone who owes the government money, never filed a return, earns above a certain dollar amount, has high audit potential, and more.
- Allow thousands of IRS agents across the country easy access to your tax return.
- Share the information on your tax return regularly with other states, cities, and federal agencies.

It seems as if each new piece of legislation designed to provide additional information from third parties about how taxpayers live whets the IRS's appetite even further. Recently, RRA '93 has required that any charitable contributions of $250 or more be acknowledged in writing by the organization receiving the money in order for it to be deductible by the giver.

What Are Your Legal Rights Against Misuse of the Information?

There is a body of law that protects private citizens by prohibiting misuse of financial information. One is the Privacy Act of 1974, another is the Computer Matching and Privacy Protection Act of 1988, Public Law 100-503.

Generally speaking, preventing misuse means making certain that only those who are allowed by law to access the information can in fact do so. It means using the information for its designated purpose, for example to verify that someone's annual income can support a specific mortgage loan amount, or to answer taxpayers' questions about their tax returns. It means ensuring that the information used is up to date. The fact that someone has declared bankruptcy, for example, must be cleared from a person's record after a period of 10 years.

If these laws are broken private citizens can legally seek redress. What if, for example, a seller accepted your bid to buy a new home and an independent private agency that verifies credit standing notified all parties concerned that your credit was unacceptable? Suppose that wasn't true. Suppose your credit rating was fine. With a credit agency, you have the right to demand a printout of the information, or to follow specific procedures to update or correct it. **With the IRS this is not possible.**

Who Is Guarding Your Privacy?

Information protection for taxpayers regarding the information collected about them and overseen by the IRS must come from two sources: the technology, which stores and manipulates the information, and the people who have access to it.

Scrupulous and precise rules for accessing information should be in place in IRS data centers to protect your interests and prevent leaks and misuse. However, there really aren't such rules.

Part of the problem, according to the IRS, is lack of resources. It takes funding to track down what systems networks within the IRS are being linked to what other IRS systems networks, and to close any gaps through which information can be accessed or "leaked." It takes time and effort to sweep each system clean of passwords used by former employees so that at least these entrypoints are locked. And, yes, it is expensive to install security-oriented software and to conduct periodic security audits.

In addition, though, the issue of computer security just doesn't seem to be a high priority at the IRS.

To reveal or not to reveal information disclosed on an individual's tax return has been debated since President Lincoln signed the first income tax into law in 1862. Almost from the beginning there were two opposing camps.

Congress's position at that time required that tax returns be published in at least four public places and for at least 15 days. (Can you imagine it!) In this way it was hoped that everyone would be kept honest. In 1914 the Supreme Court ruled that returns of individuals shall not be subject to inspection by any one except the proper officers and employees of the Treasury Department.[2]

The battle over confidentiality raged on. Each time a new revenue act was proposed, proponents of disclosure argued for the people's right to know, while the opposition argued that people have a right to privacy concerning their business affairs.

The real kicker came with the Nixon administration's abuses of individual privacy through misuse of IRS information during the early 1970's. Section 6103 of the *Internal Revenue Code* was eventually approved by Congress several years later to prevent political use of IRS-generated information by limiting the number of people and governmental agencies that could access tax information. Although this law is on the books, given the IRS's controlling, secretive nature, the reality is that an elaborate set of barriers established by Congress discourages taxpayers from seeking legal redress in the courts. The misapplication of the well-intentioned privacy law, says Burnham, has led to a situation where "lawyers are blocked from obtaining information they need to initiate suits challenging genuine IRS abuses. . . . A congressional committee empowered to investigate the IRS is partially blocked from investigating serious allegations of IRS corruption by a tortured application of the same law. The IRS has repeatedly initiated audits, leaked information, or otherwise harassed individual citizens, both in and out of government, who raised valid questions about its performance."[3]

POWER FROM THE IRS'S UNIQUE LEGAL STANDING

If you are a taxpayer suspected of violating our tax laws, you are guilty until you prove that you are not. No other area of our government operates upon this premise. In fact, the entire foundation of our civil law is based upon the assumption that one is innocent until proven guilty—except where the IRS is involved.

The IRS can accuse taxpayers of an infringement, garnishee their paychecks, put a lien on their homes, and seize their cars and businesses, all without standard procedures by lawyers, judges, or juries. Unfortunately, the accused taxpayer is fully responsible for proving his or her innocence.

POWER FROM ITS UNIQUE ROLE AS
A LAW-ENFORCEMENT AGENCY

A look, even a rather cursory one, at IRS operations since its reorganization in the early 1950's reveals an indisputable trend: the continuous expansion of the IRS's authority to penalize taxpayers for a growing laundry list of freshly created tax-related violations. In the early 1960's there were about six penalties that the IRS regularly imposed on taxpayers due to, for example, filing late, paying late, and underestimating income. **Now the IRS has the authority to penalize taxpayers and business entities for some 150 types of violations.**
Taxpayers are penalized when they

- Write checks to the IRS that bounce.
- Don't provide a Social Security number for themselves, their dependents, or other persons.
- Don't file a complete return.
- Don't report their tips to their employer.
- Pay their taxes to an unauthorized financial institution.

An entire new slew of violations and consequent penalties has been created by the phenomenon of information reporting, or, rather, inadequate information reporting. Who is liable? People or organizations that do not provide the IRS with information that Congress has deemed necessary for collecting taxes. This includes

- Tax preparers who fail to enter their federal ID number on a return they have prepared.
- Banks, real estate agencies, and securities houses that don't provide the IRS with accurate and timely information about money they are paying to taxpayers. (Fines can be stiff, up to $100,000.)
- Any business or organization that employs independent contractors or consultants and fails to file 1099 forms for payments above $600 per year.

Congress and the courts have also granted the IRS powers that have been specifically denied traditional enforcement agencies. For example, when the FBI investigates drug-related crimes or money laundering, its actions are rooted in strictly defined criminal laws. If a person's civil rights are proved to have been violated, even if the target is a major drug offender, FBI agents involved suffer the consequences.
Too often with the IRS's Criminal Investigation Division, however,

the actions guiding its special agents are what the IRS determines they should be.

The IRS and its employees are carefully protected in carrying out a range of activities that no others in the field of law enforcement would dare attempt for fear of losing their jobs or being jailed.

POWER FROM ITS UNIQUE LEGISLATION-CREATING AUTHORITY

The majority of taxpayers do not know that the IRS plays a major role in influencing and actually creating legislation through several distinct vehicles, including

- Technical advice memoranda
- Revenue rulings
- Private letter rulings
- Regulations

In addition, there are several not-so-well-known arenas in which the IRS has the ability to affect a tax bill *before* it becomes a law, and also literally to sponsor its own tax legislation.

As taxpayers, we should be cognizant of the IRS's capacity to affect and create legislation that impacts each of us. Most of these are powers that have been granted to the IRS by Congress and authorized by the *Internal Revenue Code*.

Technical Advice Memorandum

A technical advice memorandum arises from a request by an IRS district office or the Appeals Office concerning a technical or procedural question that can arise from several sources: during the examination of a taxpayer's return; in consideration of a taxpayer's claim for refund or credit, or some other matter involving a specific taxpayer under the jurisdiction of the Examination Division or Appeals Office.[4]

A technical advice memo is highly specific in its focus and is binding only upon a particular issue in a given case. If the IRS feels it has unearthed an issue that could have broader appeal, it can be developed into a revenue ruling. (For an example, see page 200.)

In 1994, the IRS made decisions on 299 technical advice memoranda; it had 132 pending as of September 30, 1995.[5]

Revenue Rulings

A revenue ruling is an official interpretation of the *Internal Revenue Code* issued to provide guidance to taxpayers and the agency itself. The subjects of revenue rulings can originate in many areas, such as rulings to taxpayers, technical advice memos, court decisions, tax articles, news reports, and suggestions submitted by tax organizations and industry specialists.

Revenue rulings are published weekly in the *Internal Revenue Bulletin* (an IRS publication) and various other tax services. They also often show up in trade publications or monthly tax newsletters where taxpayers can read about them. Specific rulings are selected for publication because

- They answer questions commonly asked by taxpayers on specific tax matters.
- The IRS believes the information presented has fairly widespread application to taxpayers in general.

Thus, without any congressional involvement, the IRS is freely empowered to interpret how a specific area of the tax law should be applied. The IRS decides, "This is the law. This is how we see it."

During 1994, the IRS made decisions on 460 revenue rulings; it had 346 pending for 1995.[6]

Private Letter Rulings

Private letter rulings are written statements issued to a taxpayer that interpret and apply the tax laws to a taxpayer's specific set of circumstances.[7] These rulings are initiated because a company or individual is considering a specific action and needs to know how the IRS would treat any tax implications involved. A company, for instance, may need to know how substantial sums should be treated on its books, e.g., as tax deductions, legitimate losses, or tax savings. The transaction in question is generally outside the normal range of categories described in the *Internal Revenue Code*.

Because they are elicited by a specific request, the rulings may be applied only by the taxpayer who receives the ruling. They cannot be relied on as precedents by other taxpayers or by IRS personnel in examining other returns.[8]

In reality private letter rulings are well known to and mainly used by businesses, especially major companies that are advised by experienced and handsomely paid tax attorneys. They are often willing to take a chance by relying on another taxpayer's private letter ruling on circumstances similar to their own particular case. These attorneys also know that the IRS often gathers several private letter rulings on a similar subject and molds them into a revenue ruling.

The IRS states that with a few exceptions, all letter rulings are available for public inspection after the deletion of all data that could identify the taxpayer.[9] **But since most people are not aware that private letter rulings exist, they are not likely to ask to see one, even though these rulings can affect broad segments of unsuspecting taxpayers.**

Private letter rulings allow the IRS broad discretion in handing down final decisions related to tax law, often to function de facto like the Supreme Court. Sometimes Congress eventually gets involved in more important cases, but it is likely to be years after the impact of the letter has been felt.

During 1994, the IRS decided on 3,221 private letter rulings; it had 1,230 pending as of September 30, 1995.[10]

Regulations

Once a tax bill is signed into law by the president, the bill is passed to the IRS. In essence, Congress says, "Here's the law, IRS. Now work out how it's going to be administered."

Regulations, or "regs," as they are known in the business, accompany about 80 percent of every new tax law. They are written by IRS attorneys and other staff who work directly with the chief counsel's office to interpret, clarify, and advise taxpayers and tax professionals about how to comply with the new law. "Regs" can appear soon after a revenue act is passed or, because the process of developing final regs is so complicated, years later. Since regulations are law, when they do appear they automatically become retroactive and taxpayers are required to file amended tax returns accordingly.

Because regulations can be hundreds of pages long for any given piece of tax law, they first appear as "proposed," then "permanent," then "final." Once issued either in temporary or final form, they are binding on all taxpayers and employees of the IRS.[11]

All regulations appear in the *Federal Register* (a daily publication of all governmental proceedings) and some commercial publications. Then they are thrown open for public comment. Most often CPA's and lobbyists send written replies to the IRS National Office suggesting how to reword or reframe them. The IRS also offers the opportunity for a public hearing on proposed regulations if a hearing is requested.[12] The IRS is supposed to consider the comments it receives before a final regulation is developed.

What do taxpayers and tax professionals use as a guide between the time when a reg is proposed and when it is finalized? They have a kind of guessing game during which they interpret the law and worry about the consequences later.

Sometimes an aspect of a new tax law may require a quick fix, especially if delaying the issuance of the final regulation(s) would mean a hardship to those affected by the new law. In this case, the IRS does not wait for the regulation process to be completed. Instead, it issues *temporary regulations* that short-circuit the usual opportunity for public comment.

Given the situation, wouldn't most taxpayers ask, "Isn't the system of creating tax laws and applying them to the taxpaying public a chaotic and virtually unregulated situation?" The answer is a definite no because basic tax laws that affect the majority of taxpayers get "fixed" right away.

In more complicated areas of the tax law, however—for example, allocations of partnership income and loss, distribution of money and property, or the intricate machinations involving how certain expenses can be recorded—regulations have been in the process of being finalized for years. In 1995 the IRS was still writing final regs for the 1986 reform act.

The favorite statement from Congress at the end of a new tax bill is "Regulations to be promulgated by the IRS." Usually no timetable is attached.

I hope the present system regarding preparation of regulations by the IRS continues. Tax professionals usually enjoy trying to think how the IRS thinks, making decisions accordingly, and patting ourselves on the back when the outcomes are confirmed by final regs.

During 1994, the IRS made decisions on 252 regulations; it had 523 pending for 1995.[13]

The Role of the IRS Before a Bill Becomes Law

Many Americans are familiar with how a revenue bill becomes a law. **But do they also know the extent to which the IRS is involved in shaping tax legislation before a bill becomes a law?**

The IRS Legislative Affairs Division is brought in to analyze and contribute to the development of pending legislation long before it comes up for a vote in Congress, and to ensure effective implementation of new legislation after it is enacted. This is actually sound management practice. But taxpayers must learn to recognize the extent to which the IRS becomes involved with new tax legislation, especially legislation the IRS doesn't like, and more, the extent to which it can massage, refine, or downright change, oppose, or block legislation to protect its own point of view, or maintain the status quo.

Here's a specific example of how this works:

In 1987 when Senator David Pryor (Democrat, Arkansas) introduced the Omnibus Taxpayer Bill of Rights legislation, the first of its kind that describes the rights private citizens should have when dealing with the IRS, he knew what he would be up against: major opposition from the IRS. He has even gone on record saying it was very difficult indeed to find members of Congress to support the bill. "I saw real fear of the possible IRS retaliation among many members of the Senate and the House of Representatives," he said at the time.[14] **In other words, other elected officials believed that if they supported his bill, the IRS would get after them in one way or another.** (For more on the "Taxpayer Bill of Rights," see chapter 7, page 161.)

When it comes to "shaping" or even rejecting new legislation that it doesn't want to see enacted into law, the IRS is not shy. It labels it as unnecessary, says it will interfere with the normal tax collection process, claims it would involve too great an imposition on the administration, and asserts it doesn't have the budget or staff to comply.

Lately, the IRS has been somewhat tempered by 1) bad reviews by the GAO; 2) scathing remarks, especially Bob Dole's "to change the IRS as we know it"; and 3) private collection companies impinging (at the insistence of Congress) in an area that was exclusively the IRS's.

IRS-Sponsored Legislation

Ensuring even greater clout in the legislative arena is the IRS's ability to sponsor legislation and to lobby Congress for IRS-backed proposals to become law. **Currently, this is the highest rung the IRS has reached in its ability to gain legislative powers almost equal to those of the U.S. Congress.**

During the hearings on the Revenue Act of 1962, the IRS uncovered the phenomenon of companies claiming large deductions for vacations, club dues, theater tickets, sports activities, business gifts, etc., from an audit of 38,000 returns. The IRS recommended remedial legislation to Congress, including substantial limitations on deductions for travel and entertainment expenses. Congress enacted the legislation, which became Section 274 of the *Internal Revenue Code* and ended up filling three pages of fine print.[15]

On January 1, 1993, newly signed legislation eliminated unreimbursed travel expenses as a deduction for taxpayers in the construction, engineering, computer, and other fields who were sent by their employers for one- to two-year assignments. Henceforth, employees in these categories could no longer claim work-related meal, lodging, and travel expenses as deductions against their income. Any payments these workers received for living costs become taxable income after one year. The IRS has had a consistent track record of voicing its displeasure and fighting taxpayers on this issue. No doubt the IRS pointed out that by eliminating this deduction, Congress could expect to increase tax revenues by $131 million over five years.

In another example, the IRS fought to make punitive damages taxable. Although some district courts ruled in favor of taxpayers (that proceeds of punitive damages were not taxable in some cases), the IRS continued to fight it until it got its way in the 1996 tax law.

In 1792, the Office of the Commissioner of Internal Revenue was established to levy and collect taxes. **Today, the IRS frequently goes head to head with Congress, creating and shaping tax legislation and challenging new and existing tax laws.**

POWER TO MAKE MISTAKES WITHOUT CONSEQUENCES

When people find themselves chatting about the IRS, one remark that inevitably surfaces is the fact that the audit rate for individual tax returns hovers between 1 and 1.5 percent. This remark is phrased to imply a certain comfort level, almost a gift to the American taxpaying public. Nothing could be further from the truth.

One percent of individual tax returns audited in 1995 translates into 1,162,298 people. Now that percentage doesn't sound so small, does it?

Just extrapolate this same thought to the numbers of taxpayers affected each year by IRS mistakes. Let's say an IRS computer mistakenly sends out a past due tax notice to only one half percent of the taxpayers in New York City. The letter charges them with penalties for failing to pay their quarterly estimated taxes in a timely manner. In fact, the computer program was malfunctioning, and most of these people did make their payments correctly.

Most taxpayers (imagine you are one of them) would naturally respond by calling their local service center, writing the necessary letter, even double-checking with their tax professional. Weeks go by, all to no avail. More letters and telephone calls later still haven't succeeded in short-circuiting the process, and now you are faced with a large collection of new IRS notices announcing dollars and penalties due.

No matter what you do, eventually your case reaches the Collection Division, where you personally fit the bill as the "cheating" taxpayer that the IRS teaches its employees about. You are trapped in IRS Problem City. The thing is—this is not happening only to you. It is *simultaneously* happening to 30,000 others, because that's one half percent of the taxpayers in New York City!

The IRS does not keep records of how many taxpayers it has abused. IRS computers can be highly effective in catching a mismatch between 1099's and 1040's. But the same technology isn't at all interested in slowing down because of IRS mistakes made along the way.

POWER FROM THE FREEDOM TO DO WHAT IT WANTS

Another aspect of IRS power comes when it decides to ignore the federal government, our judicial system, Congress, individual rights of citizens, or its own job requirements and chooses, instead, to do just exactly what it wants.

The IRS Defies the Judicial System

Dr. Nader Soliman, an anesthesiologist, who worked in three hospitals a total of 30 to 35 hours a week during the year, also set up a home office in his McLean, Virginia, apartment to maintain records, speak with patients, and study medical journals. The doctor entered the public's view when the IRS, during an audit, chose to take exception to a $2,500 home-office deduction (Section 280A of the *Internal Revenue Code*) on his 1040 form for the tax year 1983. The IRS determined that the home office wasn't his "principal place of business," which, the IRS alleged, is what the tax code requires for the deduction. Dr. Soliman appealed the IRS's decision in the U.S. Tax Court and won.

To say that the IRS was furious (because the decision was more lenient toward taxpayers than any previous home-office interpretation in that it allowed taxpayers to deduct home-office expenses even when they do not spend a majority of their time working at home) is an understatement. The IRS decided to fight, taking the case to the U.S. Court of Appeals for the Fourth Circuit in Richmond, Virginia, which upheld the Tax Court's decision.

Did the IRS try for a reversal of this position? You'll find out in chapter 7, "IRS Targets and What to Do If You're One of Them." But for now, the point to remember is when a court rules along the lines of what the IRS wishes, that's what the IRS follows. **If a court doesn't give the IRS what it wants, the IRS may not acquiesce but do what it wants anyway.** Even when different rulings are handed down by several courts on a specific issue, the IRS will follow the ruling that suits it to the exclusion of any others handed down in opposition to IRS views.

The IRS Defies the Federal Government

During the Watergate investigations, Senate Watergate Committee investigators accused the IRS of obstructing the panel's continuing inquiry by defying the Senate's resolution to provide tax returns and other data to the committee, and by refusing to provide tax data and investigative files on more than 30 individuals and corporations.[16] The IRS's underlying motivation, consistent since its inception, is tenacious and simple: **When the IRS doesn't want to do something, no matter who or what is telling it what to do, the IRS will fight long and hard to get its way.**

The IRS's ability to do what it wants despite directives from governmental bodies, individuals, and the law brings into play two particularly important laws specifically devised for and suited to the American way of life. These are the 1966 Freedom of Information Act (FOIA) and the 1974 Privacy Act, both enacted to formalize a citizen's right to request records from federal agencies.

Before enactment of the FOIA, the burden was on the individual to establish a right to examine these government records. There were no statutory guidelines or procedures to help a person seeking information, and there were no judicial remedies for those denied access.

With the passage of the FOIA, the burden of proof shifted from the individual to the government. According to a guide published by the House Committee on Government Operations, those seeking information are no longer required to show a need for information: "Instead, the 'need-to-know' standard has been replaced by a 'right-to-know' doctrine. The government now has to justify the need for secrecy."[17]

All taxpayers should know their rights in these matters, as explained in the *Citizen's Guide on Using the Freedom of Information Act and the Privacy Act of 1974 to Request Government Records*, available from the U.S. Government Printing Office, Washington, D.C. Regarding what records can be requested under the FOIA:

> The FOIA requires agencies to publish or make available for public inspection several types of information. This includes (1) descriptions of agency organization and office addresses; (2) statements of the general course and method of agency operation; (3) rules of procedure and descriptions of forms; (4) substantive rules of general applicability and gen-

eral policy statements; (5) final opinions made in the adjudication of cases; and (6) administrative staff manuals that affect the public.[18]

The IRS Defies Private Citizens

The *Internal Revenue Manual* is a major weapon against the often ludicrous situations that the IRS is known to suck taxpayers into, yet it is something most taxpayers don't know a thing about—for very good reasons. It contains IRS policies, procedures, job descriptions, and more that explain what the agency is made of. This information is exactly what the IRS hopes you won't get your hands on. You see, it is especially useful for verifying the functions of each division, for providing the parameters of specific jobs, or for spelling out specific instructions to employees on how a specific task is supposed to get done, such as seizing your assets.

In my quest to receive the *Internal Revenue Manual*, I learned firsthand how the IRS regards the FOIA and the Privacy acts. What follows describes my attempt, acting as Mr. Nice Guy taxpayer, to follow the rules so that I could glance through, in the words of the FOIA, this "administrative staff manual that affects the public."

OBTAINING THE *INTERNAL REVENUE MANUAL*

In a book about taxes, *Tax Loopholes,* a former director of the Albany and Brooklyn IRS district offices, George S. Alberts, states that someone can request a copy of the *Internal Revenue Manual* under the Freedom of Information Act from the IRS Reading Room in Washington, D.C. Furthermore, Mr. Albert says, you don't have to tell the IRS why you want the material; the fee to obtain the book is reasonable; and your action will not trigger any other actions by the IRS.[19]

Another popular tax book confirms that "each IRS District Office maintains a 'reading room' where the *Manual* is available. Copies of specific provisions of the *Manual* can also be obtained by contacting the Disclosure Officer in each district."[20]

My first step was to go to the Federal Information Center at Federal Plaza in downtown Manhattan, where I purchased the *Citizen's Guide on Using the Freedom of Information Act and the Privacy Act of 1974 to Request Government Records.* According to this publication, each act contains a provision for obtaining IRS materials, and suggests writing a letter to the agency stating that "I am willing to pay fees for this request up to a maximum of X dollars. If you estimate that the fees will exceed this limit, please inform me first."

I took no chances. I wrote two letters, one following a format suggested by Mr. Alberts, and the other following the government publication. My letters were mailed July 21, 1992; a response is required *by law* within 10 days.

I sent follow-up copies of my letters on August 21 and September 21. As of November 21, 1992, I had received no replies whatsoever.

After 30 days, on December 21, I visited the IRS district office in Manhattan and asked the person at the information desk where the IRS reading room was.

The woman began to laugh hysterically. When she caught her breath, she told me there was no reading room. There was never a reading room; she had been at her job for over 15 years and had never heard of such a thing. There was, she said, a small room upstairs where IRS employees *only* could find IRS publications. Furthermore, she informed me that she had never even heard of the *Internal Revenue Manual*.

Next I made several phone calls to IRS headquarters in Washington, D.C. No one in the IRS or the Treasury Department could find a phone number for the reading room nor did anyone know how I could obtain a copy of the *Internal Revenue Manual*.

About this time I attended a tour of the Brookhaven Service Center in Holtsville, New York. My ulterior motive was to make contact with someone who could help me in my quest to obtain this elusive book. A disclosure officer there was surprised at my tale. He immediately called the IRS in Washington, D.C., and handed me the phone, whereupon I gave my name, address, and phone number to a person responsible for filling these kinds of requests. She said that within three hours she would have an answer.

Fourteen days later I still hadn't heard a thing, despite periodic phone calls to that woman, who seemed to have disappeared.

Now I turned to the IRS historian, which, someone said, was a newly created position. This person said the *Internal Revenue Manual* was in the building next to hers (in Washington, D.C.) and if I could give her a few days, she would see what she could do.

Several days later she called me back and said the staff in the Office of Disclosure couldn't find any of my correspondence, but that if I'd send another letter, along with a check for $11, they'd send the *Manual*.

Two weeks later my check had cleared, and still no *Manual*. Finally, a full month later some photocopied pages arrived, with "Internal Revenue Manual, Tax Audit Guidelines for Internal Revenue Examiners" written across them, along with a three-hole-punched preprinted booklet entitled *Examination*.

A "Cost for copying certain Internal Revenue Manual Sections" was included in the package. Here I discovered each section of the *Internal Revenue Manual* outlined, and the corresponding cost for copying each one. The list was five pages long; if I wanted to receive information on, for example, the Collection Division, it would cost $175.95.

As a CPA, I can access the *Internal Revenue Manual* or something very close to it, with commentary, not published by the IRS or Government Printing Office but by a tax service, in a professional library closed to the public. Unfortunately, the average taxpayer will not find the task that easy.

Finally, I want to pass on to my readers information that the IRS has obviously deemed important enough to issue as an *Internal Revenue Manual Addendum:* **"In the event of a nuclear attack, to guide the conduct of all IRS employees, operations will concentrate on collecting taxes which will produce the greatest revenue yields."**[21]

I've described my epic somewhat lightheartedly, but it is not a funny story. The Freedom of Information Case List, published annually by the U.S. Department of Justice, shows the number of U.S. citizens trying to get their hands on information that can help them deal with the IRS, only to get a door slammed in their faces year after year.

Some have made the difficult decision to legally battle whatever allegations the IRS has made against them, and some of these have made a real name for themselves and become recognized experts on how the IRS administratively and otherwise resists making any information available. Most people never get very far and are forced to give up. Others do succeed in suing the IRS, winning a judgment, and getting charges against them dropped, but it takes an enormous toll in time, and often tens of thousands of dollars in legal fees.

THE BOTTOM LINE

The one lesson to be learned is: The IRS acts as if it is above and beyond the law.

Why is all of this allowed to continue? There are several rather sound reasons.

The IRS Is Good at What It Does

In 1995 the IRS collected almost $1.38 trillion in gross tax dollars, an increase of about $100 billion over the previous year. It also examined 2.1 million returns and recommended nearly $28 billion in additional taxes and penalties.[22]

Part of the reason for its effectiveness is voluntary compliance. Another part is administrative. According to one account of the development of U.S. tax policy, "In the early 1940s, many people—even highly placed officials of the Internal Revenue Service—doubted that an income tax covering almost everyone could be administered effectively."[23] But the job is being done.

The IRS Has the Government's Support

With the tax-collection machine running well (which is how the government sees it), why should it interfere? Investigations curbing the power of the IRS—in short, rocking the boat—may upset the flow of revenue; to be brutally frank, the government just doesn't want to chance it.

Congress and our legal system (the courts, judges, district attorneys) have consistently supported the IRS

- By legitimizing or ignoring the growing powers of IRS personnel.
- By seeking to punish taxpayers through a growing list of tax violations.
- By demanding ever-increasing amounts of information from an ever-growing range of third-party sources.
- By ensuring that Americans obey the IRS or face stiff consequences and penalties.

In addition, just look at how Congress has repeatedly taken the IRS under its wing,

- To protect the IRS, despite repeated cases of wrongly abused citizens, valid findings about its poor performances, and corrupt misdealings.
- To ignore instances when the IRS has skirted and gone beyond the law into realms they have no business being in.
- To give the IRS more protection from citizen suits than any other federal agency.[24]

The IRS Has the Support of the American People

If fiscal history teaches anything, it is that a successful collection system depends in large measure on the willingness of informed citizens to bear their fair share of government costs.[25]

Despite Americans' never-ending grumblings about, resistance to, and enormous fear of the IRS, the fact that federal taxes are an inescapable part of our lives is widely accepted. It is also true that the majority of Americans willingly complete and mail in their returns, and pay their taxes.

Another area of taxpayer support comes from positive perceptions that a portion of our taxes makes possible a wide range of social programs in health, education, and welfare, scientific research, and community involvement.

Sizing Up the IRS as an Opponent

True, as a taxpayer you never want to get crossways of the IRS. **What you do want to aim for is the ability to manipulate the power of the IRS through the income tax process.** You have to take extreme care doing this. It cannot be accomplished haphazardly or without sufficient knowledge. In the martial arts a small person can bring down a much heavier, stronger one. By the same token, I and thousands of other tax professionals like me continue to witness taxpayers accomplishing similar feats when dealing with the IRS.

6

IRS Technology

What Works
What Doesn't Work

Moving toward the computer age has not been easy for the IRS. Until the mid-1980's a great deal of the work—assembling millions of tax returns by year, organizing them geographically, and comparing them with third-party reports—was still being done manually. Sacks filled to the brim with tax return information sat for years in IRS corridors; massive amounts of incorrect information was disseminated to taxpayers en masse; huge numbers of tax returns would disappear, never to be found again; annually thousands of letters from taxpayers remained unanswered because they couldn't be matched up to their corresponding files; and enormous time delays for a range of requests were the norm (75 days or more instead of a promised 30).

Today the IRS computers housed in the National Computer Center (NCC) in Martinsburg, West Virginia, contain trillions of bits of information on millions of U.S. taxpayers, a capacity and collection of data unsurpassed anywhere in the world. Do images of huge storage tanks of electronic information housed in shining silver eight-foot-tall containers fill taxpayers' visions? That's exactly the image the IRS would love to have.

The current IRS technology behemoth called the Tax Systems Modernization (TSM) was initiated in the early 1990's at a cost of $8.3–10 billion. (This was on top of a previous $11-plus billion technology project.) The TSM had many laudable goals:

- To effectively execute the IRS's Information Returns Program, or matching program, in which information on all 1040 forms (Individual Tax Returns) is matched up or compared with all W-2's (Wage and Tax Statement) and the full range of 1099 documents that are sent to the IRS by third parties (i.e., employers, banks, real estate agents, loan companies, and more). This process enables the IRS to isolate underreporters and nonfilers.
- To eliminate millions of unnecessary contacts with taxpayers.
- To eliminate the confusion caused when a taxpayer continues to receive computer-generated letters because the file was not updated quickly.
- To provide copies of tax returns to taxpayers who have lost their copies and to IRS employees who are conducting audits in less than one day rather than the current 45-day average.
- To reduce by one quarter the time it takes to process cases.
- To tailor correspondence to the taxpayer's account rather than issue generic form letters.

In the tax period 1993–1994, there were strong indications that the IRS was serious regarding its efforts to build, manage, and employ technology. By 1997, however, the IRS's technology efforts have received serious criticism from the GAO and Congress (see pages 142–143).

THE PROCESSING PIPELINE

What Happens to Your Return in the Processing Pipeline

The IRS "processing pipeline" is a process your tax return goes through from the time it is dropped into the mail until a refund is issued.

Where *does* all the "other stuff" take place? Where are tax returns selected for audit? Where is the matching program run? Where are people targeted for a criminal investigation? These all take place in a vast IRS-land that has come to be called the "nonprocessing pipeline."

The problem is, for the most part this phase is not fully revealed to taxpayers. **Even explanatory material sent out by the IRS labeled "nonprocessing pipeline" is not complete. By not telling the whole story, the IRS triumphs over the taxpayer, because what transpires in the nonprocessing pipeline holds tremendous importance to anyone who files a tax return.**

First, let's take a brief look at what happens to your return in the normal processing pipeline.

Millions of mailed returns are delivered to the regional service centers, where they are fed into computerized equipment that reads the coding on the envelopes, opens the envelopes, and sorts them by type—married, single, business. (Uncoded envelopes take longer to open and sort; using a properly coded envelope will speed things up.)

Next, clerks manually remove the contents of the envelopes and sort the returns further into those with or without remittances. Payments are credited to taxpayers' accounts, payments are separated from the returns, totals are balanced, and the checks are sent to the service center's bank for deposit, eventually to end up in the U.S. Treasury.

All returns are then verified for completeness of information (the filer's signature, Social Security number, the proper forms), and coded to assist in converting the raw data directly from the return into an electronic language for computer processing. IRS personnel transcribe the data directly from the tax returns to computer disks, then the computer analyzes the information and enters error-free returns onto magnetic tapes.

If errors are encountered, they are printed on a separate report and passed on to tax examiners in the service center, who check the error records against the appropriate returns and correct what errors they can. If the errors are not easily corrected, the error is coded, indicating that the taxpayer will be sent an error notice requesting clarification.

Now the magnetic tapes containing data from all the accurate tax returns are shipped to the National Computer Center and added to the master directory of all taxpayer accounts, and updated records are sent back to each service center for further processing.

Refund tapes are sent to the Treasury Department for issuance of refund checks directly to taxpayers, and the processing pipeline ends. The total time from mailing your return to receiving your refund generally runs about six to eight weeks.

THE NONPROCESSING PIPELINE

What Happens in the Nonprocessing Pipeline
Taxpayers are kept in the dark about many phases of the nonprocessing pipeline that are quite important for them to know.

• The first round of letters is cranked out by IRS computers *only* because of missing information. If someone forgot to sign a return, if a schedule is missing, if the W-2 is not attached, these issues are handled within the first month after the return is mailed in. (All of the time periods given in these examples are for tax season, February 1 to April 15. At other times of year the turnaround time is probably shorter.)

• The next round of letters is sent to correct purely arithmetical errors. **There are generally some 6 million of these errors each filing season.** Letters of this nature are sent anywhere from two to three months after a taxpayer has mailed in his or her return.

• The Information Returns Program (IRP) or matching program is not part of the normal, tax-return-processing routine. It is run as part of the nonpipeline processing.

• The W-2, which taxpayers attach to the 1040, doesn't actually get matched to the 1040 until approximately one and one half years after it is submitted.

• Audit letters don't usually get sent out until six months to one year after the return is filed.

• No matter how spiffy the matching program sounds, the IRS itself admits that it is still a labor- and paper-intensive operation.

• **In 1992, only 2 percent of the data maintained in tax accounts was readily available on-line.** The other 98 percent was in paper files—returns filed in federal records centers or in databases without on-line retrieval capability.[1] There has been no appreciable improvement in this area since then.

Here's the full story of what happens in the nonprocessing pipeline.

Enter W-2's
W-2's, from private and public entities that report employees' salaries, are due in to the IRS the last day of January, and 1099's, from business owners, are due February 28.

Enter Inquiry Letters
It's early July and tax season has been over for about three months. Initial inquiry letters are being sent out by the service centers requesting that taxpayers send in information they inadvertently left out, and/or to correct mathematical errors. Once these situations have been corrected, one to two months later, the service centers reenter the information and create a good tape, which is then fed into the Martinsburg computer system.

Enter Audit Selection
The initial process selects tax returns whose DIF scores (Discriminate Information Function, discussed in chapter 3) mean that they fall in the audit range for one or more of the DIF items or categories. This amounts to about 10 percent of all individual returns, or about 11 million, that have audit potential. These returns are sent by Martinsburg

via tape back to the corresponding service centers, where the computer data is matched up with the hard copy, the actual tax return.

Staff in the Examination Division at the service centers manually review and select only returns that indicate the greatest potential monetary yield. As a result, at least another 90 percent of the original 10 percent are discarded, leaving less than 1 to 1.5 percent of all individual tax returns filed, or about 1.5 million chosen for audit. At this point, the tax returns targeted for correspondence audits are turned over to the Examination Division at the service centers. The balance of the tax returns are distributed to the district offices, which send out letters to taxpayers notifying them that they are being audited. This entire process takes from six months to one year after the tax return is filed.

While audit selection is taking place, so is another entire range of activities.

Enter the Social Security Administration
Did you know that the first link between you, your W-2's, and the matching process is the Social Security Administration (SSA)? Here's how this one works: The first copy of the W-2 is sent to the SSA by employers so that wages can be added to a taxpayer's lifetime earnings account. The SSA then forwards the W-2 information to the IRS on magnetic tape, where it is matched to the 1040 form and, along with the 1099's, initiates the nonprocessing pipeline.

Now the matching program can be run. The sequence of events goes something like this:

Enter Mismatches
On the basis of the data in Martinsburg, all 1040 forms (individual tax returns) are matched with W-2's and compared with over 1 billion 1099's and other third-party documents. All mismatches are downloaded onto a separate tape, which goes back to the service centers. The assigned sections in the service centers then analyze the data (see below). When a discrepancy exists indicating a mismatch among 1099's, W-2's, and 1040 forms, the case enters the collection area at the service-center level.

Enter Underreporter Notices
The service centers send out mismatch notices, "underreporter notices," or CP-2000 letters, triggered when there is a disagreement between what a taxpayer reported on the 1040 and what was reported about that person's income by one or more third-party reports. These notices propose a change to income, payments, or credits and are sent

to taxpayers about one and a half years after the tax return was filed. Apparently, the fact that the SSA uses the information first contributes to the enormous delay. In 1995 the IRS generated 2.7 million notices for underreporting.[2] This completes the matching part of the program.

Enter the Collection Division

After this, depending on how the taxpayer does or does not respond to IRS correspondence, tax assessments are made or taxpayer explanations are accepted. In any case, the collection cycle is now triggered, and the case makes its way up through the collection process, as discussed in chapter 4.

Enter the Criminal Investigation Division

At this point the Criminal Investigation Division (CID) takes center stage.

CID staff trains service center personnel to identify typical characteristics of false and fraudulent returns and potential criminal violations. If a return of this nature is recognized by someone in the service center, the case is brought to the attention of CID. From there it might head up the line, or be dismissed for lack of potential to produce either big bucks and/or a conviction.

THE REST OF THE PROCESSING PIE

Individual taxpayers are *not* the sole focus of IRS processing, so if some of the delays that occur in both pipelines seem inordinately long, one of the major reasons involves the rest of the IRS tax return–processing pie.

In 1995, the over 116.3 million individual tax returns the IRS processed represented 46.5 percent of total net dollars collected, the majority in the form of withholding. Employment taxes represented 36.6 percent, and corporation taxes were 12.3 percent of total dollars collected.[3]

The scope of the entire processing cycle is arduous, tedious, and enormous. But there is a major lesson for all taxpayers: **There are so many levels the IRS must get involved with in processing tax returns that if you learn how to prepare an unobtrusive return, chances are in your favor that it will pass through the system unnoticed.**

If you look at the three areas in the IRS that are responsible for bringing in tax dollars, you can get a good perspective on the agency's technological capability.

In 1995,

- Matching recommended $3.5 billion in additional taxes and penalties.
- Examination recommended $27.8 billion.
- Collection yielded $38.4 billion on a combination of collections on delinquent accounts and assessments on delinquent returns.[4]

The matching program, which is dependent on technology, offers the IRS widespread coverage across the taxpayer base. Nevertheless, people-dependent Examination and Collection, where IRS staff do most of the work, actually bring in far more tax dollars because of their selectivity: They select only those cases with the greatest potential for tax dollars.

So just exactly where is IRS technology performing well and what information is still sitting around or just completely unreachable, as in the old days?

WHERE THE IRS TECHNOLOGY WORKS

W-2's (Wage and Tax Statements) and 1099's (Third-Party Reports) Matched to the 1040 Form (Individual Income Tax Return)

As you know, the Information Returns Program (IRP), or matching program, allows the IRS to match up third-party information—wages, interest, dividends, and certain deductions—with the amounts taxpayers report on their 1040 form. In addition, the IRS also uses the IRP to identify nonfilers, people who have received some income (as indicated by one or more third-party reports) but nevertheless did not file a return. **The current estimate is that about 6 million people are nonfilers.** (The reasons why this segment is so large are discussed in chapter 7, "IRS Targets and What to Do If You're One of Them.")

Mismatches result from a variety of factors: mathematical errors or negligence (taxpayers do make honest mistakes), unreported name and address changes, as well as downright cheating.

Implications for Taxpayers
If you do not properly report your W-2 earnings, there is little doubt that the IRS computers will pick it up through the matching process. Therefore be honest here, to the letter.

Social Security Number Cheating Schemes

Several years ago a rash of taxpayers tried to avoid paying taxes by manipulating Social Security numbers. The incidence of fooling around with Social Security numbers increased to the point where the IRS was successful in having a law passed that requires all third-party payers to obtain corrected Social Security numbers from taxpayers when the IRS provides the payers with a list of mismatches that affects them. If a taxpayer does not comply with the third party's request for the corrected Social Security number, the institution or third party will be instructed by the IRS to begin to withhold tax from payments that person is receiving from business owners, as well as from any other third-party payments such as interest and dividends.

Starting January 1, 1993, the rate of withholding tax from this type of situation, called *backup withholding*, is 31 percent. Previously, the amount was only 20 percent, but when George Bush was president he had it raised to generate additional tax revenue from the American public without announcing a tax increase.

Among others, the requirement targets taxpayers who provide an erroneous Social Security number on their bank accounts to avoid including the sums as taxable income. This produces a mismatch on IRS computers, and triggers the backup withholding mechanism.

Once the mismatch is identified, the IRS notifies the bank, and after a two-year period, if the taxpayer hasn't stepped up to resolve the issue or offered a corrected Social Security number, the bank will automatically take 31 percent out of the account in question. So if the account earns $3,000 in yearly interest, $930 will immediately be sent to the IRS as backup withholding.

Pension Plan Distributions

The IRS's matching program regarding pension plan distributions used to have some real holes in it. With approximately half a million pension plan distributions disbursed annually, the common practice is to roll over pension funds, or place them in a qualified investment that entitles the money to remain nontaxable according to IRS requirements. If the rollover isn't followed to the letter of the *Internal Revenue Code*, the distribution is considered taxable income and the taxpayer is subject to income tax and added penalties if the distribution is taken before the taxpayer reaches age 59½.

Implications for Taxpayers

According to the *Internal Revenue Code*, when the organization holding the distribution turns it over to the taxpayer it must issue a 1099-R

(Distribution from Pensions, Annuities, Retirement or Profit-Sharing Plans, IRA's, Insurance Contracts, Etc.), which spells out the amount disbursed, and send this information to the IRS. For the most part, this reporting requirement is adhered to by companies making the pension distributions, especially since by early 1990, IRS computers became fully capable of matching up the pension-plan distribution with the roll-over amount. (For an update, see New Tax Legislation for 1996, pages 275–276.)

Form 2119 (Sale of Your Home) and Schedule D (Capital Gains and Losses)

When you sell a house, you receive a 1099-S (Proceeds from Real Estate Transactions) from the real estate broker or attorney which shows the gross sale price of your house. If no tax is due on the transaction, you might think that Form 2119 (Sale of Your Home) need not be filed. Not true. Form 2119 shows all pertinent data on the sale, and it also affects your position when you buy a new house. If you don't file this form in conjunction with your 1040, you could receive a mismatch notice for the *entire* sales proceeds and be placed at audit risk.

If you sell investment rental property, your return must include the sale on Schedule D (Capital Gains and Losses). Omitting this information could lead to an audit because the IRS has increased its search capabilities of real estate transactions and is matching that data with sales shown on Schedule D.

Disposition of Investment and Schedule D

If you have been receiving dividends from an investment and the dividend income disappears, you must show a disposition of the investment on Schedule D or be ready to prove that the company ceased the payment of dividends.

Auditors are also instructed to account for investments appearing on the previous year's tax return that have suddenly disappeared, or are not accounted for on a subsequent Schedule D. If a rental property appears on a taxpayer's 1040 one year and does not appear on the subsequent year's 1040, the auditor will suspect that you sold it and did not report the taxable gain on your 1040.

Overreporting Income

When a taxpayer submits an overpayment of tax on a check enclosed with the 1040 form, the IRS is thoroughly honest and in almost all cases will return to the taxpayer the appropriate refund. But what happens to the thousands of taxpayers who innocently overreport income?

Implications for Taxpayers

Just as underreporting income is easily detected through the matching program, so, now, is overreporting. **However, when it comes to overreporting income, the IRS does not behave as honestly as when there is an overpayment of tax.** When taxpayers overreport their income, *and* the IRS records it, the IRS doesn't tell taxpayers that they've made an error. If you pay more taxes than you owe, you will receive a refund from the IRS, but not when you overreport income.

Matching Form 941 (Employer's Quarterly Federal Tax Return) with Total Wages and Taxes Withheld on W-2's

The 941 form, filled out by employers and sent quarterly to the IRS, shows total wages, taxable Social Security wages, taxable Medicare wages, federal income tax withheld, and Social Security and Medicare taxes. Since these items all appear on each employee's W-2 at year-end, the totals reported on the employer's four quarterly 941's for the year *must* agree with the grand totals of all W-2's, also reported by the employer. **The IRS meticulously matches the W-2 totals with the 941's to ensure that businesses have legitimately paid their tax liabilities to the government in a timely manner.**

Discrepancies arise between W-2's and 941's for these reasons:

- Many 941's, year-end reconciliations, and W-2's are filled out by employers manually, not with a computer.
- Many employers do not fully understand the requirements for making payroll tax deposits.

Implications for Taxpayers

This matching process is at once a safeguard for the taxpayer (your company is not allowed to play around with money it has deducted from your salary such as Social Security and withholding), a deterrent for the employer, and also a deterrent for taxpayers who believe they can cheat the government on taxes withheld from wages earned.

It also prevents little games from being played—for example, creating a fictitious company and issuing oneself a false W-2. So why not send in a mathematically correct return with a phoney W-2 from a fictitious company, which will result in a large refund, after which the taxpayer disappears fast? Forget it. It's a major criminal offense. No one gets away with it.

As for the genuine companies and employers, those who fail to make timely payments are subject to strictly enforced penalties. They are also held personally liable for any Social Security or federal withholding taken from employees' wages that are not transmitted to the IRS. If the tax liability and required payments as shown on the 941's do not match up with the actual payments made by the employer, the IRS contacts the employer immediately.

The IRS has completely revised the 941 requirements several times over the years to cut down on deposit errors. (There was a great deal of confusion about when to send in the money.) The goal was to make depositing easier for approximately 5 million employers and eliminate most of the deposit penalties. Errors on the 941 form probably account for more than 80 percent of IRS discrepancy letters received by employers.

Beginning July 1, 1997, new rules require that employers having over $50,000 in federal payroll taxes must deposit electronically. (See New Tax Legislation for 1996, page 272.)

YOUR TAX-SAVING STRATEGY.
When a taxpayer is ready to collect retirement benefits, the Social Security Administration will use a specific formula to determine that person's monthly Social Security benefit, based on the total amount of earnings accumulated over the years.

My advice to all wage earners is to obtain a printout of your earnings account every three years by writing to your local SSA office. Verify it with the entries from your W-2's. Errors are easier to correct this way than by waiting until an error is inadvertently discovered by the Social Security Administration.

WHERE MISTAKES ARE MADE IN THE IRS MATCHING PROGRAM

Just because the technology in these areas is impressive doesn't mean that mistakes can't be made. (By the way, these mistakes are separate from instances where the IRS technology falls short, discussed further on in this chapter.) Here are the most common mistakes:

Mismatching Information on W-2 Forms with Information on the 1040 because of Nonstandardized W-2's

A tax professional who prepares personal tax returns knows that it is standard operating procedure for W-2's to be in a nonstandardized format. But have taxpayers even noticed, much less asked themselves, why the W-2, a key player in the IRS's third-party reporting system, arrives in the taxpayer's hands in all varieties of forms? Here's the answer: Employers with 250 or more employees must submit W-2 information on magnetic tape, which all appears in a standard IRS format. Almost all other employers submit the information on paper, in a format either prescribed or approved by the IRS but, unfortunately, not followed often enough. Although the requirement to use magnetic tape is strict, the format of the printed W-2, which goes directly from employers to taxpayers, was not subject to formal guidelines until March 1993, when the IRS issued instructions for the placement of the federal wage and tax data. **The end result for taxpayers was and still is a ludicrously simple situation of wrongly copied information:** Even though some of the W-2 information has to be placed in predetermined positions, the rest of the information placement and the design of the forms still vary wildly. If I had one cent each time a taxpayer miscopied information from a W-2 to a 1040 form, because the information presented on the W-2 was not in a standardized format, I'd be living in Australia and scuba-diving on the Great Barrier Reef right now. Surely the resulting error rate causes thousands of taxpayers to receive CP-2000 letters and collection notices each year because of IRS computer mismatches.

The goal of every taxpayer should be to stay out of the clutches of the IRS; any minor recording error can in a flash destroy a taxpayer's ability to fulfill this mission.

Note: Corporations are still allowed to design and print their own W-2 forms, but regulations in effect require data for W-2's to be presented in the exact order as on the preprinted IRS form. Even though these regulations break a well-entrenched pattern, we'll see how long it takes for companies large and small to completely implement the changeover.

YOUR TAX-SAVINGS STRATEGY.
If you receive income from more than one employer, take care when you transfer your income information from your W-2's to the "Wages, Salaries" line of your 1040 form. Doing it correctly means avoiding IRS scrutiny.

Mismatching Information on 1099 Forms with Information on the 1040

For self-employed persons who receive 1099's for income earned from a sole proprietorship and file Schedule C, it is inappropriate to list each 1099 separately on Schedule C. Some of my clients receive 50 or more 1099's. However, you must be absolutely sure that the total gross income from the self-employed business that you report on line 1 of Schedule C equals or exceeds the total dollar amount of the 1099's that you receive. Otherwise you will be flagged for underreporting income.

Mistakes Made Through Social Security Numbers

An incorrect Social Security number will immediately trigger a mismatch. The error might come from someone who created a bogus Social Security number that turned out to be yours. When *you* opened your last bank account, did the bank employee ask for your Social Security card to prove the validity of the Social Security number you provided to him or her? Probably not, because this isn't common practice—so a person could quite easily give an erroneous Social Security number. If some devious person just happens to give a false Social Security number to a bank or elsewhere and it turns out to be yours, you will receive a mismatch notice. The IRS will eventually notify the bank (or source) to obtain a corrected Social Security number from the person who gave yours. Unfortunately, you've been contacted by the bank or the IRS and been aggravated with unnecessary correspondence through no fault of your own.

Exempt Income Items

The IRS will sometimes select for a mismatch notice income items bearing your Social Security number that should have been excluded from your taxable income; such items might be interest earned on IRAs, interest on tax-exempt bonds, and transfers between your IRA and pension plan. An erroneous match of these exempt-income items may occur if the third-party payer submitted the information on the wrong magnetic tape.

Keypunch Errors

Sometimes an error occurs simply because of one incorrect keypunch by an IRS operator: a mispelling of your name or address or one wrong digit in your Social Security number.

WHAT TO DO IF YOU RECEIVE AN IRS "MISMATCH LETTER"

Promptly answer the IRS mismatch letter with full documentation in your first reply. Failure to do so keeps your return in front of an IRS employee unnecessarily. For example, if in the mismatch notice your income was increased by an IRA distribution that you properly rolled over within 60 days, document your answer with the statement from the financial institution that shows the receipt of the rollover money plus a copy of the canceled check, if you have it. Do not assume that the IRS employee understands the data you are sending. Include a cover letter stating all the facts.

Now that you know which areas of the IRS technology work, and also where the most common mistakes are made, let's focus on several of the IRS's sore points.

WHERE THE IRS TECHNOLOGY FALLS SHORT ON THE INCOME SIDE

We are first going to concentrate on items that show up as "income" on the 1040 form: distributions from partnerships, corporations, estates, and trusts; capital gains; and gifts and inheritances.

Schedule K-1

K-1's are schedules issued by partnerships (which report income on Form 1065), S corporations (Form 1120S), and estates and trusts (Form 1041), on which these entities show distributable amounts of income and expense that have been allocated to each partner, shareholder, or beneficiary. Information on K-1's must be reported on the partner's, shareholder's, or beneficiary's Form 1040.

Tax preparers for entities that issue K-1's are responsible for placing income and expense items on the proper line. This is not always straightforward because of the factor of *basis*. Basis is a dollar amount that represents the cost of a taxpayer's investment in an entity. Because of continuous adjustments to each taxpayer's basis in that particular entity, **the income or loss as shown on the K-1 may not reflect the true amount that must be recorded on the taxpayer's current-year Form 1040.**

If you are the recipient of a K-1 from an entity, you cannot take for granted that the income or expense as shown on the K-1 is ready to be transferred to Form 1040 as it is stated; you should rely on your tax pro to determine the correct information.

Once taxpayers are sure that they have the proper income or loss amount, they are then faced with the arduous task of transferring the K-1 information onto their Form 1040. Several lines on the K-1 are easy to comprehend and their counterparts on Form 1040 and its schedules are easily located. These include interest income and dividend income, lines 4A and 4B, respectively, which transfer to Schedule B of Form

1040; and net short-term capital gain or loss and net long-term capital gain or loss, lines 4D and 4E respectively, which transfer to Schedule D (Capital Gains and Losses).

Then there are complicated items that have their own deductibility limitations, such as Section 179, depreciation "Expense Deductions" (discussed in chapter 7, "IRS Targets and What to Do If You're One of Them"), investment interest, and low-income housing credit (Form 8586, Low-Income Housing Credit, discussed under Rule 7 in chapter 10).

To prepare a proper return, taxpayers really have to dig deeply into K-1 form instructions—which are often 10 pages long—and also examine additional schedules that explain the more complicated items being reported. Imagine it! The K-1 has up to 48 lines, some of which baffle even tax professionals. When that information is transferred to a 1040, it can appear in a number of different places on various 1040 schedules besides Schedules B and D, such as Form 6251, Alternative Minimum Tax—Individuals, and Form 8582 (Passive Activity Loss Limitations).

Implications for Taxpayers

Clearly, Schedule K-1 is inherently complex. Add to this the necessity of transferring a great deal of detailed information to the 1040 in a variety of different places, and you can understand how difficult it would be even for computers to organize, digest, and store information from the K-1 and then match it properly to the 1040. I am aware of several specific cases that demonstrate this point.

On April 15, 1988, a colleague of mine received a call from his client who said that without fail her return had to be filed on time. He told her that he couldn't do that because it was missing a partnership K-1 form. "I don't care," the client said. "What was the amount from last year?"

"It was a three-thousand-dollar loss," he replied.

"Take the same loss," she said, "and file the return on time." He did. Four months later, the K-1 arrived from the partnership indicating a $1,000 loss. Her job was transferred overseas for the next few years, and she never filed an amended tax return. She has never heard a word from the IRS.

In another case, an elderly taxpayer filing on October 15, under the latest extension possible, was missing two S corporation K-1's. The return was filed as if it were complete, except it was not noticed that the information from the K-1's was totally omitted. Three months later, the two K-1's arrived showing several items of additional income. As was his way, the elderly taxpayer buried the forms in a pile of unopened mail. An amended return should have been filed but never was, and no inquiry was ever received from the IRS.

Before we leave the K-1, I'd like to inform readers about one more thing: **K-1 reporting by the entities (the partnerships, corpora-**

tions, estates, and trusts) that issue the K-1 forms is not standardized. K-1's issued by nationally syndicated partnerships are so complicated that they tend to be accompanied by a brochure generated by each partnership explaining how taxpayers should transfer K-1 information to their 1040. Although the explanations say precisely where on the 1040 specific information should be entered, the words "Consult your tax adviser" are almost always present. For taxpayers, this is a rather indisputable indication of the difficulty of the task at hand.

Very little about the K-1 standardization predicament is news to the IRS. In 1992, during a meeting of the National Society of Public Accountants (NSPA), representatives of the Society and the IRS Tax Forms Coordinating Committee exchanged ideas and information regarding form changes. The IRS agreed that lack of K-1 standardization presents a considerable problem for both the agency and the taxpayer/practitioner communities. It also went on record as stating that the issue remains under review, and progress is likely to come only *after* the standardization of W-2/1099 reporting is complete.[5] It has been almost four years since the IRS issued new regulations regarding the standardization of W-2 forms. Who knows when the IRS will get a better hold on K-1 reporting, matching, and standardization?

Capital Gains—Sales Price of a Stock Transaction

When a person sells a stock or any type of security, the broker who sold it is required to report the sale on a 1099-B form (Proceeds from Broker and Barter Exchange Transactions). The form contains pertinent information such as the broker's name, the recipient's name and Social Security number, the trade date, gross proceeds, and a brief description of the sold item, e.g., "100 shares of XYZ Corporation stock." This information is reportable by the taxpayer on the 1040, Schedule D (Capital Gains and Losses).

There are billions of securities transactions annually, so taxpayers can understand how vital it is for the IRS to receive 1099-B information on magnetic tape from the thousands of brokers who are members of securities and commodities exchanges. Once on magnetic tape, the information is easily transferred to the IRS computer center.

There's the background. Now let's look at the reality.

The IRS requires that each security sold by a taxpayer be reported on a separate 1099-B, but it allows a great deal of latitude in how the information from the 1099-B is reported back to taxpayers. Although the IRS does have its own standardized 1099-B form, the form is used infrequently.

Essentially, reporting brokers create their own forms so there is little if any uniformity. It is not uncommon for brokers to issue substitute 1099-Bs, which can be monstrous creations that list all the securities an individual taxpayer sold in a given year on letter-size paper. Sometimes up to 40 transactions are squeezed on to a single sheet, often excluding the number of shares sold. This forces taxpayers who are looking for more detailed information to search for their original trade confirmations from their brokers. How are taxpayers to report the amount of money they receive from the sale of securities and transfer the proper information compiled by the financial institution on to Schedule D? With difficulty.

Further complications arise when a block of shares purchased as a single lot is sold at different times, or when companies split their stocks to take advantage of an opportunity to offer a lower market price to the public. For example, how does one monitor the sale of 1,000 shares of IBM purchased as a single lot, then sold on five different dates? Twenty percent of the cost would have to be assigned to each sale of 200 shares. Perhaps this sounds easy, but what if there were two or three stock splits during the time you owned the stock? You could end up with a complex math problem that might take a taxpayer hours to sort out.

Implications for Taxpayers

The information that is now being reported to the IRS by the securities industry is the sales proceeds of the transactions. Determination of the cost basis, or matching what the taxpayer paid for the security, is another matter entirely. Because this task often requires intricate and complex record keeping, computers would have to monitor detailed cost information for each taxpayer and deal with ongoing adjustments caused by stock splits and dividend reinvestment plans. It is not a surprise, therefore, that taxpayers generally do not receive notices of mismatches originating from 1099-B's. **Any technology system would be hard-pressed to sort out the quagmire of matching a 1099-B with the information on Schedule D.**

During an audit, revenue agents do not always verify the buys and sells of securities transactions. It is interesting to note that in the training materials for conducting office audits that the IRS has developed on frequently examined items, there is no pro-forma audit kit on the verification of securities.

One reason for a seeming complacency by the IRS in its examination of securities transactions could be that it has discovered in its TCMP (Taxpayer Compliance Measurement Program) examinations (the ones used to compile the Discriminate Information Function scores), that the public has been generally honest in its reporting of securities transactions and further audit measures are therefore not required.

This isn't to say that the IRS doesn't use or can't access security transaction information. It certainly does. For example, if the Criminal Investigation Division is investigating a taxpayer, special agents will track down a list of any securities transactions made by that taxpayer and trace them accordingly. But this is done as part of another or secondary investigation. It is not normally done as part of the IRS matching program.

To be perfectly frank, the entire area of securities transactions is too important a revenue source for the IRS to turn its back on. Two years ago I said that the IRS will begin to solicit the assistance of financial institutions, brokerage firms, and other companies in the securities business on this issue. As of 1997, some brokerage companies are matching cost data associated with securities transactions of their clients, and voluntarily reporting the data to the IRS in the same year that the securities are sold.

I suppose readers next want to know when all this is going to happen. That I don't know. But I do know that what I just described is probably the strongest means by which the IRS could get a good, solid grip on securities transactions.

Gifts and Inheritances

Reporting gifts and inheritances—assets received as gifts from living individuals, and inheritances passed on through decedents' estates—is another area difficult for the IRS to get its arms around. In addition to cash, the more common forms of gifts and inheritances are land, homes, jewelry, autos, and marketable securities, or stamp, art, and coin collections.

Reporting requirements for gifts and inheritances usually fall into three major categories:

- If a decedent's estate exceeds $600,000, Form 706 (U.S. Estate Tax Return) is required.
- Taxpayers who give gifts of more than $10,000 in one calendar year to one person must file Form 709 (U.S. Gift Tax Return). If a married person gives a gift of $20,000, it can be treated as a split gift, i.e., $10,000 from each spouse.
- Taxpayers who receive gifts and inheritances and ultimately dispose of the items in a taxable transaction must report them as gains or losses on Form 1040 Schedule D (Capital Gains and Losses).

When taxpayers try to determine the value or cost of a gift or inheritance, they find themselves confronted with a complex problem. The following rules are used to determine the cost basis of inherited or gifted assets: In figuring gain *or* loss of an inherited asset, generally use the fair market value at the date of death of the decedent. For gifts disposed of at a *gain*, use the donor's original cost basis. For gifts disposed of at a *loss*, use the donor's original cost basis *or* the fair market value at the time of the gift, whichever is lower.

Implications for Taxpayers

There is not a lot of information going into the IRS computers regarding the cost basis of gifts and inheritances. Therefore, in this area the IRS has to rely almost solely on taxpayer compliance. The situation has several rather far-reaching implications.

When a federal estate tax return, Form 706, is filed, the assets of the estate will be listed along with their fair market values. In this case a taxpayer could easily prove the cost of the inherited property, especially if these items are questioned during an audit, by producing the estate tax return of the decedent.

YOUR TAX-SAVING STRATEGY.

If you find yourself the recipient of an inheritance where there is *no* accompanying estate tax return, you should get an appraisal of the asset unless it is a marketable security whose value is readily obtainable. This will establish the fair market value of the item, which will allow you to properly compute gain or loss when you dispose of the asset.

Also, it is generally *not* wise for a relative to transfer assets just before passing away; rather, the assets should be in the will. This way, the cost basis of the assets you receive as a beneficiary of the estate will be valued at current fair market value, thereby reducing your tax bite when you sell.

If the transfer is made while the relative is still alive, it is classified as a gift, and upon the disposal of the asset, you will often be burdened with a significant taxable gain, since the cost basis of a gift when computing gain is the original cost to the donor and not the fair market value.

Mr. Davis's mother *gifted* her son a Florida condominium, which she purchased for $25,000. One year later, Mr. Davis sold the apartment for $40,000. The cost basis for the gift is the original $25,000 and now results in a $15,000 taxable capital gain. *On the other hand,* if Mr. Davis had *inherited* the condo after his mother's death and then sold it a few months later for $40,000, his cost basis would be $40,000 (fair market value at date of death) and there would be no taxable gain or loss.

The question is, "How can the IRS keep track of and catalog the value of bequests from an estate and gifts?" For example, could the IRS require that every person, when asked to prove the cost of inherited property, produce the estate tax return of the decedent? Although this is requested during an audit, it is not feasible to include this step in routine practice because of the relative scarcity of estates with assets that are valued in excess of $600,000, hence of estate tax returns. Sounds like another mission impossible.

It is up to the taxpayer to produce an appraisal or other proof to show fair market value, or to show a paid bill or canceled check to prove cost. Other than estate and gift tax returns, the IRS computer contains no information that will refute the documented proof that you are presenting.

To clear up a major misconception regarding tax implications of gifts and inheritances, see pages 209–210.

WHERE THE IRS TECHNOLOGY FALLS SHORT ON THE EXPENSE SIDE—MORTGAGE INTEREST AND REAL ESTATE TAX

Mortgage interest and points paid in a mortgage transaction of $600 or more are reported to taxpayers by their mortgage lenders on Form 1098 (Mortgage Interest Statement). Others besides mortgage lenders who must file this form are taxpayers who pay out $600 or more of mortgage interest in the course of conducting their trade or business, even if the taxpayer is not in the business of lending money. At tax preparation time, the taxpayers must transfer this amount to line 10 of Form 1040, Schedule A (Itemized Deductions).

Taxpayers often make errors when entering or transferring information onto their 1040. In the area of mortgage interest the chances for error are extremely high. From the taxpayer's perspective, this is extremely understandable. There are several reasons why this area has such a high error rate. Although home mortgage interest can be copied from Form 1098, most taxpayers copy both mortgage interest and real estate tax information from the annual mortgage expense statement that they receive from financial lending institutions, because Form 1098 does not contain real estate tax information. Besides information on mortgage interest and real estate taxes, other information found on annual expense statements are interest earned on tax escrows, homeowner's insurance, water charges, and late charges.

These annual statements, like the W-2 and K-1, are *not* standardized. Most are computer-generated by the reporting institutions. **As a result, when taxpayers transfer the figures to their 1040, they often transfer real estate taxes as mortgage interest and vice versa.**

Another common error is to use homeowner's insurance or water charges as a valid deduction, which of course they are not. The end result is a mismatch between the figure(s) the taxpayer entered on Schedule A, and the figure(s) supplied by the third party reporting the mortgage interest and real estate tax information.

Sounds like a simple situation and a simple mistake, and indeed, this is a *very* common error. Of course things could be clarified and subsequently made easier for the taxpayer if the IRS were to revise the 1098 form to include a line for real estate taxes. Then these two figures would at least be broken out on the same sheet of paper, which would reduce or even eliminate this particular problem altogether.

The tracking of real estate taxes is further complicated by the fact that real estate taxes are not reported only on the annual expense statement received from the lending institution.

• A taxpayer with no mortgage on his home pays his real estate taxes directly to the municipalities. In this instance, no annual expense statement is received by the taxpayer. Furthermore, since the taxpayer now has four to six checks to sort through at tax time, he will often include in his total real estate tax deduction the payment for water charges or rubbish removal (nondeductible items), because they are paid to the same payee, the municipalities.

• Mortgage interest for the short period, from the date of purchase to when the first new mortgage payment will be paid, is paid at the closing. Since this amount has been paid *before* the new account is set up, it is often not included on the annual expense statement or the 1098, both issued by the lending institution. The knowledgeable taxpayer will add up the total payments for the year, including interest and real estate taxes shown on the closing statement, and disregard the interest amount entered on the 1098. Too often, though, taxpayers forget to claim deductions for mortgage interest or real estate taxes that they are legitimately entitled to.

The IRS recognizes this problem and is trying to convince Congress to issue regulations that would require lending institutions to include these adjustments on their annual expense statements. Once this happens, taxpayers will receive more complete and understandable information from the lending institutions, which will help them claim their proper deductions.

Other possible sources of disagreement between mortgage interest as shown on Form 1098 and the deduction on Schedule A is the inclusion of late charges on the annual expense statements, incurred because the mortgage was paid after the usual 15-day grace period, and prepayment charges that accrue when you pay off your mortgage early. These charges are considered to be extra interest, *not* penalties. Accordingly, taxpayers can add the late and prepayment charges to the regular mortgage interest paid during the year.

Note that information regarding late and prepayment charges on mortgage payments is allotted two sentences in a tiny paragraph in IRS Publication 936, *Home Mortgage Interest Deduction.* Wouldn't you like to know how much revenue has been generated by the federal government because thousands of taxpayers did not realize that both of these charges were a valid deduction?

Implications for Taxpayers

If you receive a mismatch notice on mortgage interest, don't panic. Often there is just as great a chance that the error comes from the reporting institution. Answer the inquiry promptly with full documentation, including copies of your original Form 1098 and the closing statement from the purchase of your home. This will show the IRS where the extra mortgage-interest deduction can be found.

WHERE THE IRS TECHNOLOGY FALLS SHORT—NONFILERS AND UNDERREPORTERS

The GAO (General Accounting Office) does periodic studies of the IRS and usually makes specific recommendations as to how the IRS can improve its performance. The GAO studied IRS effectiveness in the area of nonfilers and underreporters, with these results:

- Nonfilers with incomes over $100,000 could more easily escape detection than those with lower incomes.
- When high-income nonfilers are pursued and they *do* file their returns, the IRS needs to scrutinize these late returns very carefully. It appears that the GAO made this very same suggestion in prior reports, but the IRS ignored it.
- The IRS should hire more employees to investigate high-income nonfilers.

- To reduce the time spent on reviewing underreporter cases that result from mistaken entries and not genuine underreporting, the IRS should change the matching program to search for reported income on as many different tax return lines as possible.
- The IRS should report to the Social Security Administration errors in wage data it finds in underreporter cases.[6]

Implications for Taxpayers

It does appear that the IRS is reducing the number of nonfilers. It remains to be seen how many of these delinquent taxpayers were contacted by the IRS because of its increased technological capabilities of the matching program versus how many voluntarily filed because they believed the IRS was on their trail; or how many were pulled in by the recent nonfiler program, or the media hype regarding leniency and so-called taxpayer amnesty.

In this area, IRS technology has a long way to go, but I believe that **by the end of the 1990s it will be extremely difficult to be a nonfiler on the loose.**

WHERE THE IRS TECHNOLOGY FALLS SHORT—LACK OF REPORTING REQUIREMENTS FOR CORPORATIONS

The biggest gap in the IRS technology infrastructure concerns payments to corporations of income, interest, dividends, rents, royalties, and capital gains. (There are several limited exceptions.) There is currently no requirement that any corporation receiving such payments be sent 1099's. According to a 1991 IRS study, small corporations voluntarily reported 81 percent of the tax they owed on such payments in 1981, but by 1987 the compliance rate dropped to only 61 percent. A new program urged by the GAO and the House Government Operations Committee would require entities that pay dividends, interest, and other payments to corporations to file 1099's with the IRS. The IRS would then attempt to catch corporations that understated income or failed to file returns.

Implications for Taxpayers

There are several valid reasons why the IRS has been dragging its feet on bringing in corporate recipients under the 1099 reporting umbrella:

- It would enormously increase the IRS processing burden of the already overworked IRS computers and staff. I estimate that more than 100 million new pieces of paper would be generated annually by payments to corporations. Also, the proponents of this arduous task have not considered the added cost to businesses, which may be as much as $1 billion annually.

• The IRS is going through a real period of growing pains. By its own admission, its new computer capabilities will not be fully operational until the end of the century. The added burden of corporate reporting might set back the current program even further.

• The task of matching bits of corporate income data to the multiple income line items that exist on Forms 1120 (Corporate Income Tax Return) and 1120S (U.S. Income Tax Return for an S Corporation) will be more formidable than matching individual income with lines on Form 1040.

• Many corporations base their books on years that end anytime between January 31 and November 30, while fiscal 1099 reporting is calculated on a calendar year. Thus, many 1099's will contain income that spans two corporate years. The only way to eliminate this problem is to require *all* corporations to convert to a calendar year. When Congress attempted exactly this procedure for S corporations in 1987, tax professionals revolted to an extent not seen since the Boston Tea Party. Being able to do fiscal year closings of books for corporations during off-peak times for accountants saves me (and no doubt countless numbers of other tax professionals) from an early death. Ultimately, Congress scaled back the calendar-year requirement just enough so that the revolt died down.

The House Government Operations Committee proposal urged the IRS to initiate corporate document matching but it was cut from the final version of RRA '93. The report said that matching could bring in significant tax revenues and have a *minimal* impact on the payer community and corporations. Based on the points just made, you can see that whoever wrote this report must have had no corporate experience or must not have been in touch with reality.

WHERE THE IRS TECHNOLOGY FALLS SHORT— THE AUDIT LEVEL

There are still the same old complaints that the IRS has trouble accessing specific information from their own computers. Information retrieval for a given year, a given tax return, or a specific piece of information may be readily available, but one never knows what will happen once a request is made. Basic tax return information takes more than a year to reach IRS computers in a readable form, and much of the technology still isn't up to where it should be. It appears as if the technology crunch is being fueled by Compliance 2000 and the Tax Systems Modernization; whatever the reason, IRS technology is still too slow to meet the needs of either IRS employees or taxpayers.

Implications for Taxpayers

Despite state-of-the-art technology, there is still too much information and not enough people and/or systems to process it. **In conclusion, there are and probably will always be gaps and lags in IRS computer capabilities.**

TECHNOLOGY OVERHAUL A FIASCO

The goals of the Tax Systems Modernization Program contrast sharply with reality. According to an article in *The Washington Post* dated March 15, 1996, "the decade-long multibillion-dollar effort to modernize the IRS's computers is badly off the track and must be rethought from top to bottom."[7] *The New York Times* has labeled the IRS's technology restructuring "a fiasco."[8] The General Accounting Office has recommended that the project be removed from the IRS and be administered instead by the Defense Department.[9] To make matters worse, the House Appropriations Subcommittee on Treasury that oversees the IRS recently approved $424.5 million in funding for the TSM for fiscal 1997, a decrease of $270.5 million from 1996 funding levels and less than half of the $850 million requested for 1997.[10]

The chairman of the subcommittee went on record: "This committee is out of the business of providing the department with billions of taxpayer dollars for what is in essence the construction of a house that lacks a blueprint."[11]

In 1988, during the planning stage, the system was expected to have been completed by 2000 at a cost of *only* $8 billion! There appears no way that the job will be done by that time, and even without the recently approved cut, the total cost will be in excess of $20 billion, including maintenance and operations expenses. The sums are so enormous they don't seem real, but they are, all U.S. tax dollars.

The biggest problems are with the electronic filing capability, the choices of software, security, and integration across the IRS's vast computer network. With outdated equipment that prevents systems from sharing files, the agency continues to rely on magnetic tapes transported between offices via trucks and planes. Is that what slows up the annual publication of the IRS's data book, which contains statistical tables that detail its operations?

One part of the new system that *is* working is 1040EZ filing (see pages 263–264). According to the IRS, taxpayers who filed this form in 1994 can continue to file their returns with only a brief phone call. Tele-Filing, too, is a continued success, along with the establishment of the IRS website on the Internet, which some 41 million people accessed to obtain more than 29,000 forms and publications daily since it opened in January 1995.

IRS commissioner Margaret Milner Richardson said that the new system "gives revenue officers on-line access to current taxpayer records . . . increasing efficiency 30 percent. The system is expected to be operating nationwide by fiscal 1999 and to result in an additional $2 billion in collections through 2004."[12] But, of course, the IRS has a track record for making projections that, at least in the area of technology, tend not to pan out.

To help sort out the mess, Arthur Gross, a seasoned tax official from New York, has been hired as the new information officer for the agency. His task is mammoth.

Although some of the newest systems ease processing, speed requests, and provide more across-the-board information on tax returns, I don't see the technology situation changing much, even by the year 2000. Taxpayers will continue to pay, and the IRS will continue to muddle through.

7

IRS Targets and What to Do
If You're One of Them

The tax compliance rate—the rate at which taxpayers willingly (although not contentedly) pay their taxes in the United States—is currently 83 percent.[1] Even so, the IRS estimates that only $83 of every $100 due in income tax is collected.[2] So despite the fact that the tax collection process brings in what seems like extraordinary sums (almost $1.4 trillion in gross collections for 1995), each year the federal government continues to be shortchanged an estimated $150 billion. (Even this is an understatement because it excludes an additional $300 billion or so of taxable income produced through drug sales, organized crime, and other illegal activities.)

In this realm of extraordinary tax evasion, very little has changed over the decades except the amounts owed and never paid, which continue to rise. Beginning in the late 1980s, however, the IRS seriously began to focus on breaking open the phenomenon that has come to be called the *underground economy* whereby a substantial number of people, businesses, and organizations do not pay their proper share, or any share at all, of their taxes.

Without a doubt the underground economy is a serious problem—for the IRS, for our society, and for honest taxpayers. **However, the IRS has taken such an aggressive position on exposing the underground economy that it is punishing innocent taxpayers and wiping out entire sectors of the independent business community.** This chapter is written for the people who are being wrongly and often unlawfully pursued.

ARE YOU IN THE LINE OF FIRE?

Individuals are responsible for about 75 percent of each year's tax shortfall, while corporations account for only 25 percent. How does the IRS identify the groups who are not paying their fair share of taxes? A great deal overlaps, duplicates, and even melds as players in the underground economy glide through avenues that facilitate evading or avoiding taxes. Easiest for the IRS to identify are

- The self-employed
- People who work out of a home office
- Independent contractors
- Cash-intensive businesses
- Nonfilers

Within each group, the two primary methods for evading tax dollars are hiding income and overstating or manipulating expenses or deductions.

TARGET: THE SELF-EMPLOYED

At the top of the IRS hit list for breaking open the underground economy are the self-employed, whether a sole proprietorship or a corporate entity. People who own a business and work full time for themselves probably have the greatest opportunities not only to hide money but also to overstate deductions.

What makes matters even more embarrassing is that the IRS knows just exactly which segments of the self-employed are the worst offenders. A 1990 GAO study named service providers as leading the list of underreporters. At the top are auto dealers, restaurateurs, and clothing store operators, who underreport nearly 40 percent of their taxable income, according to the IRS. Telemarketers and traveling salespeople have a shortfall of about 30 percent. Then come doctors, lawyers, barbers, and accountants, who understate about 20 percent of theirs.[3]

To more easily conquer this segment, as I see it, the IRS has subdivided the self-employed into three smaller groups:

- Sole proprietors
- Those who work out of a home office
- Independent contractors

Target: Sole Proprietors

A sole proprietor is defined as an unincorporated business or profession in which net income is reportable by only one person. The gamut of the self-employed runs from people who own a service business (beauticians, home services and repairs, tutors) to professionals (doctors, lawyers, tutors) to insurance agents and computer programmers and more.

How the IRS Attacks Sole Proprietors

Integral to the definition of sole proprietors is the necessity to file a Schedule C with a 1040 form. While Schedule C requires you to define the type of business you are in and/or your occupation, it also functions as a wonderful device for deducting business expenses dollar for dollar against business income (see also chapter 10, Rule 4, page 232). As a sole proprietor, via Schedule C you have every opportunity to underreport your income and lots of other opportunities to convert personal expenses to business expenses.

For these two reasons, the IRS sees the sole proprietor as a double enemy: a cheat in the underground economy *and* a prime audit target.

What Sole Proprietors Can Do to Protect Themselves

Although Schedule C affords full deductibility of business expenses, the heavy concentration of expense items are valuable indicators for the IRS, so the IRS is naturally going to focus on what you've listed. However, the IRS is *not* necessarily focusing on aggressive stances taken on expense items unless certain items jump out, such as travel being $25,000 out of a $50,000 income. **The IRS *is* focusing on the *type of business* for which the Schedule C is filed, particularly if the business type falls into one of the IRS target areas: service providers, professionals, or cash-intensive businesses.**

Here's an amazing story, the sort of thing that pops up every once in a while in the tax field, about a taxpayer who without realizing it discovered the secret to resolving the "double enemy" predicament—legally.

Sam grew up working in his father's hardware store, which was left to him after his father passed away. The normal tax procedure for this process would have been to close the estate by filing a final estate return, then to begin reporting the ongoing operations of the store on a Schedule C attached to Sam's 1040. However, the operations of the store were reported as part of a U.S. Fiduciary Income Tax Return (Form 1041), not on a 1040, and the store's net income was passed through to the son on a K-1 form (Beneficiary's Share of Income, Credits, Deductions, etc.), which is a schedule of Form 1041.

Sam continued to report income from the store through the estate on the K-1 of

Form 1041 until he retired. At no time did the IRS ever inquire why the operations of the store were included in the fiduciary income tax return. This unusual tax setup kept Sam's business virtually unnoticed by the IRS.

If you are a sole proprietor *and* are at a high risk for audit, the perfect solution, which Sam used without ever realizing it, involves the *way* you report your business activities to the IRS. By extracting yourself from the sole proprietorship/Schedule C category and transforming your business to, for example, a partnership or corporation, you can successfully remove yourself from the IRS hit list.

Because this subject is so closely linked to the audit component, the entire area will be discussed at length in chapter 8, "How to Avoid an Audit Completely."

Target: People Who Work Out of a Home Office

As many as 40 million people work at least part time at home, with about 8,000 home-based businesses starting daily. Of these, some 1.5 million claimed home-office deductions averaging $2,000 on their 1993 tax returns.[4]

How the IRS Attacks People Who Take the Home-Office Deduction

Inspired by Compliance 2000, an IRS initiative from the early 1990s to ascertain why at least 10 million individuals and businesses do not comply with tax regulations, the IRS decided that taxpayers who take the home-office deduction represented too large a segment of the underground economy. After all, a great many items taken as home-office expenses that would ordinarily be for personal use, like telephone, utilities, repairs, maintenance, and depreciation of certain items in the home, were being transformed to deductible business expenses on the 1040 form. (Home-office expenses are contrasted with out-of-pocket business expenses such as office supplies or postage, which would be incurred by a business whether it was located in a home or not.)

When a case came to light regarding a $2,500 home-office deduction taken by Dr. Soliman, an anesthesiologist who used a spare bedroom in his home to keep records and to telephone colleagues and patients, the IRS snared this as a test; it pursued Dr. Soliman relentlessly.

In Chapter 5, "Neutralizing the IRS's Power," the Soliman case was described up to the point where two lower courts had ruled against the IRS in the doctor's favor by agreeing on an interpretation that even though taxpayers did not spend most of their time in their home office, they could still take the home-office deduction as long as a substantial amount of work was performed there that couldn't be performed elsewhere.

Because this was a substantial expansion of the home-office rule as it traditionally stood, it would automatically result in a large chunk of lost tax dollars. The IRS was going to fight this to the finish, and it did, right up to the Supreme Court.

On January 19, 1993, in *Commissioner v. Soliman*, the Supreme Court reversed the two lower-court rulings and strongly reinforced the long-held IRS position, established in the Tax Reform Act of 1976, that to take a home-office deduction the site had to be used exclusively and regularly as the principal place of business.

The new ruling actually strengthened existing IRS guidelines. The Supreme Court gave the IRS an unexpected bonus because the ruling went so far in the other direction.

Let's explore how these guidelines can be, or have already been, pushed.

How to Qualify for the Home-Office Deduction
The Supreme Court decision will affect thousands of taxpayers, those who do most of their work from home, and those who do some of their work at home but typically also provide their services at other locations.

Under the "new" ruling, what stays the same, what changes, and what can be pushed or pulled into shape? **Those who *can* take the deduction are those who spend most of their working hours in the home office and conduct most of their important business there, such as meeting with customers or patients on a regular basis.** An art director who uses one room in her home or apartment as a studio and conducts her most important business there can still deduct a portion of electric, gas, heating, home repairs, maintenance, and insurance, plus depreciation or rent of the house or apartment. A doctor whose medical practice occupies a suite of rooms in his home and whose income from being self-employed comes from the practice will still be entitled to the deduction because, unlike Dr. Soliman's, his most important activities occur at the home office.

Relevant here is the concept that the space is used only for the business. An exception pertains to those who provide child care in their homes. As long as a room is used regularly in the child-care business, it need *not be used exclusively* for the person to qualify for the deduction. A woman who cooked lunch for the children in her kitchen, let them play in the family room, and had them take naps in her bedroom could take a deduction for all three rooms, even though she and her family also use those rooms.[5]

As of now, those who *cannot* take the home-office deduction are those who spend most of their hours performing services in another place (plumbers, gardeners) and who only use the home office for routine tasks such as record keeping.

A 1994 IRS revenue ruling, number 94-24, emphasized that the relevance of the business activities performed in the home office is now the key criterion for determining whether the deduction can be taken, rather than the amount of time spent there.

However, I hope you learn one thing from this book: **When it comes to the IRS, don't be deterred.** Interpreting our tax code is often an art, not a science. There will always be gray areas. Right now the Soliman ruling is again being reinterpreted, this time in Congress.

Gray Areas in the Home-Office Deduction and How to Handle Them Aggressively

You can take the home-office deduction if you bear these precautions in mind:

- Maintain a separate telephone number for business purposes only.
- Encourage some customers to visit your home office on a regular basis.
- Keep one log of all customer visits and another of the time you spend at the home office, stressing the importance of the activities performed there.
- Make sure your business correspondence is sent to your home office address rather than to some other convenient place, like one of your biggest clients.

Here's a case involving one of my clients affected by the Soliman ruling:

Ellen Stedman is an employee of a corporation whose only office is in Chicago, Illinois. But she lives in Newark, New Jersey, and uses her apartment as a home office. There she arranges customer contacts, speaks with suppliers, and performs administrative functions such as writing up sales orders and expense reports, which she mails to her employer in Chicago. Her normal workday keeps her out of her home office and on the road from nine A.M. to two P.M.

Under these circumstances the IRS might conclude that Ms. Stedman would not be entitled to take the home-office deduction because she doesn't perform her most relevant business activities at the home office.

For Ellen to keep the deduction, she has to adjust her work style somewhat. I advised her to hold several meetings with customers and suppliers at her home office during the workday and be prepared to produce a diary in which these meetings are recorded.

This enables her to secure her position with tangible evidence that she is complying with the steps necessary to qualify for the deduction under the new requirements. Call it acting wisely, or being more aggressive—the end result is that this client will be able to continue to support a position that makes the home-office deduction allowable.

How long will this work? One can't really know. The IRS is about as determined to narrow down the home-office interpretation as it was to get rid of tax shelters. So there's only so much hypothesizing one can do.

Also, don't forget that it takes the IRS a minimum of three years to develop an audit strategy on any new tax law or concept. We know, for example, that the IRS only began to collect meaningful statistics on taxpayers taking the home-office deduction in 1991, when Form 8829 (Expenses for Business Use of Your Home) was initiated (see next section). Before that, there was no effective way to collect such statistics.

The IRS probably will not begin auditing home-office returns in a wholesale manner unless the returns have other audit flags that will make it worthwhile.

Considering all the factors involved, my overall advice regarding the home-office deduction is:

- Make sure you understand the new requirements.
- Do what you have to do to meet them.
- By following both of these, you will be actively supporting your position.

Form 8829

Form 8829 is an IRS weapon for getting a grip on taxpayers taking the home-office deduction. Anyone who chooses the deduction must submit the form with Schedule C, Profit or Loss from Business (Sole Proprietorship), together with the 1040.

Although the IRS consistently denies it, Form 8829 represents another red flag that singles out your tax return for scrutiny. But just as with all other IRS forms, there are ways to interpret and fill this one out without quivering.

How to Avoid Audit Traps on Form 8829

Form 8829 is designed to contain several traps that could trigger an audit of your return.

PERCENT OF HOME SPACE USED AS AN OFFICE.

The percentage of expenses for business use of your home—insurance, utilities, repairs and maintenance, and rent, if you are a renter—that you can deduct is based on the total square footage of the residence that is used for business. Take a sensible approach in computing the percentage or you'll be caught in an audit trap. It is entirely acceptable for your business space to occupy 20 to 25 percent of your total home space, but a figure of 40 percent or more is unreasonable unless you store merchandise in your home. (For an update, see New Tax Legislation for 1996, page 271.)

NUMBER OF SQUARE FEET.

You probably should not go over the 40 percent mark regarding square footage; on the other hand, too many taxpayers operate under the wrong assumption that every piece of office furniture and equipment must be squeezed into a tiny space.

Be sure to include space you use for storage shelves, file cabinets, and other equipment. Also keep in mind that if you have merchandise inventory at home, it is not always stacked up in neat piles. With all that tax auditors have to do, it's rare for one to visit your home to verify square footage information, so utilize the greatest amount sensibly available.

DEPRECIATION OF THE HOME.

Depreciation for the portion of your home used for business, referred to as "nonresidential rental property" on Form 4562 (Depreciation and Amortization)—Part Two, is based on a write-off period of 39 years. Prior to May 13, 1993, the write-off period was 31½ years. The basis for depreciation is the original cost of your residence (excluding land cost) plus additional costs for permanent improvements, or fair market value at the time of conversion to business use, whichever is *less*. **If you use fair market value, a common mistake, your depreciation figure will show up as unnecessarily high because fair market value is generally much higher than original cost. This will attract IRS attention.**

DEPRECIATION ON EQUIPMENT AND FURNITURE.
You can depreciate the cost of new equipment and furniture over a five-
or seven-year period (depending on the item as defined and explained
in the instructions for Form 4562). In addition, anyone taking the home-
office deduction can also depreciate office machines, equipment, and
furniture that have been converted from personal (not new) to business
use. The basis for depreciation is original cost or fair market value at
the time of conversion to business use, whichever is *less*. The IRS will
not be surprised to see depreciation of this kind and will not hound you
for bills covering original items purchased since they assume you purchased them some time ago, probably as personal items.

You have several methods of depreciation to choose from:

- The *straight line method* allows you to ratably depreciate business capital assets evenly over the assets useful life.
- The *200 percent declining balance method* gives taxpayers twice
  the amount of depreciation in the earlier years. The process is described in IRS Publication 334, *Tax Guide for Small Business*, and
  Publication 534, *Depreciation*.
- Section 179 of the *Internal Revenue Code* allows taxpayers to
  write off *current-year purchases* of automobiles (with limitations) and business equipment and furniture up to $17,500 annu-
  ally through 1996 and $18,000 annually beginning in 1997,
  regardless of the item's useful life (use Form 4562). With the passage of the 1996 tax laws, Section 179 write-offs will increase in
  steps to $25,000 in 2003. So if you experience high net taxable in-
  come and can make a major purchase of office equipment or furniture in the same year, utilizing Section 179 will increase your
  expenses and reduce your net taxable income. Say you purchase
  an $8,000 copier that is normally deductible over five years accord-
  ing to the *Internal Revenue Code* for depreciation on office equipment. Under Section 179, you can deduct the entire $8,000 in the
  current year. The benefit gained is an extra $7,200 of expenses in a
  year when you have high taxable income. In the 31 percent tax
  bracket, the savings is $2,232. **Once you write off items under
  Section 179, you cannot depreciate them further.**

YOUR TAX-SAVING STRATEGY.
The Section 179 deduction cannot be used to reduce your taxable income below zero (taxable income includes the aggregate net income or
loss from all businesses you and your spouse conducted during the tax
year, *plus* any wages earned as an employee). If a Section 179 deduc-

tion would reduce your taxable income below zero, your alternative would be to use normal depreciation methods. You must depreciate autos, typewriters, computers, copiers, calculators, and the like over five years. (Autos and computers are subject to special dollar limitations.) The write-off period for office furniture (desks, files, and fixtures) and carpets is seven years.

Remember, when taking depreciation for office equipment and furniture:

- You don't need a receipt for every last cent, since you might have purchased the items a while ago.
- An IRS auditor would not be surprised to see depreciation for a desk, chair, couch, and carpeting.
- Estimates are acceptable by IRS auditors, if they are reasonable.

YOUR TAX-SAVING STRATEGY.
A computer is considered "listed property" and is subject to more stringent rules than other office equipment in order to claim any part of its cost as depreciation on a business return. To be eligible for depreciation, business use must exceed 50 percent and only that attained portion can be expensed. Where some personal usage is involved, use of a daily log to substantiate the business use is required by the IRS.

Loopholes in the Home-Office Deduction
The biggest loophole regarding the home-office deduction is available to anyone who owns an S corporation *and* uses a home office.

Owners of S corporations report income and expenses on Form 1120S (U.S. Income Tax Return for an S Corporation). **There is no special form to identify the home-office deduction.** This means that you can be the owner of an S corporation, operating fully out of your home, and there is no distinction made between your home-office expenses and any other business expenses. You avoid the home-office IRS hit list altogether. This is more fully explained in the discussion of S corporations, in chapter 8, "How to Avoid an Audit Completely" (see page 185).

YOUR TAX-SAVING STRATEGY.
Do not claim a home-office deduction in the year that you sell your home. If you sell your old residence and qualify for the deferral of any capital gain on the sale of the old residence, you will lose part of the deferral if part of your old residence was used for business (as deter-

mined by your taking the home-office deduction). Furthermore, by losing this part of the deferral, you will end up owing additional income tax in the current year—a big surprise.

Here is a final comment on Form 8829. At an American Institute of Certified Public Accountants (AICPA) seminar, an IRS presenter told the crowd that it would take an hour and 15 minutes to fill out Form 8829 and seven minutes to study the rules. This was followed by an outburst of laughter.[6]

I say there isn't a person alive who could learn anything useful about the *Internal Revenue Code* provision that governs this form in that time period. It more likely would take an entire day at a minimum.

Target: Independent Contractors

Combine downsizing and a gradual shrinking of our economy with American ingenuity, and you have millions of laid-off workers refashioning their experience and education and marketing themselves as one-person operations—independent contractors—to be hired out on an as-needed basis. By the late 1980s, this new battalion had grown to over 3 million and some of its members had joined the ranks of the underground economy. Their tax impact is an estimated shortfall of $10 billion a year.

Reclassification of Independent Contractors

By law, the IRS is entitled to receive from employers the following taxes for each employee:

- FICA tax (Social Security and Medicare), which comes to 15.3 percent of the employee's salary up to $62,700, covered equally by the employer *and* the employee, 7.65 percent each, 1.45 percent each on salary above $62,700.
- Federal withholding tax or the amount deducted from your gross wages on the basis of income level and exemptions.
- Federal unemployment insurance tax of 0.8 percent of only the first $7,000 in wages, paid by the employer. The federal unemployment insurance tax rate can be as high as 6.2 percent, which may vary according to the amount of state unemployment insurance tax paid by the employer. The rate differs in each state.

When employers hire independent contractors, these requirements and others disappear. Employers

- Are *not* required to include the contractor on the quarterly payroll tax reports. So business owners save at a minimum the employer portion of the FICA tax, or 7.65 percent of each independent contractor's gross earnings (1.45 percent on earnings above $62,700).

- Aren't subject to state unemployment insurance premiums or even increases in these premiums when a contractor is let go, since business owners who hire independent contractors are not subject to state unemployment laws. This alone represents a major consideration when deciding whether to hire an employee versus an independent contractor.
- Incur reduced compliance costs, since the federal Age Discrimination in Employment Act and the Americans with Disabilities Act of 1990 do not apply to independent contractors.
- Are *not* required by law to cover an independent contractor for worker's compensation insurance (accidents or sickness on the job), or disability insurance (accidents or sickness away from the job).
- Do *not* include independent contractors in the company's pension plan (this item alone is often as high as 10 percent of an employee's gross wages), sick leave or vacation benefits, medical coverage, stock options.

All the business owner is required to do is file a 1099-MISC and send it to the IRS at the end of the year.

When workers choose to be classified as independent contractors and/or employers choose to get rid of employees and instead hire independent contractors, the IRS is shortchanged two ways because independent contractors can

- Deduct on their tax return many items that would otherwise be considered personal: travel, entertainment, office supplies, insurance, and home-office expenses (subject to the key tests discussed earlier in this chapter). This could reasonably amount to 20 percent of one's net income.
- Set up their own pension plan, which is deductible against their income.

In turn, independent contractors *must* fulfill these obligations to the IRS:

- Pay their own FICA tax, which is about 15.3 percent of their net taxable income up to $62,700 and 2.9 percent above that, on Form 1040, Schedule SE (Self-Employment Tax).
- Pay withholding tax on their net taxable income.

The huge and growing numbers of independent contractors surging through our economy present many opportunities for workers not to pay the IRS all the money it is legislated to receive.

Are you beginning to get the picture? **Every additional worker classified as an independent contractor means the IRS loses tax dollars through unpaid FICA, withholding, and unemployment taxes, and through income tax deductions as well.**

The IRS would be delighted if all workers became classified as employees and the category of independent contractor disappeared. In its attempt to make this a reality, the IRS has initiated an all-out nationwide attack on independent contractors. One of its claims is that 92 percent of the companies they called in for a worker classification review during one recent period were assessed a higher Social Security tax, with an average assessment of $67,000 per audit.[7]

The GAO has reported that between October 1987 and December 1991, 6,900 employment tax audits resulted in $468 million of proposed assessments and reclassifications of 338,000 workers as employees.[8]

With the IRS estimating that what they call "misclassified" employees costs nearly $4 billion annually in lost revenues, it is more crucial than ever for businesses and independent contractors to recognize the IRS's aggressive tactics and how to stand protected.

IRS Attack Methods Against Independent Contractors

RECLASSIFYING INDEPENDENT CONTRACTORS.
The techniques being used by the IRS to turn independent contractors into employees include:

- A 20-factor control test
- Third-party leads (nothing more or less than informers)
- A shift in IRS Examination Division resources
- Unannounced audit blitzes by the Collection Department

Twenty Factors Control Test

The purpose of the 20 factors is to assess whether or not the relationship between a business owner and a worker exhibits a degree of control sufficient to indicate an employer-employee relationship. The factors are taken from a 1987 guide, *Revenue Ruling 87-41*, in which 20 statements are offered as a test. If a majority of the 20 statements are answered affirmatively, then the worker will probably be classified as an employee. Here are the 20 factors presented as questions:

1. Is the worker required to comply with instructions about when, where, and how the work is to be done?
2. Is the worker provided training that would enable him or her to perform a job in a particular method or manner?
3. Are the services provided by the worker an integral part of the business's operations?
4. Must the services be rendered personally?
5. Does the business hire, supervise, or pay assistants to help the worker on the job?
6. Is there a continuing relationship between the worker and the person for whom services are performed?
7. Does the recipient of the services set the work schedules?
8. Is the worker required to devote his full time to the person he performs services for?
9. Is the work performed at the place of business of the company or at specific places designated by the company?
10. Does the recipient of the services direct the sequence in which the work must be done?
11. Are regular oral or written reports required to be submitted by the worker?
12. Is the method of payment hourly, weekly, or monthly (as opposed to commission or by the job)?
13. Are business and/or traveling expenses reimbursed?
14. Does the company furnish tools and materials used by the worker?
15. Has the worker failed to invest in equipment or facilities used to provide the services?
16. Does the arrangement put the person in the position of realizing either a loss or a profit on the work?
17. Does the worker perform services exclusively for the company rather than working for a number of companies at the same time?
18. Does the worker in fact not make his services regularly available to the general public?
19. Is the worker subject to dismissal for reasons other than nonperformance of contract specifications?
20. Can the worker terminate his relationship without incurring a liability for failure to complete a job?[9]

The more control the worker has over the performance of the work and the hours worked, the less integrated the worker is in the regular routine of work. Similarly, the more the worker is motivated by profit and the less by having a long-term working relationship, the more likely that person is to be classified as an independent contractor.

Despite what appears to be rather clear guidelines, there are measures a business owner and an independent contractor can take to strengthen their respective positions.

The contract created between the business owner and the independent contractor is regarded by the IRS as a key item in assessing classification. When drawing up the contract, business owners can take several precautions.

How to Draw Up a Foolproof Independent Contractor Contract

- Specify the services to be rendered.
- Insert a starting and completion date.
- Make sure that the independent contractor is controlling the procedures necessary to accomplish the agreed-upon services. This would mean that the contractor hires additional employees of his or her own choosing to carry out the job, provides work tools, and sets payment schedules on the basis of the completion of the work, not simply on the passage of time.
- Make it clear that the independent contractor is in complete charge of supervising and directing how the work will be performed.
- Indicate that all insurance—liability, fire and theft, worker's compensation, and disability—will be provided by the independent contractor.
- Payment methods should be sporadic and vary over time, to justify treating the worker as an independent contractor.
- Do not separately state an allowance for overhead costs, such as meals and transportation; these should be included in the contract price.
- Spell out that training of workers is the full responsibility of the independent contractor.
- Do not include a provision that grants the independent contractor office or working space on the business owner's premises. This implies an employer-employee relationship. If the contractor needs office space, he'll use it. There is no need to put it in black and white.
- Avoid paying a bonus, since that isn't the nature of an independent contractor's arrangement.
- Tell the contractor that if things slow down, he will not be given

other work to do. The business owner's obligation is only for the work originally assigned and agreed upon.

In addition to the contract, business owners should make it clear to independent contractors that their responsibility is to complete the contract; they can't be fired nor can they quit the job without being at risk of a lawsuit for nonperformance of the contract.

Business owners should avoid making two common mistakes:

- Do not fill out both 1099's and W-2's for anyone working for you. An independent contractor must have payments reported by the business owner on the 1099—Miscellaneous Income, while an employee has wages filed on a W-2. Each business owner must make the decision up front as to how the payments for the worker are to be filed.
- Do not give even limited benefits to an independent contractor. It's a sure indicator that the worker is more an employee.

How to Strengthen Your Status If You Are
an Independent Contractor

- Independent contractors should always be able to take on assignments from other companies.
- The contract drawn up should never appear to be an exclusive agreement.
- Independent contractors should be able to prove that they receive income from other sources. This will help to legitimately determine their tax status as a self-employed person filing a Schedule C.
- Incorporate yourself. There is no obligation to issue a 1099 form to a corporation. As the IRS hones in on independent contractors by reviewing 1099 forms, you will no longer be included in this group.

USE OF INFORMERS.
The IRS encourages both disgruntled workers and companies that use employees rather than independent contractors to tattle on companies that use independent contractors via a "snitch sheet." This snitch sheet was distributed by an IRS official at a taxpayer association meeting in California. Reportedly the official asked technical service firms to act as "snitches" by filling out the sheet and returning it anonymously in a plain envelope. The official promised that all such leads would be followed up.[10]

The revenue officers whom the IRS turns loose for these snitch assignments are from the Collection Division. They come on sincere and act as though they're on your side. They may promise that if you help them by providing the right information, they'll help you by allowing you to retain the classification of independent contractor or by allowing your company to continue to employ independent contractors.

All of this demonstrates a wonderful knack for implying but not stating what you could easily interpret as pressure—pressure that, if you don't fess up or provide the agent with the right information, you will go down on record, somewhere, as being uncooperative or acting suspiciously.

Once you give in, and the case is open for audit, don't be surprised if these agents tell you they have acquired new information that they didn't have at the beginning of the audit and that is being used against you. The case could conclude with the agent's saying, "Even though you did as we suggested, all of your independent contractors have been reclassified as employees, and you owe $50,000 in additional FICA, withholding, and federal unemployment taxes."

Another information pool is large national firms that have actively and aggressively cooperated with the IRS in going after local firms in the same industry that treat workers as independent contractors. One national health-care agency has regularly contacted the IRS National Office regarding what they consider to be withholding-tax abuses involving the use of "independent contractors" in the supplemental nurse staffing industry.[11]

Now, however, new evidence shows that larger businesses are hiring independent contractors with the same regularity (and gaining the same benefits) as smaller firms. It is not unusual for large multinationals to hire new computer workers as independent contractors.

Despite the shift, the IRS continues to seek out independent tattletales. Tips from informers helped the IRS collect $72 million in 1989, more than twice as much as five years earlier.[12] Form No. 211, Application for Reward for Original Information, allows you to be rewarded as an informer with as much as $100,000 and have your identity kept secret. According to the IRS, in fiscal year 1995, almost $1.8 million was paid to informers.

WHAT TO DO IF YOU'RE PRESSURED TO INFORM.
If you are involved in a reclassification audit and you have every reason to believe your involvement was the result of undue pressure from a revenue agent, and the agent begins to pile up "new" information that could have been gained only through other snitches, you have every

right to cease the audit and gain professional advice. If you already have a professional on your side, your best bet is not to discuss the case any further with the auditor. Let your professional do it.

If you feel the auditor has lied in addition to applying pressure on you to inform, you can request that the auditor's group chief review the case. You can then ask the group chief to replace the auditor.

From here, you can move up the line in the appeals process. If you and your professional feel that you have a strong case, go for it. Taxpayers tend to do better at the appeals level where they face more level-headed, educated people.

SHIFT IN EXAMINATION RESOURCES.
In the Examination Division, the IRS has instructed revenue agents to look for misclassifications in the course of regular audits and has developed special training programs and audit techniques to help them do this.[13] In addition, the IRS admits to assigning over 750 revenue officers from the Collection Division to run special audits for the purpose of uncovering misclassifications. The focus of this group is businesses with assets of less than $3 million.

These investigations are nothing more than employment tax audits that are being carried out by the Collection Division instead of the audit personnel from Examination—who are *supposed* to be assigned to these tasks. Reports of incidents in the business world suggest that the way the IRS collection staff is handling these tax audits is nothing short of illegal, particularly when measured against *Your Rights as a Taxpayer*, IRS Publication 1 or, as it is generally called, the Taxpayer Bill of Rights.[14] Every taxpayer should have a copy (see Appendix D).

THE TAXPAYER BILL OF RIGHTS.
Passed in October 1988, with Senator David Pryor, Democrat from Arkansas, as its major supporter, the goal of this bill is that taxpayers be treated fairly, professionally, promptly, and courteously by Internal Revenue Service employees.

Part of this fair treatment involves being handed *Your Rights as a Taxpayer* upon *initial* contact by Examination, Collection, or any other IRS personnel, as required by law. Sometimes these pamphlets *are* given out. But too often they are handed to the taxpayer, particularly independent contractors or employers who hire them, at the *end* of a collection agent's visit, when it's too late to know which of your rights the IRS has abused.

Although the Taxpayer Bill of Rights initially appeared to have limited impact on the IRS, some significant actions have been taken on the basis of the rights defined in the publication. Furthermore, since its initial passage, the bill has gained increasing clout (more ammunition for the taxpayer) with the passage on July 30, 1996, of the *Taxpayer Bill of Rights 2*. (For an update, see New Tax Legislation for 1996, pages 278–281.)

THE UNANNOUNCED AUDIT BLITZ.

Once the IRS revamped its audit and collection resources, it came up with a new attack technique: having IRS officers from the Collection Division swoop unannounced into businesses across the country. Often these officers do not explain the purpose of their visit or what they are looking for. If they do provide an explanation, be wary. The real reasons for the visit are to uncover people who are legitimately working as independent contractors but whom the IRS would like to classify as employees, to verify the level of compliance regarding a specific reporting requirement, or to gather incriminating information on a particular industry or individual organization. The blitz is an all-purpose weapon used by the IRS to audit whichever businesses or organizations strike its fancy.

How would you feel if an IRS officer came into your company unannounced and demanded information from you, such as how the company distinguishes individual contractors from employees? **This act in and of itself is against the law and in full violation of a taxpayer's rights.** Here's what the latest version of *Your Rights as a Taxpayer* says under the section "Privacy and Confidentiality":

> You have the right to know why we are asking for information, how we will use it, and what happens if you do not provide requested information.

Under the section "Professional and Courteous Service":

> If you believe that an IRS employee has not treated you in a professional manner, you should tell that employee's supervisor. If the supervisor's response is not satisfactory, you should write to your IRS district director or service center director.

Don't try to handle the audit blitz yourself. When revenue officers know you are afraid, they will use that fear to get as much information out of you as they can. **You have the right to ask them to leave and not to answer any of their questions.** When asked, they generally do leave. They are, after all, trespassing.

Then call your tax professional, CPA, or attorney immediately. I tell my clients that the definition of an emergency is when the IRS is at your door, or inside, ready to close your business down. An unannounced audit is an emergency. Since my career began over 30 years ago, I have had only two such calls, and in both cases they were triggered by revenue officers from Collection.

LONG-AWAITED RELIEF—REAL OR NOT?

Have signs of relief arrived? With continued pressure from the business community, and a congressional subcommittee examining the independent contractor issue at a White House Conference on Small Businesses, here's what's new.

First, the Classification Settlement Program (CSP) has been initiated by the IRS to help businesses currently being examined to settle their employee classification issues by offering deals based on a graduated settlement scale ranging from a 25 to a 100 percent discount on a single year's back payroll tax liability. The offer would be made using a standard closing agreement, and participation is voluntary. A company can decline to accept a settlement and still have the right to appeal an IRS ruling. The CSP will be tried for a two-year test period, which began March 5, 1996.

Second, an early referral of employment tax issues to the Appeals Office will allow a business to hasten settlement and allegedly cut short the prohibitive penalties that build up while a case is being disputed. Requests for early referral can be made during a one-year test period, which began March 18, 1996.

Third, a new training manual has been published to provide explicit guidance to field agents on the difference between an employee and an independent contractor. The manual does not preempt the 20-question control test. Instead, it is designed to simplify and explain it, and in so doing, introduces areas that the IRS has conceded for the independent contractor.

Revised IRS Stance on Independent Contractor Status
The manual presents these new IRS positions:

- Changes over time: The IRS admits that factors in determining worker status change over time. For example, uniforms previously indicated an employer-employee relationship. Today the IRS concedes that a uniform may be necessary for an independent contractor to perform the job.

- Control: The IRS admits that even in the clearest cases, an independent contractor is not totally without control, and conversely, employees may have autonomy, previously deemed a clear indicator of independent contractor status.
- Home offices: The manual strikes a blow at using a home office as a characteristic to prove independent contractor status. Renting an office is viewed as more concrete proof because it indicates a "significant investment."
- Financial dependence: The manual points out that Congress and the Supreme Court have rejected the argument that focuses on whether or not the worker is economically dependent on or independent of the business for which services are performed and warns agents not to apply this standard.
- Hours and location: Given the current environment, the IRS no longer considers part-time versus full-time, temporary or short-term work, on- or off-site locations, or flexible hours as indicative of a worker's status.[15]

The manual also reinforces the importance of Section 530 of the Revenue Act of 1978, often referred to as the "safe harbor."

Safe Harbor—Section 530

In the Revenue Act of 1978, Congress enacted *Internal Revenue Code* Section 530, making the section a permanent part of the Tax Equity and Fiscal Responsibility Act of 1982. It became known as the "safe harbor" because it was supposed to prevent the IRS from retroactively reclassifying workers as employees if an employer consistently and in good faith classified them as independent contractors.

An employer whose workers are under scrutiny by the IRS for reclassification from independent contractors to employees can apply Section 530 if the employer has

- Not treated the worker as an employee in the past.
- Consistently treated the worker as an independent contractor on all returns filed (including Form 1099).
- A reasonable basis (reliance on authority, prior IRS audit or a long-standing industry practice) for treating the worker as an independent contractor.
- Not treated anyone else holding a substantially similar position as an employee.[16]

Any company meeting these provisions cannot be held liable for taxes not withheld after a worker is found to have been an employee rather than an independent contractor. The IRS often uses Section 530 as a bargaining tool, agreeing to its applicability only if a business reclassifies a worker. Faced with costly legal battles, which most small businesses can't afford, many accept the IRS offer.[17]

An IRS agent can seek out and offer the safe harbor option even if the employer does not.

Section 530 does not apply to an engineer, designer, draftsperson, computer programmer, systems analyst, or other similarly skilled worker if the worker's services are provided through a placement firm.[18]

The training manual *Employee or Independent Contractor* is available at no cost by writing to Douglas Izard, Dean, IRS School of Taxation, 2221 South Clark Street, Arlington, VA 22202.

WHAT ALL THIS MEANS

Settlement options aren't terrific bargains. The taxpayer still has to fork over a large sum of money just to end the aggravation. What is occurring here is quite similar to what happened in the 1980s with tax shelters. The IRS is getting so backlogged with cases that it begins to offer small bones to taxpayers just to get some cases resolved. As you already know, the IRS is smart enough to grab whatever money it can, especially if tax court cases start going against it.

There is talk that Congress is planning to formalize the independent contractor rules with new legislation that might take away some of the IRS's bite by making the delineations between employee and independent contractor clearer and more understandable. But perhaps that's hoping for too much.

The 20-point test and Section 530 are rehashes of old concepts. Taking advantage of safe harbor rules is still difficult. If you qualify, you beat the rap and the IRS can't touch you even if you employ independent contractors who really appear to be employees. The safe harbor rules, however, appear to apply mainly to larger employers, and not to too many at that.

In short, there is still not enough reason for the IRS to do anything else but continue to employ its "pay up or else" tactics. The steps taken thus far appear to be in line with the agency's usual attempt to offer some leniency in the face of mounting criticism. For an update on safe harbor legislation, see pages 270–271.

Target: Cash-Intensive Businesses

It's one thing to pursue money launderers and drug lords who are fully capable of hiding thousands, even millions, of dollars illegally. But it's another thing to treat legitimate cash-intensive businesses as if they were criminals. No doubt businesses in which large amounts of cash routinely are handed from consumers to business owners present the greatest opportunities to underreport income. This includes everything from automobile dealers, check-cashing operations, jewelers, travel agencies, brokerage houses, and real estate businesses to hair salons, bars, and restaurants. So targeting this segment of the underground economy is naturally on the IRS's agenda. But just look at how they're doing it.

IRS Attack Method Against Cash-Intensive Businesses—Form 8300

In a big push to enhance compliance, particularly among cash-intensive businesses, in 1991 the IRS issued proposed regulations that expanded cash transaction reporting requirements. Using Form 8300 (Report of Cash Payments Over $10,000 Received in Trade or Business), anyone who in the course of trade or business receives cash (cashier's checks, traveler's checks, money orders, or bank drafts) in excess of $10,000 in one separate or two or more related transactions must report the transaction(s) to the IRS. The information must be reported within 15 days of the date the cash is received and a statement must be supplied to the payer by January 31 of the following year. Owners or operators of any trade or business who do not file this form face civil and criminal penalties, including up to five years' imprisonment.

Here are some examples of how the expanded legislation works:

Through two different branches of a brokerage company, a person purchases shares of stock for $6,000 and $5,500 cash on the same day. Each branch transmits the sales information to a central unit, which settles the transactions against the person's account. The brokerage company must report the transaction because it fits the definition of being a single receipt of over $10,000 from one person.

A man buys a Rolex watch from a retail jeweler for $12,000. He pays for it with a personal check for $4,000 and a cashier's check for $8,000. The personal check is not considered cash. Thus, the amount of cash received is not more than $10,000 and the jeweler does not have to report the transaction.

Toward the end of 1991, when enforcement efforts were in full bloom, audit blitzes were conducted across the country, where IRS agents swooped into businesses unannounced.[19] The goal—to secure so-called delinquent 8300 forms and the penalties assessed for the unpaid sums. To enhance its coverage the IRS next shifted responsibilities onto the taxpaying public by requiring that businesspeople must report cash payments of over $10,000 in these kinds of situations:

For example, a travel agent receives $8,000 in cash from a customer for a trip, and the next day receives another $8,000 from the same customer to take a friend on the trip. If a customer makes two or more such purchases within a 24-hour period totaling more than $10,000, it is considered a related transaction and therefore reportable.

The IRS is also encouraging businesses to report transactions of less than $10,000 *if they appear to be suspicious*, and smaller related or multiple-cash payments that total over $10,000 in one year. Pause for a moment and think what this represents:

- The IRS is asking the private sector to do work that should be assigned to the Criminal Investigation Division.
- The business owner must now be a detective, a mindreader, and an expert administrator with systems that can track these kinds of multiple payments.
- Given the volume of business common to most of the companies that fall into this reporting category, it's likely that some transactions that should be reported would be missed, a fate not likely to be discovered until audit time when the businessman gets hit full force in the pocketbook.

According to the IRS, in 1986 only 1,200 8300 forms were received from taxpayers. By 1992, when enforcement efforts increased, that number jumped to 142,000. Since then, it has hovered around 132,0000 annually.

What to Do If You're in a Cash-Intensive Business

Stay within the law and report to the IRS cash transactions that exceed $10,000. Use as guidelines the information outlined in the instructions to Form 8300.

When the IRS carried out its audit blitzes, most of the violations uncovered were straight cash transactions that exceeded $10,000. In other words, they were blatant violations of the *Internal Revenue Code* for which the taxpayer had no defense.

Don't worry that you might miss some suspicious chain of transactions because of the volume of cash transactions in your day-to-day business operations. There is no case law that sets a precedent that you should or could know that a series of transactions are related or suspicious.

Financial Status Auditing

Despite the fact that economic reality audits have been around for years, with cash-intensive businesses as their targets, they are currently being launched into broad segments of an unsuspecting taxpaying public. Keep the term *lifestyle indicators* in your memory. During the past year the IRS realized that the vast majority of clear indications of a taxpayer's net worth—boats, cars, real estate transactions, cash on hand— do not appear on tax returns. Thus the current emphasis to determine the financial status of a taxpayer during an audit by asking some or all of 27 lifestyle questions, dreamed up by the IRS, as part of revenue agents' and tax auditors' most recent training. Along with the ones mentioned on page 53, here are some other questions:

- Did you sell any assets during the tax year? If so, what, to whom, and for how much?
- Did you receive repayments of any money lent during the tax year?
- What loans do you have besides auto and mortgage? What are your monthly payments?
- What is the largest amount of cash that you had at any one time during the tax year?
- Did you transfer funds between accounts? If so, how much and when?
- Do you have a safe-deposit box? Where? What is kept in it?

Inquiries of this nature were supposed to be asked only when there was a reasonably strong suspicion of unreported income, as in a fraud investigation. Furthermore, upon suspecting fraud, formalized procedures must be followed to protect taxpayers' civil liberties, including notifying the Criminal Investigation Division. With financial status audits, however, tax examiners are being trained "to make broad investigative inquiries before they even open the taxpayer's books" in the course of ordinary audits.[20]

There are three areas that an examiner will pursue to locate the presumed hidden income: creating a cash in–cash out equation (or, does what goes in match with what is being spent), examining personal living expense statements (as indicated on Form 4822), and gathering other internal and external data, as needed. Under this specter of fraud, "there has been speculation in the press that agents will 'have unmarked cars and trail people to see how they live and what kind of life-style they have.' Feedback from some of the IRS training sessions indicates participants were encouraged to make drive-bys of taxpayer residences, write down auto license plate numbers, and make other observations of the lifestyle enjoyed by taxpayers scheduled for audits."[21]

Just as frightening is the fact that if an audit involved fraud, a taxpayer was always forewarned so that he or she could choose to bring along a tax attorney or legal counsel. With economic reality audits, unsuspecting taxpayers enter what they think is a typical audit examination prepared for questions in a few areas of income or deductions but soon discover that they are facing what sounds like an inquisition with strong implications that fraud is suspected. Because of the lack of CPA-client privilege (see page 210), anything the taxpayer says is liable to be used later in an audit turned criminal investigation. Worse, the tax pro can subsequently be called on by the IRS to testify against his or her own client.

What to Do About Financial Status Audits

As is common with new IRS procedures, there is little control over or consistency in the execution of the financial status audits. At a July 1996 IRS Financial Status Audit Conference sponsored by The Tax Institute, School of Professional Accounting at Long Island University, with over 50 CPAs in the room, only one had come up against a financial status audit in the past 12 months. According to an IRS presenter there, these audits have been conducted for years, primarily on the East Coast, while in other areas, especially the Northwest and Midwest, these audits were rarely used. We already know that location plays a key role in determining where the IRS plays bad guy. It does, after all, go for the biggest bang for its available resources.

What we are seeing, however, is that the situation has tremendous potential and, indeed, is already beginning to get out of hand as anywhere from several to all of the lifestyle questions are being posed to unsuspecting, unprepared taxpayers.

What should you do if you are faced with this situation?

First, read chapter 8, "How to Avoid an Audit Completely," and digest the information so that you will be in the strongest position possible.

If, during an ordinary audit, the IRS presses for an economic reality audit by barraging you with financial status questions, consider legal representation to ensure attorney-client privilege. If the auditor wants to interview you without an adviser, you can request a delay until you have a professional representative. My feeling is that if you are alone, stop the audit immediately and postpone it for as long as possible. This way, the caseloads will pile up and the IRS may be forced to cut back on imposing economic reality audits, at least for a while.

If you receive correspondence in the form of an administrative summons from an IRS agent announcing an economic reality audit, contact a tax pro as soon as possible. Remember, this places you one step ahead of taxpayers who are hit with these audits on site.

If the notification of the audit arrives with Form 4822, which requires you to list all personal living expenses paid during the audited tax year (the total cost of food, housing, vacations, clothing, etc.), *you are not required to fill it out.* Consult with your representative. Be informed, however, that the tax examiner can search out additional data about you from external sources, such as social service agencies, motor vehicles databases, credit bureaus, trade associations, and court records. The examiner can also interview landlords, employers, and financial institutions.

Once you are working with a tax professional or attorney, you will need to proceed honestly. Ask your tax pro for a pre-audit evaluation to determine if a situation exists that might generate significant interest to an IRS tax examiner during an audit. Disclose as much as you can concerning what an examiner would be interested in. Work with your representative on this. Consider your "global lifestyle," including your standard of living, overall yearly consumption versus costs, and method of accumulating wealth. What does your economic history look like? Do business profits or wages match your standard of living and wealth accumulation? Are your assets and liabilities consistent with your net worth? Also be prepared to answer questions about loans, large purchases (real estate, stock transactions, personal items), lender's source of funds, and possible cash hoards, gifts, or inheritances.

Ask your tax pro to request the IRS file on you, if this hasn't already been done, to assess the basis for the investigation and to send a message to the IRS that your tax pro intends to monitor the procedure.

During the audit, if the examiner asks financial status questions, your tax pro can challenge them by asking if there is any suspicion of unreported income.

Finally, remember that an examiner cannot conduct a civil examination as if it were a criminal fraud investigation. If indication of fraud is suspected, the audit must be suspended and a fraud referral report submitted through the ranks. The case then proceeds to CID.

Since the financial status audits are attracting a great deal of public attention, professional organizations, such as the American Institute of Certified Public Accountants (AICPA), have met several times with IRS officials. AICPA's efforts to get the IRS to temper these audits and to consider the effects they are having on taxpayers' civil liberties is one of the strongest stands I have ever seen that organization take. One particularly strong request was that the IRS issue an administrative summons to force a taxpayer interview prior to the start of one of these audits so that the taxpayer can, at least, prepare. In mid-1995, all regional IRS chief compliance officers were officially informed of the AICPA's position, but, as usual, if and when these requests will filter down to the grassroots level and be adhered to by at least some examiners is another matter. IRS correspondence promises a lot but ends up doing little.

In the meantime, an IRS public relations measure is in the works to permanently change the name "economic reality auditing" to "financial status auditing" to "dispel the perception that the IRS is interfering in taxpayers' lives by making inquiries into their lifestyles."[22] Now, isn't that the truth!

TARGET: INDUSTRIES IN THE MARKET SEGMENT SPECIALIZATION PROGRAM

The Market Segment Specialization Program (MSSP) (see pages 53–54) was instituted by the IRS in 1993 to assist IRS revenue agents to shift from functioning as generalists to specialists when examining tax returns of a variety of unrelated businesses. The IRS claims that the objectives of the program are to "share MSSP expertise through educational efforts with taxpayers, involve representatives of key market segments who can deal with the underlying cause of noncompliance, and conduct tax audits using examiners skilled and knowledgeable in a particular market."[23] According to the IRS, some 20,000 tax examiners are being used in this effort.

The program is supposed to eventually replace auditing techniques that focus on geographic regions, or income ranges for individuals and asset ranges for corporations, when examining compliance problems. With the experience it provides, the program is also supposed to allow an agent to conduct audits more quickly and efficiently.

To support these goals, Audit Technique Guides are being developed by the IRS with input from industry representatives, covering almost 100 industries identified so far.

What to Do If Your Industry Is Targeted

Let's be honest. No matter what the IRS and IRS-related publications say, the MSSP is designed to tell agents whether taxpayers are paying what they should. However, the agency does appear to be going about this in a spirit of cooperation.

The guides themselves can serve as valuable assets for taxpayers. So the first thing to do is to send for the guide appropriate for you. Then become familiar with it. The more familiar you are, the more you can be on the alert to assess the direction of the audit and to work successfully with your tax pro.

This is the most current list of MSSP guides available, their order number, prices, and where to order from.

Market Segment Specialization Program (MSSP) Guide Order Form

Order No.	Guide	Price
3149-101	Ministers	4.35
3149-102	Attorneys	12.75
3149-103	Mortuaries	22.80
3149-105	Bed & Breakfast	6.00
3149-106	Pizza Restaurant	6.75
3149-107	Air Charters	3.60
3149-108	Taxicabs	3.45
3149-109	Rehabilitation Tax Credit	17.25
3149-110	Trucking Industry	18.00
3149-111	Architects	3.80
3149-112	Resolution Trust Corporation: Cancellation of Indebtedness	9.30
3149-113	The Wine Industry	15.00
3149-114	Gas Retailers (Rev. 7-95)	9.30
3149-115	Passive Activity Losses	27.90
3149-118	Bars & Restaurants	11.85
3149-119	Mobile Food Vendors	18.45
3149-120	Alaskan Commercial Fishing: Catcher Vessels—Part I	13.65
3149-121	Alaskan Commercial Fishing: Processors & Brokers—Part II	11.10
3149-122	Grain Farmers	44.40
3149-123	The Port Project	18.75
3149-124	Reforestation Industry	19.05
3149-126	Beauty & Barber Shops	5.55
3149-127	Auto Body & Repair Industry	19.05
3153-101	Entertainment—Music Industry	9.50
3153-102	Entertainment—Foreign Athletes & Entertainers	49.35
3153-103	Entertainment—Important 1040 Issues	15.75
3147-101	Tobacco Industry	12.45

	Guide	Price
3147-106	Independent Used Car Dealer	22.65
3149-125	Oil and Gas Industry	26.70
	Indian Assistance Handbook	8.40
	Classification of Workers within the TV Commercial Production and Professional Video Communication Industries	7.35
	Farmers (Noncash Renumeration for Agricultural Labor)	2.10
	Food Service Industry	1.95
	Introduction to Health Care Industry (Coursebook)	81.00

There is no charge if total amount due is less than $10.

Mail your order to: Internal Revenue Service
Freedom of Information Reading Room
P.O. Box 795
Ben Franklin Station
Washington, DC 20044

Here are several examples from already published guides to show you what to expect regarding specificity and completeness.

The beauty salon and barbershop guide states, "The [hairdressing] industry is cash intensive, . . . the majority of the workforce had a high school education and were graduates of a cosmetology school. . . . It was important to compare the type of services and the number of appointments to the income reported," and it provides a specific technique to calculate unreported tips.[24]

The architect guide gives a rule of thumb that architects "will generally be paid about 10 percent of the project cost for small jobs while for larger jobs, that may drop to 4 or 5 percent of the project cost." It points out that billings will generally be progressive rather than in lump-sum payments often tied to completion of various phases. It also notes that the plans "represent the only real leverage the architect has to secure payment of fees and therefore, will normally have billed 80 to 90 percent of the fees by the start of the construction phase."[25]

The attorney guide says, "The businesses with one person having the majority of internal control have the most audit potential, i.e., there is more opportunity to manipulate the books. . . . Furthermore, certain areas of attorney specialization are more productive than others. The personal injury area produces adjustments through the advanced client costs adjustment since, by nature of the specialty, significant client costs may be advanced prior to settlement. Criminal attorneys have more access to cash receipts than most other attorneys."[26]

The guides are thorough and well researched. No doubt a balance will be brought into play: Will the MSSP snare more taxpayers into the audit net or will the audit guides provide the right information for taxpayers to prepare their returns?

New for 1996, and attached to the MSSP, is the Market Segment Understanding (MSU) Program. According to the IRS, this is supposed to "identify a particular area of tax noncompliance where the facts, law or both are unclear, or noncompliance is widespread."[27] What is unique about the MSU is the establishment of a working group consisting of IRS and industry representatives who, together, will discuss how tax law applies to the area in question and produce a document clarifying issues that will then be made available to the public or IRS personnel.

An MSU can be initiated either by the IRS or at the request of an industry. One drawback appears to be the directive that MSU's require several levels of IRS review and approval wherever meetings are held. This initiative is too new to determine its effectiveness, but hopefully it won't end up bogged down in political positioning and paperwork.

TARGET: NONFILERS

An estimated 6 million people across the U.S. do not file any income tax returns whatsoever, down from the 9 to 10 million of about three years ago. About 64 percent of nonfilers are self-employed people who deal primarily in cash. They have been out of the system an average of four years, are in their peak earning years, and live affluently. On average, less than 25 percent of their total income is reported to the IRS by an employer, bank, or broker.

As a group, nonfilers account for almost $14 billion a year in lost revenue to the IRS and cost each of us at least $600 extra at tax time. The good news is that when it comes to the nonfiler, the IRS has for the most part proved itself to be rather trustworthy. (See also chapter 10, Rule 2, page 224, and chapter 11, "Amnesty: The Real Thing?," page 261.)

The IRS Approach for Bringing In Nonfilers
The IRS's overall thinking is that as many nonfilers as possible should be brought into the system not by threats but by cooperation. The IRS believes that once they take the first step, nonfilers will feel all the better for filing, since many are not really willful violators. It's just that they've been out of the tax collection loop for so long that they're afraid of the amounts they might owe.

The IRS has developed a nonfiler program based on this assumption. While taxpayers theoretically could be prosecuted for failing to file income tax returns, if they come forward under the new program, the IRS promises:

- Not to prosecute, but only to charge for back taxes and interest owed, and possibly penalties.
- To work out installment payments.
- To expand its "offer in compromise" terms, whereby the IRS settles for only a portion of back taxes owed, depending on the taxpayer's ability to pay.
- That the approximately 24 percent of nonfilers who are due refunds will get them if they come to their local IRS office to claim the money within three years after the due date of their tax return.

The IRS reported in 1993 that "since October 1992, more than 155,000 people telephoned the IRS about prior-year returns, and another 58,000 visited IRS offices for assistance with such returns. By the end of January 1993, more than 4 million delinquent returns from businesses and individuals were filed under the nonfiler program. Nearly 45 percent of those filing received refunds."[28]

To underscore its determination to reduce the number of nonfilers, the IRS had assigned over 2,000 of its 19,000 auditors and revenue agents to concentrate on bringing delinquents onto the tax rolls.[29] But by late 1996, according to the IRS Media Relations Department, the strong focus on nonfiler compliance was being phased out due to the successful turnout during the four-year program. Nonfilers are not, however, off the hook.

Another often overlooked way to catch nonfilers is via Form 8300 and the Currency Transaction Reports submitted by financial institutions. Both types of documents are used to report currency transactions over $10,000, and when this information is run through the IRS matching process, it has great potential to identify nonfilers and unreported income.[30]

What to Do If You're a Nonfiler

Nonfiler cases are often unique, simply because when a nonfiler walks into a tax professional's office, you never know what to expect. About 10 years ago a new client came to me with this story:

Mr. Frammer was a used-auto-parts dealer who also refurbished autos for resale. He worked out of a junkyard, was foreign born, and had come to the U.S. about 15 years before.

He had *never* filed an income tax return and sought my advice because he thought he was in trouble with the IRS. Mr. Frammer believed this was so because the previous year, a lawyer he knew had convinced him to set up a corporation so that he could limit his personal liability in selling used autos. Now the IRS was sending him notices that his corporate income tax return was past due. Incorporating had established a direct link between Mr. Frammer and IRS computers.

I filed the past-due return for him but then was curious. How could he have escaped detection for 15 years? He owned a business and he had eight children. The answer was easy.

Although Mr. and Mrs. Frammer had Social Security numbers, they never used them. They had no bank accounts, no charge cards, no bank loans, nothing that would put them within the scope of any type of third-party reporting whatsoever. His children's Social Security numbers were never used, since he didn't take them as dependents on a 1040 form.

Mr. Frammer maintained a business checking account through which he paid monthly overhead items such as telephone, electric, and rent, but he paid all other personal and business expenses in cash. As far as the IRS was concerned, the Frammer family did not exist.

This scenario would be hard to duplicate today.

In another case, two nonfilers ended up surprisingly pleased; in the words of the IRS, they were permanently brought back into the fold.

A man and a woman, both professional lawyers, came into my office saying they hadn't filed income tax returns for the past three years and now were ready to do so. Using their tax data, I computed the balances owed and refund due. The couple was quite pleased when I told them that the second year resulted in a refund of $1,000, and in the first and third years, the balances due were only $2,500 for each year.

We filed the first two years immediately and the last year a month later. On the refund return, we instructed the IRS to carry the balance over to the following year. The reason we delayed the filing of the third year was to ensure that the tax return containing the $1,000 refund had already been processed into the IRS system. When we filed the last year, we only remitted $1,500 ($2,500 minus the $1,000 refund carried forward).

When the entire process was completed, I thought I'd never see this couple again. But they have been my clients ever since, and their returns are always filed on time.

If this sounds simple, it was because the clients were able to supply me with all the necessary information. With nonfilers this is generally not the case. Much information is usually missing, which too often serves as a great deterrent for the taxpayer. Nonfilers are often motivated to file again when they understand what is required:

- Go to a tax professional.
- The tax professional will contact your local IRS office and inform them that he or she has a case of a nonfiling taxpayer who wishes to file.
- The tax professional will explain that information for the past three (or whatever) years is missing or lost because of illness, divorce, natural disaster, etc.
- The revenue officer will probably cooperate by providing the professional with income data entered under the matching program from the IRS computer listed under the taxpayer's Social Security number. This would include W-2's, 1099's for miscellaneous, interest, and dividend income, and possibly information from 1098's showing mortgage interest paid by the taxpayer. Most important, the W-2 would show the amount of federal tax that was withheld each year.
- Next the tax professional will reconstruct the 1040, enlisting the taxpayer's support to fill in information such as estimates of contributions, medical expenses, and other deductions. Revenue officers have been accepting reasonable estimates in cases like this.
- This entire process could take as little as a few weeks or as much as a few months, if items can't be found immediately.
- The IRS will add up to 25 percent in penalties plus interest to the balance due. That is to be expected. However, perhaps you will be one of the 25 percent of nonfilers who are due a refund.

The IRS continues to stress that nonfilers who do not come forward will be pursued to the point of criminal prosecution. All in all, the process of moving from being a nonfiler to a filer is not difficult. In my experience it is a great relief for taxpayers.

No one will deny that so far, the majority of the IRS's attempts to pursue the underground economy have been successful. But if you are unjustly attacked, you will be in the strongest position to hold on to what you're entitled to if you understand how the IRS moves in and out of the underground economy, and to learn your rights.

8

How to Avoid an Audit Completely

Learning what it takes to have your tax returns slide through IRS computers and past IRS scrutiny is not only possible but not even complicated. You simply must know the correct way to approach the situation. The correct way involves understanding which actions to take, and becoming familiar with the vulnerabilities and habits of the IRS. Once you know these, your fear of the IRS should drop significantly and you should be ready to proceed with a clear head and a regular pulse.

In this chapter you are going to learn how to avoid an audit through a set of clearly defined actions that apply to all taxpayers.

First a word on audit rates and how the IRS plays with them.

TO BE OR NOT TO BE AFRAID OF AUDIT STATISTICS

During most of its existence, the IRS audit rate for individual tax returns hovered between 1 and 2 percent. This may seem minuscule, but it isn't if you take into account that over 100 million personal returns are filed annually. Between 1980 and 1990, though, the audit rate for individual tax returns dropped rather steadily, from 1.77 percent, or 1.6 million individual returns, to 0.80 percent, or 883,140 individual returns.[1]

As of 1994, however, all of this changed because the IRS engaged in some substantial historical revisionism, as reported in the *IRS 1993 Annual Report*. Here's the significance of what was done:

All audit statistics were amended retroactively to include the service centers' correspondence audits. The immediate effect of this move increased the number of returns that the IRS claimed it audited, the corresponding percentages of returns audited, and the overall number of returns examined. Revisionist numbers in the *IRS 1993 Annual Report* therefore showed that the audit rate for individual returns fell below 1 percent for the first time *only* in 1993. The previous 1990 audit figure was restated as 1.04 percent audited, or 1,145,000 returns examined,[2] an increase, through some statistical manipulation, of 30 percent. How did the IRS accomplish such a herculean feat? By adding in almost 262,000 service-center correspondence contacts.[3] Imagine how this affects audit figures across the board, and think of how taxpayers, tax professionals, financial writers, and analysts will react. Sure does make the IRS look better than ever. Right?

Despite this blatant revisionism, one fact can't be hidden, or even disguised: The IRS audit rate for individuals declined steadily from 1988 to 1994, dropping from 1.57 percent to 0.92 percent, increasing slightly to 1.08 percent in 1994. Similarly, the audit rate for all returns also declined from 1.26 percent to 0.85 percent in 1993 and increased to 0.93 percent in 1994.[4] This doesn't mean, however, that the IRS brought in less money through audits of individual tax returns. Between 1988 and 1994, the IRS fairly consistently recommended additional taxes and penalties of about $6 billion a year.[5]

Now look at what happened in 1995. With a concerted effort to increase the number of audits by 45 percent,[6] along with the addition of almost 1,000 auditors, the audit rate for all returns jumped to 1.36 percent, individual audit rates reached 1.67 percent, and the total dollars recommended in additional taxes and penalties rose on individual returns to $7.8 billion.[7]

"LIVE" AUDITS ARE AIMED AT CORPORATIONS

Currently the IRS is deploying its live resources to audit returns with the highest dollar potential. Although the IRS undoubtedly misses out in lots of areas, it does know where the money is, or could come from. Acting on this, the IRS is retraining its revenue agents to audit large corporations through a new initiative: the Coordinated Examination Program (CEP), which focuses on examining 1,500 of the largest corporate taxpayers. To further emphasize this effort, for the first time the *IRS 1993 Annual Report* breaks out CEP figures, restating statistical information as far back as 1988. From that year, the figures show that corporations having $250 million or more in assets have been hit the hardest, with audit rates consistently over 50 percent.

Corporations'	*Percent Audited*		
Balance Sheet Assets	1993	1994	1995
$1–5 million	9.35	7.11	6.05
$5–10 million	19.04	15.83	14.89
$10–50 million	23.31	22.49	19.79
$50–100 million	25.56	24.69	22.04
$100–250 million	31.15	30.77	27.92
$250 million and over	52.11	55.14	51.77

Source: *IRS 1993–94 Data Book* and *IRS 1995 Data Book*, advance draft, Table 11.

By comparison, **the highest audit rate ever for individual returns was 2.3 percent, in 1975.**[8] Beginning in 1991, the audit rate for corporations earning from $1 million to $5 million was 5.81. By 1992, that figure rose to 10.08, a jump of 73 percent in only one year. Although the data show a slight decrease, in the $1 million-to-$5 million category, over 6 percent of these corporations are audited. (Audit rates for partnerships and S and small C corporations and what they tell taxpayers are discussed later in this chapter.)

Overall, you can see the enormous difference in auditing rates between individual and corporate returns. Unfortunately, one cannot conclude that the IRS has eased up on the average taxpayer. For individual returns, though, audit risk is a function not only of income levels but of the *type* of return filed.

Individuals' Income as Shown on 1040	Percent Audited			
	1992	1993	1994	1995
TPI under $25,000	0.78	0.74	1.04	1.96
$25,000–$50,000	0.70	0.58	0.53	.90
$50,000–$100,000	1.10	0.88	0.72	1.05
$100,000 and over	5.28	4.03	2.94	2.79

Income of Taxpayers Filing Schedule C	Percent Audited			
	1992	1993	1994	1995
Under $25,000	1.89	2.24	4.39	5.85
$25,000–$100,000	2.28	2.41	3.01	3.08
Over $100,000	4.17	3.91	3.57	3.47

Source: *IRS 1993–94 Data Book* and *IRS 1995 Data Book*, advance draft, Table 11.

With the overall audit rate for individual returns for 1995 at 1.67 percent, there was an unusually high audit effort spent on C filers. That effort was increased to all C filers, especially for those earning under $25,000, which nearly doubled between 1993 and 1994, and rose again to 5.85 percent in 1995, an additional increase of 33 percent in one year. As discussed in chapter 7, the IRS clearly has C filers as a target.

There are ways, however, to minimize your audit risk, no matter what schedule you file, how much you earn, or even if you are on the IRS underground-economy hit list. Part of the answer comes from taking the proper preventive steps.

HOW TO PREVENT AUDIT PROBLEMS BEFORE THEY OCCUR

Henceforth and forevermore, the first contact between your 1040 and the IRS is a computer. You can't reason with computers, so long before you get ready to fill out your 1040 or business tax return, there are certain steps to take so that your return is "prepped" to escape selection by the IRS's first technology go-around. Preventive medicine up front, such as "covering your books" (CYB), can help you avoid an audit. A rundown follows of the most effective measures for avoiding an audit and reducing its scope if you are selected.

1. Make sure that any third-party income and reports agree with your records. Verify that

- W-2's from all employers match your declared salary.
- Interest and dividend reports from your banks and securities firms match the actual interest and dividends you have received and entered on your return.
- Mortgage interest statements from your bank or lender match your mortgage interest deduction.
- Income from 1099 forms matches the appropriate income items on your return.
- If you discover an error on any of these forms, you should contact the issuer and request a corrected version immediately. If possible, try to get the information corrected before the IRS receives the incorrect version.

2. Make sure you have selected the correct forms and schedules to fill out. Ask yourself: Do the forms apply? Am I stretching the situation? Are there other credits that I am entitled to whose forms I haven't included but need to?

3. Keep track of bank deposits so that all items will be easy to trace. Write the source of the check directly on each deposit slip, especially transfers between accounts, so that these are not inadvertently counted as income. The first thing tax auditors request are your checking, savings, and investment accounts. They then proceed to do a total cash receipts analysis, comparing the total to the gross income shown on your tax return. By marking every deposit slip you know where to look for further documentation to support your notation and the auditor will have the trail in front of him or her for the source of unusual nontaxable receipts such as insurance recoveries, loans, gifts, and inheritances. It's not that much work.

Deposits into personal checking or savings accounts usually consist of one or two items, and most small- to medium-size businesses deposit a manageable number of checks on a daily basis. You would be amazed at how forgetful people can be regarding large receipts after two or three years have passed. You also need to keep copies of incoming checks that are unusual or very large.

4. Always keep your checking and savings accounts free of irregularities. Be sure you can explain large bank deposits and increases (especially sudden ones) in your net worth. At a minimum, the auditor will ask for verification of information on your return that is derived

from an institutional account, including *every* item of interest income, dividend income, and capital gains and losses.

I recently heard about an audit covering a three-year period where the taxpayer, an attorney, had great difficulty recalling the source of two large checks: A $14,000 inheritance received from the estate of an aunt, and $28,000 from the sale of her mother's condo subsequently managed by her. Because this information was not available right away, the revenue agent scheduled another audit day so that these items and a few others could be resolved. During that extra day, the auditor uncovered travel deductions totaling more than $10,000 that could not be supported and a $3,000 payment for college tuition included in charitable deductions. The taxpayer was charged an additional $5,000 in taxes, which could have been avoided if her records had been in better shape.

Warning: If you have unreported income of more than 25 percent of your adjusted gross income, the auditor may turn your case over to CID. **If you suspect this may occur, do not provide any leads to the auditor regarding the sources of unexplained deposits.** As mentioned in the discussion of CID, in a routine civil case the burden is on you to prove that certain deposits are nontaxable. In a criminal case, the burden of proof switches to the IRS. You don't have to provide leads that make their job easier.

5. Keep your business and personal bank accounts separate. Many taxpayers, especially those with sideline businesses, do not open a separate business checking account. This is a mistake. One's business account should be the depository for all business receipts and disbursements. Although there is no prohibition against paying for items that are strictly personal, they should be charged to your loan or drawing account as personal items. If you use your business account to pay for personal items on a consistent basis, an auditor will suspect that other personal items have been inadvertently, or purposely, charged to business categories. This could lead to an expanded audit, which can easily be avoided. Although it may take some discipline, the reward for keeping your business account strictly business will be to dramatically eliminate hassles in case of an audit.

6. If you know that you're going to take a business deduction, pay for it by check. Although taxpayers can pay for these things in cash, why arouse the suspicions of an auditor who is going to ask you to prove the source of all that cash? Also, it is wiser to pay for routine personal items such as bills for electricity, telephone, rent, and clothing with a check or credit cards. If these payments do not appear, the auditor assumes you used cash to pay for them and you've opened yourself up to an expanded audit.

HOW LONG SHOULD TAXPAYERS KEEP RECORDS?

Generally the IRS has only three years from the date you filed to come after you for extra tax. These are the exceptions:

- If your return omits more than 25 percent of your income, the IRS has six years to audit you.
- If you file a false and fraudulent return with intent to evade tax, there is no time limit on your being audited.

However, from a practical viewpoint, this is how long I recommend that you hold on to your records:

Business Records
Four years
  Sales invoices
  Purchases and expense bills
  Routine office correspondence
Six years
  Bank statements and canceled checks
  Accounting journals and books
Ten years
  Payroll tax returns
  Business income tax returns
Personal Records
Four years
  Receipts, bills, and canceled checks that support all deductions on Form 1040
  Records that support receipts of income, e.g., 1099's and K-1's
  Brokerage records showing purchases or sales of investments
Until four years after an asset is sold
  Records relating to home ownership (buying and selling), including home-office depreciation and deductions, receipts for improvements, repairs, appliances, and landscaping
Six years
  Bank statements and canceled checks
Forever
  Personal income tax returns and W-2 forms

HOW TO AVOID AN AUDIT COMPLETELY

The majority of taxpayers believe that the way to reduce taxable income safely is to exaggerate deductions. Wrong! Increased deductions can act as triggers that raise a taxpayer's risk for an audit.

The most important and essential step you can take to make yourself audit-proof, and the central theme of this chapter, is to remove as much information as possible from your 1040 to another place where the chances of audit are greatly diminished.

Wage earners receive their earnings primarily from W-2 income. If, in addition, they report only interest and dividend income *and follow the recommendations throughout this book*, they will successfully place themselves in a low-audit-risk category because by definition they are not on any of the IRS hit lists.

However, people who are self-employed are generally open to greater audit risk. If this group is to become audit-proof, taxpayers must choose a business entity that allows them other reporting options than, for example, a Schedule C, used by a sole proprietorship. **The most common choices of business entities available are an S corporation, a partnership, a C corporation and, gaining popularity, a limited liablity company.**

Before we discuss the best form of business entity to choose, however, I would like you to review the charts at the end of the chapter. They compare tax and legal ramifications for four of the most common types of business organizations: sole proprietorship, partnership, S corporation, and C corporation. Pick out several items that are most relevant to your own operations. This should give you a good head start in deciding which business form will offer you the most favorable tax position. Then read the discussion on S corporations and partnerships and see why both of these are the most preferred way of doing business for small to medium businesses; larger businesses that have many owners and greater potential liability typically become C corporations.

SMALL BUSINESS CORPORATIONS (S CORPORATIONS)

An S corporation is a form of organization that offers its owner the advantages of a corporation along with the favorable tax treatment of the sole proprietorship or partnership.

S corporations were first introduced in 1958. The original intention was to give mom-and-pop operations the ability to gain the advantages of incorporation (limited liability, perpetual life) and at the same time enable them to avoid the double taxation that goes with being a corporation.

Two changes in our tax law prompted the growth of S corporations, making them extremely attractive as business entities. Initially a business choosing S status could not derive more than 20 percent of its gross receipts from passive investment income such as rents, royalties, dividends, interest, annuities, and capital gains from securities or stocks. This requirement was eliminated in 1982 (subject to certain limitations). So for the first time, owners of real estate could elect S status.

Then the TRA '86 repealed the long-standing doctrine that C corporations would have only *one* tax to pay by its shareholders when it distributes property in a complete liquidation of the corporation. The new law imposed a *double tax* on a liquidating sale and distribution of assets (one tax upon the corporation and a second on its shareholders) for C corporations but *not for S corporations*. From that time, C corporations flocked to S status as a way to ensure that *only one tax* would be imposed on their shareholders.

Since 1986 it has been demonstrated to me again and again that from a tax perspective the S corporation is the best kind of business type **because it offers the many advantages of a corporation with the favorable tax treatment afforded the sole proprietorship or partnership.**

Avoiding an Audit by Setting Up an S Corporation
You are a prime candidate to be an S corporation if you

- Do not have to infuse large sums of capital into your business.
- Are a service business with modest requirements for investment in equipment.
- Invest in real estate or other rapidly appreciating assets.
- Expect to incur losses in the first year or two of operations.

Information No One Dares Tell Taxpayers About What They Can Gain by Operating an S Corporation
- The annual net income or loss of an S corporation passes through to each shareholder's 1040 on one line, which appears on Schedule E. Accordingly, no income or expense detail shows up on the 1040. You immediately avoid all the targets, triggers, and special programs that the IRS currently has in place to bring attention to taxpayers who file Schedule C's.
- There is no disclosure of home-office expenses. Although S corpo-

rations are subject to the rules regarding home-office expenses, **there is no special IRS form designed for an S corporation to list home-office expenses.** By contrast, a sole proprietor who operates out of a home office and files a 1040 must file Form 8829 along with Schedule C. You already know that Form 8829 is an audit trigger. S corporations report expenses incurred in home-office operations on the 1120S (U.S. Income Tax Return for an S Corporation). The appropriate allocations are combined with all other expenses and placed on their appropriate lines.

• The IRS does a good job of matching personal income, but corporate income reporting requirements are entirely different. **If a payment for goods purchased or services performed is made to a corporation, the entity making the payment is not legally required to file a 1099-MISC form reporting the payment.** Accordingly, when the IRS uses 1099's to audit independent contractors, you can avoid all this as an S corporation.

• Chances are that expenses that are typical audit triggers (travel, entertainment, automobile) will receive less attention on an S corporation simply because the audit rate for S corporations is considerably lower than for individuals. (See chart, "Examination Coverage of Returns Filed," page 207.)

• There has never been a better time to own a small corporation because the IRS audit function is paying the least attention to small corporations and partnerships. Currently, the potential for the IRS to extract tax dollars through the audit process is immeasurably greater with large corporations because of the Coordinated Examination Program (CEP), which focuses on auditing the largest corporate taxpayers in the country. But look what's happening to the rest of the business population (see same chart). **The lowest percentages of business returns audited are for partnerships, S corporations, and small C corporations.** For calendar year 1994, the percentage of S corporations being audited dropped slightly to .92 percent; it was only 18,839 out of 2,036,700, and only 7,072 partnerships out of 1,539,100, or 0.5 percent.[9] Partnerships continued to have the lowest audit rate, followed by C corporations (with income under $250,000) and S corporations (see chart, page 207).

• By controlling the amount of salary you take out of an S corporation, you can substantially reduce FICA taxes. For example, an S corporation with one owner-employee has a net income before salary of $50,000. If the owner takes a $50,000 salary reportable on a W-2, the combined FICA taxes for the corporation and employee will be 15.3 percent, or $7,650. But if the owner takes a reasonable salary of $30,000, the FICA taxes will be only $4,590, a savings of $3,060 to the corporation. The remaining corporate net income of $20,000 ($50,000 minus $30,000) is passed through to the owner on a K-1 form. As a result, his personal income tax remains unchanged.

• Owners of an S corporation are immune to double tax on an audit. If a C corporation is undergoing an audit, and travel and entertainment deductions are disallowed because they were found to be personal, or some officer's compensation is deemed by the auditor to be excessive, the IRS will assess a tax at both corporate *and* shareholder levels (i.e., the corporation will be charged one tax on the disallowed expense, and a second tax will be assessed upon the individual shareholder). In an S corporation, disallowed business expenses pass through to the 1040 and become taxable income to the recipients. But in this case, the IRS can levy only *one* tax—at the shareholder level. **It is my belief that this inability to double-tax an S corporation is a major reason why the audit rate is so low on S corporations.**

• There are some real advantages for S corporations that expect to incur losses in the first few years of operation. A new business usually experiences hard times initially. If you expect to incur losses in the first three months of operation, the best time to apply for or elect S corporation status would be the last three months of the calendar year. (S corporations must use the December 31 calendar year-end. There are a few exceptions but they are rarely granted.) In this way, losses pass through to the shareholders in the current year and shelter income from other sources. This is a common scenario for a taxpayer who was an employee for the first nine months of the year, and then incorporates as an S corporation, using his losses to shelter W-2 earnings.

• It is easier for the owners of an S corporation to sell the business because, unlike a C corporation, there is no corporate-level tax when the assets are sold. This makes for a preferred sale, since most buyers are only interested in the assets, not a corporation's potential liabilities.

Requirements for an S Corporation
Before 1996, basic requirements for an S corporation were:

• To have only individuals, estates, and certain trusts as shareholders; no partnerships, corporations, or nonresident aliens.
• To have no more than 35 shareholders.
• To have one class of stock.
• To be a "domestic corporation" created or organized pursuant to federal and state laws.

- To not control any other corporation or be a subsidiary of another corporation.
- To wait five years before you can make a new S corporation application (election) if you were previously an S corporation.

Some of these changed when new tax legislation was signed in 1996 (see page 272).

How to Set Up an S Corporation

1. Incorporate. Several choices are available. If you choose to use an attorney, the fees range from $600 to $1,000 depending on the size and location of the law firm. A second alternative allows you to incorporate yourself. The department of state in your home state will provide you with the required forms and fee schedule. In some states you can pay an optional "expediting fee" (about $10), which will get the paperwork returned to you in a week or two instead of three weeks to a month. Overall costs for this type of incorporation are approximately $375. For those who want a quick and more commercial route (without paying attorney's fees), there are incorporation services. At a very modest price, they offer step-by-step instructions and provide everything you need to know about legal aspects of forming your own corporation in any state of your choosing.

2. Obtain a federal identification number by filing Form SS-4 (Application for Employer Identification Number) with the IRS. You will receive your number about three weeks after you apply. If the wait is impractical because you need the number to open a commercial bank account, you can use the IRS Tele-Tin (Telephone Tax Indentification) system. To do this, first complete the SS-4, then call your local IRS service center and ask for the fax number for the Tele-Tin system. Fax the SS-4 and within 24 hours you will receive a phone call from the IRS and be given your new federal identification number.

3. File Form 2553 (Election by a Small Business Corporation) with the IRS. Generally you must apply for an S corporation, the S election, within two months and 15 days after commencing operations. For existing C corporations, the election must be filed no later than two months and fifteen days after the elected year has begun. For example, if you commence operations in 1997, the election deadline is March 15, 1997.

Once your papers are in order you should send Form 2553 to your IRS service center by certified mail, return receipt requested. This is the only proof of mailing acceptable by the IRS. It is important to file as early as possible to avoid missing the deadline and to avoid other hassles and delays.

YOUR TAX-SAVING STRATEGY.

These days, state and local taxes take a significant chunk of tax dollars. Therefore, for tax planning purposes, all taxpayers, even S corporations, must be concerned about taxation at the state and local levels.

Currently, at least 40 states recognize some form of S corporation status. New York State imposes an annual fee of $325 for S corporations, while Florida doesn't impose any. California and Illinois impose a 1.5 percent corporate tax rate on an S corporation's taxable income, but these rates are considerably less than the regular rates for non–S corporations. In participating states all the advantages that accrue to S corporations at the federal level are also recognized on the state and local levels.

New York City does not recognize S corporation status. Accordingly, the tax-planning opportunities for S corporations are limited within this jurisdiction. The optimum planning for states and localities that impose regular corporate rates is to reduce corporate net income of the S corporation to zero by increasing the salaries to the owners-employees whenever it is reasonable and proper. This results in minimal net corporate income subject to the regular corporate tax rates, and the increased salary is simply subject to individual income tax. **If at all possible, try to locate the business in an area where the S election is available at the state and local levels of taxation so that you can receive maximum benefits.**

Loopholes in the Timing of an S Election

Remember those myriad loopholes that arise out of our complex tax laws? Well, there are several that work to benefit owners of S corporations.

Let's say that you inadvertently let the 2½ month-period pass, did not file the S election, and just made up your mind to actively operate as an S corporation. For the initial year of the corporation's existence ONLY, the 2½-month period does not start until the earliest of the following:

1. Date the corporation first had shareholders.
2. Date the corporation first had assets.
3. Date the corporation began doing business.

Therefore, to still elect S status, place a date that accurately represents the actual "starting" date of the corporation in Item H on Form 2553.

Let's say you recently incorporated and started doing business as a C corporation and it was more than 2½ months ago. You are precluded from taking advantage of the first loophole. But what you can do is close off your C corporation year immediately and elect S status for the remainder of the year.

For example, the business was incorporated and started on January 5, 1997, and now, on May 10, 1997, you want S status. File the S election immediately and simply indicate in your S election, Form 2553, Item C, that the election is to be effective for the tax year beginning March 1, 1997. You will be able to operate as an S corporation beginning March 1, 1997, because you are filing within the first 2½ months of the new, short year, which began March 1, 1997. The only disadvantage to this ploy is that you must file a C corporation tax return for the short period from January 5, 1997, to February 28, 1997.

YOUR TAX-SAVING STRATEGY.
As a new corporation, try to maximize the amount of C corporation short-year expenses as start-up expenses that can be amortized later on in S corporation years. Losses incurred while you are a C corporation will remain frozen as long as you are an S corporation.

Loopholes in the Early Stages of an S Corporation

Depreciation of Assets
New corporations usually purchase furniture and equipment at the outset. Under Section 179 of the *Internal Revenue Code* (see chapter 7, page 152), you can elect to depreciate up to $17,500 of business furniture and equipment in the year of purchase through 1996 and $18,000 beginning in 1997. Therefore, even if your initial S corporation year is but a few weeks in the current year, you can deduct the full $17,500 if the assets are purchased within that period.

YOUR TAX-SAVING STRATEGY.
Section 179 deductions cannot reduce your taxable income below zero. If the S corporation's net income is approaching zero, utilize only the amount that you need to reach zero income. Or you can delay your asset purchases until the following year, when presumably there will be greater income to be offset with this deduction.

Loopholes in Reporting Income or Losses for an S Corporation

Shifting Losses

For S corporations, there is a unique way of shifting losses to a desired tax year. This brings the element of *basis* into play. Basis is a dollar amount that represents the cost of a taxpayer's investment in an entity. It can be adjusted upward or downward. S corporation losses can only be used by shareholders who have sufficient basis in the stock. If you need the losses in 1995, lend the corporation sufficient money to cover your share of the losses. If 1997 is the year you can make better use of the losses, make no additional loans until 1997. If need be, distribute loans to yourself before the end of 1996 so that your basis is minimized.

If you personally guarantee loans made to an S corporation, your basis is not increased. Therefore, borrow the money personally, and lend the proceeds to the S corporation. This will enable you to take greater losses if they become available. The key point is, S corporations provide many opportunities for the owner to handle losses.

S Corporations in the Future

For the past 10 years the IRS has been giving the public a consistent message about S corporations: "S elections and S status are cumbersome and fraught with dangers. If you are a small business person, you will be better off filing as a sole proprietor on Schedule C." **This is simply not true.** The IRS is pushing this line because it can more easily watch over the activities of small businesses using Schedule C's.

But look at what's happened: In early 1994, in separate legislation, RRA '93 enacted into law two provisions that affect S corporations. The cap on the Medicare surtax on wages (1.45 percent each on employer and employees) has been removed. Distributions of S corporation earnings are not subject to FICA or Medicare tax. So S corporations can continue to significantly reduce this tax.

In addition, RRA '93 increased the top personal tax rate to 39.6 percent, which is something S corporation owners should keep in mind, because unlike C corporations, earnings from S corporations must be included in your personal income, which could land you in a higher tax bracket. Couple this increase with the phaseout of personal exemptions and itemized deductions, and if your taxable income exceeds $263,750, you are facing an individual tax rate as high as 41 percent. Does this mean that S corporations will flock to revoke their S elections in order to take advantage of lower C corporate tax rates? I would recommend against this course of action for several reasons.

First, for taxpayers who own S corporations with modest earnings, taxable income up to $147,700 on a joint return (up to $121,300 if single) is still taxed at 31 percent or less.

Second, you may be subject to the built-in gains tax if you revoke your S election and later decide to reelect to become an S corporation. This is a corporate-level tax on appreciation of assets held by a former C corporation; it is imposed as these assets are disposed of during the first 10 years after becoming an S corporation.

Finally, why leave an S corporation now when new tax legislation passed late in 1996 makes S corporations more available and enticing than ever before and the advantages being granted to S corporations are being accelerated on a regular basis?

LIMITED LIABILITY COMPANIES AND PARTNERSHIPS

A new type of entity, called a Limited Liability Company (LLC), has emerged in the past few years. Because it is often set up in a partnership format, its name then changes to a Limited Liability Partnership (LLP). Wyoming was the first state to enact an LLC statute in 1977. As of early 1996, each state has an LLC statute.

An LLC combines two of the most important attributes that are important to business owners: pass-through taxation, where annual net income or losses pass through each shareholder's 1040 on one line, Schedule E (see pages 186, 188), and limited liability for business debts. Although these attributes are mentioned in this chapter in discussions of corporations and partnerships, for some types of businesses, setting up an LLC is more suitable. Here are some reasons why.

Whereas an S corporation must allocate income or losses in proportion to stock ownership, in an LLC agreement you can vary the sharing percentages of income and losses and not have to worry about being subject to undue scrutiny by the IRS.

Furthermore, in a partnership, investors ordinarily become limited partners so that they are liable only for the amount of their investments. Because of this, they cannot take part in the active running of the business, which is left to the general partners who *are* liable for all debts of the partnership. Under an LLP, *all* members can take an active part in the day-to-day operations of the partnership and not be subject to unlimited liability for the debts of the partnership.

The trickiest part of forming an LLC or LLP is to make sure that the IRS does not classify the entity as a regular corporation, which would stop you from being a pass-through entity. To begin with, you must follow the guidelines of the LLC statutes in your state. Next, the operating agreement must contain everything that any corporate agreement would contain plus other sections that are specifically designed for an LLC agreement.

To be recognized for tax purposes as a partnership, and to avoid being taxed as a corporation, an LLC or LLP must meet the IRS-imposed requirement of not having more (i.e., three or more) corporate characteristics than noncorporate characteristics. The four traits that the IRS considers as corporate characteristics are limited liability, continuity of life, centralization of management, and free transferability of interests.[10]

If an entity has only one or two of these corporate characteristics, it will be taxed as a partnership and be treated as a pass-through entity, which is desirable. It is important to work with an attorney who is knowledgeable in this area to set up the LLC operating agreement so that (1) it does not meet the corporate characteristics as defined by the IRS and (2) that it conforms with federal and state regulations.*

PARTNERSHIPS

A partnership is a good alternative to an S corporation.

This discussion focuses on only those general partnerships in which each partner is responsible for his or her share of partnership debts. (It does *not* include a limited partnership, which is subject to its own rules and regulations beyond the scope of this discussion. See also Limited Liability Companies, page 193.)

Advantages of a Partnership

• A partnership is easier to create than an S corporation. Two or more people just agree to be in business together. This union is made evident by a written agreement best prepared by an attorney.

• As with S corporations, a partnership has no double tax. Net income and other separately stated income and expense items, such as capital gains and contributions, are passed through to each partner via a K-1 form.

• If the partnership later decides to incorporate, the transfer will be tax-free as long as any property that is transferred to the corporation is exchanged for at least 80 percent of the corporate stock.

• It may be easier to obtain credit because one partner may provide

*These characteristics are defined in the IR Code Section 7701-2 (a)(1), and IRS Revenue Procedure 95-10.

expertise and additional net worth that could be used to guarantee partnership liabilities.

• Income or losses are allocated according to the partnership agreement, but the agreement can take into account the business efforts made by each partner. This means income can be allocated by a method that is not based on ownership percentages. But you cannot allocate income and loss merely to take advantage of the tax laws. Similarly, if you have a family partnership, you cannot allocate income to younger family members just to reduce taxes. The allocation must reflect the value of services rendered by each of the partners.

• As with S corporations, there is no special IRS form designed to list home-office expenses.

• As with S corporation shareholders, a partner's tax losses cannot exceed his or her basis (see definition on page 192).

A partner's basis

1. Increases when he pays money or contributes property to the partnership.
2. Increases by his share of income earned by the partnership.
3. Can increase or decrease as his proportionate share of partnership liabilities changes.
4. Decreases if the partnership reports losses, or if the partnership distributes money or property to the partners.

In an S corporation, basis is a more restrictive concept because it does not change as a function of the stockholder's share of general corporate liabilities.

Disadvantages of Partnerships

• A partner is personally liable for the debts of the partnership above and beyond his investment. This is characterized as unlimited liability, and it is the main reason why corporations are the preferred way of doing business. With a corporation, generally you can only lose the money and property that you contributed to the corporation.

• Although a partnership is easy to form, it is also easily dissolved, such as when a general partner who owns more than 50 percent of the entity withdraws. Thus, there is no "continuity of life." With a corporation, a withdrawing shareholder simply sells his stock to a new shareholder and the corporation continues to operate.

• Similarly, it is difficult to withdraw from a partnership if the remaining partners refuse to purchase the withdrawing partner's interest. A buy-sell agreement drawn up when the partnership is formed is highly recommended to avoid this situation. The agreement should contain a formula to measure the amount that a withdrawing partner receives, or the amount to be paid to a partner or his or her beneficiary in case of death or permanent disability.

BUSINESS VENTURES AND THE HOBBY LOSS RULE

If you're in an existing business or considering starting up a new business, besides choosing which legal entity will work best from a tax perspective, you'll also need to be aware of Section 183 of the *Internal Revenue Code*, "Activities Not Engaged In for Profit," or the Hobby Loss Rule, as it is commonly called. Ignorance or mismanagement of the Hobby Loss Rule can easily increase the chances of an IRS audit.

In order not to be subject to the Hobby Loss Rule, taxpayers need to show a profit in any three out of five consecutive tax years ending with the current tax year. This rule covers sole proprietors, partnerships, S corporations, and estates and trusts. If the IRS determines that your business activity is "not engaged in for profit," according to the Hobby Loss Rule your losses will be considered personal expenses and only expenses up to the amount of your hobby income will be deductible. Furthermore, these otherwise deductible hobby expenses will be transferred to Schedule A—Itemized Deductions (Other Miscellaneous Deductions), and be subject to a limit of 2 percent of your AGI. Mortgage interest and real estate tax are fully deductible as itemized deductions in any case. (See chapter 10, page 241, for additional information on the Hobby Loss Rule.)

What does this rule mean and how does it affect the taxpayer? Many young businesses do, after all, legitimately experience operating losses in three out of five years. But the IRS created the Hobby Loss Rule to prevent taxpayers from using personal business ventures such as horse racing, farming, or stamp and coin collecting to throw off losses used to offset other income (salaries, interest).

How to Strengthen Your Position Regarding the Hobby Loss Rule

If you are a taxpayer who could fall under the Hobby Loss Rule, you have to be ready to prove that you had an intention of earning a profit. Theoretically you could operate a business for many years and never actually earn a profit, but still be entitled to a deduction for the losses.

To strengthen your position in this direction, become familiar with these nine factors used by the IRS to determine whether or not a profit objective exists:

1. Conduct the activity in a businesslike manner. This includes keeping accurate books and records, printing business stationery and cards, keeping a separate bank account for the business, obtaining a federal identification number.

2. Obtain sufficient knowledge to operate a successful business. This is an indication that you are trying to increase the profitability of the business. Read trade journals and books on the subject, attend professional seminars and the like to gain expertise, and be able to show proof of these activities within reason.

3. Spend a sufficient amount of time in the activity so that it doesn't look as though you're dabbling (as with a hobby). If you have another full-time occupation that produces income, and most of your time is spent there, your new venture would appear to be secondary. To counteract this, you could hire competent qualified people to run the new business for you.

4. If you expect the product that you're working on to appreciate in value, this is proof that you have a profit motive. For example, if you purchase antique cars and can show that their value has risen, that in itself is proof of the profit motive.

5. Your success or lack of it in prior business ventures is a consideration. If you have previously turned an unprofitable business into a profitable one, you have proved that your mode of operation involves having a profit motive in mind even though you are currently losing money.

6. The IRS will examine your income track record in the startup business. If you had a string of successively profitable years more than five years ago, that is an indication that you have the ability and intention to turn your loss into a profit. Similarly, you may be able to show that your current losses are due to events beyond your control such as depressed market conditions or natural disasters.

7. The IRS also looks at the existence of occasional profits, if any. Profits are compared to losses over the duration of the operation; how both relate to the value of assets invested in the business is examined.

8. The wealthier you are the more likely that the activity will look like a hobby in the eyes of the IRS. If you don't have substantial income from other sources, the IRS will tend to look more favorably on your activity.

9. Does the business have a significant element of personal pleasure

or recreation? This factor is probably the one that has caused the term *hobby loss* to come into being.

Sometimes, no matter what you do, the IRS will insist that your business is a hobby. For all of us who have seen pink Cadillacs cruising down the road, this next case reminds taxpayers that part-time salespeople seeking small returns and large deductions may soon be seeing red.

Mrs. Linde began selling cosmetics in 1980 and received the use of a luxury car. For 1986 and 1987, Mrs. Linde reported her activity on Schedule C, indicating losses in excess of $25,000 per year. These losses offset the substantial income earned by her husband on their joint returns.

Using the nine-factor test, the tax court decided that the most important issue determining whether the business was a hobby or not was the manner in which the business was run. First, Mrs. Linde did very little to separate her personal and business activities. Although she presented mounds of records to prove the claimed expenses, some of the records proved that some of the deductions were taken for purely personal expenditures.

Mrs. Linde also produced summary sheets prepared by herself that the court called self-serving; it gave them no real weight. The actual books and records of her business were not organized well. After examining these, the court said it could not figure out how she computed the losses she claimed.

Lack of a profit motive was further evidenced by Mrs. Linde's failure to seek advice on how to run the business from people outside the cosmetics organization. This was particularly important because she had no prior experience in the business. The only evidence she cited to corroborate her time spent in the activity was her own testimony, which the court discounted.

Finally, the court observed that much of the time Mrs. Linde did spend in the activity involved taking people to restaurants and bars, which signified a substantial element of personal pleasure.

In summary, the court decided that Mrs. Linde's business was not a "for-profit" activity under Section 183, the Hobby Loss Rule. The result was that the taxpayer could only deduct expenses to the extent of the income from the hobby; expenses cannot reduce net operating income below zero (except for mortgage interest and real estate tax, which are deductible on Schedule A, Form 1040).

BUSINESSES THAT INCLUDE MERCHANDISE INVENTORY

If you file a business return and if you sell a product, as opposed to offering a service, one of the things the IRS computer (or audit reviewer) will focus on is the "Cost of Goods Sold" section on the statement-of-income section found on all business income tax returns. Generally the IRS will devote greater attention to a return showing a smaller gross profit than industry norms. The IRS gathers this information and reaches its conclusions by trying to identify the cost of the product being sold, or how much gross profit (sales less cost of goods sold) a business earned in a year.

There are a number of avenues the IRS can take to scrutinize this and come up with how much money it thinks a business has made on the basis of the cost of goods sold. If the gross profit percentage that you report on the business return is found to deviate greatly from what other taxpayers report in the same industry, there are some acceptable explanations.

With acceptable proof, you may show that you experienced

- More than normal returns of merchandise, which you were forced to sell at cost price or lower.
- Normal increases in the cost of acquiring or manufacturing your products, but you were unable to pass them on to your customers in the form of price increases.

How to Prepare a Closing Inventory Schedule to Minimize Audit Risk

When a tax return showing a low gross profit is being examined, the IRS auditor will most likely ask for a detailed closing inventory schedule. Taking a physical inventory is a time-consuming task, especially if you are trying to service customers or sell products during the inventory process. On the basis of your past experience, you may be able to estimate some of the inventory quantities. In so doing, you must be aware of certain things:

- The method most widely used to value inventory is the "lower of cost or market." Use of this method allows you to assign below-normal values to inventory items that are collecting dust—or are obsolete, damaged, unusable, or whose prices have dropped since you purchased them.
- A majority of the items included in an inventory should be those purchased a short time before the closing date, generally not more than one year prior to the closing date. An exception would be hard goods, e.g., hardware, that can have a normal shelf life in excess of one year.
- The items included in the ending inventory should be traceable to subsequent period sales. For example, if December 31, 1995, is the closing inventory date, then a large percentage of items should have been sold in the first half of 1996.

Therefore, it is important that the closing inventory schedule be as current as possible and be based on gross profit percentages that are normal to your industry.

SECURING A TAX-ADVANTAGED LIFE

The fact is that if you are self-employed and you incorporate you will have a tax-advantaged life that will be sheltered within a corporate environment. A technical advice memorandum, issued by the IRS in 1991, discusses an interesting case of incorporating a business.

A husband and wife operated a farm since 1949. On January 1, 1988, the husband, wife, and their son created a corporation, selling their house, automobile, crops, and farming equipment to the corporation in exchange for stock. They then became employees of the corporation. Given this situation, the family declared that providing food and shelter was not taxable income because it was required by the job.

The primary tax question that arose, therefore, was "Can the corporation deduct these as a legitimate business expense?" Normally a farmer cannot take the cost of his home and food as an expense against farm income.

The IRS agent examining the case declared this was an example of avoiding income tax. However, in a technical advice memorandum involving a lengthy analysis, the IRS ruled that *the taxpayers would have been entitled to the same deduction if a partnership and not a corporation had been formed.* It was also decided that the taxpayers were not evading or avoiding federal income tax because they were only obtaining benefits otherwise permitted under specified statutes as outlined in the *Internal Revenue Code.*

Legally, technical advice memoranda are not supposed to set any kind of precedent; as with private letter rulings, they apply only to the taxpayer who receives them, as discussed in chapter 5, page 106. But this case emphasizes the overriding principle that certain tax advantages can be gained by one's choice of a business format. The conclusions I offer taxpayers are these:

- If you want an environment in which most of your income is not reported to the IRS on a 1099 form, incorporate now.
- If you are self-employed, incorporate or form a partnership now.
- If you want to reduce IRS scrutiny of your business deductions, incorporate or form a partnership now.
- If you want to place your business income tax return in a category that is least susceptible to an IRS audit, incorporate or form a partnership now.

**A Surefire Checklist for *All* Taxpayers Who
Don't Want to Be Audited**

- Know the proper time to file. You have learned that filing late is
  not the way to avoid an audit. IRS computers aren't programmed
  to review only those returns received on or before April 15. So who
  is to say that late returns, those filed after April 15, won't be audited, or will be audited less than returns mailed earlier? All returns, late or not, go through a secondary audit potential selection
  process at the district level. All tax professionals have clients who
  filed late but were audited anyway. The days of thinking you're immune because you file late are over.
- Be thorough. Don't leave out any information that applies to you.
  Sign where you are supposed to.
- Be neat.
- Be sure your mathematics are correct.
- Be consistently accurate. Are the proper entries on the proper
  lines? Have you provided your complete address and Social Secu-
  rity number? Did you leave any lines blank that should be filled in?
- Balance out your total deductions with your income. Excessive
  and elaborate business expenses that add up to a substantial per-
  centage your income are an audit flag.
- Adjust your stated exemptions as shown on Form W-4, filed with
  your employer, so that you don't end up receiving large refunds.
  Remember, they only amount to the free loan of *your* money to the
  IRS (discussed on pages 32–37 and 209).

If you correctly follow my advice in this chapter, you will significantly
decrease your chances of being audited. Now get ready to tie it all together by learning 10 ground rules that should never be broken if you
want to win with the IRS.

Tax Considerations

	Sole Proprietorship	Partnership	S Corporation	C Corporation
Net operating income	Taxed directly to owner on 1040.	Passed through to partners' 1040 via Form K-1 whether or not distributed.	Passed through to shareholders' 1040 via Form K-1 whether or not distributed.	Double tax: once on C corporation, again when paid to shareholder as dividends.
Net operating losses	Reduces Adjusted Gross Income. Can be carried back 3 years and then forward 5 years.	Passed through to partners' 1040 via Form K-1. Losses cannot exceed partners' basis in the partnership. Subject to at-risk rules and passive-loss limitations. Losses can be carried back or forward.	Passed through to shareholders' 1040 via Form K-1. Losses cannot exceed shareholders' basis in the corporation. Subject to at-risk rules and passive loss limitations. Losses can be carried back or forward.	Deductible only against corporate net operating income. Losses can be carried back 3 years and forward 15 years.
Capital gains	Taxed directly to owner on 1040.	Passed through to partners' 1040 via Form K-1.	Passed through to shareholders' 1040 via Form K-1. Some gains are taxable under certain conditions for older S corporations.	Gains taxed at regular corporate rates.
Capital losses	Offset against capital gains + $3,000 per year. May be carried forward indefinitely.	Passed through to partners' 1040 via Form K-1.	Passed through to shareholders' 1040 via Form K-1.	Deductible only against corporate capital gains. Can be carried back 3 years or forward 15 years.
Contributions to charities	Itemized deduction on 1040.	Passed through to partners' 1040 via Form K-1.	Passed through to shareholders' 1040 via Form K-1.	Limited to 10% of corporate taxable income, as adjusted by special items. Unused can be carried forward for 5 years.
Dividends received	Taxed directly to owner on 1040.	Passed through to partners' 1040 via Form K-1.	Passed through to shareholders' 1040 via Form K-1.	Can deduct from income 70% of dividends received from domestic corporations.

Tax Considerations *(Continued)*

	Sole Proprietorship	Partnership	S Corporation	C Corporation
Tax rates	Based on taxable income: 15%–36% on first $250,000, 39.6% on amount over $263,750.	Each partner pays individual tax rate.	Each shareholder pays individual tax rate.	Based on taxable income: 15% of first $50,000 25% of next $25,000 34% of next $25,000 See instructions for amounts over $100,000.
Fringe benefits (e.g., health insurance and group term life insurance)	Partially deductible on 1040, subject to limitations.	All partners are not eligible to receive tax-free benefits.	Cannot receive tax-free benefits if shareholder owns more than 2%.	No restrictions.
Retirement plans	Keogh or SEP is available. Loans are prohibited.	Keogh or SEP is available. Loans are prohibited.	Profit-sharing or defined contribution plan is available. Loans to shareholders are prohibited.	Profit-sharing or defined contribution plan is available. Loans permitted up to ½ your vested benefits or $50,000, whichever is less.
Sale of ownership interest	Capital gain.	May be part ordinary income and part capital gain. Special election to step up basis of partnership's assets for purchaser.	Capital gain.	Capital gain.
Liquidation	N/A.	N/A.	Capital gain or loss to shareholder. Avoids double taxation. Exceptions if previously a C corporation.	Double taxation—first at corporate level, then at shareholder level.
Alternative Minimum Tax (AMT)	Subject to 26% or 28% Alternative Minimum Tax.	Partnership not subject. Preference items and adjustments passed through to partners' 1040 via Form K-1.	S corporation not subject. Preference items and adjustments passed through to shareholders via Form K-1.	Applies at corporate level—at Alternative Minimum Tax rate of 20%.

Tax Considerations (Continued)

	Sole Proprietorship	Partnership	S Corporation	C Corporation
Payroll taxes	15.3% self-employment tax on first $62,700 of taxable income, 2.9% above that. ½ of tax is deductible.	Partnership income not subject. Passed through to partners' 1040 via Form K-1, subject to self-employment tax.	Undistributed income is not subject. However, some part of distributions may be subject to payroll taxes if salary is deemed insufficient by IRS.	Corporation and its employees each pay 7.65% of FICA wages up to $62,700; 1.45% above that.
Items affecting basis	Not an issue.	(A) Income and gains increase partners' basis in partnership; losses decrease basis. (B) Capital put into partnership increases basis; distributions decrease basis. (C) General partners' share of partnership liabilities increases basis.	(A) Income and gains increase shareholders' stock basis. (B) Capital put into S corporations increases basis; distributions decrease basis. (C) Loans put into S corporation by shareholder increase stock basis. Other corporate liabilities have no effect on shareholder basis.	Not an issue.
Cash vs. accrual method for preparing taxes	Cash or accrual method.	Cash or accrual method. Must use accrual method if inventory is a factor.	Cash or accrual—no limits on annual receipts. Must use accrual method if inventory is a factor.	Cannot use cash method if annual receipts are $5 million or more, or if inventory is a factor.
Splitting of income	Not an issue.	May be allocated by partners agreement.	Allocated in proportion to number of shares owned.	Not an issue.
Tax year	Calendar year.	Must use same year as principal partners, which usually is calendar year.	New corporations must use calendar year (some limited exceptions).	Calendar or fiscal year.

Tax Considerations *(Continued)*

	Sole Proprietorship	Partnership	S Corporation	C Corporation
Accumulated earnings tax	Not subject.	Not subject.	Not subject unless S corporation had previously been a C corporation.	Unreasonable earnings above $250,000 ($150,000 for personal-service corporations) are hit with a special 39.6% tax.
Excessive compensation	Not subject.	Not subject.	Not subject.	If deemed excessive. Excess is deemed to be a nondeductible dividend.
Disallowed personal expenses on audit	Individual tax rate.	Each partner pays his individual tax rate.	Each shareholder pays his individual tax rate.	Double taxation—first at corporate level, then at shareholder level.
Personal holding company tax*	Not subject.	Not subject.	Not subject.	Subject to a special 39.6% tax under certain conditions.

All Other Considerations

	Sole Proprietorship	Partnership	S Corporation	C Corporation
Ease and cost of formation	No special actions.	No special actions. Usual arrangement is to prepare written partnership agreement.	Initial costs of $600 to $1000; $400 to $600 if you do yourself.	Same as S corporation.
Period of existence	Discretion of owner.	Termination if partners agree, or on partner's death or retirement.	Continues until dissolution. Not affected by sale of shares, unless sale is to ineligible shareholder.	Same as S corporation with no restriction on eligibility of shareholders.

*A corporation that is more than 50% owned by five or fewer individuals and 60% or more of whose ordinary gross income is derived from dividends, interest, royalties, and annuities.

All Other Considerations (Continued)

	Sole Proprietorship	Partnership	S Corporation	C Corporation
Continuing costs	Minimal.	Annual federal and state partnership tax forms. Approximately 50% increase in tax preparation fees over sole proprietor.	Annual federal and state S corporation tax forms subject to minimal taxes in some states. Approximately 50% increase in tax preparation fees over sole proprietorship.	Annual federal and state corporation tax forms plus payment of corporate-level income taxes. More tax planning is required. 50–100% increase in tax preparation fees over sole proprietorship.
Owners' exposure to business debts	Liable for all debts of business.	General partners are liable for all debts of business.	Shareholders liable only for capital contributions and debts that are personally guaranteed.	Same as S corporation.
Effect on organization upon withdrawal of taxpayer	None.	Dissolution of partnership.	After stock is disposed of, corporation continues.	Same as S corporation.
Transfer of ownership interest	N/a.	Addition of new partner requires consent of other partners.	Easy to do—just transfer stock shares to new owner.	Same as S corporation.
Limitations on ownership	N/a.	No limit on number of partners.	Limited to 35 eligible shareholders.	No limit on number and eligibility of shareholders.

Examination Coverage of Returns Filed*

	Calendar Year 1994			Calendar Year 1993			Calendar Year 1992		
	Returns Filed	Returns Examined	Percent Examined	Returns Filed	Returns Examined	Percent Examined	Returns Filed	Returns Examined	Percent Examined
Partnerships	1,539,100	7,072	.46	1,545,200	8,077	0.52	1,608,700	9,850	0.61
S corporations	2,036,700	18,839	.92	1,905,800	19,385	1.02	1,805,300	18,466	1.02
C corporations (income under $250,000)	1,557,900	12,128	.78	1,555,700	13,027	0.84	1,670,700	22,257	1.33
Schedule C (all filers)	7,229,100	298,609	4.13	6,949,000	251,496	3.62	6,761,400	182,955	2.71
Schedule C (gross receipts $100,000 and over)	1,698,600	58,912	3.47	1,619,500	57,766	3.57	1,578,700	61,768	3.91
Individuals (TPI** $100,000 and over)	4,082,000	113,982	2.79	3,745,700	110,004	2.94	3,389,600	136,908	4.03
All individuals	114,683,400	1,919,437	1.67	113,754,400	1,225,707	1.08	114,718,900	1,058,966	0.92

*Chart reflects most recent figures available, tabulated by the IRS as of September 30, 1995.

**Total Positive Income is the sum of all positive income that appears on a return, excluding losses.

9

The Thirteen Biggest Misconceptions Taxpayers Have About Their Returns

1. *Misconception: "If I am in the 31 percent tax bracket, it means that my tax liability is 31 percent of my income."*

What You Need to Know
Taxpayers in the 31 percent tax bracket operate almost across the board under the mistaken belief that because they are in that tax bracket, 31 percent of their income is being taxed. This is absolutely not true. A taxpayer in that tax bracket is actually getting taxed *less* than 31 percent. Even though you're in a 31 percent tax bracket, you pay less than that percentage because you get the benefit of being taxed at lower rates on the amounts you earn in the tax brackets that precede the bracket you are in.

Thus, a single taxpayer with $60,000 of taxable income, in the 31 percent bracket, is taxed this way: The first $24,000 of income is taxed at 15 percent, or $3,600. The next $34,150 is taxed at 28 percent, or $9,562. Only the remaining taxable income of $1,850 is taxed at 31 percent, or $573.50, and it is here, at this person's top income figure, that this taxpayer's tax bracket is determined. So even though this taxpayer is in the 31 percent tax bracket, the tax this person pays is actually just under 23 percent of $60,000, or $13,735.50.

You see, your total income tax bill accumulates as you climb up the tax rate ladder. While you are on the lower rungs, the rates being charged against your income are correspondingly lower.

The tax bracket that you finally fall into is also referred to as the marginal tax rate. Things would become much clearer to taxpayers if they viewed their top income figure as the *outside* margin, because it is this top percent that the government uses to fit the taxpayer into the tax bracket system. In no sense, however, is that percent the only one used to figure the actual amount of tax one pays.

2. *Misconception: "Isn't this great—I've just received a huge refund from the IRS. I sure know how to beat them at their own game."*

What You Need to Know
Many taxpayers prefer to overwithhold and go for a large refund as a means of forced savings, or to ensure that they do not have to make any additional payments to the IRS on or after April 15. **The fact is, taxpayers who consistently receive large refunds are actually giving the IRS an interest-free loan, and the money the IRS is borrowing is *yours*.**

The most likely candidates to be sucked into this trap of overwithholding are taxpayers with unusually high deductions (mortgage interest, contributions, taxes) who haven't properly assessed how these deductions will affect their final tax bill. These taxpayers would be better served if they reduced the amount of withholding taken out during the year and got more money each week, which adds up to the same amount as the refund check.

One final tip regarding large end-of-year refunds: Although the IRS continues to maintain that its audit selection criteria are top secret, in my opinion one of the things IRS computers *do* look at is the size of a taxpayer's refund and how it was computed.

If an average taxpayer, married with two children, had a gross income of $75,000 with $13,000 of it withheld, and ended up with a $10,000 refund, the IRS is going to be very interested in the exemptions and deductions that caused this unusually large refund. In other words, that taxpayer has made himself or herself more susceptible to an audit. The solution? It's better to have less tax withheld and reduce that year-end refund.

3. *Misconception: "When I receive my inheritance from Uncle Leo, the IRS will take out a chunk of it."*

What You Need to Know
Many people mistakenly believe that when they receive a gift or inheritance they have to pay tax on it. They don't. The provider does. Gifts and inheritances are *not* taxable to the recipient until the asset is dis-

posed of, at which point taxes are due on any capital gain. The taxpayer should obtain documentation for the cost basis of the gift or inheritance so that when he sells the item he can determine how much tax he owes.

YOUR TAX-SAVING STRATEGY.
A parent or grandparent can make tuition payments for children or grandchildren directly to a college or private school and not be subject to the $10,000 per year gift tax limit. Although this exception applies to tuition only, there is no limit on the amount.

4. *Misconception: "What a relief to confer with my accountant about my tax troubles. I know that whatever we discuss will be held in the strictest confidence."*

What You Need to Know
Under federal law, there is no such thing as accountant-client privilege. Although you trust your CPA implicitly, whatever you as a taxpayer tell your CPA cannot legally be withheld by him or her in a court of law, if it ever comes to that.

Taxpayers believe that once they hire an attorney, the professional tax preparer simply turns over all papers to that attorney, thereby securing client privilege. This is not true. **Privilege applies only for papers originated by the attorney, or through the attorney's conversations with the taxpayer.** Also, if the attorney hires an accountant (usually *not* the preparer of the original return, for obvious reasons), any information exchanged between these two people is considered privileged because the accountant prepared the data as a result of a court case. (This type of accountant is called a kovel accountant.)

5. *Misconception: "If I use the preprinted label that the IRS sends me on my tax return, my chances of being audited will be greatly increased."*

What You Need to Know
The purpose of the preprinted labels is to allow an IRS data transcriber to access an account and enter the data needed to process the return using 12 keystrokes instead of 35. As discussed in chapter 8, the Discriminate Information Function (DIF) is the primary method the IRS uses to decide the majority of returns selected for audit, along with the ever-changing audit triggers. If the IRS were to use its preprinted labels for audit selection, the average tax assessment per audit would de-

crease dramatically due to the absence of audit criteria on the label. In other words, those labels offer absolutely no indication of a taxpayer's audit potential to the IRS. With almost 206 million returns filed in 1995, the IRS must get the biggest bang for its buck. Those preprinted labels aren't even in the ballpark when the IRS considers audits.

Below is a typical label and an explanation of the information it provides the IRS.

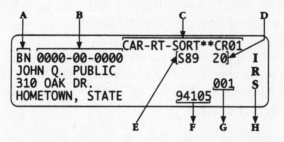

A. Two-letter "alpha code" that is computer shorthand for your name.

B. Your Social Security number. By entering the two-letter code and your Social Security number, the IRS can identify the correct account. The data-entry clerk doesn't have to type your full name and address into the computer.

C. Postal Service home delivery route.

D. Type of package mailed to the taxpayer—1040, 1040A, etc.

E. IRS Service Center where you filed your return last year—in this case, Fresno, CA. (S29 is the Ogden Service Center, Kansas City is S09, and so on.)

F. Your postal ZIP code.

G. The IRS's presort mail for the US Postal Service.

H. Certain labels, to help with mail distribution, have either PP, SS or PL directly under the "S" in IRS. *These letters indicate:*
- PP—Package (first label in a package).
- SS—Sack (first label in a sack).
- PL—Pallet (first label in a pallet).

Source: George S. Alberts, former director of the Albany and Brooklyn IRS district offices.

6. *Misconception: "When I sell my residence and realize a gain of $200,000, I can defer the payment of any income tax by buying a replacement home for at least $200,000 within two years."*

What You Need to Know

If both taxpayer and spouse are under 55 years old when they sell their home, they cannot use the one-time benefit of excluding up to $125,000 of taxable gain from their income. However, they can still be permitted to defer the gain on a sale of their primary residence if they buy a replacement home for at least the net sales price of their old home.

For example, Phil and Rachel Miller, both 50 years old, sold their Connecticut house for $600,000, which produced a realized gain of $400,000. At the time of sale, there was an unpaid mortgage of $125,000. Assuming they purchased a new house immediately for $700,000 cash (no mortgage), the entire gain of $400,000 would be deferred because the cost of the new home ($700,000) exceeded the sales price of the old home ($600,000). The adjusted basis of the new house would be $300,000 ($700,000 − $400,000). However, the $400,000 that was deferred must be taken into consideration when the new house is sold. *Note:* The amount of any mortgage on either house is irrelevent.

In another example, assume the same facts except that the Millers purchased a replacement home for only $550,000. Now $50,000 of the gain would be taxable ($600,000 − $550,000) and $350,000 ($400,000 − $50,000) would be deferred.

7. *Misconception: "Since my wife is now eligible for a pension plan where she works, we are both prohibited from making a contribution to our IRA's."*

What You Need to Know
You may still be eligible to make tax deductible contributions to your IRA's if you do not exceed certain income levels. In the above scenario, if the taxpayers' adjusted gross income is $40,000 or less ($25,000 or less for a single taxpayer), they could each contribute up to $2,000 to their IRA's. They would be eligible for a partial contribution between $40,000 and $50,000 ($25,000 and $35,000 for singles). Above $50,000 AGI ($35,000 for singles), they would not be eligible.

YOUR TAX-SAVING STRATEGY.
Even if you are ineligible to make a tax-deductible contribution to your IRA, you could make a nondeductible contribution up to $2,000. The interest on this investment would be tax deferred until retirement. Remember that you must segregate these funds from your regular IRA contributions by filing Form 8606 (Nondeductible IRAs).

8. *Misconception: "Now that I have been audited by the IRS and had money due, I will be audited every year."*

What You Need to Know
As already mentioned, tax returns are most often selected for an audit based on computer-generated criteria. The selection process is done on a year-by-year basis, with each new year standing on its own.

YOUR TAX-SAVING STRATEGY.

If one of the issues that caused a taxpayer to pay additional taxes resulted from an error, such as depreciation on a piece of office equipment, an auditor will know that this kind of error is often repeated. He or she will probably examine the prior year's return, if the statute of limitations has not expired and/or the following year's return if it is already filed. However, since these steps will normally take place immediately after the current year's audit is completed, it helps to keep your current year's return on extension (extending the filing date to October 15), if at all possible.

If the same taxpayer's return for the following year contains another red flag, such as very high travel and entertainment expenses, that return is again at risk for having a higher than normal audit potential.

9. *Misconception: "I can take more itemized deductions than I am entitled to (especially contributions and medical expenses) and not be audited as long as I stay under the national averages published by the IRS."*

What You Need to Know

Each year the IRS publishes tables of itemized deductions claimed by individuals on their tax returns and groups them by levels of adjusted gross income. These tables (see below) appear in the *Statistics of Income Bulletin (SOI).** Play this game and you'll end up playing audit roulette. To take a tax deduction, follow this simple rule: If you pay for a tax-deductible item, you can use it on your return as long as you can prove it with a canceled check or an itemized bill or receipt.

Certainly, some reasonable exceptions are allowed. You don't have to prove the first $78 of cash contributions, and you don't need every last toll or taxi receipt if you are an outside salesperson. However, deductions for taxes and interest are straightforward—if you're lacking proof, you will owe money to the IRS when audited, no matter where you fall in the national averages.

10. *Misconception: "By filing a timely Form 4868 [Application for Automatic Extension of Time To File U.S. Individual Income Tax Return], I will be excused from all penalties and interest as long as I file my tax return within the extension period and pay the balance of tax that is due."*

---

*The *SOI Bulletin* costs $14 per issue, $26 for an annual subscription. It can be obtained from the Superintendent of Documents, P. O. Box 371954, Pittsburgh, PA 15250-7954.

Average Itemized Deductions for 1994
(In order of appearance on Form 1040, Schedule A)

Adjusted Gross Income	Medical/ Dental	Taxes	Interest	Gifts to Charity	Misc. Deductions
$20,000<$25,000	2,865	2,057	4,920	1,250	2,552
$25,000<$30,000	2,924	2,351	5,134	1,195	3,657
$30,000<$40,000	4,078	2,808	5,069	1,375	2,828
$40,000<$50,000	4,531	3,372	5,678	1,520	3,171
$50,000<$75,000	5,583	4,415	6,384	1,616	3,259
$75,000<$100,000	7,788	6,208	7,626	2,380	3,942
$100,000<$200,000	8,061	10,031	10,049	4,071	6,131
$200,000 or more	17,200	29,842	18,074	11,444	14,097

Derived from the IRS *Statistics of Income Bulletin*, Fall 1995.

What You Need to Know

By filing a timely Form 4868, the only penalty that you eliminate is for filing the return late (5 percent per month, 25 percent maximum). However, you do not eliminate the penalty on the tax that is paid late (½ of 1 percent per month) or interest on the late tax payment (currently 9 percent per annum).

YOUR TAX-SAVING STRATEGY.

Here's a related matter regarding refunds. If your tax return results in a refund, you will be charged *no* penalties or interest for late filing because late-filing penalties and interest are based on the balance of tax due. In fact, you can file your refund return up to three years late and receive your refund while not being subject to penalties and interest. (Sorry, no interest is given on the refund for the length of time it takes you to file the return.)

11. *Misconception: "It doesn't pay to transfer income-producing assets to my child who is under 14 years of age. The income will still be taxed at my top income tax rate."*

What You Need to Know

This statement is true only if the child's taxable investment income exceeds $1,300. The amount of tax charged is based on a three-tiered aproach:

1. Zero to $650: Income produced at this level is wiped out since the child is entitled to a standard deduction of $650. No tax is due and no tax form or return needs to be filed by the child.

2. $651 to $1,300: Investment income above $650 is taxed at a 15 percent rate. To report this, the child must file an individual tax return.

3. $1,301 and higher: After calculating the tax on the first $1,300 of investment income as outlined in 1 and 2 above, the balance of investment income is taxed at the parents' highest tax rate. The parents must fill out Form 8615 (Tax for Children Under 14 Who Have Investment Income of More Than $1,300) and attach it to their tax return.

YOUR TAX-SAVING STRATEGY.

These rules cover investment income only. If your child earns other income, from salaries and wages, for example, that income is taxed at 15 percent to $24,000, which is the end of the 15 percent bracket for single taxpayers.

12. *Misconception: "It doesn't matter in what part of the country I live. All areas are considered equal in audit selection."*

What You Need to Know

Sadly, this is so far from the truth that it has attracted increasing media coverage of late. Even the IRS admits huge variances in audit coverage and selection based on location. As reported by the IRS in 1995, in the Los Angeles district, for example, 1.37 percent of all individual income tax returns filed were audited, compared to only 0.35 percent in Albany, New York. (See table, "Risk of Audit—Geographically," page 216.) Similarly, the number of criminal referrals of all kinds that the IRS made to the U.S. Attorney's Office also varies greatly by location. The national average is 17 referrals per one million people, administered by an average of 73 IRS agents per million residents. (See table, "Criminal Referrals Made by the IRS," page 217.)

13. *Misconception: "Our current tax system is riddled with loopholes that wealthy taxpayers take advantage of. A flat tax will not only remedy this situation and level the playing field for the rest of us, it will also simplify things dramatically. Everyone will pay the same percent of income to the government, we can say good-bye to all those complicated tax forms, and we'll finally be able to do away with the IRS along with all those CPA's who are kept in business because tax laws are so complicated."*

Risk of Audit—Geographically

IRS District	Percent of Returns Audited
Albany	0.35%
Boston	0.47%
Brooklyn	0.59%
Manhattan	1.06%
Providence	0.96%
Atlanta	1.11%
Ft. Lauderdale	0.67%
Nashville	0.53%
Cincinnati	0.32%
Cleveland	0.32%
Louisville	0.32%
Des Moines	0.50%
Dallas	1.02%
Denver	0.85%
Houston	0.78%
Phoenix	0.68%
Anchorage	1.05%
Boise	1.08%
Las Vegas	1.93%
Los Angeles	1.37%
Sacremento	1.05%
San Francisco	1.36%

Source: *IRS 1995 Data Book*, advance draft, tables 7 and 13.

What You Need to Know

Proponents of the flat tax and value-added tax have argued that the current tax system taxes investments and savings too heavily, hurts the nation's competitiveness in internationl markets, and is just too complicated to administer. However, many of these same arguments were used in support of the last major overhaul of the tax system, the Tax Reform Act (TRA) of 1986. The TRA, which was supposed to be an improvement over the existing situation, did wipe out most abusive tax shelters, but it also severely limited taxpayers' ability to use real estate investments to shelter income. The result was that the real estate industry was brought to its knees. This new weak link, created under the guise of tax reform, contributed to a recession that lasted several years.

The lesson we need to learn and remember is this: **Major tax reform often has significant side effects that are not known until some of the laws get played out.**

The most often repeated argument against the flat tax is that it would destroy the progressive nature of the tax system, in which the amount of taxes owed rises according to income earned, and load the tax bur-

Criminal Referrals Made by the IRS

Criminal referrals the IRS made to United States attorneys, ranked by referrals per million people living in the area served by each prosecutor, and the combined number of revenue agents and criminal investigators the IRS had in each district, per million residents.

City	Referrals per Million	Agents per Million	City	Referrals per Million	Agents per Million
Washington, D.C.	71	663	San Diego	14	63
Tulsa	65	95	Savannah, Ga.	14	38
Oklahoma City	55	113	Seattle	14	55
Roanoke, Va.	43	26	Atlanta	13	103
New York (Manhattan)	39	230	Greensboro, N.C.	13	49
Pittsburgh	34	59	Houston	13	92
Las Vegas, Nev.	32	89	Kansas City, Mo.	13	54
Honolulu	31	71	New Haven	13	102
Anchorage	30	109	Phoenix	13	49
Fargo	30	80	Birmingham, Ala.	12	54
Miami	30	85	Lexington, Ky.	12	44
Wilmington, Del.	30	85	Little Rock	12	61
New York (Brooklyn)	28	65	Nashville	12	80
San Antonio	27	75	Cedar Rapids	11	41
Tampa	25	55	Raleigh, N.C.	11	31
Fort Worth	23	147	Salt Lake City	11	57
Memphis, Tenn.	23	59	Boston	10	83
Mobile	22	34	Cincinnati	10	77
New Orleans	20	97	Detroit	10	66
Cheyenne	19	101	Portland, Me.	10	55
Cleveland	19	73	Syracuse	10	53
Portland, Ore.	19	52	East St. Louis	9	29
Muskogee	18	14	Milwaukee	9	77
Philadelphia	18	92	Omaha	9	73
Buffalo	17	68	Providence, R.I.	9	89
Chicago	17	106	St. Louis	9	96
Jackson, Miss.	17	50	Minneapolis	8	76
National average	**17**	**73**	Springfield, Ill.	8	49
Albuquerque	16	50	Billings	7	56
Sacramento	16	45	Shreveport	7	34
San Francisco	16	104	Spokane	6	27
Alexandria, Va.	15	55	Topeka	5	79
Baltimore	15	72	Madison, Wis.	4	22
Denver	15	98	Montgomery, Ala.	4	36
Newark	15	72	Burlington, Vt.	3	50
Los Angeles	14	86			

Source: Transactional Records Access Clearinghouse, Syracuse University.

den more heavily on the backs of the middle class. While there are economists who passionately debate both of these arguments, here are some of the potential results if a flat tax were to be enacted:

- With interest, dividends, and rental income no longer taxed, the wealthy would be able to add to their riches in a way similar to what the Vanderbilts and Rockefellers did prior to 1913; i.e., whatever interest and dividends they received from their investments, they kept—legitimately—because they were tax free.
- Tax shelters in the form of limited partnerships would lose their attractiveness, reducing needed capital sources for businesses, such as the real estate industry. This is exactly what happened with TRA 86.
- Mortgage interest and real estate tax deductions would disappear. Without these, home values would plummet.
- Sales of municipal bonds, which provide tax-sheltered interest income, would drop because with a flat tax all interest income becomes tax sheltered, thereby wiping out the advantages of municipals. The resulting shortfall in municipal revenue would be a double whammy—local property taxes would rise, which would be an additional burden on middle-class home owners, *and* these taxes would no longer be deductible on a personal income tax return.
- Charitable contributions would be eliminated. Consider the effect this would have on the level of contributions by savvy taxpayers to charitable organizations across the country!

Now let's explore how the flat tax and value-added tax proposals would affect the nation's business community.

Under the flat tax, instead of depreciating certain assets over time or being held to certain limiting thresholds, as is the case under current tax law, businesses could *immediately* write off or expense the following:

1. Amounts paid for purchases of goods, services, and materials, whether or not these are resold by year's end
2. All purchases of tangible real and personal property, such as land, buildings, and equipment (capital items)
3. Compensation, meals and entertainment, and several other limited expenses

Sounds like a real free-for-all for the business community, doesn't it? If this should become the status quo, what do you think would be needed more than ever before? How about a watchdog, *like the IRS*, to ensure that businesses comply with the new tax rules? Why? Because the temptation to bend the law will be greater than ever given the easy route open to every businessperson to avoid taxation or to defer taxes indefinitely simply by increasing the current year's purchases of goods or capital equipment and deducting the full cost. Even if done legitimately, the resulting loss of business tax revenues would transfer the tax burden right back to the middle class. Inevitably tax increases would soon follow to make up the differences.

As far as those CPA's are concerned, we are probably the largest, strongest, and most genuine group of taxpayer advocates, constantly putting ourselves on the front lines. We know the law and we also know how and where our clients, the taxpayers, are being hit the hardest by the IRS. CPA's, as I see it, are in the best position to save taxpayer dollars through their advice and daily scrutiny of individual and business returns. The American Institute of Certified Public Accountants (AICPA) and the local state CPA societies have a solid track record for establishing a viable working relationship with the IRS. If positive changes are to occur in tax laws, with the taxpayer as the beneficiary, lobbying groups such as the AICPA will be the ones to start the ball rolling.

Concerning the question regarding the demise of the IRS: Think this one through! We would still need a system to administer the collection of over $1 trillion annually. In addition, taxpayers would still need to file information in some format—although a lot less paperwork would probably be required.

Let's face it. As long as the tax-making process is intricately tied to Congress and the political machinery, the chances of having a flat tax passed into law are pretty slim. Considering the potential ramifications of a flat tax, that may be fortunate.

10

—

Ten Ground Rules Never to Break
to Win with the IRS

Wouldn't it be wonderful if every taxpayer—no matter who or what he did—could be given guidelines for avoiding the IRS altogether or for winning if confronted by it? Many worthwhile guides try to provide this information. With over 205 million tax returns processed by the IRS annually, it is impossible to provide specific answers to tax problems faced by every taxpayer. So my goal is to approach the IRS from a new vantage point.

First, you must abandon the notion that winning at taxes is about finding the right piece of information. In fact, it is about knowing as much as possible about *your own, personal tax situation*. But be wary. That information must be placed within the proper perspective, or you won't win in the end. You will only achieve the proper perspective if you move beyond your fear of the IRS and clearly see that the IRS is simply a group of people who have an enormous job to accomplish.

To continue to keep the scales between you and the IRS tipped in your favor, you must always follow these 10 ground rules for winning with the IRS.

RULE 1. ALWAYS REPORT INCOME ON YOUR TAX RETURN THAT IS BEING REPORTED TO THE IRS BY THIRD-PARTY PAYERS.

The most common include W-2's, income items on K-1's, and the entire series of 1099 forms: distributions from pension plans and individual retirement accounts (IRA's); interest and dividend income; sales of stocks, bonds, and mutual funds; state income tax refunds; and Social Security and unemployment insurance benefits.

Some of the tax laws and requirements that govern third-party disclosures are

- Withholding law (Tax Payment Act of 1943).
- Requirement to report miscellaneous income totaling $600 or more in a year (1099-MISC).
- Requirement to report payments of interest and dividend income totaling $10 or more (1099-DIV, 1099-INT).
- Any of the other tax laws governing information reporting that bring into play the full series of 1099 forms, eleven in all.

But as usual, when it comes to practicing the law, people don't always meet their legal obligations uniformly. Exceptions occur because people misinterpret, manipulate, or simply ignore what is requested. As a result, you must pay attention to more than the letter of these laws and be prepared for the following circumstances in adhering to this ground rule.

Some Employers Report All Payments

Be aware that many business owners report *all* payments on 1099-MISC to the IRS, even if they are less than $600. What implication does this have for taxpayers? To follow the letter of the law, taxpayers should report all income received, even if the amount is below $600 annually.

In fact, taxpayers should learn to assume responsibility for keeping track of all their own earnings. At least then they can be certain that a comparison between what they say they earn and the 1099's provided by payers will be accurate.

Payment Methods

A worker can be paid "on the books" or "off the books." "Regular employees" and independent contractors are paid on the books. Regular employees receive a salary from the entity they work for and have their income reported directly to the IRS by that entity on a W-2 form. Independent contractors have their income reported to the IRS by the entity that pays them on a 1099-MISC, if their remuneration is over $600 per year.

All payment methods—cash, checks, barter—are treated equally under the law. **No matter what the form of payment, including barter, the business owner is legally bound to report the amount paid to the IRS on a W-2, a 1099-MISC, or on any of the other 10**

1099 forms. This information is carefully matched up on IRS computers, so if you don't report it, you place yourself at audit risk.

Workers who so choose or are talked into it are paid "off the books," in cash—and usually no reporting requirements are fulfilled by the entity to the IRS. This group usually believes they're getting a bargain. Not true.

When You Are Paid "Off the Books"

Fifteen or 20 years ago "off the books" meant taking your earnings home with no taxes deducted. Today all of that has changed because of information technology and reporting requirements. **Anyone who accepts this method of payment becomes an independent contractor in the eyes of the IRS and is liable for all of the taxes independent contractors must pay.**

If your teenage daughter tells you she'll be working part-time, "off the books," what is really going on is probably not the "classic" definition just described, but something more like this: Mr. and Mrs. Owner are the only "employees" listed on the company's payroll records. All others whom they employ are issued 1099's at the end of the year. Since 1099's represent payments to nonemployees, no taxes are withheld from these payments, and the worker is treated like an independent contractor. Thus your daughter could earn $5,500 with no taxes withheld but end up being liable for paying FICA taxes of $777.13.

If she were treated as an employee, the FICA tax deduction from her salary would be $420.75 (7.65 percent of $5,500), a net savings of $356.-38. In both instances, she would owe no income tax because she would be earning below the $6,550 threshold for a single person. The $5,500 is wiped out by a personal exemption of $2,550 and a standard deduction for a single person amounting to $4,000.

In short, if you are a part-time or summer worker, insist you be paid "on the books," receiving full benefits, paying your share of taxes. A student is generally subject only to the withholding of FICA tax. If you are working full-time on a permanent basis and are not self-employed or are not inclined to file your tax return as a self-employed person, also insist that you be treated as a regular employee.

The Greed Factor

Dealing in cash presents temptations. Once you have been tempted, it's often difficult to overcome the *greed factor*. Problems arise when business owners pocket cash and fail to report it to the IRS, or get involved in schemes for hiding income. Why would a business owner report the *full* amount of cash payments made to workers on 1099's but only report *part* of the cash income to the IRS? To reduce the company's net taxable income. (If the income goes directly into the owner's pocket, the IRS can't tax it, right?) None of this is news to the IRS, so don't let the greed factor get you.

The only major reporting exception for business owners is something many tax professionals consider to be a major weakness in the IRS's reporting system: **The IRS does not require business owners to prepare 1099-MISC forms for payments to corporations.** That means if you are an independent contractor or self-employed *and you incorporate,* anyone who pays you is *not* required to file a 1099-MISC with the IRS. (See also the discussion of advantages of an S corporation, pages 185–193, in chapter 8, "How to Avoid an Audit Completely.")

What Happens When You Don't Receive a 1099?

Some people actually believe that if they don't receive a Form 1099, it means that it was not mailed to the IRS and therefore they don't have to include that income on their tax return. Nothing could be further from the truth. It is vital that you follow Ground Rule 1 even if you do not actually receive your 1099 form telling you how much income you received from a particular job.

Why Business Owners Don't Send 1099's

Occasionally business owners are unfamiliar with the rules governing payments for labor and services and fail to prepare the required 1099 paperwork. Or sometimes they inadvertently forget to mail the 1099 to the recipient. But the primary reasons business owners "forget" to prepare 1099's are these:

- They are fearful that the independent contractors they use will be reclassified by the IRS as employees. What better way to avoid reclassification than by not mailing the 1099's to the IRS?
- They believe that the less the IRS knows about their operation in general, the better off they are. If they do get audited and the IRS discovers that they didn't file 1099's, they would rather risk paying the penalties ($100 per nonfiling of a 1099) than revealing more of their business operations to the IRS.

An IRS auditor does not often impose a penalty for failure to file 1099's. Even if one does, though, the $100 per item nonfiling penalty is small compared to the possible costly reclassification of some or all of the business owner's workers as employees. However, if the IRS can prove *intentional* disregard of the filing rules by the business owner, there is no maximum penalty per information return.

The bottom line for workers is this: If you do *not* receive a 1099, ask the business owner if one is forthcoming. Then be prepared. You may have inadvertently alerted that person to a new responsibility, something he or she didn't know about (no kidding) until you mentioned it.

RULE 2. NEVER INCLUDE OTHER FORMS THAT ARE *NOT* REQUIRED WITH YOUR TAX RETURN. DO NOT VOLUNTEER ADDITIONAL INFORMATION.

This ground rule applies to a number of situations, some involving several very specific (and many newly created) IRS forms, some applying to cases in which taxpayers owe the IRS money and negotiations are a possibility, and some applying to audits.

Form 8275 (Disclosure Statement) and Form 8275-R (Regulation Disclosure Statement)

The IRS would love it if all taxpayers used Forms 8275 and 8275-R more often because they are supposed to be filed with a 1040 if a taxpayer knowingly takes a position on the return that is questionable. Both forms look extremely harmless and provide minimal direction. Form 8275 states, "Do not use this form to disclose information that is contrary to treasury regulations." Form 8275-R states, "Use this form only to disclose items or positions that are contrary to treasury regulations." Following each sentence is blank space. The IRS designed Forms 8275 and 8275-R this way to give taxpayers enough rope to hang themselves.

In 1993, I said that by electing to use these forms, you are notifying the IRS that you're probably doing something wrong. In 1995, the IRS finally admitted it.

The instructions for Form 8275 and 8275-R require that you support your position through revenue rulings, revenue procedures, tax court cases, and the like. This means that you need to locate, from thousands of pages in our current tax code, previous laws and decisions that support your position.

According to the IRS there is a plus side to all of this: If you attach Form 8275 or 8275-R to your return, and if the return is subsequently audited, *and* the issue is decided against you, you won't have to pay any penalties. However, you will still have to pay additional tax, plus interest.

Form 8275 and 8275-R are nifty tools devised by the IRS to ease the burden of the Examination Department. **Instead of IRS personnel manually sorting through thousands of returns to come up with**

questionable issues, with these forms, taxpayers are now flagging questionable items for the IRS of their own free will. Why should you be the one to start the ball rolling?

The fact is that you can disregard these forms entirely and still take the same position regarding income and expenses, and rely on the same rulings or procedures, which your tax professional may already be familiar with.

There's something else to consider when it comes to Forms 8275 and 8275-R. **The consensus of tax pros regarding both of these forms is that the IRS wants to make it tougher on tax preparers if they take aggressive positions on their clients' tax returns.** Existing IRS regulations say that when a tax preparer takes a questionable position on a return, one that stands less than one chance in three of being accepted by the IRS, the tax preparer must describe the position taken and then include support for it by using Form 8275. If the use of a borderline justification is not disclosed in this way, and the return is found unacceptable, the instructions to Form 8275 indicate that the taxpayer is subject to additional tax, and the preparer can be charged with a $250 penalty as well.

Who's to judge whether the tax preparer has one in three chances that the position taken on a client's 1040 will be accepted? The regulation goes on to say that the final decision will be based on a "reasonable and well-informed analysis by a person knowledgeable in tax law." If you were to bet on which decision would win, the one taken by the IRS or the taxpayer, which would you choose?

My advice is that if your tax pro suggests including Form 8275 or Form 8275-R with your return, be sure that he or she justifies why the form is being used and convinces you that it is being used for your benefit and not just to cover your tax professional's own exposure.

Form 5213 (Election to Postpone Determination as to Whether the Presumption That an Activity Is Engaged in for Profit Applies)

If you file taxes as an individual, partnership, S corporation, or an estate or trust (pass-through entities) that has incurred or is expected to incur net operating losses for three out of five years, you can elect to file Form 5213.

If an activity is presumed to be engaged in for profit, the activity must show a net profit for three out of five years. Conversely, if you have net losses for three out of the first five years, your activity will be presumed to be a hobby and on an audit deductions will be allowed only to the extent of income reported from the activity. That is, you will be able to reduce the income to but not below zero. Here is a case that demonstrates the use of 5213 and the tax rulings associated with it.

During an audit, a client of mine, a small producer of documentary films, showed a string of losses for five years amounting to approximately $15,000 per year. Although she had only small amounts of income and large expenses, she was still actively seeking distribution outlets for the films she produced. In her favor was the fact that three years prior to the five years showing losses, she showed a substantial profit in two out of three years.

During the past five years, however, she was living off her savings. Careful documentation provided to the tax auditor showed that she was making an honest attempt to sell her films. For example, many of the travel expenses charged to the business were in pursuit of this effort.

After a half-day audit that covered a two-year period, the agent concluded that my client had demonstrated an honest profit motive.

This goes to the heart of the Hobby Loss Provision. Losses in three out of five years merely *indicate* that you're not in it to make a profit. If you can *prove* the profit motive (time spent, investigation before starting, expertise, lack of other income to offset losses, etc.), then the losses will stand. The IRS would have loved my client to have filled out Form 5213 when she began producing films. This could have led the IRS to believe that this occupation was a hobby—which in reality it wasn't.

The IRS is trying to sell you on Form 5213 by attaching a bonus to it: If you file Form 5213, you can postpone the determination by the IRS as to whether or not you are engaged in an activity for profit. That is, you cannot be audited during the initial five-year test period. **This may sound good, but it's not, for two reasons.**

First, there is nothing automatic about the Hobby Loss Provision. If you show net losses for three or four consecutive years, you may not hear from the IRS. **By filing the form you are actually informing the IRS that you are afraid that your losses will be disallowed.** Why put yourself on record that you might be subject to the Hobby Loss Provision? Let the IRS discover your losses on its own. If you don't file Form 5213, you still retain all your rights to refute the IRS that you have engaged in the activity not to make a profit.

Second, when you file Form 5213 you are also agreeing to extend the period for tax assessment (statute of limitations) for two years after the due date of the return in question for the first tax year of the five-year test period. For example, if the test period is 1991 through 1995, the IRS would normally have until April 15, 1995, to initiate an audit of the 1991 return. However, if you file a 5213, the IRS has until April 15, 1997, an extra two years. **This could mean giving the IRS five years to assess you for additional tax instead of the normal three!** It's better not to fill out the form.

Form SS-8 (Determination of Employee Work Status for Purposes of Federal Employment Taxes and Income Tax Withholding

Form SS-8 was formerly called Independent Contractor Status. As explored in chapter 7, the IRS is currently very focused on reclassifying independent contractors as employees. As you recall, reclassification enables the IRS to recoup huge amounts of tax dollars.

To file an SS-8 would be to admit that there is some doubt in your status as an independent contractor or, if the form is being filed by an employer, the status of your workers. Based on what you have already learned about the IRS, why would you want to place doubt on your own working status, or on the working status of your workers? The form is also quite complicated and cumbersome, even for professionals.

If you do not file Form SS-8, your status, or your workers' status, will probably come into question *only* **during an audit.**

Form 872 (Consent to Extend the Time to Assess Tax) and Form 872-A (Special Consent to Extend the Time to Assess Tax)

When an audit has been going on for six months or more and the statute of limitations, normally three years, will be up in one year or less, the auditor may ask you to sign Form 872 or 872-A. Before you even think about signing either one, you should consider that the wrong choice could hurt you badly.

If, at an audit, you are asked to sign one of the forms, you almost have no choice. If you don't agree to an extension of the statute of limitations, the IRS will send you a Statutory Notice of Deficiency, which will force you to end up in Tax Court or at least have the IRS commence collection actions against you. In addition, if it looks as though you can't settle your case with the auditor at this point and you're thinking of taking your case to Appeals, signing an extension for at least one year is usually required.

So now the question is, which one do you sign? **Under no circumstances should you choose Form 872-A, which leaves the extension date open-ended.** This gives the IRS an unlimited amount of time to complete your examination. Needless to say, the IRS *will* take its time. The case could end up at the bottom of the pile and the clock will tick away as interest charges mount up. I know of cases like this that have gone on for seven years or more.

Therefore, when signing an extension, choose Form 872, which defines the end of the extension period. And you absolutely want to limit this period to one additional year.

One more thing: Make sure the agent doesn't "inadvertently" hand you the 872-A instead. I've had that happen to me.

Form 9465 (Installment Agreement Request)

In the last few years the IRS has accepted an increasing number of 9465 forms to create an installment agreement between the IRS and taxpayers who have balances due on their 1040's. Before the changeover to this form, taxpayers had to receive a tax bill *before* they could ask to set up a payment agreement.

Now taxpayers can attach Form 9465 to the 1040 and specify the amount of the proposed monthly payment. A response from the IRS to accept, deny, or request more information regarding the terms is supposed to arrive within 30 days. The terms of the agreement are negotiated between the IRS and the taxpayer.

Form 9465 actually offers an enormous advantage: The old form required taxpayers to disclose their current financial status to the IRS, about four pages of it, including a full list of all assets and liabilities. In an effort to streamline paperwork, the IRS says, the new form omits this requirement for tax liabilities under $10,000. **At least taxpayers can now pay their bills without disclosing their ready assets to the IRS, which could implicate them if they have sufficient means to pay their obligation in full.**

There's another advantage. If the liability is under $10,000 and if taxpayers adhere to the terms of the payment schedule, no tax liens will be filed against the taxpayers' property.

The IRS says it has decided to take this new approach to reduce the number of taxpayers who do not file at all because of money owed, and in the hopes that taxpayers will file returns even if they cannot pay the balance due immediately.

However, there are some drawbacks to installment agreements as well. First, they are binding. Second, penalties and interest are due on the unpaid balance. Essentially taxpayers who file Form 9465 are locked in to a late-payment penalty of one half percent a month plus interest on unpaid amounts. Taken together the cost comes to 13 percent a year. This is less interest than on a credit card, but you still need to think it through before you sign. You may end up owing more than you expect and if you don't meet your monthly payment, the IRS will come after you. In addition, if your income goes up, the IRS can insist that monthly payments be increased. However, if your income drops, you must submit new financial information before the IRS will, *at its discretion*, consider lowering your payments.

Next, how benevolent the IRS will be when negotiating the installment terms remains unknown. Add to this that all functions within the IRS have the authority to grant installment agreements up to $10,000. Previously only the Collection Division could work with accounts over $5,000. Now employees in Appeals, Employee Plans and Exempt Organizations, Examination, Problem Resolution, Returns Processing (in the service centers), and Taxpayer Service can help in resolving accounts.[1] With the 1996 passage of the Taxpayer Bill of Rights 2, at least the IRS is now required to notify taxpayers *before* changing the terms of an installment agreement (see page 279).

Another way to look at this is that there will probably be a lack of uniformity from division to division in handling installment requests.

How to Pay Off the IRS on Your Terms
Without Using IRS Installment Agreements

Rather than lock yourself into a 9465 installment agreement, I recommend the following short-term fix to ease out of tax money due.

- Send in some money as soon as you receive your first notice of tax due.
- Follow the payment up with some more money each time you receive another collection notice.
- With each notice, include a short note explaining why you cannot pay the full balance right now, such as illness or loss of your job.
- Be sure to tell the IRS that you will continue to try your best to pay as much as you can.

Using this method, you could get away with paying a fairly small amount for three to four months. **If you file a 9465, you will soon be strapped with a strict payment schedule that will be fraught with penalties if you don't make all the payments on time.** Hopefully, after the first few months you'll be in better shape to pay off the balance.

The Fallacy of Giving the IRS Backup Data for Deductions

Many tax preparers suggest including backup data with your return when you have taken a larger than normal deduction. For example, they suggest that if you have sustained a large casualty loss, you should include repair bills and appraisals. My advice to you is this: **Do not include this data.** The only thing you accomplish by including backup data is to bring the questionable items to the attention of IRS reviewers. Also, if the return *is* selected for a review, by the time it reaches the reviewer your backup data may be incomplete after having gone through mail and sorting machines and being handled by lots of different people.

Let the IRS carry out its audit function its way. If your return is selected for a correspondence audit to verify one glaring item, you can submit all your documentary proof at that time.

RULE 3. USE TO YOUR ADVANTAGE THE FACT THAT THE IRS SYSTEM FOR DOCUMENT RETRIEVAL IS ARCHAIC.

David Burnham reports that "during the year ending in October 1987, IRS employees made 41 million requests for tax returns and other documents that had previously been provided to the agency under the requirements of law. Because of faulty filing procedures and poorly trained personnel, however, the agency was unable to locate 2 million of the requested documents. Even where the documents were located, the searches often required an inordinate time to complete. In more than one third of the cases, IRS employees had not received the documents 45 days after making their initial request."[2]

This situation—the inability of the IRS to retrieve tax returns—has not changed much over the years. The negative implications continue to be far-reaching. **Hundreds of thousands of individual taxpayers, as well as IRS staff from Examination, Collection, and CID who work directly with taxpayers, are all stymied by the archaic retrieval system.** But probably the most visible person who has to deal with this embarrassing mess, aside from the taxpayer and the taxpayer's representative, is the IRS auditor who is preparing for an upcoming audit, or who is in the midst of one. Not being able to locate a specific tax return consistently affects an auditor's role, behavior, and performance.

Mrs. Raymond hired me as her accountant in 1992 and asked whether I could assist her in obtaining a home equity loan. This was not an easy task, since the IRS had placed a lien on her house and I have not yet come across a mortgage lender who will provide a borrower with any funds if the IRS has a lien on that person's property.

I discovered that the IRS had disallowed a tax shelter deduction from Mrs. Raymond's 1983 tax return. After the tax was assessed, the IRS filed the lien in October 1988.

Further investigation made me increasingly suspicious. Each time I phoned the IRS all I got were indirect answers. I also wondered why the IRS had not sent Mrs. Raymond even one collection letter during the past three years. I did find out that the tax Mrs. Raymond owed, including penalties and interest, amounted to over $100,000.

I finally reached an auditor at the IRS office in Mrs. Raymond's hometown who had been assigned to the case and who admitted to me that Mrs. Raymond's entire file had been lost! He had turned the situation over to his supervisor because it was "too hot to handle." The supervisor delayed for another three months while he insisted on a thorough search of the storage warehouse where Mrs. Raymond's file might have been sent in error—a warehouse in Passaic, New Jersey.

When the search proved fruitless, the supervisor would not take the responsibility of excusing a $100,000 case simply because a file had been misplaced. He forwarded the case to the regional Problems Resolution Office (PRO), obviously hoping for a miracle. Nothing was solved, but at least the matter was out of his hands.

Everyone I dealt with at the IRS tried to hide this information trail from me as long as they could.

After only 30 days—PRO is the most efficient unit in the entire IRS—a credit was put through for the entire $100,000. A short while later, Mrs. Raymond's equity loan cleared.

Auditors *like* to have some independent corroboration of items of income so they can verify what the taxpayer has previously included on the tax return being examined. After all, they are trained to look for information that may be missing, altered, or omitted intentionally, and part of their job is *not* automatically to accept what the taxpayer or the taxpayer's representative is handing over.

But any IRS auditor knows that when a request for a copy of a tax return is made, the return may not be received until *after* the audit is completed, or too late in the audit process for it to be useful.

A successful, self-employed insurance agent, Mr. Franklyn was being audited for 1989. His business operations were filed on Form 1040, Schedule C, and an 1120S (Income Tax Return for an S Corporation), since he also owned part of an S corporation.

During the audit, the agent requested copies of Mr. Franklyn's 1040's for 1988 and 1990 and the 1120S's for 1988 and 1989. I gave the auditor Mr. Franklyn's 1040 for 1990 and the 1120S for 1989 (which was the final return filed for this corporation), and said we didn't have copies of the 1040 or 1120S for 1988. The returns had been misplaced when Mr. Franklyn moved to a new office. The auditor naturally said he'd try to retrieve them from the IRS system.

Expecting that the IRS would take a minimum of 45 days to get the copies, if they ever got them, I made my next and final date with the auditor less than 30 days later. At that meeting, the auditor still had not received the requested tax returns, so he proceeded with the audit disallowing $15,000 of items on Mr. Franklyn's business return (specifically travel and entertainment), and then closed the case. If the missing returns contained any information that could have been damaging to Mr. Franklyn, the IRS will never know.

How to Take Advantage of the IRS's Ancient Retrieval System
The implications of this situation for taxpayers are particularly important if you are facing or involved in an audit. *Take your time* locating a copy of an earlier return if you think that a prior return will

- Contradict any information on the return being audited.
- Provide reasons for the auditor to examine additional areas for which you have less than adequate proof.

You are playing for time here, because time is most likely on your side, as we just discussed. For example, you may know that something on a past or current return will show up as an inconsistency—a K-1 from a rental property that no longer appears, or dividend income on an investment for which the dividend is no longer reported *and* there is no reported sale of the investment. There may be adequate explanations for these inconsistencies, but you should conclude the audit as soon as possible *before* the auditor receives the requested information from the IRS.

RULE 4. IF ANY INFORMATION THAT YOU ARE PUTTING ON A TAX RETURN IS A "GRAY" AREA, GO FOR AS CLOSE TO FULL DEDUCTIBILITY AS POSSIBLE.

Often the data taxpayers are planning to include on a return is not a perfect fit for the category or line that they think it belongs on. For example, a variety of expenses can appear on more than one place on Form 1040. The secret is knowing which schedule to choose to gain the biggest tax advantage and how to support your claims. This also applies if you are filing as a partnership or an S or C corporation.

The majority of taxpayers choose to report expenses on three schedules, all used in connection with the 1040 form: Schedule C (Profit or Loss from Business), Schedule E (Supplemental Income and Loss [from rental real estate, royalties, partnerships, S corporations, estates, trusts, REMIC's, etc.]), and Schedule A (Itemized Deductions).

The essential differences among these is that many expenses listed on Schedule A are subject to formulas that limit deductibility such as percentage of adjusted gross income. In contrast, expenses listed on Schedule C and Schedule E are fully deductible, with the exception of certain restraints such as home-office expenses on Schedule C and passive loss amounts on Schedule E, both of which are sometimes not fully deductible on their respective schedules.

Form 1040, Schedule C (Profit or Loss from Business)

Form 1040, Schedule C (Profit or Loss From Business) is used to report the income from a business operated by a self-employed person, the income of someone who renders part- or full-time service as an independent contractor, or of someone who carries on a trade or business as a proprietor. In the audit chapter, taxpayers were advised to reduce their 1040 line items by eliminating Schedule C in its entirety. **If you must continue to use Schedule C, there are certain flexibilities you should know about.** (The following information can apply to all business entities, such as partnerships, S corporations, and C corporations.)

Schedule C contains about 25 listed expense items and an unlimited amount of other miscellaneous expense categories and it provides taxpayers with ample opportunities to increase business deductions. Some line items are more flexible than others.

Listed Items

Advertising
Car and truck expenses
Legal and professional services

Other Expenses

Telephone

You can use these items to your advantage.

Advertising

You're self-employed, and you decide to print up some résumés and place ads for your services in your local newspaper, at a total cost of $2,500. As a self-employed person you can report this as a business expense on Schedule C and take a full $2,500 deduction.

If these or other job-related expenses are incurred while you are an employee, they must be reported on Schedule A in a section titled "Job Expenses and Most Other Miscellaneous Deductions." Here, however, the total amount of your deductions is subject to a reduction of an amount equal to 2 percent of your adjusted gross income (AGI). If you are single with an AGI of $60,000 and in the 28 percent tax bracket, 2 percent is $1,200, so your deduction would be reduced by this amount, and would be only $1,300.

Car and Truck Expenses

No matter what type of business you are in, you probably use your car some of the time for business reasons. Taxpayers in this position have two choices for computing and reporting vehicle expenses.

The simplest and safest way to report these expenses is by using the *mileage method.* To do this simply multiply business miles driven by the allowable mileage rate (currently 31 cents), add tolls and parking expenses, and you have your deduction. If you use your car for a mere 5,000 miles, this will provide you with a $1,550 deduction.

Using the alternative *direct method,* you simply add up all your auto expenses—gas and oil, repairs, and insurance—plus depreciation. You then must factor in the number of days per week the car is used for business purposes. If it's Monday to Friday, then you can deduct 5⁄7 of the auto expenses. The remainder of the costs represent those incurred for personal use and are not deductible.

Since many business owners often use their cars on Saturdays and perhaps even on an occasional Sunday to greet an out-of-town customer or supplier, deduct 6⁄7 of the total car expenses and present your position if you are audited.

To decide which works best, compare the direct-method costs with the mileage costs and go with the one that offers the largest deduction. You should also factor in one further consideration: If you are audited, with the direct method you have to document every last item of expense with receipts, and maintain a diary that shows full details of your business miles. With the mileage method, a diary that shows your business miles is all that is required. *Warning:* If you lease your car, you *must* use the direct method–substitute lease payments for depreciation (also see page 251).

Legal and Professional Services

The IRS wants you to apportion deductible legal and accounting fees to each appropriate schedule on your return: Schedules A, C, and E; or "Other Income," line 21 on page 1 of the 1040. Since a tax professional usually spends a considerable amount of time preparing the business part of your return, it is perfectly acceptable for you to request that the bill be weighted in favor of Schedule C, where it is deductible in full without limitations. If a legal fee is personal in nature and doesn't relate to the business, exclude it. For example, preparation of a will is personal, but tax advice that was part of a discussion with the attorney is deductible. Speak to the attorney *before* the bill arrives and explain that you're tax-savvy and insist that the tax advice be clearly shown on the bill.

The greatest advantage for taxpayers is achieved by including expenses for legal and professional services in a schedule that offers 100 percent deductibility. This is what a detailed bill and its traceable deductions might include:

Where to List Legal and Professional Services for Maximum Deductibility

Item	Schedule
Professional fees in pursuit of back alimony	Line 21, page 1 of 1040
Audit fees to uncover hidden assets of ex-spouse relating to alimony	Line 21, page 1 of 1040
Attorney's fees on purchase of a new home	Add to cost basis of home
Legal fees to collect back rent*	Schedule E, Part 1
Tax preparer's fees for preparation of business payroll tax returns	Schedule C
Attorney's fees for setting up a new business	Schedule C
Planning advice in reference to a new business venture	Schedule C

*The last four items are also generally deductible by partnerships and corporations.

Telephone Expenses

Generally speaking, you can take a more aggressive position if you use estimates to supplement actual receipts. For example, since there are no receipts available for coins put into public telephones, working people who spend a lot of time on the road can conceivably declare they spend as much as $30 a week on business calls from pay phones. Even if you have a telephone credit card or a cellular phone, it is more economical to use coins for calls under one dollar. Because items such as telephone calls are not a major expense, IRS auditors spend little time in this area, so reasonable estimates are usually accepted.

If you have a dedicated business phone, most IRS auditors will accept your deduction as a 100 percent business cost. Don't worry, auditors generally will not test your honesty by calling specific telephone numbers.

For a smaller business, where your previously personal telephone has been switched over to both business and personal use, you have to determine which portion is now business-related and which long-distance calls are to your Aunt Minerva. However, an auditor will not usually compare your usage of the telephone now that you are in business to the time when your phone was strictly personal. So estimate generously in favor of business use.

Expenses for Business Use of Your Home
As you learned in the chapter on the underground economy, this is a very hot topic for the 1990's. Before 1991, taxpayers were able to deduct home-office expenses directly on Schedule C. Now all of this is done on Form 8829, a new IRS device/weapon. (For a full discussion of how to obtain the maximum benefit from Form 8829, see page 151 in chapter 7.)

Form 1040, Schedule E (Supplemental Income and Loss)
Another useful schedule that allows taxpayers flexibility regarding the gray areas of deductions is Schedule E, Part 1. This schedule is used to report income or loss from real estate rentals and royalties.

Bear in mind that many of the considerations concerning expenses that taxpayers can place on Schedule C are also appropriate for Schedule E. An expense on Part 1 of Schedule E is fully deductible against rental income. So the IRS is on the lookout for expenses that may be more personal than business and that should rightfully be placed on Schedule A (Itemized Deductions) or some other schedule that, because of the threshold of the deductible, will reduce the expense to a meaningless amount. (See "Legal and Other Professional Fees," below.)

Direct expenses that are deductible against rental income are easy to identify. These include cleaning, maintenance, utilities, commissions, insurance, mortgage interest, and real estate taxes. To give owners of rental property the greatest advantage, the following discussion focuses on items that are subject to interpretation, and how an aggressive position regarding these expenses may be possible.

Auto Expenses
To arrive at the maximum amount that you can deduct as a proper business-related auto expense on Schedule E, you have to ask yourself

some questions that an IRS auditor would ask: Do you use your car to visit your properties? How often? How far is the round trip? Even if you do not run the day-to-day operations, do you drive to a specific location to meet with the managing agent, or sign new leases, or collect rents directly from tenants? Certainly, you would make a personal visit if one of the properties was sold or if you were purchasing a new rental property.

If you answer yes to some of these questions, you can deduct your auto expenses on Schedule E. You can determine how much to deduct by using the mileage method; total up the business miles and multiply by the allowable mileage rate. As usual, to back up your figures, keep a diary of trips associated with the rental property. (See also "Car and Truck Expenses," page 234.)

Travel Expenses

Is your rental property in another state? Many residents of one state have rental properties in another and have to travel there periodically by air to buy or sell a property, or to take care of an existing problem. If you decide to stay a little longer and vacation for a few days, your air travel plus the cost of hotels and meals while you are involved in the business-related activities are still 100 percent deductible against rental income. If your spouse is a co-owner of the property, then his or her expenses are also deductible if she accompanies you.

Keep an accurate diary of your business activities so that you have clear and convincing evidence that the trip was not solely personal in nature. Since a deduction like this is usually substantial, have all expenditures fully documented. Estimates are not appropriate in this situation.

Legal and Other Professional Fees

Sometimes it's hard to differentiate between a fee for ordinary legal services, which is deductible in one year, compared to a fee for legal services in connection with a purchase of property, which must be added to the cost basis of the property and depreciated over a period of years, or in connection with a sale of property when a legal fee decreases the capital gain generated from the sale.

Your attorney may be performing services for you on an ongoing basis and your bill may not provide an adequate explanation of the services rendered. If this is the case, ask your attorney for a bill with the services listed. If you can't obtain a more descriptive bill, take an aggressive position by deducting a reasonable part of the entire bill as being applicable toward your business activities.

Repairs

The cost of repairs to a property used in a trade or business is deductible as an ordinary and necessary business expense. Capital expenditures must be depreciated over a period of years. Generally, improvements, additions, or replacements that extend the property's life or increase its value must be capitalized. How do you determine whether the property value increased or if the property's useful life was extended? You should approach your local real estate appraiser, who may provide you with an appraisal that indicates no change in the property's value, which allows you to write off the entire repair in the current year.

YOUR TAX-SAVING STRATEGY.

If you do not need additional write-offs, the best approach is to capitalize the expenditure (add to the property's cost basis), and depreciate it over 27½ years (residential) or 39 years (nonresidential). That way you avoid a potential argument with an IRS auditor, since a common IRS position is to push for capitalization of large items rather than expense the items in their entirety in the current year.

Form 1040, Schedule A (Itemized Deductions)

If you're not sure about what and how much to deduct on Schedules C and E, a more appropriate place for your expenses may be Schedule A. Relocating expenses from Schedule C or E to Schedule A will probably reduce the items' deductibility because of the many limitations. However, the trade-off is greater peace of mind and a decreased chance that you'll be audited.

The chart below lists the most common expenses taken on Schedule A and explains their limitations.

Typical Expenses on Schedule A Subject to Limitations

Description of Expenses	Location on Schedule A	How It Works
Medical and dental	Lines 1–4	Otherwise deductible medical and dental expenses must be decreased by 7½ percent of Adjusted Gross Income (AGI).

Typical Expenses on Schedule A (Continued)

Description of Expenses	Location on Schedule A	How It Works
Investment interest	Line 13	Deductible only to the extent of net investment income. Unused portion can be carried over to future years.
Contributions by cash or check	Line 15	Donations to public charities are limited to 50 percent of AGI. Unused portion can be carried over for five years. A detailed receipt is required for items $250 or higher.* (see next page)
Contributions other than by cash or check	Line 16	Form 8283 (Noncash Charitable Contributions). If you make noncash charitable contributions in excess of $500, you must include Form 8283 with your return. If the noncash deduction exceeds $5,000, you will also have to include a separate appraisal on the item donated.
Casualty and theft losses	Line 19	Must be reduced by 10 percent of AGI *plus* $100.

Typical Expenses on Schedule A (Continued)

Description of Expenses	*Location on Schedule A*	*How It Works*
Job expenses and most other miscellaneous deductions, including unreimbursed employee business expenses	Lines 20, 21, 22	The total of lines 20 through 22 must be reduced by 2 percent of AGI and the net amount entered on line 26.

*YOUR TAX-SAVING STRATEGY.

The new rule is that cash contributions of $250 or more require a detailed receipt from the charitable organization. Based on this, it was obvious that taxpayers were making these two mistakes: 1. After obtaining the detailed receipt, they were attaching it *to* the 1040. The only requirement is that you actually *have it* when the return is filed. 2. Taxpayers were obtaining detailed receipts if their *total* cash contributions were $250 or higher. You only need the detailed receipt for *single* cash contributions of $250 or higher.

What Wage Earners Can Do

Attention everyone out there who earns W-2 income from a salary: You can receive some of the financial benefits that come from loopholes in our tax laws by relocating income and expense items to Schedules E and C.

To do this, you should try to find a way to create self-employment income. As you know from the Hobby Loss Rule, the IRS is constantly monitoring "businesses" that don't have a profit motive and are carried on as a hobby. So there's no point in creating something that *looks* like a hobby. What I am suggesting here is the creation of a bona fide business that stems from a personal interest.

Some taxpayers actively pursue a hobby that can easily be turned into a business venture. For example, someone I know, Carl Jennings, a high school teacher, loved to tinker with clocks. He decided to put his free time to better use by beginning a clock-repair service. He began to visit local stores that both sold and repaired clocks and informed the store owners that he was "open for business." Three months later, he was so busy he had to turn down new work.

There's no reason why you can't do it too. Follow these guidelines:

1. Develop a new source of income, something you always wanted to do but never did. The tax benefits you will gain should give you plenty of motivation and incentive to pull this together.
2. Set up your new business so you can work when you want to.
3. If the business mushrooms, incorporate as an S corporation.
4. Make your home your full-time place of business where most of your relevant business activities occur and follow the suggestions in this book, which allow you the complete array of home-office deductions.
5. Take out-of-pocket costs, such as supplies and tools that were previously considered personal items, as items fully deductible against your self-employment income.
6. When traveling to suppliers or customers, take deductions for the business use of your auto.
7. If possible, make contributions to a self-employed Keogh Retirement Plan, which will eventually supplement your retirement pay from your nine-to-five pension plan.

Before we leave this discussion of how to achieve full deductibility by using Schedules C, E, or A, there's something you need to be warned about: The IRS is constantly on the lookout for taxpayers who use Schedules C and E to load up on expenses that are not fully deductible elsewhere or not deductible at all. Because expenses listed on these two schedules are fully deductible against income, taxpayers tend to abuse this capability. **As a result, Schedules C and E have become popular audit triggers (C more so than E).** Going too far can get you into trouble. The IRS generally allows reasonable leeway when taxpayers estimate expenses, but you need to avoid crossing the line between a generous estimate of a deduction and downright abuse. Always be prepared with some reasonable explanation for why you have chosen to place your expenses on Schedule C.

Hobby Loss Rule

Also be aware that the IRS is looking for personal expenses that taxpayers disguise as business expenses when they look at Schedule C. One of the most significant measures the IRS uses to assess the distinction between what constitutes a business versus a hobby is known as the Hobby Loss Rule or Provision. (See also chapter 8, pages 196–198.)

Accordingly, the IRS scrutinizes Schedule C's that show large deductions that reduce gross income down to a minimal profit, or produce a net loss. If a business shows a net loss for three out of five years, the IRS presumes that it is a hobby and losses may be disallowed. In this case, it is up to the taxpayer to prove that the activity is not a hobby. Conversely, if a business shows minimal profits in three out of five years, then it is up to the IRS to prove that the business is a hobby. If you can prove a profit motive, then your business expenses will be fully deductible even if they produce a net loss.

Knowing when to be aggressive, especially regarding the opportunities available to taxpayers on Schedules C, E, and A, can save you money *and* hold up against IRS scrutiny.

RULE 5. FILE YOUR PERSONAL TAX RETURN BY APRIL 15. USE AN EXTENSION ONLY IF ABSOLUTELY NECESSARY.

The idea that your return will slip by unnoticed because you file later than April 15 is no longer valid.

Computers are slaves. On April 10, they will process 100,000 returns each day at the same rate as on August 10, when they may process only 5,000 returns.

Some tax professionals argue that workloads are set and returns are selected for audit by the end of August, so if you file in September or October, your return will not be selected for audit. This is a fallacy. **A return can be selected for audit at any time.** Furthermore, if your return contains some unusually large deductions, the chances of its being selected for audit will not diminish simply because you wait until October to file.

Another theory suggests that the IRS likes to review a return for audit potential when it has leisure time. Therefore, if you file four or five months after April 15, you are giving the IRS what it wants—more time to make up its mind about your return.

There are other more substantial reasons why you are *not* well served by delaying the filing of your return. For one thing, hiring a tax professional anytime in April or after is expensive: no doubt 25 to 30 percent higher than normal. This is because the taxpayer must still make a good-faith effort to compute and pay all taxes by April 15 even with the extension form in hand. For the tax professional, the extension requires an unavoidable duplication of effort. The tax professional must first go through all items of income and expense to prepare a reasonable guesstimate. Then weeks or months later, the same job must be repeated in even greater detail.

Also, if you have a refund due, instead of receiving it on time, about six weeks after April 15, you won't receive it until six months after your extended filing date. So you lose four to six months' worth of interest.

Furthermore, for those who pay estimated quarterly taxes, filing late complicates the following year's payments. If you file on August 1, you have already missed the following year's estimated tax due dates of April 15 and June 15. Since you did not have accurate figures to work with based on the previous year's return, you may have underpaid these estimates and be subject to underpayment penalties.

RULE 6. IF YOU ARE INVOLVED WITH IRS PERSONNEL IN ANY WAY, BEHAVE DECENTLY.

When dealing with revenue officers in particular, do not make them angry by complaining about the IRS in general terms, by treating them rudely, lying to them, or insisting that you're being treated unfairly. If you do, they will be more prone to use their arsenal of weapons—liens, levies, seizures, and sales of property—in an arbitrary and capricious manner.

If you receive any correspondence from the IRS, answer it promptly. If you have received a notice of tax due and you do not agree with it, or if you know for a fact that the IRS is wrong, do not disregard the notice or the IRS. Send a letter to the IRS with the notice explaining why you feel the tax is incorrect. If you can't pay the tax, send in a token payment and say that more money will be coming shortly.

This way you are appealing to the human side of the person who reads your response. You can appease that person for a while as long as he or she does not think that you are a renegade. You also have ample opportunity to restate your case to his or her supervisor or to an appeals officer, if you choose.

This is the perfect place for me to reinforce one of the major themes of this book: learning about the IRS personality. Don't forget, with an IRS auditor you're usually dealing with a civil service employee who is just trying to get through the day without making waves. Most often, these IRS staff are not ambitious enough to go through the extra effort required to make life miserable for you. But if you anger them with a poor attitude, they will probably try harder to get the added proof needed to show that you are not telling the truth.

RULE 7. DON'T WORRY ABOUT BEING UNABLE TO INTERPRET OR DECIPHER THE REALLY COMPLEX IRS TAX FORMS. MANY IRS AUDITORS DON'T UNDERSTAND THEM EITHER.

A great deal has been said in this book about the complexity of our tax *laws*. It is no surprise, therefore, that this same complexity characterizes many of our tax *forms*. Here are the most complex ones and what to do about them:

Form 6251 (Alternative Minimum Tax—Individuals)

Computing taxable income is based on either the IRS tax table or the alternative minimum tax (AMT) method. The higher of the two is the tax you pay. **All taxpayers are supposed to compute their taxes on the basis of these two methods.** Determining who is subject to the AMT and who is less likely to be affected by it gets extremely complicated. But if you don't compute AMT you're placing yourself at a risk. Here's why.

The alternative minimum tax method, which was started in the late 1970's, was originally designed to force people with tax shelters to pay additional taxes to balance out the advantage obtained by the enormous losses they were taking. Because the IRS has been voracious in adding "add-on's" over the years, the AMT has been expanded many times. When the concept of passive losses was created in the TRA '86, for example, they became another item on Form 6251 to prevent taxpayers with passive losses from gaining an income tax advantage over those who didn't have them. In essence, the alternative minimum tax functions as a leveling device to ensure that everyone who files ends up paying some income taxes, especially those who are able to reduce their regular taxable income to zero.

To complete Form 6251 using the AMT method, you start with your regular taxable income, then make adjustments on the basis of approximately 20 items. The more common add-on's are personal exemptions, standard deduction (if used), state and local taxes, certain interest expense, part of medical expenses, and passive-activity losses. Then you add on "tax preference" items (about 10 in all), special tax deductions given to a select group of taxpayers many of whom are partners in oil and gas enterprises and real estate investments, whose tax information is passed through via K-1's. If the resulting "Alternative Minimum Taxable Income" (AMTI) exceeds $45,000 for a joint return ($33,750 for single or head of household), then the AMTI is subject to tax at a rate of 26 percent on the first $175,000 and 28 percent on AMTI greater than $175,000.

The entire process is so complicated that each IRS district office has *only* one or two people who know enough about the alternative minimum tax to teach the rules to other tax auditors. **But nowadays the computer does the work for them so if you are subject to the AMT and you didn't fill out Form 6251, you can be sure the IRS** will recompute your tax as submitted on your 1040 and send you a bill for the difference.

Form 8582 (Passive Activity Loss Limitations)

Form 8582 is another terribly complex form—10 pages of instructions—that impacts hundreds of thousands of taxpayers. This form is used by people who have investments in any passive activity, such as oil and gas or real estate. The form measures available passive losses for the current year and the amount to be carried over to future years.

The process of filling out this form is a nightmare. First, data must be gathered from your current year and prior year's returns and grouped into two broad categories: "rental real estate activities with active participation" and "all other passive activities." Then activities with net income must be segregated from those with net losses.

Before reporting the information, you must first complete up to *six* preliminary work sheets preprinted by the IRS that accompany the form. Interestingly enough, the IRS does *not* require that you submit the work sheets with your return, but they must be made available if your return is subsequently examined. You see, unless the losses described on Form 8582 stem from unincorporated real estate activities that you operate yourself, much of the input for these work sheets originates from K-1's that taxpayers receive from partnership and S corporation investments. Remember that the IRS has difficulty matching this part of the K-1 to taxpayer returns.

The form determines the amount of passive losses you can deduct this year and how much has to be deferred to future years. So no matter what, if you are a passive investor, you really must go through this exercise and determine whether you are entitled to any current deductions.

Form 8586 (Low-Income Housing Credit) and Form 8582-CR (Passive Activity Credit Limitations)

Tax shelters may be a thing of the past, but investing in low-income housing increased at least 500 percent in the early 1990's and for 1995 and 1996 has again risen dramatically. Any taxpayer who owns part of a residential rental project that provides low-income housing is subject to two other complex nightmares, Form 8586 and Form 8582-CR. The investment is usually marketed through major brokerage firms, and like any other investment, it has advantages and disadvantages that should be fully researched before you invest.

Taxpayers who qualify and choose to take the low-income housing credit will feel as if they're walking through an endless maze as they embark on the tax computation for it. Most tax credits begin with a base figure that is provided to you from the partnership as listed on Schedule K-1. To this base, you normally apply a percentage, which produces a tentative tax credit. Not in this case. Similar to passive-activity losses, you must first complete three preliminary work sheets to achieve the first required amount of credit.

Two stages and up to *six* more work sheets later, you arrive at the tentative current-year credit, which can be used *only* against regular income tax and not against the alternative minimum tax (AMT). Therefore if you do not plan in advance and you are subject to the AMT, you will lose part or all of the benefit of the low-income housing credit for the current year. In the end, if you add up the tax credit and cash distributions, a good investment will produce a 10 percent return on your investment. Therefore, it makes sense to fill out Forms 8586 and 8582-CR, and take a shot at the credit.

The only plus side to complex forms such as these is this: **If you attempt to complete them, you can be confident that an IRS auditor will understand only a little more than you do.**

RULE 8. STRIVE TO BE NEAT.

I have been telling my clients for years that neat returns, especially computerized ones, are less likely to be audited than handwritten or sloppy ones. Even the IRS has gone on record stating that computerized returns are preferable.

As I see it, computerized returns look more correct than handwritten ones. Today's tax software programs enable computers to produce extremely complicated schedules (e.g., passive losses) instantaneously. The assumption is that computer-prepared returns are less likely to be selected for audit than hand-prepared returns, which often contain errors or are illegible causing them to be selected for further review. Accordingly, a whole new industry has opened up supplying computer software specifically designed for nonprofessional use, such as Personal Tax Edge by Parsons Technology.

There are several other areas where neatness and good organization can and should be applied.

When you have been asked to submit material to a tax auditor, the auditor should be handed well-organized records pertaining *only* to the matter being questioned with an adding machine tape on the top. The more time an auditor spends on your case, the more pressure she is under to collect additional taxes.

Also, when submitting a diary intended to show a detailed log of your travels, be sure that the diary entries are as neat as possible. In most cases, where a diary is being used as evidence, adequate information contained in the diary will, for IRS purposes, support deductions for entertainment, auto expenses, airline travel, auto rentals, hotels, taxicabs, and local travel.

Records should be in perfect order for corporate audits as well. The IRS revenue agent usually reviews corporate records such as minutes, capital stock certificates, stockholder loan agreements, and related promissory notes. When the corporation has made loans, each disbursement should be covered by a separate promissory note and a set of corporate minutes of the meeting in which the loan was authorized, as well as complete details as to the rate of interest and repayment dates.

RULE 9. MAKE IT YOUR BUSINESS TO KNOW WHICH TAX LOOPHOLES APPLY TO YOUR PERSONAL TAX SITUATION.

By now you know that hundreds of loopholes in our tax laws exist. Creating a complete list of these is impossible. Tax newsletters, sent by subscription only, are full of them. Here are some loopholes that one doesn't often see elsewhere. They are arranged by general subject, and if any apply to you, take advantage of them.

You're Facing Bankruptcy

According to the Bankruptcy Reform Act of 1994, taxpayers can file a bankruptcy petition, which must be done with the help of a professional. Although this can be expensive and complicated to execute, here's what it can for you.

It can bring collection activities to a halt. The government cannot issue a notice of intent to levy, nor can the government seize your property and sell it for the payment of taxes.

In our current on-and-off sluggish economic environment, many taxpayers have been falling behind in paying their bills. Ultimately many file for personal and/or business bankruptcy. Since one of the ultimate creditors is bound to be the IRS, there are steps taxpayers can take to ease their burden if they fall on financially hard times.

YOUR TAX-SAVING STRATEGY.
If you are married, you and your spouse should file separate returns. If you file jointly, the IRS can go after either spouse to collect any unpaid tax assessments. If they file separate returns, each spouse is responsible only for his/her own tax liability. This allows at least one spouse to remain debt-free.

The disadvantages in this are that separate return rates are higher and itemized deductions such as mortgage interest and real estate tax can be deducted only by the spouse who pays for them. But with a little forethought and planning, you can end up in a better place if the spouse who earns the highest income pays for these kinds of major deductions.

YOUR TAX-SAVING STRATEGY.
If you cannot pay your taxes promptly and cannot work out an installment agreement with the IRS, your IRA can be seized. Furthermore, when the financial institution holding your IRA pays over the money to the IRS, it is considered a taxable distribution to the taxpayer and subject to a possible 10 percent early-distribution penalty if the taxpayer is under 59½ years of age.

If you feel that the seizure of your IRA by the IRS is imminent, withdraw the money immediately and send in an estimated tax payment representing the income tax and penalty on the withdrawal. You then at least have control over the balance of the proceeds.

You Are Incorporated as a C Corporation and the Corporation Is Discontinued Because of Heavy Losses

YOUR TAX-SAVING STRATEGY.
A shareholder can take the loss of his capital investment on his 1040 as an ordinary loss and not as a capital loss by using Section 1244 of the *Internal Revenue Code*. On a joint return, you can deduct losses from the sale or worthlessness of Section 1244 stock up to $100,000 ($50,000 on separate returns). Any excess above the threshold is a capital loss. This provision is limited to companies whose original capitalization is under $1 million and covers only regular operating businesses, not tax shelters or real estate. Note: There are no disadvantages to using this provision. If your business does well, Section 1244 will be forgotten.

You Are Disposing of Your Entire Interest in a Passive Activity

Any taxpayer in this situation has a wonderful opportunity to take advantage of one of the few possibilities for double tax benefits. To begin with, both current and deferred losses come to the surface and the accumulated losses wipe out any gain you are recognizing on the disposition of the investment. Then the balance of unused losses can be used to offset other nonpassive income such as salaries and interest income. If the gain on the disposition is higher than the accumulated losses, you can use passive losses allocated to other activities to reduce the gain even further, until you reach zero gain. Therefore, if you fully dispos̄ a passive investment, make sure you deduct all the losses that you ar̄ entitled to.

The next part comes into play if the gain on the disposition is a capital gain. If this is so, the gain is both capital gain and passive income at the same time. This entitles you to further benefits. Not only can you take passive losses to offset the passive income, but if you have unused capital losses (because of the $3,000 annual limitation), you can offset these capital losses dollar for dollar against the capital gain as well. For example, if you have a capital gain of $25,000 recognized upon sale of a passive activity, $25,000 in passive losses will be allowed to offset the gain. Because the character of the income is capital gain, up to $28,000 in capital losses, if available, can also be deducted currently.

You Are Drawing Salaries from Two or More Corporations Under One Roof

This situation is referred to as a *common paymaster* because although the corporations may be involved in different businesses, all payrolls are derived from the same source and are usually paid by the same bookkeeper or controller. The taxpayer can take advantage of the little-known common paymaster rule, the privilege of withholding FICA taxes from one salary only.

The general rule for FICA tax is that 6.2 percent of the first $62,700 of salary is withheld for the Social Security portion of the tax, and 1.45 percent of all salary, no limit, is withheld for Medicare. The corporation must match these withheld amounts and remit the total to the IRS. The common paymaster rule cannot be used to avoid reaching the maximum FICA tax, but it can be used to avoid the payment of a double FICA tax. Here's how this works:

Mr. Jones receives annual salaries of $175,000 from ABC Corporation and $150,000 from DEF Corporation. He owns 100 percent of both corporations. Both salaries are paid from the same office location by the same bookkeeper. Using conventional withholding tax rules, the bookkeeper is obligated to withhold 6.2 percent of the first $62,700 from *each* salary ($3,887.40 × 2, or $7,774.80), *and* Medicare tax of 1.45 percent of both salaries—1.45 percent of $325,000, or $4,712.50. The bookkeeper then matches the total of $12,487.30 and remits $24,974.60 to the IRS ratably over the year as the salaries are paid.

When the common paymaster rule is used, ABC Corporation pays the entire $325,000 to Mr. Jones and withholds from his salary the same 6.2 percent of $62,700, or $3,887.40, for just one salary, and 1.45 percent of $325,000 ($4,712.50), a total of $8,599.90. The bookkeeper matches this

l7,199.80 to the IRS. Thus, the common paymaster
saving of $7,748.80 ($24,974.60 − $17,199.80).
reimburses ABC Corporation for its share of Mr.
l taxes. In the end, DEF Corporation receives an
...ng of $3,887.40, representing the employer's share of the
...ax. And Mr. Jones has avoided the double withholding of FICA tax
in the amount of $7,774.80.

You Operate as a Sole Proprietorship or S Corporation and You Want to Hire Your Dependent Child

The major advantage to hiring your dependent child (under 18 years of age) to work in your sole proprietorship is that you don't have to pay FICA and Medicare taxes. (Of course the salary must be paid for actual services rendered.) Remember that the first $4,000 of wages paid is not subject to income tax because that is the standard deduction for single taxpayers. As of 1996, the next $24,000 is taxed at 15 percent.

You and your child can save some additional money if he or she contributes $2,000 to an IRA—for example, to save for college. (Even though taxes and a penalty would have to be paid when the money is withdrawn early—before your child reaches retirement age—the benefit of the current deduction still makes it worthwhile.) Assuming the child's taxable income is not more than $24,000, you will be able to save about $300 on federal taxes, because no tax will have to be paid on the $2,000 paid into the IRA.

This discussion concerns wages, or earned income, of a dependent. Don't confuse this scenario with the "kiddie tax," which is a tax on the investment income (interest and dividends) of children under age 14 and is based on the parents' tax rates. (See discussion on page 214.)

If you pay wages to your children from an S corporation, you must pay FICA and Medicare taxes, because all corporate wages are subject to these taxes. But there is another advantage with an S corporation: You can reduce your tax bill by splitting income with other members of your family. This is accomplished by allowing each family member to own stock in the corporation. Each person reports his or her share of income on the 1040, including children who will probably be in the lowest tax bracket.

Warning: This arrangement works best with children over 14 years of age, who are not subject to the "kiddie tax."

Warning: In this situation, parents/owners cannot take an unreasonably low salary to reduce personal taxable income because if this is discovered during an audit, the IRS can reallocate income among family members.

You Want to Lease an Automobile for
Business Purposes Instead of Buying One

Since TRA '86, annual depreciation for an auto used for business has been greatly diminished. For automobiles "placed in service" in 1996 (any automobile used for business purposes), you can take maximum depreciation of $3,060 for the first year, $4,900 for the second year, $2,950 for the third year, and $1,775 for each succeeding year. These dollar caps are applicable if the automobile is used 100 percent for business.

If you lease a car that has a fair market value in excess of $15,500, you are required to include in your W-2 income an amount specified for that market value in the *Internal Revenue Code*, Section 280F-7. Theoretically this additional W-2 income treats leased autos the same as purchased autos for tax purposes. **In actual practice, though, you obtain a much greater tax savings when you lease an auto, especially if the lease is for at least four years.** For example, if you leased a car in 1996 valued at $27,000 for four years at a rate of $400 per month, over four years you'd pay a total of $19,200. According to the IRS's "leasing inclusion table," assuming the car could be claimed as 100 percent business use, you would have to add back to your income $898 over the four-year period. Therefore, your net tax deduction for the four years is $18,302.

If instead you purchased the car for $27,000, your monthly payments would be considerably higher and the depreciation deductions on your business tax return would be only $12,685. The extra write-off ($18,302 – $12,685) is $5,617, and if you are in the 31 percent tax bracket, this is a tax savings of $1,741.

The only downside to leasing is that if you buy a new car, you can probably use it for seven or eight years. The advantage of leasing is that you get the luxury of driving a new car every four years, along with a substantial business lease deduction that is more advantageous than if you bought a vehicle.

RULE 10: WHEN ALL ELSE FAILS, WRITE TO YOUR CONGRESSPERSON

Almost every congressperson has a contact in the IRS who is dedicated to being responsive to taxpayers. If you have been involved with an IRS issue that just isn't getting resolved, try writing to your congressperson. I have recommended this many times with good results. Typically, someone in the congressperson's office calls, followed by someone in the IRS, and in a matter of weeks the issue gets resolved.

Taking this route, however, has its pitfalls. In your first letter, you must fully document the case so that it is clear and accurate. The congressperson will forward your letter to his or her contact in the IRS.

After this the IRS will treat you strictly according to the letter of the law. The IRS is not particularly fond of this approach because it is both a pressure tactic and leaves them no way to wiggle out. However, this should get you the response you've been waiting for.

To learn the name or phone number of your member of Congress, call the U.S. Capitol switchboard: (202) 224-3121 for Senate inquiries; (202) 225-3121 for House inquiries. Tell the operator your ZIP code and she can give you the phone number of your senator or representative. Give your name, city, and state, and ask for the caseworker on staff.[3]

11

Where the IRS Is (or Isn't) Going and What *to* Do, or *Not* Do, About It

What more comforting gift than a glimpse into the future could someone give to taxpayers who want every assurance possible when it comes to the IRS? An educated look could successfully extend a taxpayer's horizons far beyond the pages of this book. Our journey into the IRS, or perhaps more precisely, our attempt to establish a new approach for taxpayers regarding their relationship with the IRS, now leaves us at the door to the future.

A shift in the IRS's approach appeared likely with the publication in 1994 of *A Plan for Reinventing the IRS*, which defined three goals:

- Increasing voluntary compliance
- Reducing taxpayer burden
- Improving quality-driven productivity and customer satisfaction[1]

THE IRS'S PREVENTIVE MEDICINE

Regarding its operations, the IRS declared that it would

- Reduce paper submissions, with a target of more than 80 million electronically filed returns and electronic payments.
- Start programs designed to increase voluntary compliance from 82.7 percent to more than 90 percent. (Every added percentage point would bring $7 billion into the U.S. Treasury.)

- Employ information systems that give IRS employees instant access to all relevant information, thereby reducing the time it takes to resolve issues and errors.
- Implement a one-stop-shopping approach that allows taxpayers to have 95 percent of their needs met with one phone call.[2] (Currently, at least 40 percent of callers don't get through to the IRS on the first call.)

Two years later, electronic filing has increased, but not as much as the IRS had hoped or predicted. Voluntary compliance, as measured through audit rates, has increased, spurred by amnesty-type measures and new thrusts in examination (financial status auditing and the Market Segment Segmentation Program). The shortcomings of the IRS's Tax Systems Modernization Program, however, are blatant and overshadow the other improvements.

From an organizational perspective, the IRS planned to reduce its 12 computing sites to three super sites, at Martinsburg, West Virginia, Detroit, Michigan, and Memphis, Tennessee, by the year 2000.[3] The IRS also hoped to streamline its record keeping through the use of telecommunications and smaller computers. The new centers would receive and process all electronic and magnetic submissions of tax data, assign work electronically to IRS locations, update taxpayer information, identify possible problems or issues in tax returns, and route them for proper action.[4]

In addition, the 44 IRS locations that have telephone operations (remember the Automated Collection System discussed in chapter 3?) will be condensed into 23 customer service centers modeled after the IRS's current 10 service centers.

This overhaul is the IRS's biggest in 40 years, but before you are lulled into a false sense of security, look at these future trends and see how they will affect you.

FUTURE TREND—ELECTRONIC FILING

When taxpayers hear the term "electronic filing," they usually envision themselves sitting in front of a computer in their home or office, typing in numbers on a 1040 on their screen, making one telephone call, and then transmitting their 1040 directly into the IRS computers. This is not the way it happens.

Electronic filing, which began in 1986, has slowly developed to the point where data is sent in code via a modem to IRS computers, eliminating the task of keyboarding entries. This doesn't mean that these returns are filed by taxpayers themselves, but rather by tax professionals whose equipment and software have been certified by the IRS for performing electronic filing for clients. The IRS will not accept electronic filing directly from taxpayers, and does not expect to do so soon, because it fears it will be flooded with disks and electronic transmissions.[5]

Electronic filing, which became nationwide in 1990, allows taxpayers' federal and state returns to be filed in one transmission to the IRS, which in turn relays the relevant data to state tax collectors.

What to Do About Electronic Filing

Lower Error Rate
The greatest benefit for taxpayers who file electronically is a dramatically lower error rate. Computer-assisted returns are generally far more accurate than those prepared by hand. The accuracy shows up in the mathematics and through general neatness. As a result, the error rate on electronic returns is about 2.8 percent, compared with 18 percent for paper returns.

This is what error reduction does for the average taxpayer:

- It ensures your anonymity.
- It helps you avoid a mismatch and subsequent flagging of your return for review.
- It eliminates the possibility of having your refund check delayed or of your being charged penalties that later have to be rectified.

Faster Refunds
Another benefit for people who file electronically is that a refund may arrive faster, in about three weeks or less. The reason for the time saved is not that an electronically filed return is processed more quickly than a paper 1040, but that the refund may be deposited in a taxpayer's bank account electronically, similar to the way many Social Security payments are made.[6] A check sent through the mail may take six or eight weeks, according to the IRS.

Essentially, electronic filing is just another method for transmitting returns to the IRS. Tax preparers who do a high volume of returns are offering electronic filing for an extra fee. For some clients the extra fee is worth it.

Nationally, the number of electronic returns went from 7.5 million in 1991 to 12.3 million in 1993, a 64 percent increase, and rose again to 13.5

in 1994, an 80 percent increase in 3 years.[7] According to the Statistics of Income office, as of June 21, 1996, the total number of 1040 forms electronically filed was 13.6 million, an insignificant increase since 1994.(It is doubtful that 60 percent of returns will be filed electronically by the year 2000, as the IRS predicts, or 80 million returns by the year 2001.)

The GAO is really pushing the IRS to develop a nationwide strategy for making electronic filing more appealing and available.

The present strategy has resulted in a program that primarily attracts individuals who file simple returns, are due refunds, and are willing to pay the fees associated with electronic filing to get those refunds sooner.[8]Although the record shows that the IRS does not abide by all the GAO's recommendations, there is no doubt that electronic filing will be *the* filing method of the future. As usual, though, while we get there taxpayers will be paying for all this efficiency by having to hire a preparer who has the service, which is costly to set up. Eventually, as a standard technology is established, these costs will level out.

FUTURE TREND—FORM 1040PC

In keeping with the IRS's push to increase the use of electronics, in a onetime effort the 1040 package mailed to taxpayers in 1993 included information about the new 1040PC form. The 1040PC is essentially a condensed paper format of the 1040 that is prepared and printed on a personal computer. To produce the form, an individual taxpayer must have a computer and the willingness to purchase one of the many tax preparation software programs sold in computer stores. The form is not available from the IRS.

The software package will walk you through the 1040 form line by line, so that in the end you have a return tailored to your specific tax situation. This capability often allows a taxpayer to boil a 12-page return down to two pages.

What to Do About Form 1040PC

The 1040PC provides taxpayers with benefits similar to those derived from filing returns electronically: A significantly lower error rate and, for those who are due one, a refund that comes sooner. In addition, the IRS claims that the 1040PC is easier for data transcribers to process and more accurate. These benefits alone make it worth taking advantage of.

The Brookhaven Service Center reported a 300 percent increase in 1040PC returns between 1992 and '93.[9] As of April 8, 1994, 2.5 million taxpayers discovered the 1040PC tax return.[10] The IRS expected that

for the 1994 filing season, six million tax returns woul⟨
printouts prepared on taxpayers' personal computers,[11]
ful thinking on their part. For 1995, however, over 7 m⟨
turns *were* filed, according to the IRS Media Relations Depa⟨⟩

FUTURE TREND—TELEPHONE FILING (TELEFILING)

Initially instituted on a test basis with about 126,000 eligible taxpayers in Ohio, telephone filing was first tried during the 1992 tax season. The experiment was limited mainly to single taxpayers who used Form 1040EZ, earned less than $50,000 a year, claimed no dependents, and had had the same address for two filing years. Six more states tested TeleFiling in 1994 and in 1995 some 700,000 taxpayers in 10 states filed by phone.[12] As of June 24, 1996, according to the Statistics of Income office, 2.8 million taxpayers filed by telephone, an increase of more than 300 percent over the number who filed similarly one year prior.

Currently you can file by phone if you:

- Are single with no dependents.
- Have taxable income less than $50,000.
- Have filed a tax return previously and been at the same address as last year.
- Have a Touch-Tone telephone.
- Do not have more than five W-2's.
- Meet requirements 3 through 7 listed on page 9 for filing Form 1040EZ.
- Have all wages, salaries, tips, and taxable scholarship or fellowship grants shown on W-2's.

The benefits of TeleFiling are these: You receive a refund within two weeks from the date you call; the service is free; and the IRS does the math for you, determining your refund or the amount you owe and if you can claim the earned income credit.

Taxpayers can call toll-free, 24 hours a day. If your tax package was sent to you in one of the following states, call **1-800-829-5166:** Alabama, Connecticut, Delaware, District of Columbia, Georgia, Indiana, Kentucky, Louisiana, Maine, Maryland, Massachusetts, Michigan, Mississippi, New Hampshire, New Jersey, New York, North Carolina, Ohio, Pennsylvania, Rhode Island, South Carolina, Tennessee, Vermont, Virginia, West Virginia. If your tax package was sent to you in one of the following states, call **1-800-585-5345:** Alaska, Arizona, Arkansas, Caliornia, Colorado, Florida, Hawaii, Idaho, Illinois, Iowa, Kansas, Minnesota, Missouri, Montana, Nebraska, Nevada, New Mexico, North Dakota, Oklahoma, Oregon, South Dakota, Texas, Utah, Washington, Wisconsin, Wyoming.

Be aware that you probably cannot use TeleFile if you received any unemployment compensation in 1996.

What to Do About TeleFiling

Telefiling is an advantage to anyone who files a simple, relatively routine return. If you just have earnings from a W-2 and some interest and dividend slips, you should use this simple filing method.

FUTURE TREND—TAXLINK/ELECTRONIC FEDERAL TAX PAYMENT SYSTEM

To increase the use of electronic filing and to reduce the burden on business taxpayers, TaxLink, test-piloted in 1992, has become a reality. Now called the Electronic Federal Tax Payment System (EFTPS), it was enacted as part of the North American Free Trade Agreement of 1993 (NAFTA). Designed to speed the flow of funds to the U.S. Treasury, EFTPS requires employers to deposit federal payroll taxes electronically. The IRS initially predicted that TaxLink could eliminate 80 million paper coupons each year along with the typical problems associated with burdensome paper filing. EFTPS, which is being phased in over several years, could make this come true.

Here's what's new: If you are one of the more than one million employers who were subject to federal payroll tax deposits of $50,000 or more for calendar year 1995, you will no longer be able to make payments using a Federal Tax Deposit coupon. You *must* use EFTPS. You can expect to receive notification from the IRS, and it is best to enroll in the program immediately, since the process may take months to complete. Once you become part of the system, you must electronically pay business taxes owed not only on Form 941 (Employer's Quarterly Federal Tax Return) but also on Form 1120 (U.S. Corporate Income Tax Return), Form 940 (Employer's Annual Federal Unemployment—FUTA—Tax Return), and eight other infrequently used federal business tax returns.

You have three payment options:
1. Call your bank, which debits your account.
2. Call the IRS, which debits your bank account.

3. Use Fedwire, especially for companies required to make large deposits; offers same-day debits.

The starting date for these new EFTPS regulations was on or before January 1, 1997. (See New Tax Legislation for 1996, page 272, for an update.)

NOTE: The penalty for noncompliance is 10 percent for each payment not made through EFTPS.

What to Do About TaxLink/EFTPS

Evaluation of TaxLink is ongoing. But if my clients are good indicators of the reduced error rate and fewer penalties paid each year, the TaxLink/EFTPS system could save business taxpayers millions of dollars annually. Why? It would eliminate all of the time and energy offices like mine spend answering IRS queries regarding inadequate or untimely deposits made with Form 941. We receive more questions from the IRS on this than on any other business-tax area.

FUTURE TREND—INCREASING VOLUNTARY COMPLIANCE

In a genuine attempt to meet its goal of producing a more compliant taxpayer, the IRS has taken several initiatives. It has:

- Changed the rules for Form 4868 (Application for Automatic Extension of Time to File U.S. Individual Income Tax Return).
- Put in place revised approaches for negotiating monies owed.
- Tried to ease the taxpayer's burden through education and tax simplification.

AUTOMATIC EXTENSIONS—FORM 4868 (APPLICATION FOR AUTOMATIC EXTENSION OF TIME TO FILE U.S. INDIVIDUAL INCOME TAX RETURN)

During 1993, the IRS tampered with Form 4868 by allowing an automatic four-month extension from April 15 until August 16 for taxpayers who owed money. As a result, extensions surged from 4.8 million in the 1992 season to 5.5 million in 1993.[13]

Three years later, there's more tampering.

What to Do About Automatic Extensions

With Form 4868 you are forced to make a conscientious effort to estimate your total tax liability by April 15. However, prior to the 1996 tax filing season (for 1995 personal returns), if you submitted less than the full amount of tax you had estimated you owed, your request could have been deemed invalid by the IRS. Therefore, once the completed 1040 was filed, the taxpayer might be facing a rejected extension and a late-filing penalty.

Furthermore, upon rejection you could be prevented from using several important tax breaks when the return is eventually filed. A self-employed person who files late without a valid extension cannot deduct contributions to a Keogh retirement account paid between April 16 and August 15. If you are subsequently audited, any tax assessed will be subject to greater penalties because your return was not filed in a timely manner (no extension).

A recent and *big* change is that the extension will now be deemed valid *even if* you do not pay the balance due by April 15, as long a you make a reasonable, conscientious effort to report on Form 4868 how much you think your total tax liability will be.

If, for example, your estimated total tax liability is $7,500 but the actual amount turns out to be $8,500, the IRS will probably accept your payment with no further recriminations.

What are the benefits of using Form 4868? Despite the new leeway afforded by the IRS, I agree with current professional advice: If at all possible, rather than borrowing the money you owe from the government (by not paying the full tax that is due), borrow it instead from your family, a friend, or a bank. Hopefully the interest rate will be lower, and potential collection efforts should not be as severe.

For a major misconception regarding Form 4868, see chapter 9, page 213.

FORM 1127 (APPLICATION FOR EXTENSION OF TIME FOR PAYMENT OF TAX)

Prior to the IRS's benevolence regarding amounts due with extensions, Form 1127 was used when taxpayers simply could not pay what they owed. Because of the 1993 filing season fluke, the importance of Form 1127 decreased. But who's to say it won't reappear for some future filing season? You'd better know what's in store.

Form 1127 allows taxpayers to file a maximum extension of six months to pay the full amount of tax owed in a onetime payment. This form is *not* about installments. For the IRS to accept this form, taxpayers must, among other things:

- Prove undue hardship.
- Show they will experience substantial financial loss on the day the payment is due.
- Indicate they have no borrowing power except under terms that will cause severe difficulties.

The two major disadvantages to Form 1127 are:

- Taxpayers must disclose their full financial data, so that if you don't fulfill the terms of the agreement, the IRS will know exactly where to attack your assets.
- The IRS requests collateral, such as the deed to your house, on the amount promised. If you don't pay when Form 1127 states you will, the collateral is subject to a lien, seizure, and sale.

If Form 1127 does resurface, I recommend using it only if you are in dire financial straits.

AMNESTY: THE REAL THING?

The essence of tax amnesty legislation is to encourage nonfilers to come forward and negotiate a means to pay or begin to pay what they owe over a period of time without being criminally prosecuted.

The IRS finally took a good look at this situation, and about two months before April 15, 1993, the IRS actually announced some genuine amnesty-type measures for nonfilers based on a new philosophy that it is more sensible to encourage taxpayers to come forward and offer some payment than to threaten them and receive nothing.

Amnesty-Type Vehicles—Offer in Compromise and Form 9465 (Installment Agreement Request)

An *offer in compromise* is used when the IRS agrees to settle for less than the amount owed because it seems unlikely that any more can be collected from the taxpayer. According to the IRS, offers in compromise increased an astounding 377 percent for the first six months of fiscal 1993.[14] Furthermore, the number of compromise offers accepted by the IRS more than doubled in 1992 and the acceptance rate for such offers increased from 25 percent to 45 percent.[15] (See chapter 10, pages

228–229, for a discussion of Form 9465.) As of May 8, 1993, the IRS received some 800,000 9465 forms. In 1994, the IRS approved 2.6 million of these installment agreement requests in contrast to 1991, when only 1.1 million were approved.[16] By comparison, only 4,356 offers in compromise were accepted by the IRS in 1992 which rose to 18,020 in 1993, 25,019 in 1994, and in fiscal 1995 reached 26,668, the latest figures available from the IRS. With the 1996 passage of the Taxpayer Bill of Rights 2, the acceptance rate should accelerate even further because IRS attorneys are getting involved *only* if the amount owed is $50,000 or more, compared to $500 previously.

What to Do About an Offer in Compromise

The question that needs to be asked is "Is amnesty really what is going on?" If you look closely, the IRS never had an amnesty program per se. The word was *initially* passed around but it was quickly dropped, replaced by "nonfiler program." The bottom line, which seems to have hit the IRS right where it hurts, is:

- The IRS wants to get paid what it is owed.
- To realize this, it must encourage nonfilers to come in out of the cold.

Nonfilers do have greater opportunities now to come clean, but taxpayers in this situation should think through any steps before signing installment agreements and locking themselves into strict payment schedules.

FUTURE TREND—REACHING OUT THROUGH EDUCATION AND TAX SIMPLIFICATION

"Simplify taxes" has been a great cry for years from tax professionals and taxpayers. The American Institute of Certified Public Accountants has an entire initiative devoted solely to tax simplification. "Tax complexity is as bad for CPA's as it is for taxpayers," is its motto. Errors and mistakes have become the norm simply because following instructions and doing the right thing are so difficult to accomplish.

Are Simplified Tax Forms for You?

In its effort to move toward simplification, the IRS has included a series of supposedly less complicated forms designed for certain groups of taxpayers:

- Schedule C-EZ for those filing a Schedule C with their 1040.
- A streamlined 1040A and 1040EZ for simplified individual returns.
- An 1120A.
- A proposed single wage reporting system for employers.

As of now these signify just a small start in the right direction.

Schedule C-EZ (Net Profit from Business)

This form is designed for sole proprietors who have gross receipts of any amount and business expenses of $2,500 or less with the following limitations: The cash method of accounting must be used, and the company *cannot have* inventory, a net loss, employees, depreciation, or home-office expenses, and must meet a few other more minor qualifications.

What to Do About Schedule C-EZ

According to the IRS, about 3 million taxpayers can use this new form, a substantial number despite the form's limitations. The major benefit is its ease: You just fill in a single dollar amount of total expenses. Although the audit rate for Schedule C filers has increased for 1993 and 1994, the focus was *not* on Schedule C-EZ filers.

Form 1040A (U.S. Individual Income Tax Return) and Form 1040EZ (Income Tax Return for Single and Joint Filers with No Dependents)

Both of these forms are designed to make it easier for taxpayers by giving them an option to bypass the standard 1040. The 1040A and 1040EZ are both shorter, quicker, and supposedly easier to fill out.

What to Do About Forms 1040A and 1040EZ

They may have been designed for ease of use, but inherent in the design is a laundry list of strict filing requirements. Built-in limitations keep the forms simple. You can't blame the IRS for trying, but you must be aware of the limitations and what they could do to your tax position.

Form 1040EZ has the tightest restrictions. In 1993, it was expanded to include couples filing jointly and in 1995 to include people who received unemployment compensation. But you must

- Have no dependents.
- Be under 65 years of age and not be blind.
- Have a taxable income less than $50,000.
- Derive your income from wages, salary, and tips and have taxable interest income of $400 or less.

- Have total wages not exceeding $62,700 (one spouse's wages) if that spouse works for more than one employer and if you are filing jointly.
- Have no advanced payments of the Earned Income Credit.
- Not take any adjustments against your income such as IRA's or Keoghs.
- Not itemize deductions.

By comparison, Form 1040A allows you to take an IRA deduction, file as head of household, report household employment taxes, and take various other credits such as earned income, child care, and a credit for the elderly. But it, too, has its drawbacks. Most glaring are the directions in the 1040A "Forms and Instructions" package, which are more difficult to read and follow. Even an extensive chart that lists qualifications and limitations to filing the form doesn't help much.

Another drawback to both the 1040EZ and 1040A is that taxpayers are limited to the standard deduction that is based on filing status (single, married, head of household): $4,000 for most single people and $6,700 for married taxpayers filing jointly. Therefore, if you have higher itemized deductions, it is wiser to use Form 1040.

Despite its dramatic technology failures, the IRS claims that "23 million single tax payers who filed 1040EZ in 1995 can file their returns in 1996 with a phonecall, using Telefile, in less than 10 minutes."[17] Generally, both the 1040EZ and 1040A are worthwhile if you prepare your own return. They save you from going over sections that do not apply to the majority of taxpayers and may not apply to you. To determine whether you should use these forms, you first have to decide whether you fit the bill on the basis of the qualifications. If you do, then decide what the trade-offs are by asking, "What, if anything, am I giving up for ease of filing?"

Form 1120-A (U.S. Corporation Short-Form Income Tax Return)

This abbreviated form of the 1120 (U.S. Corporation Income Tax Return) is two pages long instead of four. Nineteen qualifications are listed, the three most important being that gross receipts, total income, and total assets have to be under $500,000. The other 16 rarely come into play for small corporations.

What to Do About Form 1120-A

Basically, this one is simpler to prepare and will make your life a bit easier.

Single Wage Reporting

Currently, employers report annual employee wages on W-2's to numerous state and federal agencies. To eliminate the multiple steps, paperwork, and time it takes for employers to complete a W-2 and send it to multiple agencies, the IRS is working with the Social Security Administration to develop a single wage reporting system.

What to Do About Single Wage Reporting

Over the years, employers have become accustomed to the W-2 format, which is easy to fill out. If the IRS wants to allocate money and slim down the wage-reporting process, there's no harm in it. But perhaps the money would be better directed to something that really needs work, such as K-1 reporting or the multiple reporting formats of 1099-B's. Remember? The ones that brokerage companies mail to taxpayers in any, usually unrecognizable, format they wish.

In any case, as of August 1995, the IRS, the Social Security Administration, and the Department of Labor have created the Simplified Tax and Wage Reporting System (STAWRS). The objective is to reduce the tax- and wage-reporting burden on employers while improving the efficiency and effectiveness of each agency's operations.[18] For 1997, perhaps employers can expect a prototype that will allow them to submit all major reports, such as 941, W-2, and state unemployment insurance, electronically or on magnetic media.

Do-It-Yourself Audits

Several years ago, the IRS decided to test a plan allowing 2,000 taxpayers to audit specific entries on their 1989 returns. A sample of taxpayers was chosen in New England and upstate New York; all reported incomes between $50,000 and $100,000 and had already been chosen for audits.

These taxpayers received correspondence from the IRS that asked them to take another look at their 1989 federal income tax return, which, it seemed, had some items omitted or incorrectly reported. They could spare themselves a visit to an IRS office for an audit by choosing to audit their own returns within 30 days. If they found that additional taxes were due, they were to complete an amended return and remit the money. If they believed that their return was correct, they could choose to take that position. Anyone who ignored the letter would automatically be asked to come to an IRS office for an audit.

What could the IRS hope to achieve with this escapade? A savings of the average $1,295 cost of an audit, shifting the job of auditing to taxpayers, and eliminating the need for an IRS audit while simultaneously allowing taxpayers to examine their returns at a time and place of their choosing.[19] There was one catch: Even if a taxpayer chose to audit, amend, and pay additional tax, that person could still be called in for a face-to-face audit.

What to Do About Do-It-Yourself Audits

The IRS's self-audit scheme failed miserably. Seventy percent ignored the IRS request and two thirds of those who did answer said that their returns were correct.[20] The IRS accounts for this poor response with a wild surmise—behind each of the taxpayers selected for the self-audit program was a tax professional advising them to ignore the request because explaining deductions by letter was just too complicated.

The IRS has dropped the idea of self-audits.

FUTURE TREND—MODERNIZING OPERATIONS

By spending billions of dollars on the Tax Systems Modernization (TSM), the IRS hopes to achieve, among other things, a "one-stop-shopping" service. This would allow IRS staff to make on-the-spot decisions based on information from a computer screen regarding inquiries from over 35 million telephone calls they receive annually.

What to Do About One-Stop Shopping

With the details of your 1040 in front of them, IRS personnel will be able to help taxpayers understand a mismatch notice, a math error, or an overpayment of taxes over the phone. They will also be able to make minor corrections and updates to files immediately. In the past, help was available only at the IRS center where the return was filed, meaning that answers were weeks and months in coming; even minor decisions could only be made by revenue agents and employees further up the ladder. New IRS plans are supposed to give service-center auditors immediate computer access to any taxpayer's account, but, by early 1997, that hasn't happened.

Yes, the thought of having these kinds of tax issues resolved quickly sounds wonderful. But remember, the IRS receives over 110 million phone calls a year.[21] **So how positive do you feel about giving people unfamiliar with your tax situation all the data on a computer screen that they need to make decisions regarding your taxes, especially given the IRS track record?**

In line with the IRS's modernization efforts that allow some 56,000 of its employees access to at least some part of the retrieval system to resolve discrepancies with a single phone call, a recent minor exposé indicated that "more than 1,300 IRS employees around the country were investigated for possible improper use of IRS computers to snoop on taxpayers."[22]

Despite discharges, suspensions, reprimands, admonishments, and counseling sessions, you already know that the likelihood of this problem ever disappearing is probably nil. Is the appointment of a specialist in the Privacy Act and Freedom of Information Act, by Margaret Richardson, commissioner of Internal Revenue under President Clinton, who will act as the IRS's first privacy advocate a consolation?

To be fair, a similar program encompassing details on business payroll tax returns, Form 941 (Employer's Quarterly Federal Tax Return), has been in effect for a few years. This program places on-line account data in front of IRS employees. So when the tax professional or taxpayer calls, the problem is usually resolved then and there. In my experience, this is one program the IRS can be proud of. But all 941s look exactly alike, which will not be the case when the staff begins working with a 1040, where the differences can be staggering. Therefore, we'll have to wait and see if the IRS will be as helpful with this more complex form.

So far, the IRS claims that the Tax Systems Modernization has eliminated more than 900,000 unnecessary taxpayer contacts annually, and will eventually eliminate some 7 million. The estimate is that TSM will save taxpayers and their representatives 5.9 billion hours and at least 1.1 billion dollars.[23]

How will this affect future taxpayers? The key for you will be to try and tune in to a source that keeps you updated about where IRS technology is working and where it isn't. **No matter how spiffy aspects of the technology may be, there will continue to be holes along the tax-processing pipelines.** Tax professionals will be especially familiar with these and will be able to advise clients accordingly.

FUTURE TREND—NEW TAX LEGISLATION FOR 1996

Four separate acts, signed by President Clinton in July and August 1996, contain a wide variety of new tax laws that affect taxpayers on many levels. The four acts are: the Health Insurance Portability and Accountability Act; the Small Business Job Protection Act; the Personal Responsibility and Work Opportunity Reconciliation Act (referred to as the Welfare Reform Act); and the Taxpayer Bill of Rights 2. The almost overwhelming number of topics and caveats tucked into each act has, as usual, a numbing effect on anyone trying to use or make sense out of these new laws. As a result, I have chosen to discuss sections of each act that have the broadest application to taxpayers, as well as to readers of *What the IRS Doesn't Want You to Know*. To find out if any of the very specific tax implications contained in these four acts affect you, or to get more complete information in any one area, you will need to ask a tax pro, or get summaries of the tax laws from your local library.

The Health Insurance Portability and Accountability Act

This section of the new legislation covers tax issues relating to life insurance and long-term care insurance; boosting health insurance deductions for the self-employed; using IRA monies for medical purposes; establishing medical savings accounts; and much more. Here are some of the broader, less intricate tax aspects of the new law.

Boosting Health Insurance Deductions for the Self-Employed

Under the previous law, self-employed people were allowed to deduct 30 percent of their health insurance premiums from their adjusted gross income. The new law increases this deduction to 40 percent in 1997, 45 percent in 1998, 50 percent in 1999, and will ultimately level off at 80 percent in 2006.

This is obviously a plus for anyone owning a business. It also makes for a sweeter package of incentives currently available to the dramatically growing number of small-business owners as well as for those who work at home.

Offering New Tax-Free Life Insurance Benefits

Previously, if a terminally ill person chose to withdraw much-needed money from his life insurance policy in excess of his basis (i.e., usually an amount above premiums paid), that money was considered taxable income. The new law provides that if someone is terminally ill (expected to die within 24 months), the money drawn from that person's life insurance after 1996 is *not* taxable. The provision also allows someone who is "chronically ill" to use life insurance money withdrawn, again, in excess of basis, to provide for long-term care without that money being taxable. Now insurers are free to offer this feature without any doubts as to tax treatment. Best of all, the new law gives significant relief for those in this situation because it provides necessary funds while eliminating the burden incurred if those funds were taxable.

Offering Penalty-Free Withdrawals from IRA's for Medical Expenses and Medical Insurance

Under the new law, you can take early distributions from an IRA without the previous 10 percent penalty as long as the distributions are for medical expenses that exceed 7.5 percent of the taxpayer's adjusted gross income and are used for the taxpayer, the taxpayer's spouse, or dependents. Among other things, the money can be used to hire a nurse, to pay for prescription drugs, and even to purchase eyeglasses, hearing aids, and dentures. These penalty-free withdrawals are available beginning in 1997.

NOTE: The amount withdrawn will be subject to income tax that can be offset by taking a corresponding medical expense deduction if it is itemized on Schedule A (Itemized Deductions).

Early distributions can also be made from IRA's penalty-free to pay for medical insurance for the taxpayer, the taxpayer's spouse, or dependents *without regard to the 7.5 percent minimum of adjusted gross income* if the individual has received federal or state unemployment compensation for at least 12 weeks, and the withdrawal is made in the year the unemployment compensation is received or in the following year.

Setting up Tax-Favored Medical Savings Accounts

In what appears to be an interesting pilot program running from 1997 to 2000, a limited number of self-employed people, and those covered by a small employer's high-deductible or catastrophic health plan, may be eligible for a new item: a medical savings account (MSA). A small employer is defined as having no more than 50 employees during the preceding or second preceding year. Under the program, taxpayers would be allowed to make tax-deductible contributions, with certain restrictions, to an MSA if they satisfy various requirements. Although taxpayers with other health insurance plans generally won't be able to establish an MSA, the law has included some fine-line descriptions (if you have Medicare supplemental insurance, per-diem hospitalization coverage, or if the majority of coverage relates to liabilities incurred under workers compensation, etc.), so check with a tax pro to see if and where you fit in.

Contributions to an MSA for employees are tax-deductible, tax-free, and not subject to payroll tax withholding as long as they are made by the taxpayer's employer and the amount does not exceed the individual's compensation. In the case of the self-employed, contributions are deductible from adjusted gross income and cannot exceed that person's earned income. Earnings on contributions for both employees and the self-employed are tax-free, and amounts could be withdrawn tax- and penalty-free if used for specified medical purposes. The maximum annual contribution is 65 percent of the deductible under the high-deductible plan for individual coverage and 75 percent of the deductible for family coverage. Taxpayers of any income level may take advantage of this deduction, but the number of taxpayers benefiting from an MSA during the pilot period is limited to 750,000 in any year.

Since taxpayers at any income level are eligible for an MSA, and it is free of income tax if paid by your employer, it pays to check with your tax adviser to see if you fit the profile.

NOTE: Unlike flexible spending accounts, where an employee must use the full dollar amount for medical purposes by a certain time or lose it, MSA's do not contain this negative provision.

The Small Business Job Protection Act

The majority of these laws—reinstating tax credits for research, changes to S corporation rules, expansion of home office deductions, new income exclusions for injury or sickness, creation of a simplified retirement plan for small businesses, taxability of punitive damages in personal injury or sickness cases, simplification of pension plans covering the self-employed—are designed for small businesses. Let's look at several significant changes.

Providing Small Business Incentives

MODIFYING SAFE HARBOR RULES FOR TREATMENT OF EMPLOYEES AND INDEPENDENT CONTRACTORS.

What the IRS had previously suggested to revenue agents regarding Section 530 of the Revenue Act of 1978—that they advise taxpayers undergoing a worker classification audit (independent contractor or employee) that the safe harbor rules exist—has now become, in the new law, obligatory. IRS agents *must* inform taxpayers of the existence of the provisions in Section 530.

In another safe harbor change, on a more negative note, a taxpayer undergoing a worker classification audit could previously rely on *any* previous income tax audit to use as an example of worker status. In the new law, a prior audit may be used as proof of status *only* if that audit discussed whether or not the worker was treated as an employee of the taxpayer. The somewhat saving grace is that taxpayers may still rely on the prior audit rule if the audit began before 1997, even if it was not related to employment tax matters.

After years of quibbling about what degree of industry practice could be relied on to prove the necessity of using independent contractors as workers (instead of hiring full-time employees), the new law clearly states that no fixed percentage of the industry in question must be shown, and in no case will an employee undergoing a worker classification audit be required to show that the practice of hiring an independent contractor is followed by more than 25 percent of that industry. This ruling is highly favorable to independent contractors and employers who hire them, because it lowers the percentages necessary to constitute standard practice. In addition, to determine if an industry practice is long-standing enough for the employer to rely on its classification of workers, no fixed length of time is required. The IRS was pushing for a 10-year requirement in this case, but they have been over-ruled—a genuine win for independent contractors and their employers.

In a recent case, a used-car dealer who established that a significant segment of the used-car sales business treated salespeople as independent contractors, rather than as employees, demonstrated a reasonable basis for such treatment. Thus he was entitled to safe harbor relief under Section 530.[24]

And finally, if an employer has established a reasonable basis for treating a worker as an independent contractor, the burden of proof shifts to the IRS to prove otherwise. Now, although this may sound like a major breakthrough, it isn't; the law sets up several conditions, simultaneously stringent yet vague, that leave IRS behavior too open-ended.

In the end, as I have said previously, the establishment of an independent contractor safe harbor is very hard to prove, and these new changes in the law are only designed to provide clearer, more uniform standards to reduce costly litigation.

CREATING NEW HOME-OFFICE DEDUCTION.
The tax allowance that provides deductions for items pertaining to space allocated on a regular basis in the taxpayer's home office has been extended to include storage of product samples. The deduction is available for expenses incurred beginning after December 31, 1995.

This extension is particularly beneficial to businesses whose inventory and samples, because of their size or numbers, take up substantial space.

NOTE: Taxpayers should remember to make a distinction between product samples and inventory, the latter being already allowable in the existing home-office deduction.

Delaying Electronic Funds Transfer Requirement

After all the talk about expanding TaxLink into the Electronic Federal Tax Payment System (EFTPS), where employers who deposited more than $50,000 in 1995 were required to begin using this electronic form of deposit by January 1, 1997, the new tax law has placed a 6-month delay on the process, postponing it until July 1, 1997. It seems that more than meets the taxpayer's and the IRS's eye is required to complete the paperwork, sort out loose ends, and have the technology up to speed to accommodate the estimated 58.3 percent of employers, or 1.2 million businesses, expected to pay withheld income and FICA taxes, their portion of FICA taxes, excise taxes, and corporate estimated payments directly to the U.S. Treasury.

To a large extent the postponement is due to the efforts of the National Society of Public Accountants working with other practitioner organizations and small business associations to get the IRS to realize that the point of readiness for such a major changeover has not, as yet, been reached. The delay allows businesses more time to make their federal tax deposits with traditional paper coupons while they learn more about how the new electronic system works. Although the IRS has already sent the letters and forms needed to enroll in the EFTPS to the affected 1.2 million businesses, much concern has been raised by the national banks coordinating the project and the local banks where clients have their accounts regarding confusing and conflicting information received from the IRS.[25]

The IRS has agreed not to penalize businesses that fail to begin making their deposits electronically by January 1, 1997.[26]

Changing S Corporation Rules

Despite some improvements over the years, restrictions to S corporations remained. Shareholders were limited to 35—individuals, estates, or certain types of trusts; in comparison, other types of businesses have no such limitations. For example, C corporations are not limited in number of shareholders, which can be other corporations, partnerships, and tax-exempt organizations. Another limitation was that S corporations could not own more than 80 percent of another corporation. Also, if a corporation decided to choose or elect S corporation status (see pages 185–193), and an eligibility or timing rule was mistakenly broken during the application phase, the corporation involved was subject to disqualification without being given another chance to remedy the situation and was forced to wait until the following year to refile, this time, hopefully, without error.

These restrictions made S corporations less attractive to investors, created artificial restraints on how day-to-day business was conducted, and, in general, did not properly reflect today's business environment where other forms of businesses operate with greater freedoms.

Some of the areas in the 1996 law that change this situation for the better are:

- Facilitating ownership in an S corporation by family members, employees, venture capitalists, and others by increasing the number of shareholders from 35 to 75, beginning January 1, 1997. Some restrictions on the composition of the shareholders have also been lifted to include, for example, certain tax-exempt organizations such as qualified pension and profit-sharing plans, and certain types of trusts that are used in estate planning. Now an S corporation is not only more attractive for investment purposes, it also offers greater estate-planning opportunities to reduce estate taxes.
- Terminating the previous requirement of waiting up to five years to reelect S status, and replacing it with the provision that any termination of an S election in a tax year beginning before January 1997 will not be taken into account. In other words, a corporation that has chosen not to become an S corporation and then changes its mind will be allowed to reelect S status immediately.
- Permitting an S corporation to own 80 percent or more of a C corporation as well as become an owner of other kinds of business entities, including wholly owned S corporation subsidiaries beginning January 1, 1997.

  NOTE: The subsidiary does not have to file its own corporate tax return but can file a combined return with its parent S corporation. In other words, the parent S corporation can own a "qualified subchapter S subsidiary" that will not be treated as a separate corporation for tax purposes. This opens up the field tremendously for S corporation owners to place separate operations in subsidiary companies with significant tax advantages to boot.

  These new laws make it more beneficial than ever to become an S corporation (see pages 185–193 in chapter 8). Now that S corporation restrictions are being lifted, expect more to follow. This is *not* the right time to switch out of S corporation status.

Changing the Laws Relating to Pensions

ALLOWING FULL IRA DEDUCTION FOR NONWORKING SPOUSES.
The maximum amount allowable for an IRA contribution for a spouse who does not work outside the home had been $250.00. The new law

raises that maximum to $2,000, which makes the contribution equal to the spouse who works outside the home. This provision is effective beginning after December 31, 1996.

SIMPLIFYING DEFINITION OF HIGHLY COMPENSATED EMPLOYEE.
In the previous law, employees who were considered "highly compensated" could not contribute proportionately more to their 401(k) plans than lower-paid workers, because the maximum allowable for a highly compensated employee was a set percent topped off with a dollar limit of $9,500 (indexed for inflation). In other words, the amount that a highly paid employee could contribute was usually less than the $9,500 maximum. The definition of the so-called highly compensated employee was anyone who owned 5 percent of the company, or earned more than $66,000 annually and was in the top 20 percent of a company's earners. To make the situation more just, the new law changes the definition of a highly compensated employee to someone owning 5 percent of the company or earning more than $80,000, allowing the employer to eliminate the requirement that the company use the "top 20 percent" compensation test. This means that anyone earning between $66,000 and $80,000 will probably now be able to contribute the full $9,500 to their 401(k). As a result of this new definition, employers face a reduced administrative burden because they can elect to no longer perform what often amounted to endless calculations for determining their "top 20 percent" earners.

NOTE: This is a particularly complicated section of the law, and if you fall into this category, it is a good idea to check with your personnel department to see exactly how much of your salary you can save in the 401(k). Also discuss this with your tax pro.

Repealing 5-year Averaging
Under the new law, lump-sum distributions from qualified pension plans are no longer eligible for 5-year averaging. But don't think you have to rush to retire to take advantage of the old law. Although the new distribution rules become effective after 1999, the new law has *not* altered that part of the Tax Reform Act of 1986 that still allows the possibility for certain individuals to manage this aspect of their income tax burden by electing 10-year averaging and capital gains for lump-sum distributions. Furthermore, why force yourself into taking a lump sum? Control your own destiny. After age 59½ you can choose to take one fifth, one quarter, one third, etc., each year from your IRA balance, thereby receiving the same benefits as were offered by the 5-year averaging provision.

Changing When to Begin Withdrawals from Tax-Deferred Retirement Accounts

The previous law required that anyone participating in a qualified tax-deferred retirement plan must begin to withdraw the money by age 70½. Under the new law, you can begin to withdraw the money at that age or you can keep your money in the account as long as you're employed, i.e., until you retire. This change does *not* apply to distributions from IRA's. The only exception is for someone who is a 5 percent owner of the company, in which case the money must begin to be distributed no later than April 1 of the calendar year following the year in which that person reaches age 70½.

This is clearly a boon for those tens of thousands still earning salaries who don't need their pension money. Now their money can remain untouched, tax-deferred, and growing. This law becomes effective after December 31, 1996.

NOTE: If you have already elected to begin taking pension money and want to take advantage of the new law, your pension plan will be permitted to stop your distributions until required to do otherwise. Some good advice that anyone can give regarding this new law is to immediately start making careful plans about how you want to take and manage the money.

Offering New Retirement Plans

In an effort to increase the flexibility of retirement plans, the new law establishes a retirement plan for small businesses called the Savings Incentive Match Plans for Employees (SIMPLE). In short, this is a new kind of simplified IRA or 401(k) plan. SIMPLE plans can be adopted by self-employed individuals, and employers having 100 or fewer employees who received at least $5,000 in compensation for the preceding year and who do not maintain another employer-sponsored retirement plan. Employees who earned at least $5,000 from the employer in any two preceding years before the SIMPLE plan was offered and who also are expected to receive at least $5,000 in compensation for the current year are eligible to participate. Employees' contributions, which are generally matched by the employer up to 3 percent, cannot exceed $6,000 per year. The SIMPLE can be adopted as an IRA or as part of a 401(k) salary-deferral plan, and, as such, it involves typically intricate and sometimes confusing rules for employers matching specific sums, vesting, and how contributions and distributions are made, including associated tax implications.

It is important to review the fine print for this plan, but generally it looks like a good incentive for small businesses and their employees. Some benefits for both employees and employers are:

- SIMPLE plans are not subject to the nondiscrimination rules as other qualified pension plans are. This means that the amount of money an individual earns or a person's ownership percentage of a company does not control or limit the amount that person can contribute to the plan.
- Contributions are deductible by the employer and are excludable from the employee's income.
- Contributions are immediately vested, i.e., the money is yours to keep even if your employment is terminated.

NOTE: Unlike other Keogh and 401(k) plans, 40 percent of all eligible employees do *not* have to elect to participate. An employer may establish a SIMPLE even if no employees wish to participate, but the employer *must* notify employees of their right to do so. Generally speaking, this should be an easier plan for employers to adopt and administer, and less expensive as well.

A significant drawback for employees is that if you withdraw money in the first two years, you are subject to a 25 percent withdrawal penalty (on SIMPLE IRA's only), which is 15 percent more than normal IRA's.

For employers, a major drawback is that they must continue to match at least 1 percent of employees' compensation even if the business is doing poorly. There are many other intricate benefits and drawbacks that need to be examined before you make a choice.

The SIMPLE is available after January 1, 1997.

Extending Certain Expiring Provisions

EXTENDING EDUCATIONAL ASSISTANCE EXCLUSION.
Tax relief has been granted for people who receive reimbursements from their employers for educational costs. The tax provision granting an employer the ability to pay for an employee's education, which is deductible up to $5,250 annually on a business return yet is not taxable income to the employee, had expired at the end of 1994. The new law extended that provision retroactively to January 1, 1995. This should prove especially good news for an estimated 800,000 people who receive education assistance from their employers.

NOTE: This provision is again short-lived and scheduled to expire after May 31, 1997. It does not apply to courses beginning after June 30, 1997, or to graduate-level courses beginning after June 30, 1996.

YOUR TAX-SAVING STRATEGY.

Because the educational assistance provision expired at the end of 1994, many employees were paid this benefit during 1995, and the amounts were added to their W-2 wages as taxable income, since at that time the benefit was *not* tax-free. With the new law, if workers included educational assistance on their personal returns for 1995, they should file amended returns. This will enable them to receive refunds of income taxes, Social Security taxes, and Medicare taxes. Employers must file corrected W-2 forms and provide copies to affected employees. Employers are also entitled to receive refunds on their 1995 Social Security and Medicare taxes. The employer should follow a similar procedure to receive refunds on 1996 federal payroll taxes.

Providing Tax Breaks for Adoptions

A nonrefundable tax credit of up to $5,000 of qualified adoption expenses for both domestic and foreign adoptions can be taken by taxpayers who adopt an "eligible adoptee," who is, according to the IRS, someone under 18, or someone who cannot care for himself or herself either physically or mentally. For an adoptee with special needs, further defined in the law, the credit can be increased to $6,000. The credit is reduced for taxpayers with adjusted gross incomes above $75,000 and is not available for those with incomes over $115,000.

Repealing Exclusion of Employer-Provided Death Benefits

The $5,000 exclusion for death benefits provided by an employer has been repealed in the new law. This means that the estate or beneficiary of a deceased employee can no longer exclude up to $5,000 in benefits paid by or on behalf of an employer. That amount will now be considered taxable income in the hands of the recipient.

The Personal Responsibility and Work Opportunity Reconciliation Act (Welfare Reform Act)

Although this act is designed to reform welfare through broad cash grants made available to the states, it also encompasses child protection and child care programs, foster care, adoption assistance, and food stamp distribution. An essential tax aspect of the act pertains to the Earned Income Credit.

Tightening Restrictions on the Earned Income Credit

The Welfare Reform Act requires that anyone applying for the Earned Income Credit (EIC) must use a taxpayer identification number (TIN), i.e., a Social Security number, on the return. If the applicant is married, the spouse's TIN must also be included. This requirement aims to deny the EIC to anyone not authorized to be employed in the United States. This provision becomes effective for returns due 30 days after the enactment of the Welfare Reform Act.

Two other restrictions concern disqualified income (taxable and tax-exempt interest, dividends, rent and royalties) and adjusted gross income. Under the new law, an individual is *not* eligible for the EIC if disqualified income exceeds a certain amount, and that threshold has been lowered from $2,350 to $2,200. Further tightening comes from a new definition of disqualified income expanded to include capital gains and passive income (e.g., tax shelters, rents). It would appear that a person receiving income from interest, dividends, rent, and royalties is not one who fits the EIC profile.

In addition, certain losses that a taxpayer could once apply to lower his adjusted gross income to qualify for the EIC have been disallowed. Some of these include capital losses, losses from trusts and estates, and nonbusiness rents and royalties. The disqualified income and AGI provisions are effective after December 31, 1996.

Clearly, Congress is tightening the reins on the money it had heretofore been almost happy to give away under the EIC.

The Taxpayer Bill of Rights 2 (TBOR2)

From considerable struggles to heady politicking, which characterized the rather arduous passage of the first Taxpayer Bill of Rights, with Public Law 104-168 (or the TBOR2) taxpayers have working for them a substantial piece of tax legislation. It provides over 40 pro-taxpayer rights to, hopefully (only time will tell), level the playing field between taxpayers and the IRS. These are the most significant provisions:

- *Instituting a Taxpayer Advocate.* A taxpayer advocate (TA) to help taxpayers "expeditiously resolve problems" with the IRS will replace the taxpayer ombudsman. The TA, appointed by and reporting directly to the IRS commissioner, has broad authority to modify or rescind taxpayer assistance orders and to intervene and take positive action for taxpayers who would otherwise suffer significant hardship, including help with refunds, because of the way the IRS is administering tax laws.
- *Expediting Offers in Compromise.* Allows the IRS to more easily expedite an offer in compromise if the taxpayer cannot pay the full tax, the IRS cannot collect the tax, or the liability itself is doubtful. Prior to this act, if a taxpayer owed over $500, the payment could be accepted only if the reasons for acceptance were documented

in detail and supported by the IRS chief counsel's opinion. TBOR2 increased the chief counsel review threshold to $50,000, effective on the date of enactment, which should dramatically facilitate the process of accepting offers in compromise.

- *Shifting Burden of Proof to the Government for Attorney's Fees.* TBOR2 switches the burden of proof to the IRS to show that its position was justified in an action by a taxpayer for attorney's fees and litigation costs. Key here is that the IRS will not be considered justified if it does not follow procedure as published in its regs, revenue rulings, revenue procedures, information releases, private letter rulings, etc.
- *Increasing Limit on Civil Damages.* Prior to TBOR2, a taxpayer victimized by "reckless" collection action could sue the government for damages caused by an officer or employee of the IRS for up to $100,000. The new law increases this limit to $1,000,000.
- *Modifying Installment Agreements.* The IRS must now notify taxpayers at least 30 days before altering, modifying, or terminating an installment agreement for any reason except when tax collection is in jeopardy. Taxpayers can use the time to challenge IRS actions. This provision will be effective January 30, 1997.
- *Waiving a Penalty for Payroll Tax Deposit.* A waiver of penalty for inadvertently failing to make payroll tax deposits is now possible under certain conditions: if the depositing entity is a small business, i.e., an individual whose net worth is not over $2 million at the time the act was filed, an organization whose net worth is not over $7 million and that doesn't have more than 500 employees, according to the Equal Access to Justice Act; if the failure to deposit takes place during the first quarter that employment tax deposits were required; if the employment tax return was filed on time. The penalty can also be abated if a first-time depositor inadvertently sends the deposit to the IRS instead of to the required government depository.
- *Switching from Separate to Joint Filing Without Full Tax Payment.* The requirement that full payment of tax must be paid before the expiration of the three-year period for making an election to file jointly, as a precondition to switching from separate to joint filing status, has been repealed. This represents a savings for those who, after filing separately, determine that they would pay less tax by filing jointly.
- *Disclosing Collection Activities for Joint Filers.* If a tax deficiency is assessed on a joint return and the filers are divorced or not living together, the IRS is now required to disclose in writing,

in response to a written request by one of the individuals, whether attempts are being made to collect from either spouse, the nature of the collection activities, and the amount collected.

- *Studying Joint Return Issues of Separated and Divorced.* The Department of the Treasury and the General Accounting Office are to conduct detailed studies examining possible changes to the joint and several liability standard* in order to better protect the rights of separated or divorced couples. It is hoped that this small step in the right direction will do away with the "innocent spouse syndrome," where the tax burdens of a philandering spouse are placed upon the spouse who may or may not have known that tax and penalties were being incurred.

- *Modifying "Responsible Person" Penalty Rules for Payroll Tax Penalties.* The IRS is now required to notify a person it has identified as the "responsible person" (one who is responsible for paying certain FICA and withholding taxes in a timely manner to the IRS) at least 60 days before contacting that person for taxes and penalties owed. Previously, the IRS could contact a person without any notice and collect 100 percent from *any* "responsible person" without bothering to go after other guilty culprits. (This is similar to where the IRS can still go after an innocent spouse for all the tax and penalties incurred and owed by that spouse's guilty partner on a joint return.) The new law also requires that the IRS must disclose the identity of others deemed responsible for not paying payroll taxes to the IRS to those already identified as culpable. The IRS must also commence an action against the other responsible parties to pay their share of the amounts owed. This new law could ensure, for example, that a low-salaried employee who was deemed by the IRS to be the "responsible person" doesn't take the fall for the head of a company who may be the real culprit. A step in the right direction, to say the least.

- *Increasing Levy Exemption.* The amount the IRS *cannot* levy against a taxpayer has been increased from $1,650 to $2,500 for personal property, and from $1,100 to $1,250 for books and business tools as indexed for inflation, starting in 1997. This allows taxpayers who owe money to keep a little more for themselves.

- *Extending Payment of Tax.* The interest-free period for a delinquent tax payment of less than $100,000 (includes taxes, penalties, additional amounts or additions to tax for which interest is im-

---

*If a spouse has a tax liability, the IRS can collect the *full* amount from *either* party if a joint return is filed.

posed) has been extended from 10 to 21 calendar days. The new law applies to notices issued after 1996.

- *Private Delivery Service.* At last the IRS has caught up with the times (at least regarding private delivery services) by allowing taxpayers to use services like Federal Express to prove timely filing of returns. Expect an approved list of carriers, published by the IRS, to follow.

No doubt by the time this third edition of *What the IRS Doesn't Want You to Know* is published, we will be hearing a great deal about these changes, plus the other, more specialized laws also included in this 1996 tax package.

IRS DOWNSIZING

Additional late-breaking news to appear just before this book went to press was the announcement of a substantial downsizing facing the IRS. Based on the imminent IRS budget cuts, already discussed, the loss of 5,000 IRS employees was not shocking. Projections show approximately 2,400 national office positions disappearing and the remainder of the reduction occurring in the field.[27] I would hesitate a guess that given the deliberate increase made in audits, revenue agents and tax auditors need not worry about losing their jobs.

IRS USING PRIVATE TAX COLLECTORS

In a one-year pilot program aimed at bringing in some of the $200 billion owed the government, the IRS has just hired five private collection firms to go after 125,000 tax truants in 13 western states.[28] But the prognosis doesn't look good. In a 1996 study of a similar program, the Federation of Tax Administrators, a group of state tax officials, reported that only a third of the 30 states with private collection programs were successful. And according to a previous report issued in 1994 by the General Accounting Office, of the 24 states that hired firms, only about 6 percent of outstanding tax payments were recovered.[29] Keep an eye out for legislation on this issue currently being pushed by the House.

In my opinion, no one has the clout that the IRS has, and given the fact that many of the cases the private collectors have been handed are up to 10 years old, that's another strike against success. But heck, it's only taxpayer money, so we should probably be cheering the new hires on.

THE IRS AND THE INTERNET

Did you know that just like many other businesses in this age of on-line services, the IRS, too, has a website? In August 1996, it announced that it intends to enhance its offerings on the information superhighway: the *Internal Revenue Manual* (I tend to think this doubtful, but perhaps some sections may appear. See my *Internal Revenue Manual* saga, page 114); its Market Segment Specialization Program Audit Technique Guides (see pages 53–54 and 172–174); a database of tax-exempt organizations; news from local IRS offices; and a downloadable tax calendar showing due dates for various forms.[30]

FUTURE TREND—A HUMANIZED IRS

By delving into the reasons why taxpayers don't comply with income tax laws, the IRS has not only grasped but simultaneously admitted what tax professionals have believed all along: The majority of taxpayers want to file their income taxes correctly, but complex laws, badly designed forms, indecipherable instructions, and an adversarial relationship with those to whom those taxes are being paid stand in their way.

What to Do About the Humanized IRS

There is no way to determine whether the quintessential IRS personality is going to disappear in the process of rethinking, reshaping, and enhancing the operation and the organization. To be a success, every IRS employee must be trained in the principles espoused for Compliance 2000. This would require tremendous funding and an enormous feat of superb management and organizational skills. We are talking about key information filtering down to 106,000 employees across the nation so that all receive and absorb the same message for the most part.

The IRS admits "that change can be difficult. We are preparing our workforce for the enormous challenge that lies ahead and the substantial changes that will occur in the nature of our work. We are committed to providing all employees with the information, training and tools they will need to perform the jobs of the future."[31]

All of this sounds and may be well and good. **However, the single biggest fault I have seen regarding IRS policies is its inability to bring national policies down to the grassroots of its own organization.**

Even if this could be done, teaching principles is not the same as changing attitudes. How will the 20-year IRS professional respond to this dosage of healthy thinking? With cooperation or sabotage? Holding on to the way it's always been and dealing with taxpayers accordingly is too easy a path to take, especially in an organization that has not only abhorred but also battled change throughout its history.

Two programs that have succeeded in the IRS's new and friendly approach are the offers in compromise and the installment agreements. Perhaps in these two areas, something is going right so that IRS employees are treating taxpayers consistently and fairly. But even though the increase in offers in compromise is dramatic, too many of them are still turned down on the judgment or whim of an IRS employee.

The power IRS employees have as a result of decentralization will continue to have a very real impact on any future IRS plans. The size of the organization and the fact that substantial power is divided among so many leads to an ongoing inadequacy, visibly evident throughout its entire history: **IRS employees who deal directly with taxpayers have proved incapable of achieving a consistent standard for administering IRS policies fairly and effectively.**

Even upper-echelon policy-makers are unable to find a way to ensure that policies are carried out in an evenhanded manner.

Closely related to the difficulties in presenting a consistent operating ethic is another major problem: the lack of uniformity in the behavior of revenue officers. Some are cooperative while others are threatening and immediately fill the citizen with a sense of foreboding. Such officers fail miserably in carrying out the IRS's national policy of recognizing the rights of all taxpayers.

Studies and data have always borne out the high degree of compliance among American taxpayers. Using cooperation and honey instead of threats to shape a more compliant taxpayer is, perhaps, just beginning to catch on at the most senior IRS levels. The question is, will these new attitudes ever filter down whole and intact or will they be distorted—proving again the vulnerabilities of the IRS?

HAS ANYTHING REALLY CHANGED?

Despite the fact that many of these IRS advances are positive and decent-sounding, do not for a moment think that you are looking at a complete about-face. The IRS knows that cheaters will never disappear from the tax rolls. For each transgression, the IRS has and will continue to have a set penalty. In 1995, from the tardy, the negligent, and the fraudulent, the IRS exacted 19.6 million penalties, worth over $3.3 billion.[32] These are civil penalties alone. Make no mistake, the IRS has no plans to shrink its Examination, CID, or even internal security divisions. Enforcement will still be the name of the game.

For the majority of taxpayers, those of us who want to comply honestly, the signs coming from IRS national headquarters regarding changes in attitudes, solid new programs, and what appears to be a genuine reaching out and desire to improve are positive. These signs, which are no small feat for the IRS, signify some measure of a breakthrough and, in some cases, a break for taxpayers.

But—and it's a large but—despite some good intentions and initiatives backing it up, the IRS is still so weighted down with the enormity of its job (which isn't going to change) and the lack of strong, effective internal management, that too much gets stymied along the way. Watch the IRS continue to plod along with budget cuts, reduced manpower, an inevitable new commissioner every four-odd years, and almost nonstop reorganizations. (Call up the IRS and ask for an organization chart; you'll have a hard time finding anyone who knows where the latest one is.)

Then, of course, there's the matter of deciphering the 1996 tax laws embedded in the Health Insurance Portability and Accountability Act, the Small Business Job Protection Act, and the Personal Responsibility and Work Opportunity Reconciliation Act (the Welfare Reform Act). Typically, as with all new tax laws, it will take professionals, practitioners, IRS personnel, and taxpayers from several months to two or more years for the tax implications of these laws to trickle down to the level of understanding so that they can be used for their intended purposes. We'll find some items new and different and better than before; we'll find some items new and different and worse or more complicated; and there will be other, bigger items that will be just that—big—without being different from previous years except for a new name or a change in a small clause. Most of the material will be revealed over time, and with professionals working it out for taxpayers.

Now for the Taxpayer Bill of Rights 2. Stay carefully tuned to the IRS's reaction. TBOR2 continues to offer encouragement for the IRS to clean up some of its act. Will old-line attitudes and behavior resist, or will the more recent efforts aimed at cooperating with the business community and taking suggestions from professional accounting organizations prevail?

Glaring bungles in its technology program, which have squandered billions of taxpayer dollars, and its steadily lagging ability to make available to the public timely statistics of its operations should leave us with sufficient ill will, concern, and even anger as to why the IRS isn't structured, organized, and led to accomplish a great deal more. To end on a happier note, since the first edition of this book was written, over three years ago, it can be said that there appears to be a positive shift in the IRS's behavior and attitude that lets taxpayers know, as does a cool breeze on a hot day, that relief is possible—though sporadic.

APPENDIXES

Appendix A: Most Important Tax Forms
Discussed in This Book
Appendix B: Guide to Free Tax Services
Appendix C: Your Rights as a Taxpayer
(Taxpayer Bill of Rights)
Appendix D: Practitioner Hot Line Telephone
Numbers

APPENDIX A: MOST IMPORTANT
TAX FORMS
DISCUSSED IN THIS BOOK

The IRS forms included in this book are for reference purposes only. If you need a specific form, it is best to obtain it and the accompanying instructions directly from the IRS. Call the taxpayer assistance telephone number for your area (listed in Appendix B, page 386).

Almost all IRS tax forms remain identical from year to year, except that a new year is printed on the form. All forms shown are dated 1994 or 1995.

Form **1040**

Department of the Treasury—Internal Revenue Service
U.S. Individual Income Tax Return (0) 19**95**

IRS Use Only—Do not write or staple in this space.

For the year Jan. 1–Dec. 31, 1995, or other tax year beginning _____ , 1995, ending _____ , 19 ___ | OMB No. 1545-0074

Label

(See instructions on page 11.)

Use the IRS label. Otherwise, please print or type.

L A B E L H E R E

Your first name and initial | Last name | **Your social security number**

If a joint return, spouse's first name and initial | Last name | **Spouse's social security number**

Home address (number and street). If you have a P.O. box, see page 11. | Apt. no.

City, town or post office, state, and ZIP code. If you have a foreign address, see page 11.

For Privacy Act and Paperwork Reduction Act Notice, see page 7.

Presidential Election Campaign (See page 11.)

Yes | No | Note: Checking "Yes" will not change your tax or reduce your refund.

Do you want $3 to go to this fund? . . . .
If a joint return, does your spouse want $3 to go to this fund? . . . . .

Filing Status

(See page 11.)

Check only one box.

1 | Single
2 | Married filing joint return (even if only one had income)
3 | Married filing separate return. Enter spouse's social security no. above and full name here. ▶ _____
4 | Head of household (with qualifying person). (See page 12.) If the qualifying person is a child but not your dependent, enter this child's name here. ▶ _____
5 | Qualifying widow(er) with dependent child (year spouse died ▶ 19___). (See page 12.)

Exemptions

(See page 12.)

If more than six dependents, see page 13.

6a | ☐ **Yourself.** If your parent (or someone else) can claim you as a dependent on his or her tax return, **do not** check box 6a. But be sure to check the box on line 33b on page 2
b | ☐ **Spouse** . . . .

No. of boxes checked on 6a and 6b

c | **Dependents:**

(1) First name Last name	(2) Dependent's social security number. If born in 1995, see page 13.	(3) Dependent's relationship to you	(4) No. of months lived in your home in 1995

No. of your children on 6c who:

• lived with you
• didn't live with you due to divorce or separation (see page 14)

Dependents on 6c not entered above

d | If your child didn't live with you but is claimed as your dependent under a pre-1985 agreement, check here ▶ ☐
e | Total number of exemptions claimed

Add numbers entered on lines above ▶

Income

Attach Copy B of your Forms W-2, W-2G, and 1099-R here.

If you did not get a W-2, see page 14.

Enclose, but do not attach, your payment and payment voucher. See page 33.

7 | Wages, salaries, tips, etc. Attach Form(s) W-2 . . . . | 7
8a | **Taxable** interest income (see page 15). Attach Schedule B if over $400 . . | 8a
b | Tax-exempt interest (see page 15). DON'T include on line 8a | 8b
9 | Dividend income. Attach Schedule B if over $400 . . . . . . | 9
10 | Taxable refunds, credits, or offsets of state and local income taxes (see page 15) . | 10
11 | Alimony received . . . . | 11
12 | Business income or (loss). Attach Schedule C or C-EZ . . . . . | 12
13 | Capital gain or (loss). If required, attach Schedule D (see page 16) . . | 13
14 | Other gains or (losses). Attach Form 4797 . . . . | 14
15a | Total IRA distributions . | 15a | b Taxable amount (see page 16) | 15b
16a | Total pensions and annuities | 16a | b Taxable amount (see page 16) | 16b
17 | Rental real estate, royalties, partnerships, S corporations, trusts, etc. Attach Schedule E | 17
18 | Farm income or (loss). Attach Schedule F . . . . | 18
19 | Unemployment compensation (see page 17) . . . . | 19
20a | Social security benefits | 20a | b Taxable amount (see page 18) | 20b
21 | Other income. List type and amount—see page 18 . . . . | 21
22 | Add the amounts in the far right column for lines 7 through 21. This is your **total income** ▶ | 22

Adjustments to Income

23a | Your IRA deduction (see page 19) . . . . . | 23a
b | Spouse's IRA deduction (see page 19) . . . . . | 23b
24 | Moving expenses. Attach Form 3903 or 3903-F . . . | 24
25 | One-half of self-employment tax . . . . . . | 25
26 | Self-employed health insurance deduction (see page 21) | 26
27 | Keogh & self-employed SEP plans. If SEP, check ▶ ☐ | 27
28 | Penalty on early withdrawal of savings . . . . . | 28
29 | Alimony paid. Recipient's SSN ▶ _____ | 29
30 | Add lines 23a through 29. These are your **total adjustments** . . . . ▶ | 30

Adjusted Gross Income

31 | Subtract line 30 from line 22. This is your **adjusted gross income.** If less than $26,673 and a child lived with you (less than $9,230 if a child didn't live with you), see "Earned Income Credit" on page 27 ▶ | 31

Cat. No. 11320B

Form **1040** (1995)

Tax Computation

(See page 23.)

32	Amount from line 31 (adjusted gross income)	32
33a	Check if: ☐ **You** were 65 or older, ☐ Blind; ☐ **Spouse** was 65 or older, ☐ Blind. Add the number of boxes checked above and enter the total here . . . . ▶ 33a	
b	If your parent (or someone else) can claim you as a dependent, check here . ▶ 33b ☐	
c	If you are married filing separately and your spouse itemizes deductions or you are a dual-status alien, see page 23 and check here. . . . . ▶ 33c ☐	

34 Enter the larger of your:
Itemized deductions from Schedule A, line 28, **OR**
Standard deduction shown below for your filing status. **But if you checked any box on line 33a or b,** go to page 23 to find your standard deduction. If you checked **box 33c,** your standard deduction is zero.
- Single—$3,900   • Married filing jointly or Qualifying widow(er)—$6,550
- Head of household—$5,750   • Married filing separately—$3,275

		34
35	Subtract line 34 from line 32	35
36	If line 32 is $86,025 or less, multiply $2,500 by the total number of exemptions claimed on line 6e. If line 32 is over $86,025, see the worksheet on page 23 for the amount to enter .	36
37	**Taxable income.** Subtract line 36 from line 35. If line 36 is more than line 35, enter -0-	37

If you want the IRS to figure your tax, see page 35.

38	Tax. Check if from a ☐ Tax Table, b ☐ Tax Rate Schedules, c ☐ Capital Gain Tax Worksheet, or d ☐ Form 8615 (see page 24). Amount from Form(s) 8814 ▶ e _____	38
39	Additional taxes. Check if from a ☐ Form 4970 b ☐ Form 4972	39
40	Add lines 38 and 39 . . . . ▶	40

Credits

(See page 24.)

41	Credit for child and dependent care expenses. Attach Form 2441 .	41
42	Credit for the elderly or the disabled. Attach Schedule R . .	42
43	Foreign tax credit. Attach Form 1116	43
44	Other credits (see page 25). Check if from a ☐ Form 3800 b ☐ Form 8396 c ☐ Form 8801 d ☐ Form (specify) _____	44
45	Add lines 41 through 44	45
46	Subtract line 45 from line 40. If line 45 is more than line 40, enter -0- . . . ▶	46

Other Taxes

(See page 25.)

47	Self-employment tax. Attach Schedule SE	47
48	Alternative minimum tax. Attach Form 6251	48
49	Recapture taxes. Check if from a ☐ Form 4255 b ☐ Form 8611 c ☐ Form 8828 .	49
50	Social security and Medicare tax on tip income not reported to employer. Attach Form 4137	50
51	Tax on qualified retirement plans, including IRAs. If required, attach Form 5329 .	51
52	Advance earned income credit payments from Form W-2	52
53	Household employment taxes. Attach Schedule H	53
54	Add lines 46 through 53. This is your **total tax** . . . . ▶	54

Payments

Attach Forms W-2, W-2G, and 1099-R on the front.

55	Federal income tax withheld. If any is from Form(s) 1099, check ▶ ☐	55
56	1995 estimated tax payments and amount applied from 1994 return .	56
57	**Earned income credit.** Attach Schedule EIC if you have a qualifying child. Nontaxable earned income: amount ▶ _____ and type ▶ _____	57
58	Amount paid with Form 4868 (extension request)	58
59	Excess social security and RRTA tax withheld (see page 32)	59
60	Other payments. Check if from a ☐ Form 2439 b ☐ Form 4136	60
61	Add lines 55 through 60. These are your **total payments** . . . . ▶	61

Refund or Amount You Owe

62	If line 61 is more than line 54, subtract line 54 from line 61. This is the amount you **OVERPAID.** . .	62
63	Amount of line 62 you want **REFUNDED TO YOU.** . . . . ▶	63
64	Amount of line 62 you want **APPLIED TO YOUR 1996 ESTIMATED TAX** ▶ 64	
65	If line 54 is more than line 61, subtract line 61 from line 54. This is the **AMOUNT YOU OWE.** For details on how to pay and use **Form 1040-V,** Payment Voucher, see page 33 . . ▶	65
66	Estimated tax penalty (see page 33). Also include on line 65 66	

Sign Here

Keep a copy of this return for your records.

Under penalties of perjury, I declare that I have examined this return and accompanying schedules and statements, and to the best of my knowledge and belief, they are true, correct, and complete. Declaration of preparer (other than taxpayer) is based on all information of which preparer has any knowledge.

Your signature	Date	Your occupation
▶		
Spouse's signature. If a joint return, BOTH must sign.	Date	Spouse's occupation
▶		

Paid Preparer's Use Only

Preparer's signature ▶	Date	Check if self-employed ☐	Preparer's social security no.
Firm's name (or yours if self-employed) and address ▶		EIN	
		ZIP code	

✿ **Printed on recycled paper**

*U.S. Government Printing Office: 1995 - 389-188

SCHEDULES A&B (Form 1040) Department of the Treasury Internal Revenue Service (O)	**Schedule A—Itemized Deductions** (Schedule B is on back) ▶ Attach to Form 1040. ▶ See Instructions for Schedules A and B (Form 1040).	OMB No. 1545-0074 19**95** Attachment Sequence No. **07**

Name(s) shown on Form 1040 | Your social security number

Medical and Dental Expenses		Caution: *Do not include expenses reimbursed or paid by others.*		
	1	Medical and dental expenses (see page A-1)	1	
	2	Enter amount from Form 1040, line 32. 2		
	3	Multiply line 2 above by 7.5% (.075)	3	
	4	Subtract line 3 from line 1. If line 3 is more than line 1, enter -0-		4
Taxes You Paid (See page A-1.)	5	State and local income taxes	5	
	6	Real estate taxes (see page A-2)	6	
	7	Personal property taxes	7	
	8	Other taxes. List type and amount ▶ _____	8	
	9	Add lines 5 through 8		9
Interest You Paid (See page A-2.)	10	Home mortgage interest and points reported to you on Form 1098	10	
	11	Home mortgage interest not reported to you on Form 1098. If paid to the person from whom you bought the home, see page A-3 and show that person's name, identifying no., and address ▶		
Note: Personal interest is not deductible.	11	_____	11	
	12	Points not reported to you on Form 1098. See page A-3 for special rules	12	
	13	Investment interest. If required, attach Form 4952. (See page A-3.)	13	
	14	Add lines 10 through 13		14
Gifts to Charity If you made a gift and got a benefit for it, see page A-3.	15	Gifts by cash or check. If you made any gift of $250 or more, see page A-3	15	
	16	Other than by cash or check. If any gift of $250 or more, see page A-3. If over $500, you **MUST** attach Form 8283	16	
	17	Carryover from prior year	17	
	18	Add lines 15 through 17		18
Casualty and Theft Losses	19	Casualty or theft loss(es). Attach Form 4684. (See page A-4.)		19
Job Expenses and Most Other Miscellaneous Deductions (See page A-5 for expenses to deduct here.)	20	Unreimbursed employee expenses—job travel, union dues, job education, etc. If required, you **MUST** attach Form 2106 or 2106-EZ. (See page A-5.) ▶ _____	20	
	21	Tax preparation fees	21	
	22	Other expenses—investment, safe deposit box, etc. List type and amount ▶ _____	22	
	23	Add lines 20 through 22	23	
	24	Enter amount from Form 1040, line 32. 24		
	25	Multiply line 24 above by 2% (.02)	25	
	26	Subtract line 25 from line 23. If line 25 is more than line 23, enter -0-		26
Other Miscellaneous Deductions	27	Other—from list on page A-5. List type and amount ▶ _____		27
Total Itemized Deductions	28	Is Form 1040, line 32, over $114,700 (over $57,350 if married filing separately)? **NO.** Your deduction is not limited. Add the amounts in the far right column for lines 4 through 27. Also, enter on Form 1040, line 34, the **larger** of this amount or your standard deduction. **YES.** Your deduction may be limited. See page A-5 for the amount to enter.		28

For Paperwork Reduction Act Notice, see Form 1040 instructions.   Cat. No. 11330X   Schedule A (Form 1040) 1995

APPENDIX A

OMB No. 1545-0074   Page **2**

Name(s) shown on Form 1040. Do not enter name and social security number if shown on other side. | Your social security number

Schedule B—Interest and Dividend Income

Attachment
Sequence No. **08**

		Amount

Part I
Interest
Income

(See
pages 15
and B-1.)

Note: If you
received a Form
1099-INT, Form
1099-OID, or
substitute
statement from
a brokerage firm,
list the firm's
name as the
payer and enter
the total interest
shown on that
form.

Note: If you had over $400 in taxable interest income, you must also complete Part III.

1 List name of payer. If any interest is from a seller-financed mortgage and the buyer used the property as a personal residence, see page B-1 and list this interest first. Also, show that buyer's social security number and address ▶

2 Add the amounts on line 1 . . . .   **2**

3 Excludable interest on series EE U.S. savings bonds issued after 1989 from Form 8815, line 14. You MUST attach Form 8815 to Form 1040 . . . .   **3**

4 Subtract line 3 from line 2. Enter the result here and on Form 1040, line 8a ▶   **4**

Part II
Dividend
Income

(See
pages 15
and B-1.)

Note: If you
received a Form
1099-DIV or
substitute
statement from
a brokerage
firm, list the
firm's name as
the payer and
enter the total
dividends
shown on that
form.

Note: If you had over $400 in gross dividends and/or other distributions on stock, you must also complete Part III.

		Amount

5 List name of payer. Include gross dividends and/or other distributions on stock here. Any capital gain distributions and nontaxable distributions will be deducted on lines 7 and 8 ▶

6 Add the amounts on line 5 . . . .   **6**

7 Capital gain distributions. Enter here and on Schedule D* .   **7**

8 Nontaxable distributions. (See the inst. for Form 1040, line 9.)   **8**

9 Add lines 7 and 8 . . . .   **9**

10 Subtract line 9 from line 6. Enter the result here and on Form 1040, line 9 . ▶   **10**

If you do not need Schedule D to report any other gains or losses, see the instructions for Form 1040, line 13, on page 16.

Part III
Foreign
Accounts
and
Trusts

(See
page B-2.)

If you had over $400 of interest or dividends **or** had a foreign account or were a grantor of, or a transferor to, a foreign trust, you must complete this part. | Yes | No |

11a At any time during 1995, did you have an interest in or a signature or other authority over a financial account in a foreign country, such as a bank account, securities account, or other financial account? See page B-2 for exceptions and filing requirements for Form TD F 90-22.1 . . . .

  b If "Yes," enter the name of the foreign country ▶

12 Were you the grantor of, or transferor to, a foreign trust that existed during 1995, whether or not you have any beneficial interest in it? If "Yes," you may have to file Form 3520, 3520-A, or 926 .

For Paperwork Reduction Act Notice, see Form 1040 instructions.   ✪ *Printed on recycled paper*   **Schedule B (Form 1040) 1995**

*U.S. Government Printing Office: 1995 - 389-194

SCHEDULE C
(Form 1040)

Department of the Treasury
Internal Revenue Service (O)

Profit or Loss From Business
(Sole Proprietorship)

▶ **Partnerships, joint ventures, etc., must file Form 1065.**

▶ **Attach to Form 1040 or Form 1041.**   ▶ **See Instructions for Schedule C (Form 1040).**

OMB No. 1545-0074

19**95**

Attachment
Sequence No. **09**

Name of proprietor

Social security number (SSN)

A Principal business or profession, including product or service (see page C-1)

B Enter principal business code
(see page C-6) ▶

C Business name. If no separate business name, leave blank.

D Employer ID number (EIN), if any

E Business address (including suite or room no.) ▶ ....
City, town or post office, state, and ZIP code

F Accounting method: **(1)** ☐ Cash   **(2)** ☐ Accrual   **(3)** ☐ Other (specify) ▶ ....

G Method(s) used to value closing inventory: **(1)** ☐ Cost   **(2)** ☐ Lower of cost or market   **(3)** ☐ Other (attach explanation)   **(4)** ☐ Does not apply (if checked, skip line H)   Yes | No

H Was there any change in determining quantities, costs, or valuations between opening and closing inventory? If "Yes," attach explanation . . . . . .

I Did you "materially participate" in the operation of this business during 1995? If "No," see page C-2 for limit on losses. . .

J If you started or acquired this business during 1995, check here . . . . ▶ ☐

Part I   Income

1	Gross receipts or sales. **Caution:** If this income was reported to you on Form W-2 and the "Statutory employee" box on that form was checked, see page C-2 and check here . . . . ▶ ☐	**1**	
2	Returns and allowances	**2**	
3	Subtract line 2 from line 1	**3**	
4	Cost of goods sold (from line 40 on page 2)	**4**	
5	**Gross profit.** Subtract line 4 from line 3	**5**	
6	Other income, including Federal and state gasoline or fuel tax credit or refund (see page C-2) . . .	**6**	
7	**Gross income.** Add lines 5 and 6 . . . . ▶	**7**	

Part II   Expenses. Enter expenses for business use of your home **only** on line 30.

8	Advertising	**8**		**19** Pension and profit-sharing plans	**19**	
9	Bad debts from sales or services (see page C-3) .	**9**		**20** Rent or lease (see page C-4):		
10	Car and truck expenses (see page C-3) . . .	**10**		**a** Vehicles, machinery, and equipment .	**20a**	
				b Other business property . .	**20b**	
11	Commissions and fees. . .	**11**		**21** Repairs and maintenance . .	**21**	
12	Depletion.	**12**		**22** Supplies (not included in Part III) .	**22**	
				23 Taxes and licenses	**23**	
13	Depreciation and section 179 expense deduction (not included in Part III) (see page C-3) . .	**13**		**24** Travel, meals, and entertainment:		
				a Travel	**24a**	
14	Employee benefit programs (other than on line 19) . . .	**14**		**b** Meals and entertainment .		
15	Insurance (other than health) .	**15**		**c** Enter 50% of line 24b subject to limitations (see page C-4) .		
16	Interest:					
a	Mortgage (paid to banks, etc.) . .	**16a**		**d** Subtract line 24c from line 24b .	**24d**	
b	Other	**16b**		**25** Utilities	**25**	
17	Legal and professional services	**17**		**26** Wages (less employment credits) .	**26**	
18	Office expense	**18**		**27** Other expenses (from line 46 on page 2)	**27**	

28	**Total expenses** before expenses for business use of home. Add lines 8 through 27 in columns. . . ▶	**28**	
29	Tentative profit (loss). Subtract line 28 from line 7	**29**	
30	Expenses for business use of your home. Attach **Form 8829**	**30**	
31	**Net profit or (loss).** Subtract line 30 from line 29.		
	• If a profit, enter on **Form 1040, line 12,** and ALSO on **Schedule SE, line 2** (statutory employees, see page C-5). Estates and trusts, enter on Form 1041, line 3.	**31**	
	• If a loss, you MUST go on to line 32.		
32	If you have a loss, check the box that describes your investment in this activity (see page C-5).		
	• If you checked 32a, enter the loss on **Form 1040, line 12,** and ALSO on **Schedule SE, line 2** (statutory employees, see page C-5). Estates and trusts, enter on Form 1041, line 3.	**32a** ☐ All investment is at risk.	
	• If you checked 32b, you MUST attach **Form 6198.**	**32b** ☐ Some investment is not at risk.	

For Paperwork Reduction Act Notice, see Form 1040 instructions.   Cat. No. 11334P   Schedule C (Form 1040) 1995

SCHEDULE C-EZ
(Form 1040)

Department of the Treasury
Internal Revenue Service   (O)

Net Profit From Business

(Sole Proprietorship)

▶ Partnerships, joint ventures, etc., must file Form 1065.

▶ Attach to Form 1040 or Form 1041. ▶ See instructions on back.

OMB No. 1545-0074

1995

Attachment
Sequence No. **09A**

Name of proprietor | Social security number (SSN)

Part I   General Information

You May Use This Schedule Only If You:

- Had gross receipts from your business of $25,000 or less.
- Had business expenses of $2,000 or less.
- Use the cash method of accounting.
- Did not have an inventory at any time during the year.
- Did not have a net loss from your business.
- Had only one business as a sole proprietor.

And You:

- Had no employees during the year.
- Are not required to file **Form 4562**, Depreciation and Amortization, for this business. See the instructions for Schedule C, line 13, on page C-3 to find out if you must file.
- Do not deduct expenses for business use of your home.
- Do not have prior year unallowed passive activity losses from this business.

A Principal business or profession, including product or service

B Enter principal business code (see page C-6) ▶

C Business name. If no separate business name, leave blank.

D Employer ID number (EIN), if any

E Business address (including suite or room no.). Address not required if same as on Form 1040, page 1.

City, town or post office, state, and ZIP code

Part II   Figure Your Net Profit

1 **Gross receipts.** If more than $25,000, you **must** use Schedule C.
Caution: *If this income was reported to you on Form W-2 and the "Statutory employee" box on that form was checked, see **Statutory Employees** in the instructions for Schedule C, line 1, on page C-2 and check here* . . . . ▶ ☐ | **1**

2 **Total expenses.** If more than $2,000, you **must** use Schedule C. See instructions . . . . . | **2**

3 **Net profit.** Subtract line 2 from line 1. If less than zero, you **must** use Schedule C. Enter on **Form 1040, line 12,** and ALSO on **Schedule SE, line 2.** (Statutory employees **do not** report this amount on Schedule SE, line 2. Estates and trusts, enter on Form 1041, line 3.) . . . . . | **3**

Part III   Information on Your Vehicle. Complete this part ONLY if you are claiming car or truck expenses on line 2.

4 When did you place your vehicle in service for business purposes? (month, day, year) ▶ ..... / ..... / ..... .

5 Of the total number of miles you drove your vehicle during 1995, enter the number of miles you used your vehicle for:

a Business .... **b** Commuting .... **c** Other ....

6 Do you (or your spouse) have another vehicle available for personal use? . . . . ☐ Yes ☐ No

7 Was your vehicle available for use during off-duty hours? . . . . ☐ Yes ☐ No

8a Do you have evidence to support your deduction? . . . . ☐ Yes ☐ No

b If "Yes," is the evidence written? . . . . ☐ Yes ☐ No

For Paperwork Reduction Act Notice, see Form 1040 instructions.   Cat. No. 14374D   Schedule C-EZ (Form 1040) 1995

Schedule D
(Form 1040)

Department of the Treasury
Internal Revenue Service (99)

Capital Gains and Losses

► **Attach to Form 1040.** ► **See instructions for Schedule D (Form 1040).**

► **Use lines 20 and 22 for more space to list transactions for lines 1 and 9.**

OMB No. 1545-0074

1995

12

Name(s) Shown on Form 1040

Your Social Security Number

t

Part I — Short-Term Capital Gains and Losses — Assets Held One Year or Less

(a) Description of property (Example: 100 shares 'XYZ' Co)	(b) Date acquired (Mo, day, yr.)	(c) Date sold (Mo, day, yr.)	(d) Sales price	(e) Cost or other basis	(f) LOSS If (e) is more than (d), subtract (d) from (e)	(g) GAIN If (d) is more than (e), subtract (e) from (d)
1						

2 Enter your short-term totals, if any, from line 21 . . . . **2**

3 **Total short-term sales price amounts.** Add column (d) of lines 1 and 2 . . . . **3**

4 Short-term gain from Forms 2119 and 6252, and short-term gain or loss from Forms 4684, 6781, and 8824 . . . . **4**

5 Net short-term gain or loss from partnerships, S corporations, estates, and trusts from Schedule(s) K-1 . . . . **5**

6 Short-term capital loss carryover. Enter the amount, if any, from line 9 of your 1994 Capital Loss Carryover Worksheet **6**

7 Add lines 1 through 6 in columns (f) and (g) **7**

8 **Net short-term capital gain or (loss).** Combine columns (f) and (g) of line 7 . . . . ► **8**

Part II — Long-Term Capital Gains and Losses — Assets Held More Than One Year

9						

10 Enter your long-term totals, if any, from line 23 . . . . **10**

11 **Total long-term sales price amounts.** Add column (d) of lines 9 and 10 . . . . **11**

12 Gain from Form 4797; long-term gain from Forms 2119, 2439, and 6252; and long-term gain or loss from Forms 4684, 6781, and 8824 . . . . **12**

13 Net long-term gain or loss from partnerships, S corporations, estates, and trusts from Schedule(s) K-1 . . . . **13**

14 Capital gain distributions **14**

15 Long-term capital loss carryover. Enter the amount, if any, from line 14 of your 1994 Capital Loss Carryover Worksheet **15**

16 Add lines 9 through 15 in columns (f) and (g) **16**

17 **Net long-term capital gain or (loss).** Combine columns (f) and (g) of line 16 . . . . ► **17**

Part III — Summary of Parts I and II

18 Combine lines 8 and 17. If a loss, go to line 19. If a gain, enter the gain on Form 1040, line 13.
Note: *If both lines 17 and 18 are gains, see the* **Capital Gain Tax Worksheet** *in the instructions* **18**

19 If line 18 is a loss, enter here and as a (loss) on Form 1040, line 13, the **smaller** of these losses:
a the loss on line 18; **or**
b ($3,000) or, if married filing separately, ($1,500) **19**

Note: *See the* **Capital Loss Carryover Worksheet** *in the instructions if the loss on line 18 exceeds the loss on line 19 or if Form 1040, line 35, is a loss.*

BAA **For Paperwork Reduction Act Notice, see Form 1040 instructions.**

Schedule D (Form 1040) 1995

FDIA0612 10/25/95

SCHEDULE E	**Supplemental Income and Loss**	OMB No. 1545-0074
(Form 1040)	(From rental real estate, royalties, partnerships, S corporations, estates, trusts, REMICs, etc.)	**19 95**
Department of the Treasury Internal Revenue Service (O)	▶ **Attach to Form 1040 or Form 1041.** ▶ **See Instructions for Schedule E (Form 1040).**	Attachment Sequence No. **13**

Name(s) shown on return | Your social security number

Part I **Income or Loss From Rental Real Estate and Royalties** Note: *Report income and expenses from your business of renting personal property on **Schedule C** or **C-EZ** (see page E-1). Report farm rental income or loss from **Form 4835** on page 2, line 39.*

1 Show the kind and location of each **rental real estate property:**

A ....

B ....

C ....

2 For each rental real estate property listed on line 1, did you or your family use it for personal purposes for more than the greater of 14 days or 10% of the total days rented at fair rental value during the tax year? (See page E-1.)

	Yes	No
A		
B		
C		

Income:		Properties			Totals (Add columns A, B, and C.)
		A	**B**	**C**	
3 Rents received	**3**				**3**
4 Royalties received	**4**				**4**
Expenses:					
5 Advertising	**5**				
6 Auto and travel (see page E-2)	**6**				
7 Cleaning and maintenance	**7**				
8 Commissions	**8**				
9 Insurance	**9**				
10 Legal and other professional fees	**10**				
11 Management fees	**11**				
12 Mortgage interest paid to banks, etc. (see page E-2)	**12**				**12**
13 Other interest	**13**				
14 Repairs	**14**				
15 Supplies	**15**				
16 Taxes	**16**				
17 Utilities	**17**				
18 Other (list) ▶....................	**18**				
19 Add lines 5 through 18	**19**				**19**
20 Depreciation expense or depletion (see page E-2)	**20**				**20**
21 Total expenses. Add lines 19 and 20	**21**				
22 Income or (loss) from rental real estate or royalty properties. Subtract line 21 from line 3 (rents) or line 4 (royalties). If the result is a (loss), see page E-2 to find out if you must file **Form 6198**	**22**				
23 Deductible rental real estate loss. **Caution:** *Your rental real estate loss on line 22 may be limited. See page E-3 to find out if you must file* **Form 8582.** *Real estate professionals must complete line 42 on page 2*	**23**	( )	( )	( )	

24 **Income.** Add positive amounts shown on line 22. **Do not** include any losses . . . . | **24** |

25 **Losses.** Add royalty losses from line 22 and rental real estate losses from line 23. Enter the total losses here . | **25** ( ) |

26 Total rental real estate and royalty income or (loss). Combine lines 24 and 25. Enter the result here. If Parts II, III, IV, and line 39 on page 2 do not apply to you, also enter this amount on Form 1040, line 17. Otherwise, include this amount in the total on line 40 on page 2 . . . . | **26** |

For Paperwork Reduction Act Notice, see Form 1040 instructions.   Cat. No. 11344L   Schedule E (Form 1040) 1995

Schedule E (Form 1040) 1995 | Attachment Sequence No. **13** | Page **2**

Name(s) shown on return. Do not enter name and social security number if shown on other side. | **Your social security number**

Note: *If you report amounts from farming or fishing on Schedule E, you must enter your gross income from those activities on line 41 below. Real estate professionals must complete line 42 below.*

Part II **Income or Loss From Partnerships and S Corporations** Note: *If you report a loss from an at-risk activity, you MUST check either column (e) or (f) of line 27 to describe your investment in the activity. See page E-4. If you check column (f), you must attach Form 6198.*

27	(a) Name	(b) Enter **P** for partnership; **S** for S corporation	(c) Check if foreign partnership	(d) Employer identification number	Investment At Risk?	
					(e) All is at risk	(f) Some is not at risk
A						
B						
C						
D						
E						

	Passive Income and Loss		Nonpassive Income and Loss		
	(g) Passive loss allowed (attach **Form 8582** if required)	(h) Passive income from **Schedule K-1**	(i) Nonpassive loss from **Schedule K-1**	(j) Section 179 expense deduction from **Form 4562**	(k) Nonpassive income from **Schedule K-1**
A					
B					
C					
D					
E					
28a Totals					
b Totals					

29	Add columns (h) and (k) of line 28a	29	
30	Add columns (g), (i), and (j) of line 28b	30	( )
31	Total partnership and S corporation income or (loss). Combine lines 29 and 30. Enter the result here and include in the total on line 40 below	31	

Part III **Income or Loss From Estates and Trusts**

32	(a) Name	(b) Employer identification number
A		
B		

	Passive Income and Loss		Nonpassive Income and Loss	
	(c) Passive deduction or loss allowed (attach **Form 8582** if required)	(d) Passive income from **Schedule K-1**	(e) Deduction or loss from **Schedule K-1**	(f) Other income from **Schedule K-1**
A				
B				
33a Totals				
b Totals				

34	Add columns (d) and (f) of line 33a	34	
35	Add columns (c) and (e) of line 33b	35	( )
36	Total estate and trust income or (loss). Combine lines 34 and 35. Enter the result here and include in the total on line 40 below	36	

Part IV **Income or Loss From Real Estate Mortgage Investment Conduits (REMICs)—Residual Holder**

37	(a) Name	(b) Employer identification number	(c) Excess inclusion from **Schedules Q**, line 2c (see page E-4)	(d) Taxable income (net loss) from **Schedules Q**, line 1b	(e) Income from **Schedules Q**, line 3b

38	Combine columns (d) and (e) only. Enter the result here and include in the total on line 40 below	38	

Part V **Summary**

39	Net farm rental income or (loss) from **Form 4835**. Also, complete line 41 below	39	
40	TOTAL income or (loss). Combine lines 26, 31, 36, 38, and 39. Enter the result here and on Form 1040, line 17 ▶	40	

41	**Reconciliation of Farming and Fishing Income.** Enter your **gross** farming and fishing income reported on Form 4835, line 7; Schedule K-1 (Form 1065), line 15b; Schedule K-1 (Form 1120S), line 23; and Schedule K-1 (Form 1041), line 13 (see page E-4)	41	
42	**Reconciliation for Real Estate Professionals.** If you were a real estate professional (see page E-3), enter the net income or (loss) you reported anywhere on Form 1040 from all rental real estate activities in which you materially participated under the passive activity loss rules . .	42	

♻ *Printed on recycled paper*

SCHEDULE EIC
(Form 1040A or 1040)

Department of the Treasury
Internal Revenue Service   (O)

Earned Income Credit
(Qualifying Child Information)
▶ Attach to Form 1040A or 1040.
▶ See instructions on back.

OMB No. 1545-0074

1995

Attachment
Sequence No. **43**

Name(s) shown on return

Your social security number

Before You Begin . . .

- Answer the questions on page 47 of the Form 1040A instructions or page 27 of the Form 1040 instructions to see if you can take this credit.
- If you can take the credit, fill in the worksheet on page 48 (1040A) or page 28 (1040) to figure your credit. **But if you want the IRS to figure it for you, see page 42 (1040A) or page 35 (1040).**

Then, you **must** complete and attach Schedule EIC only if you have a qualifying child (see boxes on back).

Information About Your Qualifying Child or Children

If you have more than two qualifying children, you only have to list two to get the maximum credit.

Caution: If you don't attach Schedule EIC and fill in all the lines that apply, it will take us longer to process your return and issue your refund.	**(a) Child 1**	**(b) Child 2**
	First name Last name	First name Last name
1 Child's name		
2 Child's year of birth	19___	19___
3 If the child was born **before 1977** AND—		
a was **under age 24** at the end of 1995 **and** a student, check the "Yes" box, **OR**	☐ Yes	☐ Yes
b was permanently and totally disabled (see back), check the "Yes" box	☐ Yes	☐ Yes
4 Enter the child's social security number. If born in 1995, see instructions on back		
5 Child's relationship to you (for example, son, grandchild, etc.) .		
6 Number of months child lived with you in the United States in 1995	months	months

TIP: Do you want the earned income credit added to your take-home pay in 1996? To see if you qualify, get **Form W-5** from your employer or by calling the IRS at 1-800-TAX-FORM (1-800-829-3676).

For Paperwork Reduction Act Notice, see Form 1040A or 1040 instructions.   Cat. No. 13339M   **Schedule EIC (Form 1040A or 1040) 1995**

Schedule H
(Form 1040)

Department of the Treasury
Internal Revenue Service

Household Employment Taxes

(For Social Security, Medicare, Withheld Income, and Federal
Unemployment (FUTA) Taxes)

► **Attach to Form 1040, 1040A, 1040NR, 1040NR-EZ, 1040-SS, 1040-T, or 1041.**
► **See separate instructions.**

OMB No. 1545-0074

1995

44

Name of Employer (as shown on return)

Social Security Number

Employer Identification Number

A Did you pay **any one** household employee cash wages of $1,000 or more in 1995? (If any household employee was your spouse, your child under age 21, your parent, or anyone under age 18, see the line A instructions before you answer this question.)

☐ **Yes.** Skip questions B and C and go to Part I.
☐ **No.** Go to question B.

B Did you withhold federal income tax during 1995 for any household employee?

☐ **Yes.** Skip question C and go to Part I.
☐ **No.** Go to question C.

C Did you pay **total** cash wages of $1,000 or more in **any** calendar **quarter** of 1994 or 1995 to household employees? (**Do not** count cash wages paid in 1994 or 1995 to your spouse, your child under age 21, or your parent.)

☐ **No.** **Stop.** Do not file this schedule.
☐ **Yes.** Skip Part I and go to Part II.

Part I   **Social Security, Medicare, and Income Taxes**

1 Total cash wages subject to social security taxes (see instructions)	1	
2 Social security taxes. Multiply line 1 by 12.4% (.124)	**2**	
3 Total cash wages subject to Medicare taxes (see instructions)	3	
4 Medicare taxes. Multiply line 3 by 2.9% (.029)	**4**	
5 Federal income tax withheld, if any	**5**	
6 Add lines 2, 4, and 5	**6**	
7 Advance earned income credit (EIC) payments, if any	**7**	
8 **Total social security, Medicare, and income taxes.** Subtract line 7 from line 6	**8**	

9 Did you pay **total** cash wages of $1,000 or more in **any** calendar **quarter** of 1994 or 1995 to household employees? (**Do not** count cash wages paid in 1994 or 1995 to your spouse, your child under age 21, or your parent.)

☐ **No.** **Stop.** Take the amount from line 8 above and enter it on Form 1040, line 53, or Form 1040A, line 27. If you are not required to file Form 1040 or 1040A, see the line 9 instructions.

☐ **Yes.** Go to Part II.

BAA For Paperwork Reduction Act Notice, see Form 1040 instructions.   Schedule H (Form 1040) 1995

FDIA9412 12/13/95

302

Schedule H (Form 1040) 1995   Page **2**

Part II   Federal Unemployment (FUTA) Tax

		Yes	No
10	Did you pay unemployment contributions to only one state?		
11	Did you pay all state unemployment contributions for 1995 by April 15, 1996? Fiscal year filers, see instructions		
12	Were all wages that are taxable for FUTA tax also taxable for your state's unemployment tax?		

Next: If you answered **'Yes'** to **all** of the questions above, complete Section A.
If you answered **'No'** to **any** of the questions above, skip Section A and complete Section B.

Section A

13   Name of state where you paid unemployment contributions .... ▶

14   State reporting number as shown on state unemployment tax return .... ▶

15   Contributions paid to your state unemployment fund (see instructions) ... **15**

16   Total cash wages subject to FUTA tax (see instructions) **16**

17   **FUTA tax.** Multiply line 16 by .008. Enter the result here, skip Section B, and go to Part III **17**

Section B

18   Complete all columns below that apply (if you need more space, see instructions):

(a) Name of State	(b) State reporting no. as shown on state unemployment tax return	(c) Taxable wages (as defined in state act)	(d) State experience rate period		(e) State experience rate	(f) Multiply column (c) by .054	(g) Multiply column (c) by column (e)	(h) Subtract column (g) from column (f). If zero or less, enter -0-.	(i) Contributions paid to state unemployment fund
			From	To					

19   Totals **19**

20   Add columns (h) and (i) of line 19 .... **20**

21   Total cash wages subject to FUTA tax (see instructions) **21**

22   Multiply line 21 by 6.2% (.062) **22**

23   Multiply line 21 by 5.4% (.054) **23**

24   Enter the **smaller** of line 20 or line 23 .... **24**

25   **FUTA tax.** Subtract line 24 from line 22. Enter the result here and go to Part III **25**

Part III   Total Household Employment Taxes

26   Enter the amount from line 8 .... **26**

27   Add line 17 (or line 25) and line 26 .... **27**

28   Are you required to file Form 1040 or 1040A?

  ☐ **Yes. Stop.** Take the amount from line 27 above and enter it on Form 1040, line 53, or Form 1040A, line 27. **Do not** complete Part IV below.

  ☐ **No.** You may have to complete Part IV. See instructions.

Part IV   Address and Signature — Complete this part **only** if required. See instructions.

Address (number and street) or P.O. Box if Mail is Not Delivered to Street Address | Apt, Room, or Suite Number

City, Town or Post Office, State, and ZIP Code

Under penalties of perjury, I declare that I have examined this schedule, including accompanying statements, and to the best of my knowledge and belief, it is true, correct, and complete. No part of any payment made to a state unemployment fund claimed as a credit was, or is to be, deducted from the payments to employees.

▶ _____   ▶ _____

  Employer's Signature   Date

Form **1040A**	Department of the Treasury—Internal Revenue Service		

U.S. Individual Income Tax Return (O) **1995**   IRS Use Only—Do not write or staple in this space.

OMB No. 1545-0085

Label
(See page 19.)

Use the IRS label. Otherwise, please print or type.

L A B E L   H E R E

Your first name and initial | Last name

Your social security number

If a joint return, spouse's first name and initial | Last name

Spouse's social security number

Home address (number and street). If you have a P.O. box, see page 19. | Apt. no.

City, town or post office, state, and ZIP code. If you have a foreign address, see page 19.

For Privacy Act and Paperwork Reduction Act Notice, see page 11.

Presidential Election Campaign Fund (See page 19.)   Yes | No
Do you want $3 to go to this fund? . . . .
If a joint return, does your spouse want $3 to go to this fund?

Note: Checking "Yes" will not change your tax or reduce your refund.

Check the box for your filing status
(See page 20.)
Check only one box.

1 ☐ Single
2 ☐ Married filing joint return (even if only one had income)
3 ☐ Married filing separate return. Enter spouse's social security number above and full name here. ▶
4 ☐ Head of household (with qualifying person). (See page 21.) If the qualifying person is a child but not your dependent, enter this child's name here. ▶
5 ☐ Qualifying widow(er) with dependent child (year spouse died ▶ 19). (See page 22.)

Figure your exemptions
(See page 22.)

If more than seven dependents, see page 25.

6a ☐ **Yourself.** If your parent (or someone else) can claim you as a dependent on his or her tax return, **do not** check box 6a. But be sure to check the box on line 18b on page 2.

b ☐ **Spouse**

No. of boxes checked on 6a and 6b ____

c **Dependents:**

(1) First name Last name	(2) Dependent's social security number. If born in 1995, see page 25.	(3) Dependent's relationship to you	(4) No. of months lived in your home in 1995

No. of your children on 6c who:
• lived with you ____
• didn't live with you due to divorce or separation (see page 26) ____

Dependents on 6c not entered above ____

d If your child didn't live with you but is claimed as your dependent under a pre-1985 agreement, check here . . . . ▶ ☐

e Total number of exemptions claimed.

Add numbers entered on lines above ____

Figure your adjusted gross income
Attach Copy B of your Forms W-2 and 1099-R here. If you didn't get a W-2, see page 27. Enclose, but do not attach, any payment.

7 Wages, salaries, tips, etc. This should be shown in box 1 of your W-2 form(s). Attach Form(s) W-2. | 7

8a **Taxable** interest income (see page 28). If over $400, attach Schedule 1. | 8a

b **Tax-exempt** interest. DO NOT include on line 8a. | 8b

9 Dividends. If over $400, attach Schedule 1. | 9

10a Total IRA distributions. | 10a | **10b** Taxable amount (see page 29). | 10b

11a Total pensions and annuities. | 11a | **11b** Taxable amount (see page 29). | 11b

12 Unemployment compensation (see page 32). | 12

13a Social security benefits. | 13a | **13b** Taxable amount (see page 33). | 13b

14 Add lines 7 through 13b (far right column). This is your **total income.** ▶ | 14

15a Your IRA deduction (see page 35). | 15a

b Spouse's IRA deduction (see page 35). | 15b

c Add lines 15a and 15b. These are your **total adjustments.** | 15c

16 Subtract line 15c from line 14. This is your **adjusted gross income.** If less than $26,673 and a child lived with you (less than $9,230 if a child didn't live with you), see "Earned income credit" on page 47. ▶ | 16

Cat. No. 11327A

1995 Form 1040A page 1

Department of the Treasury—Internal Revenue Service

Form 1040EZ

Income Tax Return for Single and Joint Filers With No Dependents **1995**

OMB No. 1545-0675

Use the IRS label here

Your first name and initial | Last name

If a joint return, spouse's first name and initial | Last name

Home address (number and street). If you have a P.O. box, see page 11. | Apt. no.

City, town or post office, state, and ZIP code. If you have a foreign address, see page 11.

Your social security number

Spouse's social security number

See instructions on back and in Form 1040EZ booklet.

Presidential Election Campaign (See page 11.)

Note: *Checking "Yes" will not change your tax or reduce your refund.*

Do you want $3 to go to this fund? ▶

If a joint return, does your spouse want $3 to go to this fund? ▶

Yes No

Dollars | Cents

Income

Attach Copy B of Form(s) W-2 here. Enclose, but do not attach, any payment with your return.

1 Total wages, salaries, and tips. This should be shown in box 1 of your W-2 form(s). Attach your W-2 form(s). **1**

2 Taxable interest income of $400 or less. If the total is over $400, you cannot use Form 1040EZ. **2**

3 Unemployment compensation (see page 14). **3**

4 Add lines 1, 2, and 3. This is your **adjusted gross income.** If less than $9,230, see page 15 to find out if you can claim the earned income credit on line 8. **4**

Note: *You must check Yes or No.*

5 Can your parents (or someone else) claim you on their return?

☐ **Yes.** Do worksheet on back; enter amount from line G here.

☐ **No.** If **single,** enter 6,400.00. If **married,** enter 11,550.00. For an explanation of these amounts, see back of form. **5**

6 Subtract line 5 from line 4. If line 5 is larger than line 4, enter 0. This is your **taxable income.** ▶ **6**

Payments and tax

7 Enter your Federal income tax withheld from box 2 of your W-2 form(s). **7**

8 **Earned income credit** (see page 15). Enter type and amount of nontaxable earned income below.

Type | $ **8**

9 Add lines 7 and 8 (don't include nontaxable earned income). These are your **total payments.** **9**

10 **Tax.** Use the amount on **line 6** to find your tax in the tax table on pages 29–33 of the booklet. Then, enter the tax from the table on this line. **10**

Refund or amount you owe

11 If line 9 is larger than line 10, subtract line 10 from line 9. This is your **refund.** **11**

12 If line 10 is larger than line 9, subtract line 9 from line 10. This is the **amount you owe.** See page 22 for details on how to pay and what to write on your payment. **12**

Sign your return

Keep a copy of this form for your records.

I have read this return. Under penalties of perjury, I declare that to the best of my knowledge and belief, the return is true, correct, and accurately lists all amounts and sources of income I received during the tax year.

Your signature | Spouse's signature if joint return

Date | Your occupation | Date | Spouse's occupation

For IRS Use Only — Please do not write in boxes below.

1 2 3 4 5

6 7 8 9 10

For Privacy Act and Paperwork Reduction Act Notice, see page 7.

Cat. No. 11329W

Form 1040EZ (1995)

Form **1040X**	Department of the Treasury—Internal Revenue Service	
(Rev. October 1994)	**Amended U.S. Individual Income Tax Return**	OMB No. 1545-0091
	▶ **See separate instructions.**	

This return is for calendar year ▶ 19_____ , OR fiscal year ended ▶ _____ , 19_____ .

Please print or type		
Your first name and initial	Last name	Your social security number
If a joint return, spouse's first name and initial	Last name	Spouse's social security number
Home address (number and street). If you have a P.O. box, see instructions.	Apt. no.	Telephone number (optional) ( )
City, town or post office, state, and ZIP code. If you have a foreign address, see instructions.		For Paperwork Reduction Act Notice, see page 1 of separate instructions.

Enter name and address as shown on original return. If same as above, write "Same." If changing from separate to joint return, enter names and addresses from original returns.

A Service center where original return was filed
B Has original return been changed or audited by the IRS? ☐ Yes ☐ No
If "No," have you been notified that it will be? . . . . ☐ Yes ☐ No
If "Yes," identify the IRS office ▶

C If you are amending your return to include any item (loss, credit, deduction, other tax benefit, or income) relating to a tax shelter required to be registered, attach **Form 8271**, Investor Reporting of Tax Shelter Registration Number, and check here . . . . ▶ ☐

D Filing status claimed. **Note:** *You cannot change from joint to separate returns after the due date has passed.*
On original return ▶ ☐ Single ☐ Married filing joint return ☐ Married filing separate return ☐ Head of household ☐ Qualifying widow(er)
On this return ▶ ☐ Single ☐ Married filing joint return ☐ Married filing separate return ☐ Head of household ☐ Qualifying widow(er)

Income and Deductions (see instructions) USE PART II ON PAGE 2 TO EXPLAIN ANY CHANGES		**A.** As originally reported or as previously adjusted (see instructions)	**B.** Net change—Increase or (Decrease)—explain on page 2	**C.** Correct amount
1 Adjusted gross income (see instructions)	1			
2 Itemized deductions or standard deduction	2			
3 Subtract line 2 from line 1	3			
4 Exemptions. If changing, fill in Parts I and II on page 2 . .	4			
5 Taxable income. Subtract line 4 from line 3	5			
6 Tax (see instructions). Method used in col. C _____	6			
7 Credits (see instructions)	7			
8 Subtract line 7 from line 6. Enter the result but not less than zero .	8			
9 Other taxes (such as self-employment tax, alternative minimum tax, etc.)	9			
10 Total tax. Add lines 8 and 9	10			
11 Federal income tax withheld and excess social security, Medicare, and RRTA taxes withheld. If changing, see instructions	11			
12 Estimated tax payments	12			
13 Earned income credit	13			
14 Credits for Federal tax paid on fuels, regulated investment company, etc.	14			
15 Amount paid with Form 4868, Form 2688, or Form 2350 (application for extension of time to file) .	15			
16 Amount of tax paid with original return plus additional tax paid after it was filed	16			
17 Total payments. Add lines 11 through 16 in column C	17			

Refund or Amount You Owe

18 Overpayment, if any, as shown on original return or as previously adjusted by the IRS	18	
19 Subtract line 18 from line 17 (see instructions)	19	
20 **AMOUNT YOU OWE.** If line 10, column C, is more than line 19, enter the difference and see instructions .	20	
21 If line 10, column C, is less than line 19, enter the difference	21	
22 Amount of line 21 you want **REFUNDED TO YOU**	22	
23 Amount of line 21 you want **APPLIED TO YOUR 19_____ ESTIMATED TAX** ▏ 23		

Sign Here
Keep a copy of this return for your records.

Under penalties of perjury, I declare that I have filed an original return and that I have examined this amended return, including accompanying schedules and statements, and to the best of my knowledge and belief, this amended return is true, correct, and complete. Declaration of preparer (other than taxpayer) is based on all information of which the preparer has any knowledge.

Your signature	Date	Spouse's signature. If a joint return, BOTH must sign.	Date

Paid Preparer's Use Only

Preparer's signature ▶	Date	Check if self-employed ☐	Preparer's social security no.
Firm's name (or yours if self-employed) and address ▶		E.I. No. ZIP code	

Cat. No. 11360L   Form **1040X** (Rev. 10-94)

Form SS-4
(Rev. December 1995)
Department of the Treasury
Internal Revenue Service

Application for Employer Identification Number

(For use by employers, corporations, partnerships, trusts, estates, churches, government agencies, certain individuals, and others. See instructions.)

▶ Keep a copy for your records.

EIN

OMB No. 1545-0003

Please type or print clearly.

1 Name of applicant (Legal name) (See instructions.)

2 Trade name of business (if different from name on line 1)

3 Executor, trustee, "care of" name

4a Mailing address (street address) (room, apt., or suite no.)

5a Business address (if different from address on lines 4a and 4b)

4b City, state, and ZIP code

5b City, state, and ZIP code

6 County and state where principal business is located

7 Name of principal officer, general partner, grantor, owner, or trustor—SSN required (See instructions.) ▶

8a Type of entity (Check only one box.) (See instructions.)
☐ Sole proprietor (SSN) _____
☐ Partnership   ☐ Personal service corp.
☐ REMIC   ☐ Limited liability co.
☐ State/local government   ☐ National Guard
☐ Other nonprofit organization (specify) ▶ _____
☐ Other (specify) ▶

☐ Estate (SSN of decedent) _____
☐ Plan administrator-SSN _____
☐ Other corporation (specify) ▶ _____
☐ Trust   ☐ Farmers' cooperative
☐ Federal Government/military   ☐ Church or church-controlled organization
_____ (enter GEN if applicable) _____

8b If a corporation, name the state or foreign country (if applicable) where incorporated

State

Foreign country

9 Reason for applying (Check only one box.)
☐ Started new business (specify) ▶ _____
☐ Hired employees
☐ Created a pension plan (specify type) ▶

☐ Banking purpose (specify) ▶ _____
☐ Changed type of organization (specify) ▶ _____
☐ Purchased going business
☐ Created a trust (specify) ▶ _____
☐ Other (specify) ▶

10 Date business started or acquired (Mo., day, year) (See instructions.)

11 Closing month of accounting year (See instructions.)

12 First date wages or annuities were paid or will be paid (Mo., day, year). **Note:** *If applicant is a withholding agent, enter date income will first be paid to nonresident alien. (Mo., day, year)* . . . . ▶

13 Highest number of employees expected in the next 12 months. **Note:** *If the applicant does not expect to have any employees during the period, enter -0-. (See instructions.)* . . . ▶

Nonagricultural	Agricultural	Household

14 Principal activity (See instructions.) ▶

15 Is the principal business activity manufacturing? . . . . ☐ Yes ☐ No
If "Yes," principal product and raw material used ▶

16 To whom are most of the products or services sold? Please check the appropriate box.   ☐ Business (wholesale)
☐ Public (retail)   ☐ Other (specify) ▶   ☐ N/A

17a Has the applicant ever applied for an identification number for this or any other business? . . . . ☐ Yes ☐ No
Note: *If "Yes," please complete lines 17b and 17c.*

17b If you checked "Yes" on line 17a, give applicant's legal name and trade name shown on prior application, if different from line 1 or 2 above.
Legal name ▶   Trade name ▶

17c Approximate date when and city and state where the application was filed. Enter previous employer identification number if known.
Approximate date when filed (Mo., day, year) | City and state where filed   Previous EIN

Under penalties of perjury, I declare that I have examined this application, and to the best of my knowledge and belief, it is true, correct, and complete.

Business telephone number (include area code)

Fax telephone number (include area code)

Name and title (Please type or print clearly.) ▶

Signature ▶   Date ▶

Note: *Do not write below this line. For official use only.*

Please leave blank ▶	Geo.	Ind.	Class	Size	Reason for applying

For Paperwork Reduction Act Notice, see page 4.   Cat. No. 16055N   Form **SS-4** (Rev. 12-95)

Form **SS-8** (Rev. July 1993) Department of the Treasury Internal Revenue Service	**Determination of Employee Work Status for Purposes of Federal Employment Taxes and Income Tax Withholding**	OMB No. 1545-0004 Expires 7-31-96

Paperwork Reduction Act Notice

We ask for the information on this form to carry out the Internal Revenue laws of the United States. You are required to give us this information. We need it to ensure that you are complying with these laws and to allow us to figure and collect the right amount of tax.

The time needed to complete and file this form will vary depending on individual circumstances. The estimated average time is: **recordkeeping,** 34 hr., 55 min., **learning about the law or the form,** 6 min. and **preparing and sending the form to IRS,** 40 min. If you have comments concerning the accuracy of these time estimates or suggestions for making this form more simple, we would be happy to hear from you. You can write to both the **Internal Revenue Service,** Attention: Reports Clearance Officer, T:FP, Washington, DC 20224; and the **Office of Management and Budget,** Paperwork Reduction Project (1545-0004), Washington, DC 20503. **DO NOT** send the tax form to either of these offices. Instead, see **General Information** for where to file.

Purpose

Employers and workers file Form SS-8 to get a determination as to whether a worker is an employee for purposes of Federal employment taxes and income tax withholding.

General Information

This form should be completed carefully. If the firm is completing the form, it should be completed for **ONE** individual who is representative of the class of workers whose status is in question. If a written determination is desired for more than one class of workers, a separate Form SS-8 should be completed for one worker from each class whose status is typical of that class. A written determination for any worker will apply to other workers of the same class if the facts are not materially different from those of the worker whose status was ruled upon.

Please return Form SS-8 to the Internal Revenue Service office that provided the form. If the Internal Revenue Service did not ask you to complete this form but you wish a determination on whether a worker is an employee, file Form SS-8 with your District Director.

*Caution: Form SS-8 is **not** a claim for refund of social security and Medicare taxes or Federal income tax withholding. Also, a determination that an individual is an employee does not necessarily reduce any current or prior tax liability. A worker must file his or her income tax return even if a determination has not been made by the due date of the return.*

Name of firm (or person) for whom the worker performed services	Name of worker
Address of firm (include street address, apt. or suite no., city, state, and ZIP code)	Address of worker (include street address, apt. or suite no., city, state, and ZIP code)

Trade name	Telephone number (include area code) ( )	Worker's social security number – –

Telephone number (include area code) ( )	Firm's taxpayer identification number	

Check type of firm for which the work relationship is in question:
☐ **Individual** ☐ **Partnership** ☐ **Corporation** ☐ **Other** (specify) ▶

Important Information Needed to Process Your Request

This form is being completed by: ☐ Firm ☐ Worker

If this form is being completed by the worker, the IRS **must** have your permission to disclose your name to the firm.

Do you object to disclosing your name and the information on this form to the firm? . . . . ☐ Yes ☐ No
If you answer "Yes," the IRS cannot act on your request. **DO NOT complete the rest of this form unless the IRS asks for it.**

Under section 6110 of the Internal Revenue Code, the information on this form and related file documents will be open to the public if any ruling or determination is made. However, names, addresses, and taxpayer identification numbers must be removed before the information can be made public.

Is there any other information you want removed? . . . . ☐ Yes ☐ No
If you check "Yes," we cannot process your request unless you submit a copy of this form and copies of all supporting documents showing, in brackets, the information you want removed. Attach a separate statement telling which specific exemption of section 6110(c) applies to each bracketed part.

*This form is designed to cover many work activities, so some of the questions may not apply to you. **You must answer ALL items or mark them "Unknown" or "Does not apply."** If you need more space, attach another sheet.*

Total number of workers in this class. (Attach names and addresses. If more than 10 workers, attach only 10.) ▶ _____

This information is about services performed by the worker from _____ to _____
                                                                (month, day, year)   (month, day, year)

Is the worker still performing services for the firm? . . . . ☐ Yes ☐ No

If "No," what was the date of termination? ▶ _____
                                           (month, day, year)

Cat. No. 16106T   Form **SS-8** (Rev. 7-93)

APPENDIX A

1a Describe the firm's business ....

  b Describe the work done by the worker ....

....

2a If the work is done under a written agreement between the firm and the worker, attach a copy.

  b If the agreement is not in writing, describe the terms and conditions of the work arrangement ....

....

  c If the actual working arrangement differs in any way from the agreement, explain the differences and why they occur ....

....

3a Is the worker given training by the firm? . . . . □ **Yes** □ **No**
    If "Yes": What kind? ....
    How often? ....

  b Is the worker given instructions in the way the work is to be done (exclusive of actual training in 3a)? . □ **Yes** □ **No**
    If "Yes," give specific examples. ....

  c Attach samples of any written instructions or procedures.

  d Does the firm have the right to change the methods used by the worker or direct that person on how to
    do the work? . . . . □ **Yes** □ **No**
    Explain your answer ....

....

  e Does the operation of the firm's business require that the worker be supervised or controlled in the
    performance of the service? . . . . □ **Yes** □ **No**
    Explain your answer ....

....

4a The firm engages the worker:
    □ To perform and complete a particular job only
    □ To work at a job for an indefinite period of time
    □ Other (explain) ....

  b Is the worker required to follow a routine or a schedule established by the firm? . . . . □ **Yes** □ **No**
    If "Yes," what is the routine or schedule? ....

....

  c Does the worker report to the firm or its representative?. . . . . □ **Yes** □ **No**
    If "Yes": How often? ....
    For what purpose? ....
    In what manner (in person, in writing, by telephone, etc.)? ....
    Attach copies of report forms used in reporting to the firm.

  d Does the worker furnish a time record to the firm?. . . . . □ **Yes** □ **No**
    If "Yes," attach copies of time records.

5a State the kind and value of tools, equipment, supplies, and materials furnished by:
    The firm ....

....

    The worker ....

....

  b What expenses are incurred by the worker in the performance of services for the firm? ....

  c Does the firm reimburse the worker for any expenses? . . . . □ **Yes** □ **No**
    If "Yes," specify the reimbursed expenses ....

6a Will the worker perform the services personally? . . . . □ **Yes** □ **No**

  b Does the worker have helpers? . . . . □ **Yes** □ **No**
    If "Yes": Who hires the helpers? □ Firm □ Worker
    If hired by the worker, is the firm's approval necessary? . . . . □ **Yes** □ **No**
    Who pays the helpers? □ Firm □ Worker
    Are social security and Medicare taxes and Federal income tax withheld from the helpers' wages? . . □ **Yes** □ **No**
    If "Yes": Who reports and pays these taxes? □ Firm □ Worker
    Who reports the helpers' incomes to the Internal Revenue Service? □ Firm □ Worker
    If the worker pays the helpers, does the firm repay the worker? . . . . □ **Yes** □ **No**
    What services do the helpers perform?

APPENDIX A

7 At what location are the services performed? ☐ Firm's ☐ Worker's ☐ Other (specify) ....

8a Type of pay worker receives:
☐ Salary ☐ Commission ☐ Hourly wage ☐ Piecework ☐ Lump sum ☐ Other (specify) ....

b Does the firm guarantee a minimum amount of pay to the worker? . . . . ☐ Yes ☐ No

c Does the firm allow the worker a drawing account or advances against pay? . . . . ☐ Yes ☐ No
If "Yes": Is the worker paid such advances on a regular basis? . . . . ☐ Yes ☐ No

d How does the worker repay such advances? ....

9a Is the worker eligible for a pension, bonus, paid vacations, sick pay, etc.? . . . . ☐ Yes ☐ No
If "Yes," specify ....

b Does the firm carry workmen's compensation insurance on the worker? . . . . ☐ Yes ☐ No

c Does the firm deduct social security and Medicare taxes from amounts paid the worker? . . . . . ☐ Yes ☐ No

d Does the firm deduct Federal income taxes from amounts paid the worker? . . . . ☐ Yes ☐ No

e How does the firm report the worker's income to the Internal Revenue Service?
☐ Form W-2 ☐ Form 1099-MISC ☐ Does not report ☐ Other (specify) ....
Attach a copy.

f Does the firm bond the worker? . . . . ☐ Yes ☐ No

10a Approximately how many hours a day does the worker perform services for the firm? ....
Does the firm set hours of work for the worker? . . . . ☐ Yes ☐ No
If "Yes," what are the worker's set hours? _____ am/pm to _____ am/pm (Circle whether am or pm)

b Does the worker perform similar services for others? . . . . ☐ Yes ☐ No ☐ **Unknown**
If "Yes": Are these services performed on a daily basis for other firms? . . . . ☐ Yes ☐ No ☐ **Unknown**
Percentage of time spent in performing these services for:
This firm .... % Other firms .... % ☐ **Unknown**
Does the firm have priority on the worker's time? . . . . ☐ Yes ☐ No
If "No," explain ....

c Is the worker prohibited from competing with the firm either while performing services or during any later
period? . . . . ☐ Yes ☐ No

11a Can the firm discharge the worker at any time without incurring a liability? . . . . ☐ Yes ☐ No
If "No," explain ....

b Can the worker terminate the services at any time without incurring a liability? . . . . ☐ Yes ☐ No
If "No," explain ....

12a Does the worker perform services for the firm under:
☐ The firm's business name ☐ The worker's own business name ☐ Other (specify) ....

b Does the worker advertise or maintain a business listing in the telephone directory, a trade
journal, etc.? . . . . ☐ Yes ☐ No ☐ **Unknown**
If "Yes," specify ....

c Does the worker represent himself or herself to the public as being in business to perform
the same or similar services? . . . . ☐ Yes ☐ No ☐ **Unknown**
If "Yes," how? ....

d Does the worker have his or her own shop or office? . . . . ☐ Yes ☐ No ☐ **Unknown**
If "Yes," where? ....

e Does the firm represent the worker as an employee of the firm to its customers? . . . . ☐ Yes ☐ No
If "No," how is the worker represented? ....

f How did the firm learn of the worker's services? ....

13 Is a license necessary for the work? . . . . ☐ Yes ☐ No ☐ **Unknown**
If "Yes," what kind of license is required? ....
By whom is it issued? ....
By whom is the license fee paid? ....

14 Does the worker have a financial investment in a business related to the services performed? ☐ **Yes** ☐ No ☐ **Unknown**
If "Yes," specify and give amounts of the investment ....

15 Can the worker incur a loss in the performance of the service for the firm? . . . . ☐ Yes ☐ No
If "Yes," how? ....

16a Has any other government agency ruled on the status of the firm's workers? . . . . ☐ Yes ☐ No
If "Yes," attach a copy of the ruling.

b Is the same issue being considered by any IRS office in connection with the audit of the worker's tax
return or the firm's tax return, or has it recently been considered? . . . . ☐ Yes ☐ No
If "Yes," for which year(s)?

APPENDIX A

17 Does the worker assemble or process a product at home or away from the firm's place of business? ☐ **Yes** ☐ **No**
If "Yes":

    Who furnishes materials or goods used by the worker? ☐ Firm ☐ Worker
    Is the worker furnished a pattern or given instructions to follow in making the product? . . . . . ☐ **Yes** ☐ **No**
    Is the worker required to return the finished product to the firm or to someone designated by the firm? . ☐ **Yes** ☐ **No**

Answer items 18a through n only if the worker is a salesperson or provides a service directly to customers.

18a Are leads to prospective customers furnished by the firm? . . . . ☐ **Yes** ☐ **No** ☐ **Does not apply**
  b Is the worker required to pursue or report on leads? . . . . ☐ **Yes** ☐ **No** ☐ **Does not apply**
  c Is the worker required to adhere to prices, terms, and conditions of sale established by the firm? . . ☐ **Yes** ☐ **No**
  d Are orders submitted to and subject to approval by the firm? . . . . ☐ **Yes** ☐ **No**
  e Is the worker expected to attend sales meetings? . . . . ☐ **Yes** ☐ **No**
    If "Yes": Is the worker subject to any kind of penalty for failing to attend? . . . . ☐ **Yes** ☐ **No**
  f Does the firm assign a specific territory to the worker? . . . . ☐ **Yes** ☐ **No** ☐ **Does not apply**
  g Who does the customer pay? ☐ Firm ☐ Worker
    If worker, does the worker remit the total amount to the firm? . . . . ☐ **Yes** ☐ **No**
  h Does the worker sell a consumer product in a home or establishment other than a permanent retail establishment? ☐ **Yes** ☐ **No**
  i List the products and/or services distributed by the worker, such as meat, vegetables, fruit, bakery products, beverages (other than milk), or laundry or dry cleaning services. If more than one type of product and/or service is distributed, specify the principal one. ....
  j Did the firm or another person assign the route or territory and a list of customers to the worker? . . ☐ **Yes** ☐ **No**
    If "Yes," enter the name and job title of the person who made the assignment. ....
    ....
  k Did the worker pay the firm or person for the privilege of serving customers on the route or in the territory? ☐ **Yes** ☐ **No**
    If "Yes," how much did the worker pay (not including any amount paid for a truck or racks, etc.)? $ ....
    What factors were considered in determining the value of the route or territory? ....
  l How are new customers obtained by the worker? Explain fully, showing whether the new customers called the firm for service, were solicited by the worker, or both. ....
  m Does the worker sell life insurance? . . . . ☐ **Yes** ☐ **No**
    If "Yes":
    Is the selling of life insurance or annuity contracts for the firm the worker's entire business activity? . . ☐ **Yes** ☐ **No**
    If "No," list the other business activities and the amount of time spent on them ....
    Does the worker sell other types of insurance for the firm? . . . . ☐ **Yes** ☐ **No**
    If "Yes," state the percentage of the worker's total working time spent in selling other types of insurance .... %
    At the time the contract was entered into between the firm and the worker, was it their intention that the worker sell life insurance for the firm: ☐ on a full-time basis ☐ on a part-time basis
    State the manner in which the intention was expressed. ....
  n Is the worker a traveling or city salesperson? . . . . ☐ **Yes** ☐ **No**
    If "Yes": From whom does worker principally solicit orders for the firm? ....
    If the worker solicits orders from wholesalers, retailers, contractors, or operators of hotels, restaurants, or other similar establishments, specify the percentage of the worker's time spent in this solicitation. .... %
    Is the merchandise purchased by the customers for resale or for use in their business operations? If used by the customers in their business operations, describe the merchandise and state whether it is equipment installed on their premises or a consumable supply. ....

19 Attach a detailed explanation of any other reason why you believe the worker is an independent contractor or is an employee of the firm.

Under penalties of perjury, I declare that I have examined this request, including accompanying documents, and to the best of my knowledge and belief, the facts presented are true, correct, and complete.

Signature ▶   Title ▶   Date ▶

If this form is used by the firm in requesting a written determination, the form must be signed by an officer or member of the firm.
If this form is used by the worker in requesting a written determination, the form must be signed by the worker. If the worker wants a written determination about services performed for two or more firms, a separate form must be completed and signed for each firm.
Additional copies of this form may be obtained from any Internal Revenue Service office or by calling 1-800-TAX-FORM (1-800-829-3676).

*U.S. Government Printing Office: 1995 — 387-095/20102

a Control number			OMB No. 1545-0008	
b Employer's identification number			1 Wages, tips, other compensation	2 Federal income tax withheld
c Employer's name, address, and ZIP code			3 Social security wages	4 Social security tax withheld
			5 Medicare wages and tips	6 Medicare tax withheld
			7 Social security tips	8 Allocated tips
d Employee's social security number			9 Advance EIC payment	10 Dependent care benefits
e Employee's name, address, and ZIP code			11 Nonqualified plans	12 Benefits included in box 1
			13 See Instrs. for box 13	14 Other

15 Statutory employee ☐	Deceased ☐	Pension plan ☐	Legal rep. ☐	Hshld. emp. ☐	Subtotal ☐	Deferred compensation ☐

16 State	Employer's state I.D. No.	17 State wages, tips, etc.	18 State income tax	19 Locality name	20 Local wages, tips, etc.	21 Local income tax

(O)

Department of the Treasury—Internal Revenue Service

Form **W-2** **Wage and Tax Statement** **1996**

This information is being furnished to the Internal Revenue Service.

Copy B To Be Filed With Employee's FEDERAL Tax Return

Notice to Employee

Refund.—Even if you do not have to file a tax return, you should file to get a refund if box 2 shows Federal income tax withheld, or if you can take the earned income credit.

Earned Income Credit (EIC).—You must file a tax return if any amount is shown in box 9.

You may be able to take the EIC for 1996 if **(1)** you do not have a qualifying child and you earned less than $9,500, **(2)** you have one qualifying child and you earned less than $25,078, or **(3)** you have more than one qualifying child with valid SSNs and you earned less than $28,495. Also, you cannot claim the EIC if you have more than $2,350 in investment income. **Any EIC that is more than your tax liability is refunded to you, but only if you file a tax return.** If you have at least one qualifying child, you may get as much as $1,291 of the EIC in advance by completing Form W-5.

Caution: At the time this notice was printed, Congress was considering changes to the EIC. See your 1996 income tax return instructions and Pub. 596 for a detailed explanation of EIC and any changes made to it. You can get these items by calling 1-800-TAX-FORM (829-3676).

Corrections.—If your name, social security number (SSN), or address is incorrect, correct Copies B, C, and 2 and ask your employer to correct your employment record. Be sure to ask the employer to file **Form W-2c,** Statement of Corrected Income and Tax Amounts, with the Social Security Administration (SSA) to correct any name, amount, or SSN error reported to the SSA on Copy A of Form W-2. If your name and SSN are correct but are not the same as shown on your social security card, you should ask for a new card at any Social Security office or call 1-800-SSA-1213.

Credit for Excess Taxes.—If more than one employer paid you wages during 1996 and more than the maximum social security employee tax, railroad retirement (RRTA) tax, or combined social security and RRTA tax was withheld, you may claim the excess as a credit against your Federal income tax. See your income tax return instructions.

Box 1.—Enter this amount on the wages line of your tax return.

Box 2.—Enter this amount on the Federal income tax withheld line of your tax return.

Box 8.—This amount is **not** included in boxes 1, 5, or 7. For information on how to report tips on your tax return, see your tax return instructions.

Box 9.—Enter this amount on the advance earned income credit payment line of your tax return.

Box 10.—This amount is the total dependent care benefits your employer paid to you (or incurred on your behalf). Any amount over $5,000 is included in box 1. This amount may be taxable unless you complete Schedule 2 of Form 1040A or Form 2441.

Box 11.—This amount is a distribution made to you from a nonqualified deferred compensation or section 457 plan and is included in box 1. Or, it may be a contribution by your employer to a nonqualified deferred compensation plan that is included in box 3 and/or 5.

Box 12.—You may be able to deduct expenses that are related to fringe benefits; see the instructions for your tax return.

Box 13.—The following list explains the codes shown in box 13. You may need this information to complete your tax return.

A—Uncollected social security tax on tips (see "Total tax" in Form 1040 instructions)

B—Uncollected Medicare tax on tips (see "Total tax" in Form 1040 instructions)

C—Cost of group-term life insurance coverage over $50,000

D—Elective deferrals to a section 401(k) cash or deferred arrangement

E—Elective deferrals to a section 403(b) salary reduction agreement

F—Elective deferrals to a section 408(k)(6) salary reduction SEP

G—Elective and nonelective deferrals to a section 457(b) deferred compensation plan

H—Elective deferrals to a section 501(c)(18)(D) tax-exempt organization plan (see Form 1040 instructions for how to deduct)

J—Sick pay not includible as income

K—Tax on excess golden parachute payments

L—Nontaxable part of employee business expense reimbursements

M—Uncollected social security tax on cost of group-term life insurance coverage over $50,000 (former employees only) (see Form 1040 instructions)

N—Uncollected Medicare tax on cost of group-term life insurance coverage over $50,000 (former employees only) (see Form 1040 instructions)

P—Excludable moving expense reimbursements

Q—Military employee basic quarters, subsistence, and combat pay

Box 15.—If the "Pension plan" box is checked, special limits may apply to the amount of IRA contributions you may deduct. If the "Deferred compensation" box is checked, the elective deferrals in box 13 (for all employers, and for all such plans to which you belong) are generally limited to $9,500. Elective deferrals for section 403(b) contracts are limited to $9,500 ($12,500 in limited circumstances, see Pub. 571). The limit for section 457(b) plans is $7,500. Amounts over that must be included in income. See instructions for Form 1040.

Form W-4 (1996)

Want More Money In Your Paycheck?
If you expect to be able to take the earned income credit for 1996 and a child lives with you, you may be able to have part of the credit added to your take-home pay. For details, get Form W-5 from your employer.

Purpose. Complete Form W-4 so that your employer can withhold the correct amount of Federal income tax from your pay. Because your tax situation may change, you may want to refigure your withholding each year.

Exemption From Withholding. Read line 7 of the certificate below to see if you can claim exempt status. *If exempt, only complete lines 1, 2, 3, 4, 7, and sign the form to validate it.* No Federal income tax will be withheld from your pay. Your exemption expires February 18, 1997.

Note: *You cannot claim exemption from withholding if (1) your income exceeds $650*

and includes unearned income (e.g., interest and dividends) and (2) another person can claim you as a dependent on their tax return.

Basic Instructions. If you are not exempt, complete the Personal Allowances Worksheet. Additional worksheets are on page 2 so you can adjust your withholding allowances based on itemized deductions, adjustments to income, or two-earner/two-job situations. Complete all worksheets that apply to your situation. The worksheets will help you figure the number of withholding allowances you are entitled to claim. However, you may claim fewer allowances than this.

Head of Household. Generally, you may claim head of household filing status on your tax return only if you are unmarried and pay more than 50% of the costs of keeping up a home for yourself and your dependent(s) or other qualifying individuals.

Nonwage Income. If you have a large amount of nonwage income, such as interest or dividends, you should consider making estimated tax payments using Form 1040-ES.

Otherwise, you may find that you owe additional tax at the end of the year.

Two Earners/Two Jobs. If you have a working spouse or more than one job, figure the total number of allowances you are entitled to claim on all jobs using worksheets from only one W-4. This total should be divided among all jobs. Your withholding will usually be most accurate when all allowances are claimed on the W-4 filed for the highest paying job and zero allowances are claimed for the others.

Check Your Withholding. After your W-4 takes effect, use **Pub. 919,** Is My Withholding Correct for 1996?, to see how the dollar amount you are having withheld compares to your estimated total annual tax. Get Pub. 919 especially if you used the Two Earner/Two Job Worksheet and your earnings exceed $150,000 (Single) or $200,000 (Married). To order Pub. 919, call 1-800-829-3676. Check your telephone directory for the IRS assistance number for further help.

Sign This Form. Form W-4 is not considered valid unless you sign it.

Personal Allowances Worksheet

A Enter "1" for **yourself** if no one else can claim you as a dependent . . . . **A** _____

B Enter "1" if:
- You are single and have only one job; or
- You are married, have only one job, and your spouse does not work; or
- Your wages from a second job or your spouse's wages (or the total of both) are $1,000 or less.

. . **B** _____

C Enter "1" for your **spouse.** But, you may choose to enter -0- if you are married and have either a working spouse or more than one job (this may help you avoid having too little tax withheld) . . . . **C** _____

D Enter number of **dependents** (other than your spouse or yourself) you will claim on your tax return . . . . . . **D** _____

E Enter "1" if you will file as **head of household** on your tax return (see conditions under **Head of Household** above) . **E** _____

F Enter "1" if you have at least $1,500 of **child or dependent care expenses** for which you plan to claim a credit . . **F** _____

G Add lines A through F and enter total here. **Note:** This amount may be different from the number of exemptions you claim on your return ▶ **G** _____

For accuracy, do all worksheets that apply.
- If you plan to **itemize or claim adjustments to income** and want to reduce your withholding, see the Deductions and Adjustments Worksheet on page 2.
- If you are **single** and have **more than one job** and your combined earnings from all jobs exceed $30,000 OR if you are **married** and have a **working spouse or more than one job,** and the combined earnings from all jobs exceed $50,000, see the Two-Earner/Two-Job Worksheet on page 2 if you want to avoid having too little tax withheld.
- If **neither** of the above situations applies, **stop here** and enter the number from line G on line 5 of Form W-4 below.

- - - - - - - - - - - - - - - - - Cut here and give the certificate to your employer. Keep the top portion for your records. - - - - - - - - - - - - - - - - - -

Form **W-4** Department of the Treasury Internal Revenue Service	**Employee's Withholding Allowance Certificate** ▶ **For Privacy Act and Paperwork Reduction Act Notice, see reverse.**	OMB No. 1545-0010 **1996**

1	Type or print your first name and middle initial	Last name	2	Your social security number

Home address (number and street or rural route)

3 ☐ Single ☐ Married ☐ Married, but withhold at higher Single rate.
Note: *If married, but legally separated, or spouse is a nonresident alien, check the Single box.*

City or town, state, and ZIP code

4 If your last name differs from that on your social security card, check here and call 1-800-772-1213 for a new card . . . . . ▶ ☐

5 Total number of allowances you are claiming (from line G above or from the worksheets on page 2 if they apply) . **5** _____

6 Additional amount, if any, you want withheld from each paycheck . . . . **6** $ _____

7 I claim exemption from withholding for 1996 and I certify that I meet **BOTH** of the following conditions for exemption:
- Last year I had a right to a refund of **ALL** Federal income tax withheld because I had **NO** tax liability; **AND**
- This year I expect a refund of **ALL** Federal income tax withheld because I expect to have **NO** tax liability.

If you meet both conditions, enter "EXEMPT" here . . . . ▶ **7** _____

Under penalties of perjury, I certify that I am entitled to the number of withholding allowances claimed on this certificate or entitled to claim exempt status.

Employee's signature ▶ _____ **Date** ▶ _____ , 19 ___

8	Employer's name and address (Employer: Complete 8 and 10 only if sending to the IRS)	9	Office code (optional)	10	Employer identification number

Cat. No. 10220Q

APPENDIX A

Deductions and Adjustments Worksheet

Note: *Use this worksheet only if you plan to itemize deductions or claim adjustments to income on your 1996 tax return.*

1 Enter an estimate of your 1996 itemized deductions. These include qualifying home mortgage interest, charitable contributions, state and local taxes (but not sales taxes), medical expenses in excess of 7.5% of your income, and miscellaneous deductions. (For 1996, you may have to reduce your itemized deductions if your income is over $117,950 ($58,975 if married filing separately). Get Pub. 919 for details.) **1** $ _____

2 Enter: $6,700 if married filing jointly or qualifying widow(er)
$5,900 if head of household
$4,000 if single
$3,350 if married filing separately **2** $ _____

3 Subtract line 2 from line 1. If line 2 is greater than line 1, enter -0- **3** $ _____

4 Enter an estimate of your 1996 adjustments to income. These include alimony paid and deductible IRA contributions **4** $ _____

5 **Add** lines 3 and 4 and enter the total **5** $ _____

6 Enter an estimate of your 1996 nonwage income (such as dividends or interest) **6** $ _____

7 **Subtract** line 6 from line 5. Enter the result, but not less than -0- **7** $ _____

8 **Divide** the amount on line 7 by $2,500 and enter the result here. Drop any fraction **8** _____

9 Enter the number from Personal Allowances Worksheet, line G, on page 1 **9** _____

10 **Add** lines 8 and 9 and enter the total here. If you plan to use the Two-Earner/Two-Job Worksheet, also enter this total on line 1 below. Otherwise, **stop here** and enter this total on Form W-4, line 5, on page 1 **10** _____

Two-Earner/Two-Job Worksheet

Note: *Use this worksheet only if the instructions for line G on page 1 direct you here.*

1 Enter the number from line G on page 1 (or from line 10 above if you used the Deductions and Adjustments Worksheet) **1** _____

2 Find the number in **Table 1** below that applies to the **LOWEST** paying job and enter it here **2** _____

3 If line 1 is **GREATER THAN OR EQUAL TO** line 2, subtract line 2 from line 1. Enter the result here (if zero, enter -0-) and on Form W-4, line 5, on page 1. **DO NOT** use the rest of this worksheet **3** _____

Note: *If line 1 is **LESS THAN** line 2, enter -0- on Form W-4, line 5, on page 1. Complete lines 4–9 to calculate the additional withholding amount necessary to avoid a year end tax bill.*

4 Enter the number from line 2 of this worksheet **4** _____

5 Enter the number from line 1 of this worksheet **5** _____

6 Subtract line 5 from line 4 **6** _____

7 Find the amount in **Table 2** below that applies to the **HIGHEST** paying job and enter it here **7** $ _____

8 **Multiply** line 7 by line 6 and enter the result here. This is the additional annual withholding amount needed **8** $ _____

9 Divide line 8 by the number of pay periods remaining in 1996. (For example, divide by 26 if you are paid every other week and you complete this form in December 1995.) Enter the result here and on Form W-4, line 6, page 1. This is the additional amount to be withheld from each paycheck **9** $ _____

Table 1: Two-Earner/Two-Job Worksheet

Married Filing Jointly				All Others	
If wages from **LOWEST** paying job are—	Enter on line 2 above	If wages from **LOWEST** paying job are—	Enter on line 2 above	If wages from **LOWEST** paying job are—	Enter on line 2 above
0 - $3,000	0	39,001 - 50,000	9	0 - $4,000	0
3,001 - 6,000	1	50,001 - 55,000	10	4,001 - 10,000	1
6,001 - 11,000	2	55,001 - 60,000	11	10,001 - 14,000	2
11,001 - 16,000	3	60,001 - 70,000	12	14,001 - 19,000	3
16,001 - 21,000	4	70,001 - 80,000	13	19,001 - 23,000	4
21,001 - 27,000	5	80,001 - 90,000	14	23,001 - 45,000	5
27,001 - 31,000	6	90,001 and over	15	45,001 - 60,000	6
31,001 - 34,000	7			60,001 - 70,000	7
34,001 - 39,000	8			70,001 and over	8

Table 2: Two-Earner/Two-Job Worksheet

Married Filing Jointly		All Others	
If wages from **HIGHEST** paying job are—	Enter on line 7 above	If wages from **HIGHEST** paying job are—	Enter on line 7 above
0 - $50,000	$380	0 - $30,000	$380
50,001 - 100,000	710	30,001 - 60,000	710
100,001 - 130,000	790	60,001 - 120,000	790
130,001 - 240,000	920	120,001 - 240,000	920
240,001 and over	1,010	240,001 and over	1,010

  Printed on recycled paper

☆U.S. Government Printing Office: 1996 389-119

1996 Form W-5

![IRS logo] **Department of the Treasury**
Internal Revenue Service

Instructions

A Change To Note

If you expect your 1996 investment income to be more than $2,350, you **cannot** claim the earned income credit (EIC) for 1996. As used on this form, **investment income** includes taxable interest and dividends and tax-exempt interest. It also includes rental and royalty income after subtracting the total deductible related expenses. But rents and royalties received in a trade or business are not investment income.

Caution: *At the time these instructions were printed, Congress was considering legislation that would change the EIC rules for 1996. If this legislation results in changes to the advance EIC rules, the IRS will issue a revised 1996 Form W-5. For information on the changes, get Pub. 553, Highlights of 1995 Tax Changes. You can get it by calling 1-800-TAX-FORM (1-800-829-3676).*

Purpose

Use Form W-5 if you are eligible to get part of the EIC in advance with your pay and choose to do so. The amount you can get in advance generally depends on your wages. If you are married, the amount of your advance EIC payments also depends on whether your spouse has filed a Form W-5 with his or her employer. However, your employer cannot give you more than $1,291 throughout 1996 with your pay.

If you do not choose to get advance payments, you can still claim the EIC on your 1996 tax return.

What Is the EIC?

The EIC is a credit for certain workers. It reduces tax you owe. It may give you a refund even if you don't owe any tax. For 1996, the EIC can be as much as $2,152 if you have one qualifying child; $3,556 if you

have more than one qualifying child; $323 if you don't have a qualifying child. But you **cannot** get **advance** EIC payments unless you have a qualifying child. See **Who Is a Qualifying Child?** on this page.

Who Is Eligible To Get Advance EIC Payments?

You are eligible to get advance EIC payments if **all three** of the following apply.

1. You have at least one qualifying child.

2. You expect that your 1996 earned income and adjusted gross income will each be less than $25,078. Include your spouse's income if you plan to file a joint return. As used on this form, earned income does not include amounts inmates in penal institutions are paid for their work.

3. You expect to be able to claim the EIC for 1996. To find out if you may be able to claim the EIC, answer the questions on page 2.

How Do I Get Advance EIC Payments?

If you are eligible to get advance EIC payments, fill in the Form W-5 at the bottom of this page. Then, detach it and give it to your employer. If you get advance payments, you **must** file a 1996 Federal income tax return.

You may have only **one** Form W-5 in effect with a current employer at one time. If you and your spouse are both employed, you should file separate Forms W-5.

This Form W-5 expires on December 31, 1996. If you are eligible to get advance EIC payments for 1997, you must file a new Form W-5 next year.

(TIP) *You may be able to get a larger credit when you file your 1996 return. For details, see **Additional Credit** on page 2.*

Who Is a Qualifying Child?

Any child who meets **all three** of the following conditions is a **qualifying child**.

1. The child is your son, daughter, adopted child, stepchild, foster child, or a descendant (for example, your grandchild) of your son, daughter, or adopted child.

Note: *An **adopted child** includes a child placed with you by an authorized placement agency for legal adoption even if the adoption isn't final. A **foster child** is any child you cared for as your own child.*

2. The child is under age 19 at the end of 1996, or under age 24 at the end of 1996 and a full-time student, or any age at the end of 1996 and permanently and totally disabled.

3. The child lives with you in the United States for over half of 1996 (for all of 1996 if a foster child). If the child does not live with you for the required time because the child was born or died in 1996, the child is considered to have lived with you for all of 1996 if your home was the child's home for the entire time he or she was alive in 1996.

Note: *Temporary absences such as for school, medical care, or vacation count as time lived at home. Members of the military on extended active duty outside the United States are considered to be living in the United States.*

Married child.—If the child is married at the end of 1996, that child is a qualifying child only if you may claim him or her as your dependent, **or** the following **Exception** applies to you.

Exception. You are the custodial parent and would be able to claim the child as your dependent, but the noncustodial parent claims the child as a dependent because—

1. You signed **Form 8332**, Release of Claim to Exemption for Child of Divorced

(Continued on page 2)

✂ *Give the lower part to your employer; keep the top part for your records.* ✂

·· *Detach here* ··

Form **W-5**	**Earned Income Credit**	OMB No. 1545-1342
Department of the Treasury Internal Revenue Service	**Advance Payment Certificate** ⚬ **Give this certificate to your employer.** ⚬ **This certificate expires on December 31, 1996.**	**1996**

Type or print your full name	Your social security number

Note: *If you get advance payments of the earned income credit for 1996, you **must** file a 1996 Federal income tax return. To get advance payments, you **must** have a qualifying child and your filing status must be any status **except** married filing a separate return.*

		Yes	No
1	I expect to be able to claim the earned income credit for 1996, I do not have another Form W-5 in effect with any other current employer, and I choose to get advance EIC payments		
2	Do you have a qualifying child?		
3	Are you married?		
4	If you are married, does your spouse have a Form W-5 in effect for 1996 with any employer?		

Under penalties of perjury, I declare that the information I have furnished above is, to the best of my knowledge, true, correct, and complete.

Signature ⚬ _____   Date ⚬ _____

Cat. No. 10227P

Form W-5 (1996)   Page **2**

Questions To See if You May Be Able To Claim the EIC for 1996

Caution: *You cannot claim the EIC if you plan to file either Form 2555 or Form 2555-EZ (relating to foreign earned income) for 1996. You also cannot claim the EIC if you are a nonresident alien for any part of 1996 unless you are married to a U.S. citizen or resident and elect to be taxed as a resident alien for all of 1996.*

1   Do you have a qualifying child? Read **Who Is a Qualifying Child?** on page 1 before you answer this question. If the child is married, be sure you also read **Married child** on page 1.

☐ **No. Stop.** You may be able to claim the EIC but you **cannot** get advance EIC payments.

☐ **Yes.** Go to question 2.

Caution: *If the child is a qualifying child for both you and another person, the child is your qualifying child only if you expect your 1996 adjusted gross income to be higher than the other person's adjusted gross income. If the other person is your spouse and you expect to file a joint return for 1996, this rule doesn't apply.*

2   Do you expect your 1996 filing status to be Married filing a separate return?

☐ **Yes. Stop.** You **cannot** claim the EIC.

☐ **No.** Go to question 3.

(TIP)   *If you expect to file a joint return for 1996, include your spouse's income when answering questions 3 and 4.*

3   Do you expect that your 1996 earned income and adjusted gross income will each be less than $25,078 (less than $28,495 if you have more than one qualifying child)? To find out what is included in adjusted gross income, you can look at page 1 of your 1995 tax return (Form 1040EZ, Form 1040A, etc.).

☐ **No. Stop.** You **cannot** claim the EIC.

☐ **Yes.** Go to question 4. But remember, you **cannot** get advance EIC payments if you think your 1996 earned income or adjusted gross income will be $25,078 or more.

4   Do you expect that your 1996 investment income (defined on page 1) will be more than $2,350?

☐ **Yes. Stop.** You **cannot** claim the EIC.

☐ **No.** Go to question 5.

5   Do **you** expect to be a qualifying child of another person for 1996?

☐ **No.** You may be able to claim the EIC.

☐ **Yes.** You **cannot** claim the EIC.

---

or Separated Parents, or a similar statement, agreeing not to claim the child for 1996, **or**

2. You have a pre–1985 divorce decree or separation agreement that allows the noncustodial parent to claim the child and he or she gives at least $600 for the child's support in 1996.

Qualifying child of more than one person.—If the child is a qualifying child of more than one person, only the person with the **highest** adjusted gross income for 1996 may treat that child as a qualifying child. If the other person is your spouse and you plan to file a joint return for 1996, this rule doesn't apply.

Reminder.—You must get a social security number for a qualifying child unless the child was born after November 30, 1996.

What If My Situation Changes?

If your situation changes after you give Form W-5 to your employer, you will probably need to file a new Form W-5. For example, you should file a new Form W-5 if any of the following applies for 1996.

You no longer have a qualifying child. Check **"No"** on line 2 of your new Form W-5.

You no longer expect to be able to claim the EIC for 1996. Check **"No"** on line 1 of your new Form W-5.

You no longer want advance payments. Check **"No"** on line 1 of your new Form W-5.

Your spouse files Form W-5 with his or her employer. Check **"Yes"** on line 4 of your new Form W-5.

Note: *If you get the EIC with your pay and find you are not eligible, you must pay it back when you file your 1996 Federal income tax return.*

Additional Information

How To Claim the EIC

If you are eligible, claim the EIC on your 1996 tax return. See your 1996 instruction booklet.

Additional Credit

You may be able to claim a larger credit when you file your 1996 tax return because your employer cannot give you more than $1,291 of the EIC throughout the year with your pay. You may also be able to claim a larger credit if you have more than one qualifying child. But you must file your 1996 tax return to claim any additional credit.

Privacy Act and Paperwork Reduction Act Notice

We ask for the information on this form to carry out the Internal Revenue laws of the United States. Internal Revenue Code sections 3507 and 6109 and their regulations require you to provide the information requested on Form W-5 and give the form to your employer if you want advance payment of the EIC. As provided by law, we may give the information to the Department of Justice and other Federal agencies. In addition, we may give it to cities, states, and the District of Columbia so they may carry out their tax laws.

The time needed to complete this form will vary depending on individual circumstances. The estimated average time is: **Recordkeeping,** 7 min.; **Learning about the law or the form,** 9 min.; and **Preparing the form,** 27 min.

If you have comments concerning the accuracy of these time estimates or suggestions for making this form simpler, we would be happy to hear from you. You can write to the Tax Forms Committee, Western Area Distribution Center, Rancho Cordova, CA 95743-0001. **DO NOT** send the form to this address. Instead, give it to your employer.

⊛   *Printed on recycled paper*

Department of the Treasury
Internal Revenue Service
Publication 1693 (Rev. 7-96)
Catalog Number 15060W

APPENDIX A

Form **433-A**
(Rev. September 1995)

Department of the Treasury — Internal Revenue Service

Collection Information Statement for Individuals

NOTE: **Complete all blocks, except shaded areas, Write "N/A"** *(not applicable)* in those blocks that do not apply.
Instructions for certain line items are in Publication 1854.

1. Taxpayer(s) name(s) and address	2. Home phone number ( )	3. Marital status
County _____	4.a. Taxpayer's social security number	b. Spouse's social security number

Section I. Employment Information

5. Taxpayer's employer or business *(name and address)*	a. How long employed	b. Business phone number ( )	c. Occupation
	d. Number of exemptions claimed on Form W-4 _____	e. Pay period: ☐ Weekly ☐ Bi-weekly ☐ Monthly ☐ _____ Payday: _____ (Mon - Sun)	f. *(Check appropriate box)* ☐ Wage earner ☐ Sole proprietor ☐ Partner
6. Spouse's employer or business *(name and address)*	a. How long employed	b. Business phone number ( )	c. Occupation
	d. Number of exemptions claimed on Form W-4 _____	e. Pay period: ☐ Weekly ☐ Bi-weekly ☐ Monthly ☐ _____ Payday: _____ (Mon - Sun)	f. *(Check appropriate box)* ☐ Wage earner ☐ Sole proprietor ☐ Partner

Section II. Personal Information

7. Name, address and telephone number of next of kin or other reference	8. Other names or aliases	9. Previous address(es)

10. Age and relationship of dependents living in your household *(exclude yourself and spouse)*

11. Date of Birth ▶	a. Taxpayer	b. Spouse	12. Latest filed income tax return *(tax year)*	a. Number of exemptions claimed	b. Adjusted Gross Income

Section III. General Financial Information

13. Bank accounts *(include savings & loans, credit unions, IRA and retirement plans, certificates of deposit, etc.)* Enter bank *loans* in item 28.

Name of Institution	Address	Type of Account	Account No.	Balance
			Total *(Enter in Item 21)*	

Cat. No. 20312N

Form **433-A** (Rev. 9-95)

Section III - *continued*   General Financial Information

14. Charge cards and lines of credit from banks, credit unions, and savings and loans. List all other charge accounts in item 28.

Type of Account or Card	Name and Address of Financial Institution	Monthly Payment	Credit Limit	Amount Owed	Credit Available
Totals *(Enter in Item 27)* ▶					

15. Safe deposit boxes rented or accessed *(List all locations, box numbers, and contents)*

16. **Real Property** *(Brief description and type of ownership)*	Physical Address
a.	
	County _____
b.	
	County _____
c.	
	County _____

17. **Life Insurance** *(Name of Company)*	Policy Number	Type	Face Amount	Available Loan Value
		☐ Whole ☐ Term		
		☐ Whole ☐ Term		
		☐ Whole ☐ Term		
	Total *(Enter in Item 23)* ▶			

18. Securities *(stocks, bonds, mutual funds, money market funds, government securities, etc.)*:

Kind	Quantity or Denomination	Current Value	Where Located	Owner of Record

19. Other information relating to your financial condition. If you check the yes box, please give dates and explain on page 4, Additional Information or Comments:

a. Court proceedings ☐ Yes ☐ No	b. Bankruptcies ☐ Yes ☐ No
c. Repossessions ☐ Yes ☐ No	d. Recent sale or other transfer of assets for less than full value ☐ Yes ☐ No
e. Anticipated increase in income ☐ Yes ☐ No	f. Participant or beneficiary to trust, estate, profit sharing, etc. ☐ Yes ☐ No

Form **433-A**   **page 2**   (Rev. 9-95)

Section IV.   Assets and Liabilities

Description	Current Market Value	Current Amount Owed	Equity in Asset	Amount of Monthly Payment	Name and Address of Lien/Note Holder/Lender	Date Pledged	Date of Final Payment
20. Cash							
21. Bank accounts *(from Item 13)*							
22. Securities *(from Item 18)*							
23. Cash or loan value of insurance							
24. Vehicles *(model, year, license, tag#)*							
a.							
b.							
c.							
25. Real property *(From Section III, item 16)* a.							
b.							
c.							
26. Other assets							
a.							
b.							
c.							
d.							
e.							
27. Bank revolving credit *(from Item 14)*							
28. Other Liabilities *(Including bank loans, judgments, notes, and charge accounts not entered in Item 13.)* a.							
b.							
c.							
d.							
e.							
f.							
g.							
29. Federal taxes owed (prior years)							
30. **Totals**			$	$			

Internal Revenue Service Use Only Below This Line

Financial Verification/Analysis

Item	Date Information or Encumbrance Verified	Date Property Inspected	Estimated Forced Sale Equity
Personal Residence			
Other Real Property			
Vehicles			
Other Personal Property			
State Employment *(Husband and Wife)*			
Income Tax Return			
Wage Statements *(Husband and Wife)*			
Sources of Income/Credit *(D&B Report)*			
Expenses			
Other Assets/Liabilities			

Form **433-A**   **page 3**   (Rev. 9-95)

Section V.   Monthly Income and Expense Analysis

Total Income			Necessary Living Expenses		
Source	**Gross**			**Claimed**	*(IRS use only)* **Allowed**
31. Wages/Salaries *(Taxpayer)*	$		42. National Standard Expenses[1]	$	$
32. Wages/Salaries *(Spouse)*			43. Housing and utilities[2]		
33. Interest - Dividends			44. Transportation[3]		
34. Net business income *(from Form 433-B)*			45. Health care		
35. Rental Income			46. Taxes *(income and FICA)*		
36. Pension *(Taxpayer)*			47. Court ordered payments		
37. Pension *(Spouse)*			48. Child/dependent care		
38. Child Support			49. Life insurance		
39. Alimony			50. Secured or legally-perfected debts *(specify)*		
40. Other			51. Other expenses *(specify)*		
41. Total Income	$		**52. Total Expenses**	$	$
			53. *(IRS use only)* Net difference *(income less necessary living expenses)*	$	

Certification   Under penalties of perjury, I declare that to the best of my knowledge and belief this statement of assets, liabilities, and other information is true, correct, and complete.

54. Your signature	55. Spouse's signature *(if joint return was filed)*	56. Date

Notes

1. Clothing and clothing services, food, housekeeping supplies, personal care products and services, and miscellaneous.

2. Rent or mortgage payment for the taxpayer's principal residence. Add the average monthly payment for the following expenses if they are *not* included in the rent or mortgage payment: property taxes, homeowner's or renter's insurance, parking, necessary maintenance and repair, homeowner dues, condominium fees and utilities. Utilities includes gas, electricity, water, fuel oil, coal, bottled gas, trash and garbage collection, wood and other fuels, septic cleaning and telephone.

3. Lease or purchase payments, insurance, registration fees, normal maintenance, fuel, public transportation, parking and tolls.

Additional information or comments:

Internal Revenue Service Use Only Below This Line

Explain any difference between Item 53 and the installment agreement payment amount:

Name of originator and IDRS assignment number:	Date

Form **433-A**   **page 4**   (Rev. 9-95)   *U.S. Government Printing Office: 1995 — 387-109/21883

How to prepare a
Collection Information Statement (Form 433-A)

Complete all blocks, except shaded areas. Write "N/A" (Not Applicable) in those blocks that do not apply to you. *If you don't complete the form, we won't be able to help determine the best method for you to pay the amount due.* The areas explained below are the ones we have found to be the most confusing to people completing the form.

Section III

Item 13—Bank Accounts
Enter all accounts even if there is currently no balance. *Do Not* enter bank loans.

Item 14—Bank Charge Cards, Lines of Credit, etc.
Enter only credit issued by a bank, credit union, or savings and loan (MasterCard, Visa, overdraft protection, etc.). List other charge accounts such as oil companies and department stores in Item 28.

Item 16—Real Property Description and Ownership
List all real property that you own or are purchasing. Include the address, county, and type of buildings on the property. List the names of all owners and type of ownership (such as joint tenants, tenant in common, etc.)

Section IV

Items 24 thru 26—Vehicles, Real Property, and Other Assets

Current Market Value - Indicate the amount you could sell the asset for today.

Equity in Asset - Subtract liability (current amount owned) from current market value.

Date Pledged - Enter the date the loan was originally taken out or property given as security.

Date of Final Payment - Enter the date the loan will be fully paid. If you are behind in payments, enter "Behind."

List other assets you own such as campers, boats, jewelry, antiques, etc. in item 26.

Item 28—Other Liabilities
List all other liabilities, including charge accounts, bank loans and notes, personal loans, medical bills, etc.

Section V

If only one spouse has a tax liability, but both have income, list the total household income and expenses.

Items 31 and 32—Wages and Salaries
Enter your *gross* monthly wages and/or salaries. Do not deduct withholding, or allotments you elect to take out of your pay such as insurance payments, credit union deductions, car payments, etc. List these expenses in Section IV and Section V.

Item 34—Net Business Income
Enter your monthly *net* business income, that is, what you earn after you have paid your ordinary and necessary monthly business expenses.

Necessary Living Expenses

To be necessary, expenses must provide for the health and welfare of you and your family and/or provide for the production of income, and must be reasonable in amount. You may be asked to provide substantiation of certain expenses.

Item 42—National Standard Expenses
This category includes clothing and clothing services, food, housekeeping supplies, personal care products and services, and miscellaneous. Enter the amount you are allowed, based on your total monthly gross income and the size of your family, from the chart on the back of these instructions. If you claim a higher amount, you must substantiate why a higher amount is necessary for each item included in this category.

Item 43—Housing and Utilities
Enter the monthly rent or mortgage payment for your principal residence. Add the average monthly payment for the following expenses if they are *not* included in your rent or mortgage payment: property taxes, homeowner's or renter's insurance, parking, necessary maintenance and repair, homeowner dues, condominium fees, and utilities. Utilities includes gas, electricity, water, fuel oil, coal, bottled gas, trash and garbage collection, wood and other fuels, septic cleaning and telephone.

Item 44—Transportation
Enter your average monthly transportation expenses. Transportation expenses include: lease or purchase payments, insurance, registration fees, normal maintenance, fuel, public transportation, parking and tolls.

Item 50—Secured or Legally-perfected Debts
Do not enter mortgage payment entered in Item 43, or lease or purchase payments entered in Item 44.

Item 51—Other Expenses
Enter your average monthly payments for any other *necessary* expenses.

Item 53—Net Difference
Do not show an entry in this space. IRS use only.

Certification

For joint income tax liabilities, both husband and wife should sign the statement.

Department of the Treasury
Internal Revenue Service
Publication **1854** (Rev. 9-95)
Catalog No. 21563Q

National Standard Expenses
(Item 42)

Total Monthly Income	Number of Persons in Household				
	One	Two	Three	Four	Over Four
Less than $830	315	509	553	714	+120
$830 to $1,249	383	517	624	723	+130
$1,250 to $1,669	448	569	670	803	+140
$1,670 to $2,499	511	651	731	839	+150
$2,500 to $3,329	551	707	809	905	+160
$3,330 to $4,169	590	840	948	1,053	+170
$4,170 to $5,829	665	913	1,019	1,177	+180
$5,830 and over	923	1,179	1,329	1,397	+190

Expenses include: Housekeeping supplies
Clothing and clothing services
Personal care products and services
Food
Miscellaneous

To find the amount you are allowed, read down the Total Gross Monthly Income Column until you find your income, then read across to the column for the number of persons in your family.

If there are more than four persons in your family, multiply the number of additional persons by the amount in the "Over Four" column and add the result to the amount in the "Four" column. (For example total monthly income of $830 to $1,249 for six persons would equal a monthly national standard of 723 + 130 + 130, or 983.

Normally, expenses should be allowed only for persons who can be claimed as exemptions on your income tax return.

Dollar amounts are derived from Bureau of Labor Statistics (BLS) Consumer Expenditure Survey, 1992-93, Tables 1, 3, 4, and 5.

*U.S. Government Printing Office: 1995 — 387-109/21884

Form **433-B** (Rev. June 1991)	Department of the Treasury — Internal Revenue Service **Collection Information Statement for Businesses** *(If you need additional space, please attach a separate sheet)*

NOTE: Complete all blocks, except shaded areas. Write "N/A" *(not applicable)* in those blocks that do not apply.

1. Name and address of business	2. Business phone number ( )

3. *(Check appropriate box)*
☐ Sole proprietor ☐ Other *(specify)*
☐ Partnership _____
☐ Corporation _____

County _____

4. Name and title of person being interviewed	5. Employer Identification Number	6. Type of business

7. Information about owner, partners, officers, major shareholder, etc.

Name and Title	Effective Date	Home Address	Phone Number	Social Security Number	Total Shares or Interest

Section I. General Financial Information

8. Latest filed income tax return ▶	Form	Tax Year ended	Net income before taxes

9. Bank accounts *(List all types of accounts including payroll and general, savings, certificates of deposit, etc.)*

Name of Institution	Address	Type of Account	Account Number	Balance
	Total *(Enter in Item 17)*		▶	

10. Bank credit available *(Lines of credit, etc.)*

Name of Institution	Address	Credit Limit	Amount Owed	Credit Available	Monthly Payments
Totals *(Enter in Items 24 or 25 as appropriate)*		▶			

11. Location, box number, and contents of all safe deposit boxes rented or accessed

Section I - *continued*   General Financial Information

12. Real property

Brief Description and Type of Ownership	Physical Address
a.	County _____
b.	County _____
c.	County _____
d.	County _____

13. Life insurance policies owned with business as beneficiary

Name Insured	Company	Policy Number	Type	Face Amount	Available Loan Value
		Total *(Enter in Item 19)*		▶	

14a. Additional information regarding financial condition *(Court proceedings, bankruptcies filed or anticipated, transfers of assets for less than full value, changes in market conditions, etc.; include information regarding company participation in trusts, estates, profit-sharing plans, etc.)*

b. If you know of any person or organization that borrowed or otherwise provided funds to pay net payrolls:

a. Who borrowed funds?

b. Who supplied funds?

15. Accounts/Notes receivable *(Include current contract jobs, loans to stockholders, officers, partners, etc.)*

Name	Address	Amount Due	Date Due	Status
		$		
	Total *(Enter in Item 18)* ▶	$		

Form 433-B (Rev. 6-91)

Section II.   Asset and Liability Analysis

Description (a)	Cur. Mkt. Value (b)	Liabilities Bal. Due (c)	Equity in Asset (d)	Amt. of Mo. Pymt. (e)	Name and Address of Lien/Note Holder/Obligee (f)	Date Pledged (g)	Date of Final Pymt. (h)
16. Cash on hand							
17. Bank accounts							
18. Accounts/Notes receivable							
19. Life insurance loan value							
20. Real property *(from Item 12)* a.							
b.							
c.							
d.							
21. Vehicles *(Model, year, and license)* a.							
b.							
c.							
22. Machinery and equipment *(Specify)* a.							
b.							
c.							
23. Merchandise inventory *(Specify)* a.							
b.							
24. Other assets *(Specify)* a.							
b.							
25. Other liabilities *(Including notes and judgments)* a.							
b.							
c.							
d.							
e.							
f.							
g.							
h.							
26. Federal taxes owed							
27. **Total**							

Section III.   Income and Expense Analysis

The following information applies to income and expenses during the period _____ to _____		Accounting method used	
Income		**Expenses**	
28. Gross receipts from sales, services, etc.	$	34. Materials purchased	$
29. Gross rental income		35. Net wages and salaries Number of Employees _____	
30. Interest		36. Rent	
31. Dividends		37. Allowable installment payments *(IRS use only)*	
32. Other income *(Specify)*		38. Supplies	
		39. Utilities/Telephone	
		40. Gasoline/Oil	
		41. Repairs and maintenance	
		42. Insurance	
		43. Current taxes	
		44. Other *(Specify)*	
33. Total Income ▶	$	45. Total Expenses *(IRS use only)* ▶	$
		46. Net difference *(IRS use only)* ▶	$

Certification   Under penalties of perjury, I declare that to the best of my knowledge and belief this statement of assets, liabilities, and other information is true, correct, and complete.

47. Signature	48. Date

Internal Revenue Service Use Only Below This Line

Financial Verification/Analysis

Item	Date Information or Encumbrance Verified	Date Property Inspected	Estimated Forced Sale Equity
Sources of Income/Credit (D&B Report)			
Expenses			
Real Property			
Vehicles			
Machinery and Equipment			
Merchandise			
Accounts/Notes Receivable			
Corporate Information, if Applicable			
U.C.C. : Senior/Junior Lienholder			
Other Assets/Liabilities:			

Explain any difference between Item 46 (or P&L) and the installment agreement payment amount:

Name of Originator and IDRS assignment number	Date

Form **656**
(Rev. Sept. 1993)

Department of the Treasury—Internal Revenue Service

Offer in Compromise

▶ **See Instructions**
Page 5

(1) Name and Address of Taxpayers

For Official Use Only

Offer is *(Check applicable box)*
☐ Cash *(Paid in full)*
☐ Deferred payment

Serial Number

(Cashier's stamp)

(2) Social Security Number

(3) Employer Identification Number

Alpha CSED Ind. _____

Amount Paid
$

To: **Commissioner of Internal Revenue Service**

(4) I/we (includes all types of taxpayers) **submit this offer to compromise the tax liabilities plus any interest, penalties, additions to tax, and additional amounts required by law (tax liability)** for the tax type and period checked below: (Please mark "X" for the correct description and fill-in the correct tax period(s), adding additional periods if needed.)

☐ Income tax for the year(s) 19_____, 19_____, 19_____, and 19_____

☐ Trust fund recovery penalty (formerly called the 100-percent penalty) as a responsible person of _____
_____(enter business name) for failure to pay withholding and Federal Insurance Contributions Act taxes (Social Security taxes) for the period(s) ended _____ /_____ /_____ , _____
/_____ /_____ , _____ /_____ /_____ , _____ /_____ /_____ (for example - 06/30/92)

☐ Withholding and Federal Insurance Contributions Act taxes (Social Security taxes) for the period(s) ended _____ /_____
/_____ , _____ /_____ /_____ , _____ /_____ /_____ , _____ /_____ /_____ (for example - 06/30/92)

☐ Federal Unemployment Tax Act taxes for the year(s) 19_____, 19_____, 19_____, and 19_____

☐ Other (Be specific.) _____

(5) I/we offer to pay $ _____ .

If you aren't making full payment with your offer, describe below when you will make full payment (for example – within ten (10) days from the date the offer is accepted): See the instructions for Item 5.

_____

_____

_____

As required by section 6621 of the Internal Revenue Code, the Internal Revenue Service (IRS) will add interest to the offered amount from the date IRS accepts the offer until the date you completely pay the amount offered. IRS compounds interest daily, as required by section 6622 of the Internal Revenue Code.

(6) I/we submit this offer for the reason(s) checked below:

☐ Doubt as to collectibility ("I can't pay.") You must include a completed financial statement (Form 433-A and/or Form 433-B).

☐ Doubt as to liability ("I don't believe I owe this tax.") You must include a detailed explanation of the reason(s) why you believe you don't owe the tax.

IMPORTANT: SEE REVERSE FOR TERMS AND CONDITIONS

I accept waiver of the statutory period of limitations for the Internal Revenue Service.	Under penalties of perjury, I declare that I have examined this offer, including accompanying schedules and statements, and to the best of my knowledge and belief, it is true, correct and complete.	
Signature of authorized Internal Revenue Service Official	(8a) Signature of Taxpayer-proponent	Date
Title Date	(8b) Signature of Taxpayer-proponent	Date

Dispose of prior issues.

Part 1 IRS Copy

Cat. No. 16728N

Form **656** (Rev. 9-93)

Form **709**	**United States Gift (and Generation-Skipping Transfer) Tax Return**	
(Rev. November 1993)	(Section 6019 of the Internal Revenue Code) (For gifts made after December 31, 1991)	OMB No. 1545-0020
Department of the Treasury Internal Revenue Service	**Calendar year 19** .... ▶ **See separate instructions. For Privacy Act Notice, see the Instructions for Form 1040.**	Expires 5-31-96

Part 1—General Information

1 Donor's first name and middle initial	2 Donor's last name	3 Donor's social security number

4 Address (number, street, and apartment number)	5 Legal residence (Domicile) (county and state)

6 City, state, and ZIP code	7 Citizenship

		Yes	No
8	If the donor died during the year, check here ▶ ☐ and enter date of death .... , 19		
9	If you received an extension of time to file this Form 709, check here ▶ ☐ and attach the Form 4868, 2688, 2350, or extension letter		
10	Enter the total number of separate donees listed on Schedule A—count each person only once . . . . ☐		
11a	Have you (the donor) previously filed a Form 709 (or 709-A) for any other year? If the answer is "No," do not complete line 11b .		
11b	If the answer to line 11a is "Yes," has your address changed since you last filed Form 709 (or 709-A)?		
12	Gifts by husband or wife to third parties.—Do you consent to have the gifts (including generation-skipping transfers) made by you and by your spouse to third parties during the calendar year considered as made one-half by each of you? (See instructions.) (If the answer is "Yes," the following information must be furnished and your spouse must sign the consent shown below. **If the answer is "No," skip lines 13–18 and go to Schedule A.)**		
13	Name of consenting spouse **14** SSN		
15	Were you married to one another during the entire calendar year? (see instructions)		
16	If the answer to 15 is "No," check whether ☐ married ☐ divorced or ☐ widowed, and give date (see instructions) ▶		
17	Will a gift tax return for this calendar year be filed by your spouse?		
18	**Consent of Spouse**—I consent to have the gifts (and generation-skipping transfers) made by me and by my spouse to third parties during the calendar year considered as made one-half by each of us. We are both aware of the joint and several liability for tax created by the execution of this consent.		

Consenting spouse's signature ▶   Date ▶

Part 2—Tax Computation

1	Enter the amount from Schedule A, Part 3, line 15	1		
2	Enter the amount from Schedule B, line 3	2		
3	Total taxable gifts (add lines 1 and 2)	3		
4	Tax computed on amount on line 3 (see Table for Computing Tax in separate instructions). . .	4		
5	Tax computed on amount on line 2 (see Table for Computing Tax in separate instructions). . .	5		
6	Balance (subtract line 5 from line 4)	6		
7	Maximum unified credit (nonresident aliens, see instructions)	7	192,800	00
8	Enter the unified credit against tax allowable for all prior periods (from Sch. B, line 1, col. C) . . .	8		
9	Balance (subtract line 8 from line 7)	9		
10	Enter 20% (.20) of the amount allowed as a specific exemption for gifts made after September 8, 1976, and before January 1, 1977 (see instructions)	10		
11	Balance (subtract line 10 from line 9)	11		
12	Unified credit (enter the smaller of line 6 or line 11)	12		
13	Credit for foreign gift taxes (see instructions)	13		
14	Total credits (add lines 12 and 13)	14		
15	Balance (subtract line 14 from line 6) (do not enter less than zero)	15		
16	Generation-skipping transfer taxes (from Schedule C, Part 3, col. H, total)	16		
17	Total tax (add lines 15 and 16)	17		
18	Gift and generation-skipping transfer taxes prepaid with extension of time to file.	18		
19	If line 18 is less than line 17, enter BALANCE DUE (see instructions)	19		
20	If line 18 is greater than line 17, enter AMOUNT TO BE REFUNDED	20		

Under penalties of perjury, I declare that I have examined this return, including any accompanying schedules and statements, and to the best of my knowledge and belief it is true, correct, and complete. Declaration of preparer (other than donor) is based on all information of which preparer has any knowledge.

Donor's signature ▶   Date ▶

Preparer's signature (other than donor) ▶   Date ▶

Preparer's address (other than donor) ▶

Attach check or money order here.

For Paperwork Reduction Act Notice, see page 1 of the separate instructions for this form.   Cat. No. 16783M   Form **709** (Rev. 11-93)

APPENDIX A

		In Reply Refer To:
Form **872** (Rev. August 1988)	Department of the Treasury—Internal Revenue Service **Consent to Extend the Time to Assess Tax**	SSN or EIN

(Name(s))

taxpayer(s) of _____
(Number, Street, City or Town, State, ZIP Code)

and the District Director of Internal Revenue or Regional Director of Appeals consent and agree to the following:

(1) The amount of any Federal _____ tax due on any return(s) made by
(Kind of tax)

or for the above taxpayer(s) for the period(s) ended _____

_____

may be assessed at any time on or before _____ . However, if
(Expiration date)

a notice of deficiency in tax for any such period(s) is sent to the taxpayer(s) on or before that date, then the time for assessing the tax will be further extended by the number of days the assessment was previously prohibited, plus 60 days.

(2) This agreement ends on the earlier of the above expiration date or the assessment date of an increase in the above tax that reflects the final determination of tax and the final administrative appeals consideration. An assessment for one period covered by this agreement will not end this agreement for any other period it covers. Some assessments do not reflect a final determination and appeals consideration and therefore will not terminate the agreement before the expiration date. Examples are assessments of: (a) tax under a partial agreement; (b) tax in jeopardy; (c) tax to correct mathematical or clerical errors; (d) tax reported on amended returns; and (e) advance payments. In addition, unassessed payments, such as amounts treated by the Service as cash bonds and advance payments not assessed by the Service, will not terminate this agreement before the expiration date.

This agreement ends on the above expiration date regardless of any assessment for any period includible in a report to the Joint Committee on Taxation submitted under section 6405 of the Internal Revenue Code.

(3) The taxpayer(s) may file a claim for credit or refund and the Service may credit or refund the tax within 6 months after this agreement ends.

(SIGNATURE INSTRUCTIONS AND SPACE FOR SIGNATURE ARE ON THE BACK OF THIS FORM) Form **872** (Rev. 8-88)

Cat.No. 20755I

Form **872-A** (Rev. October 1987)	Department of the Treasury — Internal Revenue Service **Special Consent to Extend the Time to Assess Tax**	In reply refer to: SSN or EIN

_____
(Name(s))

taxpayer(s) of _____
(Number, Street, City or Town, State, ZIP Code)

and the District Director of Internal Revenue or Regional Director of Appeals consent and agree as follows:

   (1) The amount(s) of any Federal_____tax due on any return(s) made by or
(Kind of tax)

for the above taxpayer(s) for the period(s) ended _____
may be assessed on or before the 90th (ninetieth) day after: (a) the Internal Revenue Service office considering the case receives Form 872-T, Notice of Termination of Special Consent to Extend the Time to Assess Tax, from the taxpayer(s); or (b) the Internal Revenue Service mails Form 872-T to the taxpayer(s); or (c) the Internal Revenue Service mails a notice of deficiency for such period(s); except that if a notice of deficiency is sent to the taxpayer(s), the time for assessing the tax for the period(s) stated in the notice of deficiency will end 60 days after the period during which the making of an assessment is prohibited. A final adverse determination subject to declaratory judgment under sections 7428, 7476, or 7477 of the Internal Revenue Code will not terminate this agreement.

   (2) This agreement ends on the earlier of the above expiration date or the assessment date of an increase in the above tax or the overassessment date of a decrease in the above tax that reflects the final determination of tax and the final administrative appeals consideration. An assessment or overassessment for one period covered by this agreement will not end this agreement for any other period it covers. Some assessments do not reflect a final determination and appeals consideration and therefore will not terminate the agreement before the expiration date. Examples are assessments of: (a) tax under a partial agreement; (b) tax in jeopardy; (c) tax to correct mathematical or clerical errors; (d) tax reported on amended returns; and (e) advance payments. In addition, unassessed payments, such as amounts treated by the Service as cash bonds and advance payments not assessed by the Service, will not terminate this agreement before the expiration date determined in (1) above. This agreement ends on the date determined in (1) above regardless of any assessment for any period includible in a report to the Joint Committee on Taxation submitted under section 6405 of the Internal Revenue Code.

   (3) This agreement will not reduce the period of time otherwise provided by law for making such assessment.

   (4) The taxpayer(s) may file a claim for credit or refund and the Service may credit or refund the tax within 6 (six) months after this agreement ends.

(Signature instructions and space for signature are on the back of this form)   Form **872-A** (Rev. 10-87)

Form **911** (Rev. January 1994)	Department of the Treasury – Internal Revenue Service **Application for Taxpayer Assistance Order** *(ATAO)* (Taxpayer's Application for Relief from Hardship)	If sending Form 911 with another form or letter, put Form 911 on top.

Note: If you have not tried to obtain relief from the IRS office that contacted you, use of this form may not be necessary. Use this form only after reading the instructions for When To Use This Form. Filing this application may affect the statutory period of limitations. (See instructions for line 14.)

Section I.   **Taxpayer Information**

1. Name*(s)* as shown on tax return	2. Your Social Security Number	4. Tax form
	3. Social Security of Spouse Shown in 1.	5. Tax period ended

6. Current mailing address (number & street). For P.O. Box, see instructions	Apt. No.	8. Employer identification number, if applicable.
7. City, town or post office, state and ZIP Code		9. Person to contact

If the above address is different from that shown on latest filed tax return and you want us to update our records with this new address, check here........☐	10. Daytime telephone number ( )	11. Best time to call

12. Description of significant hardship *(If more space is needed, attach additional sheets.)*

13. Description of relief requested *(If more space is needed, attach additional sheets.)*

A
T
A
O

14. Signature of taxpayer or Corporate Officer *(See instructions.)*	15. Date	16. Signature of spouse shown in block 1	17. Date

Section II.   **Representative Information** *(If applicable)*

18. Name of authorized representative (Must be same as on Form 2848 or 8821)	22. Firm name
19. Centralized Authorization File (CAF) number	23. Mailing address
20. Daytime telephone number ( )	21. Best time to call	
24. Representative Signature	25. Date

Section III.   **(For Internal Revenue Service only)**

26. Name of initiating employee	27. ☐ IRS Identified ☐ Taxpayer request	28. Telephone ( )	29. Function	30. Office	31. Date

Cat. No. 16965S

Form **911** (Rev. 1-94)

Form **941**		**Employer's Quarterly Federal Tax Return**	

(Rev. January 1996)
Department of the Treasury
Internal Revenue Service (O)

4141 ▶ See separate instructions for information on completing this return.
Please type or print.

Enter state code for state in which deposits made . ▶ ☐ (see page 3 of instructions).

Name (as distinguished from trade name)	Date quarter ended	OMB No. 1545-0029
Trade name, if any	Employer identification number	T / FF / FD / FP / I / T
Address (number and street)	City, state, and ZIP code	

If address is different from prior return, check here ▶ ☐

IRS Use

1 1 1 1 1 1 1 1 1 1   2   3 3 3 3 3 3   4 4 4

5 5 5   6   7   8 8 8 8 8 8   9 9 9   10 10 10 10 10 10 10 10 10

If you do not have to file returns in the future, check here ▶ ☐ and enter date final wages paid ▶

If you are a seasonal employer, see **Seasonal employers** on page 1 of the instructions and check here ▶ ☐

1	Number of employees (except household) employed in the pay period that includes March 12th ▶		
2	Total wages and tips, plus other compensation	**2**	
3	Total income tax withheld from wages, tips, and sick pay	**3**	
4	Adjustment of withheld income tax for preceding quarters of calendar year	**4**	
5	Adjusted total of income tax withheld (line 3 as adjusted by line 4—see instructions) . . .	**5**	
6a	Taxable social security wages	$ × 12.4% (.124) =	**6a**	
b	Taxable social security tips	$ × 12.4% (.124) =	**6b**	
7	Taxable Medicare wages and tips	$ × 2.9% (.029) =	**7**	
8	Total social security and Medicare taxes (add lines 6a, 6b, and 7). Check here if wages are not subject to social security and/or Medicare tax . . . . ▶ ☐	**8**	
9	Adjustment of social security and Medicare taxes (see instructions for required explanation) Sick Pay $ _____ ± Fractions of Cents $ _____ ± Other $ _____ =	**9**	
10	Adjusted total of social security and Medicare taxes (line 8 as adjusted by line 9—see instructions)	**10**	
11	**Total taxes** (add lines 5 and 10)	**11**	
12	Advance earned income credit (EIC) payments made to employees, if any	**12**	
13	Net taxes (subtract line 12 from line 11). **This should equal line 17, column (d) below** (or line D of Schedule B (Form 941))	**13**	
14	Total deposits for quarter, including overpayment applied from a prior quarter	**14**	
15	**Balance due** (subtract line 14 from line 13). See instructions	**15**	
16	**Overpayment,** if line 14 is more than line 13, enter excess here ▶ $ _____ and check if to be: ☐ Applied to next return OR ☐ Refunded.		

- **All filers:** If line 13 is less than $500, you need not complete line 17 or Schedule B.
- **Semiweekly schedule depositors:** Complete Schedule B and check here . . . . ▶ ☐
- **Monthly schedule depositors:** Complete line 17, columns (a) through (d), and check here. . . . . . ▶ ☐

17	**Monthly Summary of Federal Tax Liability.**		
(a) First month liability	**(b)** Second month liability	**(c)** Third month liability	**(d)** Total liability for quarter

Sign Here

Under penalties of perjury, I declare that I have examined this return, including accompanying schedules and statements, and to the best of my knowledge and belief, it is true, correct, and complete.

Signature ▶   Print Your Name and Title ▶   Date ▶

For Paperwork Reduction Act Notice, see page 1 of separate instructions.   Cat. No. 17001Z   Form **941** (Rev. 1-96)

Form **1041**	Department of the Treasury—Internal Revenue Service **U.S. Income Tax Return for Estates and Trusts**	**1995**	

For calendar year 1995 or fiscal year beginning , 1995, and ending , 19 — OMB No. 1545-0092

A Type of entity:	Name of estate or trust (If a grantor type trust, see page 7 of the instructions.)	**C** Employer identification number
☐ Decedent's estate		
☐ Simple trust		**D** Date entity created
☐ Complex trust		
☐ Grantor type trust	Name and title of fiduciary	**E** Nonexempt charitable and split-interest trusts, check applicable boxes (see page 9 of the instructions):
☐ Bankruptcy estate–Ch. 7		
☐ Bankruptcy estate–Ch. 11	Number, street, and room or suite no. (If a P.O. box, see page 7 of the instructions.)	
☐ Pooled income fund		☐ Described in section 4947(a)(1)
B Number of Schedules K-1 attached (see instructions) ▶	City or town, state, and ZIP code	☐ Not a private foundation ☐ Described in section 4947(a)(2)

F Check applicable boxes: ☐ Initial return ☐ Final return ☐ Amended return ☐ Change in fiduciary's name ☐ Change in fiduciary's address

G Pooled mortgage account (see page 9 of the instructions): ☐ Bought ☐ Sold Date:

Income

1	Interest income	1	
2	Dividends	2	
3	Business income or (loss) (attach Schedule C or C-EZ (Form 1040))	3	
4	Capital gain or (loss) (attach Schedule D (Form 1041))	4	
5	Rents, royalties, partnerships, other estates and trusts, etc. (attach Schedule E (Form 1040))	5	
6	Farm income or (loss) (attach Schedule F (Form 1040))	6	
7	Ordinary gain or (loss) (attach Form 4797)	7	
8	Other income. List type and amount	8	
9	**Total income.** Combine lines 1 through 8 ▶	9	

Deductions

10	Interest. Check if Form 4952 is attached ▶ ☐	10	
11	Taxes	11	
12	Fiduciary fees	12	
13	Charitable deduction (from Schedule A, line 7)	13	
14	Attorney, accountant, and return preparer fees	14	
15a	Other deductions NOT subject to the 2% floor (attach schedule)	15a	
b	Allowable miscellaneous itemized deductions subject to the 2% floor	15b	
16	**Total.** Add lines 10 through 15b	16	
17	Adjusted total income or (loss). Subtract line 16 from line 9. Enter here and on Schedule B, line 1 ▶	17	
18	Income distribution deduction (from Schedule B, line 17) (attach Schedules K-1 (Form 1041))	18	
19	Estate tax deduction (including certain generation-skipping taxes) (attach computation)	19	
20	Exemption	20	
21	**Total deductions.** Add lines 18 through 20 ▶	21	

Tax and Payments

22	Taxable income. Subtract line 21 from line 17. If a loss, see page 13 of the instructions	22	
23	**Total tax** (from Schedule G, line 8)	23	
24	**Payments: a** 1995 estimated tax payments and amount applied from 1994 return	24a	
b	Estimated tax payments allocated to beneficiaries (from Form 1041-T)	24b	
c	Subtract line 24b from line 24a	24c	
d	Tax paid with extension of time to file: ☐ Form 2758 ☐ Form 8736 ☐ Form 8800	24d	
e	Federal income tax withheld. If any is from Form(s) 1099, check ▶ ☐	24e	
	Other payments: **f** Form 2439 ....; **g** Form 4136 ....; Total ▶	24h	
25	**Total payments.** Add lines 24c through 24e, and 24h ▶	25	
26	Estimated tax penalty (see page 14 of the instructions)	26	
27	**Tax due.** If line 25 is smaller than the total of lines 23 and 26, enter amount owed	27	
28	**Overpayment.** If line 25 is larger than the total of lines 23 and 26, enter amount overpaid	28	
29	Amount of line 28 to be: **a Credited to 1996 estimated tax** ▶ ; **b Refunded** ▶	29	

Please Sign Here

Under penalties of perjury, I declare that I have examined this return, including accompanying schedules and statements, and to the best of my knowledge and belief, it is true, correct, and complete. Declaration of preparer (other than fiduciary) is based on all information of which preparer has any knowledge.

Signature of fiduciary or officer representing fiduciary	Date	EIN of fiduciary if a financial institution (see page 3 of the instructions)

Paid Preparer's Use Only

Preparer's signature ▶	Date	Check if self-employed ▶ ☐	Preparer's social security no.
Firm's name (or yours if self-employed) and address ▶		EIN ▶	
		ZIP code ▶	

For Paperwork Reduction Act Notice, see page 1 of the separate instructions.   Cat. No. 11370H   Form **1041** (1995)

| SCHEDULE K-1
(Form 1041)

Department of the Treasury
Internal Revenue Service | Beneficiary's Share of Income, Deductions, Credits, etc.
for the calendar year 1995, or fiscal year
beginning .... , 1995, ending .... , 19 ....
▶ Complete a separate Schedule K-1 for each beneficiary. | OMB No. 1545-0092

1995 |

Name of trust or decedent's estate
☐ Amended K-1
☐ Final K-1

Beneficiary's identifying number ▶	Estate's or trust's EIN ▶
Beneficiary's name, address, and ZIP code	Fiduciary's name, address, and ZIP code

	(a) Allocable share item		(b) Amount	(c) Calendar year 1995 Form 1040 filers enter the amounts in column (b) on:
1	Interest.	1		Schedule B, Part I, line 1
2	Dividends	2		Schedule B, Part II, line 5
3a	Net short-term capital gain	3a		Schedule D, line 5, column (g)
b	Net long-term capital gain	3b		Schedule D, line 13, column (g)
4a	Annuities, royalties, and other nonpassive income before directly apportioned deductions	4a		Schedule E, Part III, column (f)
b	Depreciation	4b		Include on the applicable line of the appropriate tax form
c	Depletion	4c		
d	Amortization	4d		
5a	Trade or business, rental real estate, and other rental income before directly apportioned deductions (see instructions) .	5a		Schedule E, Part III
b	Depreciation	5b		Include on the applicable line of the appropriate tax form
c	Depletion	5c		
d	Amortization	5d		
6	Income for minimum tax purposes	6		
7	Income for regular tax purposes (add lines 1 through 3b, 4a, and 5a)	7		
8	Adjustment for minimum tax purposes (subtract line 7 from line 6).	8		Form 6251, line 12
9	Estate tax deduction (including certain generation-skipping transfer taxes)	9		Schedule A, line 27
10	Foreign taxes.	10		Form 1116 or Schedule A (Form 1040), line 8
11	Adjustments and tax preference items (itemize):			
a	Accelerated depreciation	11a		Include on the applicable line of Form 6251
b	Depletion	11b		
c	Amortization	11c		
d	Exclusion items	11d		1996 Form 8801
12	Deductions in the final year of trust or decedent's estate:			
a	Excess deductions on termination (see instructions)	12a		Schedule A, line 22
b	Short-term capital loss carryover	12b		Schedule D, line 5, column (f)
c	Long-term capital loss carryover	12c		Schedule D, line 13, column (f)
d	Net operating loss (NOL) carryover for regular tax purposes	12d		Form 1040, line 21
e	NOL carryover for minimum tax purposes	12e		See the instructions for Form 6251, line 20
f	....	12f		Include on the applicable line of the appropriate tax form
g	....	12g		
13	Other (itemize):			
a	Payments of estimated taxes credited to you . .	13a		Form 1040, line 56
b	Tax-exempt interest	13b		Form 1040, line 8b
c	....	13c		Include on the applicable line of the appropriate tax form
d	....	13d		
e	....	13e		
f	....	13f		
g	....	13g		
h	....	13h		

For Paperwork Reduction Act Notice, see page 1 of the Instructions for Form 1041.   Cat. No. 11380D   **Schedule K-1 (Form 1041) 1995**

Form **1065**	**U.S. Partnership Return of Income**	OMB No. 1545-0099
Department of the Treasury Internal Revenue Service	For calendar year 1995, or tax year beginning .... , 1995, and ending .... , 19 .... . ▶ See separate instructions.	**19 95**

A Principal business activity	Use the IRS label. Other- wise, please print or type.	Name of partnership	D Employer identification number
B Principal product or service		Number, street, and room or suite no. (If a P.O. box, see page 10 of the instructions.)	E Date business started
C Business code number		City or town, state, and ZIP code	F Total assets (see page 10 of the instructions) $

G Check applicable boxes: **(1)** ☐ Initial return **(2)** ☐ Final return **(3)** ☐ Change in address **(4)** ☐ Amended return

H Check accounting method: **(1)** ☐ Cash **(2)** ☐ Accrual **(3)** ☐ Other (specify) ▶ ....

I Number of Schedules K-1. Attach one for each person who was a partner at any time during the tax year ▶ ....

Caution: *Include only trade or business income and expenses on lines 1a through 22 below. See the instructions for more information.*

Income	**1a** Gross receipts or sales	1a		
	b Less returns and allowances.	1b	1c	
	2 Cost of goods sold (Schedule A, line 8)		2	
	3 Gross profit. Subtract line 2 from line 1c.		3	
	4 Ordinary income (loss) from other partnerships, estates, and trusts *(attach schedule)* . .		4	
	5 Net farm profit (loss) *(attach Schedule F (Form 1040))*		5	
	6 Net gain (loss) from Form 4797, Part II, line 20.		6	
	7 Other income (loss) *(attach schedule)*		7	
	8 **Total income (loss).** Combine lines 3 through 7		8	

Deductions (see page 11 of the instructions for limitations)	**9** Salaries and wages (other than to partners) (less employment credits)	9	
	10 Guaranteed payments to partners	10	
	11 Repairs and maintenance	11	
	12 Bad debts	12	
	13 Rent	13	
	14 Taxes and licenses	14	
	15 Interest	15	
	16a Depreciation (if required, attach Form 4562) . . . . . . [16a]	16c	
	b Less depreciation reported on Schedule A and elsewhere on return [16b]		
	17 Depletion **(Do not deduct oil and gas depletion.)**	17	
	18 Retirement plans, etc.	18	
	19 Employee benefit programs	19	
	20 Other deductions *(attach schedule)*	20	
	21 **Total deductions.** Add the amounts shown in the far right column for lines 9 through 20 .	21	
	22 **Ordinary income (loss)** from trade or business activities. Subtract line 21 from line 8 . .	22	

Please Sign Here	Under penalties of perjury, I declare that I have examined this return, including accompanying schedules and statements, and to the best of my knowledge and belief, it is true, correct, and complete. Declaration of preparer (other than general partner or limited liability company member) is based on all information of which preparer has any knowledge.
	▶ _____ ▶ _____
	Signature of general partner or limited liability company member Date

Paid Preparer's Use Only	Preparer's signature ▶	Date	Check if self-employed ▶ ☐	Preparer's social security no.
	Firm's name (or yours if self-employed) and address ▶		EIN ▶	
			ZIP code ▶	

For Paperwork Reduction Act Notice, see page 1 of separate instructions.   Cat. No. 11390Z   Form **1065** (1995)

SCHEDULE K-1 (Form 1065)	Partner's Share of Income, Credits, Deductions, etc.	OMB No. 1545-0099
Department of the Treasury Internal Revenue Service	▶ See separate instructions. For calendar year 1995 or tax year beginning , 1995, and ending , 19	1995

Partner's identifying number ▶   **Partnership's identifying number** ▶

Partner's name, address, and ZIP code   **Partnership's name, address, and ZIP code**

A This partner is a ☐ general partner ☐ limited partner ☐ limited liability company member

B What type of entity is this partner? ▶ ....

C Is this partner a ☐ domestic or a ☐ foreign partner?

D Enter partner's percentage of: (i) Before change or termination   (ii) End of year
Profit sharing . . . . % .... %
Loss sharing . . . . % .... %
Ownership of capital . . . . % .... %

E IRS Center where partnership filed return:

F Partner's share of liabilities (see instructions):
Nonrecourse . . . . $ ....
Qualified nonrecourse financing . $ ....
Other . . . . $ ....

G Tax shelter registration number . ▶ ....

H Check here if this partnership is a publicly traded partnership as defined in section 469(k)(2) . . . . ☐

I Check applicable boxes: **(1)** ☐ Final K-1 **(2)** ☐ Amended K-1

J Analysis of partner's capital account:

(a) Capital account at beginning of year	(b) Capital contributed during year	(c) Partner's share of lines 3, 4, and 7, Form 1065, Schedule M-2	(d) Withdrawals and distributions	(e) Capital account at end of year (combine columns (a) through (d))
			( )	

	(a) Distributive share item		(b) Amount	(c) 1040 filers enter the amount in column (b) on:
Income (Loss)	**1** Ordinary income (loss) from trade or business activities . . .	**1**		See pages 5 and 6 of Partner's Instructions for Schedule K-1 (Form 1065).
	2 Net income (loss) from rental real estate activities	**2**		
	3 Net income (loss) from other rental activities	**3**		
	4 Portfolio income (loss):			
	a Interest	**4a**		Sch. B, Part I, line 1
	b Dividends	**4b**		Sch. B, Part II, line 5
	c Royalties	**4c**		Sch. E, Part I, line 4
	d Net short-term capital gain (loss)	**4d**		Sch. D, line 5, col. (f) or (g)
	e Net long-term capital gain (loss).	**4e**		Sch. D, line 13, col. (f) or (g)
	f Other portfolio income (loss) (attach schedule)	**4f**		Enter on applicable line of your return.
	5 Guaranteed payments to partner	**5**		See page 6 of Partner's Instructions for Schedule K-1 (Form 1065).
	6 Net gain (loss) under section 1231 (other than due to casualty or theft)	**6**		
	7 Other income (loss) (attach schedule)	**7**		Enter on applicable line of your return.
Deductions	**8** Charitable contributions (see instructions) (attach schedule) . .	**8**		Sch. A, line 15 or 16
	9 Section 179 expense deduction.	**9**		See page 7 of Partner's Instructions for Schedule K-1 (Form 1065).
	10 Deductions related to portfolio income (attach schedule) . . .	**10**		
	11 Other deductions (attach schedule).	**11**		
Investment Interest	**12a** Interest expense on investment debts	**12a**		Form 4952, line 1
	b (1) Investment income included on lines 4a, 4b, 4c, and 4f above	**b(1)**		See page 7 of Partner's Instructions for Schedule K-1 (Form 1065).
	(2) Investment expenses included on line 10 above	**b(2)**		
Credits	**13a** Low-income housing credit:			
	(1) From section 42(j)(5) partnerships for property placed in service before 1990	**a(1)**		
	(2) Other than on line 13a(1) for property placed in service before 1990	**a(2)**		
	(3) From section 42(j)(5) partnerships for property placed in service after 1989	**a(3)**		Form 8586, line 5
	(4) Other than on line 13a(3) for property placed in service after 1989	**a(4)**		
	b Qualified rehabilitation expenditures related to rental real estate activities	**13b**		
	c Credits (other than credits shown on lines 13a and 13b) related to rental real estate activities.	**13c**		See page 8 of Partner's Instructions for Schedule K-1 (Form 1065).
	d Credits related to other rental activities	**13d**		
	14 Other credits	**14**		

For Paperwork Reduction Act Notice, see Instructions for Form 1065.   Cat. No. 11394R   **Schedule K-1 (Form 1065) 1995**

APPENDIX A

RECIPIENT'S/LENDER'S name, street address, city, state, and ZIP code	* The amount shown may not be fully deductible by you on your Federal income tax return. Limitations based on the cost and value of the secured property may apply. In addition, you may only deduct an amount of mortgage interest to the extent it was incurred by you, actually paid by you, and not reimbursed by another person.	OMB No. 1545-0901 19**96** Form **1098**	**Mortgage Interest Statement**
RECIPIENT'S Federal identification no.	PAYER'S social security number	1 Mortgage interest received from payer(s)/borrower(s)* $	**Copy B** **For Payer**
PAYER'S/BORROWER'S name		2 Points paid on purchase of principal residence (See **Box 2** on back.) $	The information in boxes 1, 2, and 3 is important tax information and is being furnished to the Internal Revenue Service. If you are required to file a return, a negligence penalty or other sanction may be imposed on you if the IRS determines that an underpayment of tax results because you overstated a deduction for this mortgage interest or for these points or because you did not report this refund of interest on your return.
Street address (including apt. no.)		3 Refund of overpaid interest (See **Box 3** on back.) $	
City, state, and ZIP code		4	
Account number (optional)			

Form **1098**   (Keep for your records.)   Department of the Treasury - Internal Revenue Service

Instructions for Payer/Borrower

A person (including a financial institution, a governmental unit, and a cooperative housing corporation) who is engaged in a trade or business and, in the course of such trade or business, received from you at least $600 of mortgage interest (including certain points) on any one mortgage in the calendar year must furnish this statement to you.

If you received this statement as the payer of record on a mortgage on which there are other borrowers entitled to a deduction for the interest and points shown on this form, please furnish each of the other borrowers with information about the proper distribution of these amounts. Each borrower is entitled to deduct only the amount he or she paid and points paid by the seller that represent his or her share of the amount allowable as a deduction for mortgage interest and points.

If your mortgage payments were subsidized by a government agency, you may not be able to deduct the amount of the subsidy.

Box 1.—Shows the mortgage interest received by the interest recipient during the year. This amount includes interest on any obligation secured by real property, including a home equity, line of credit, or credit card loan. This amount does not include points, government subsidy payments, or seller payments on a "buy-down" mortgage. Such amounts are deductible by you only in certain circumstances. **Caution:** If you prepaid interest in 1996 that accrued in full by January 15, 1997, this prepaid interest may be included in box 1. However, even though the prepaid amount may

be included in box 1, you cannot deduct the prepaid amount in 1996. For more information, see **Pub. 936,** Home Mortgage Interest Deduction. If you are a mortgage credit certificate holder who can claim the mortgage interest credit, see **Form 8396,** Mortgage Interest Credit. If the interest was paid on a mortgage, home equity, line of credit, or credit card loan secured by your personal residence, you may be subject to a deduction limitation as explained in the instructions for your tax return.

Box 2.—Not all points are reportable to you. This form shows points you or the seller paid this year for the purchase of your principal residence that are required to be reported to you. Generally, these points are fully deductible in the year paid, but you must subtract seller-paid points from the basis of your residence. Other points not reported in this box may be deductible. See Pub. 936. Also see the instructions for your tax return.

Box 3.—**Do not deduct this amount.** It is a refund (or credit) from the interest recipient/lender for overpayment(s) of interest you made in a prior year or years. Generally, list the total amount shown in box 3 on the "Other income" line on your 1996 tax return. However, do not report the refund as income if you did not itemize deductions in the year(s) you paid the interest. No adjustment to your prior year(s) tax return(s) is necessary. For more information, see Pub. 936 and **Pub. 525,** Taxable and Nontaxable Income.

Box 4.—This box is for use by the interest recipient to furnish other information to you, such as real estate taxes or insurance paid from escrow.

APPENDIX A

LENDER'S name, street address, city, state, and ZIP code		OMB No. 1545-0877	**Acquisition or Abandonment of Secured Property**
		1996 Form **1099-A**	
	1 Date of lender's acquisition or knowledge of abandonment	**2** Balance of principal outstanding $	**Copy B For Borrower**
LENDER'S Federal identification number	BORROWER'S identification number		This is important tax information and is being furnished to the Internal Revenue Service. If you are required to file a return, a negligence penalty or other sanction may be imposed on you if taxable income results from this transaction and the IRS determines that it has not been reported.
BORROWER'S name	**3**	**4** Fair market value of property $	
Street address (including apt. no.)	**5** Was borrower personally liable for repayment of the debt? ☐ Yes ☐ No		
City, state, and ZIP code	**6** Description of property		
Account number (optional)			

Form **1099-A**   (Keep for your records.)   Department of the Treasury - Internal Revenue Service

Instructions for Borrower

Certain lenders who acquire an interest in property that was security for a loan or who have reason to know that such property has been abandoned must provide you with this statement. You may have reportable income or loss because of such acquisition or abandonment. Gain or loss from an acquisition generally is measured by the difference between your adjusted basis in the property and the amount of your debt canceled in exchange for the property, or, if greater, the sale proceeds. If you abandoned the property, you may have income from the discharge of indebtedness in the amount of the unpaid balance of your canceled debt. You may also have a loss from abandonment up to the adjusted basis of property at the time of abandonment. Losses on acquisitions or abandonments of property held for personal use are not deductible. See **Pub. 544,** Sales and Other Dispositions of Assets, for information about foreclosures and abandonments.

Property means real property, such as a personal residence, intangible property, or tangible personal property held for investment or used in a trade or business.

If you borrowed money on this property with someone else, each of you should receive this statement.

Box 1.—For a lender's acquisition of property that was security for a loan, the date shown is generally the earlier of the date title was transferred to the lender or the date possession and the burdens and benefits of ownership were transferred to the lender. This may be the date of a foreclosure or execution sale or the date your right of redemption or objection expired. For an abandonment, the date shown is the date on which the lender first knew or had reason to know that the property was abandoned or the date of a foreclosure, execution, or similar sale.

Box 2.—Shows the amount of the debt (principal only) owed to the lender on the loan at the time the interest in the property was acquired by the lender or on the date the lender first knew or had reason to know that the property was abandoned.

Box 4.—Shows the fair market value of the property. If the amount in box 4 is less than the amount in box 2, and your debt is canceled, you may have cancellation of debt income.

Box 5.—Shows whether you were personally liable for repayment of the loan at the time the debt was created or, if modified, at the time of the last modification.

Box 6.—Shows the description of the property acquired by the lender or abandoned by you. If "CCC" is shown, the form indicates the amount of any Commodity Credit Corporation loan outstanding when you forfeited your commodity.

APPENDIX A

☐ CORRECTED (if checked)

PAYER'S name, street address, city, state, and ZIP code		1a Date of sale	OMB No. 1545-0715	**Proceeds From Broker and Barter Exchange Transactions**
		1b CUSIP No.	19**96** Form **1099-B**	
		2 Stocks, bonds, etc. $	Reported to IRS } ☐ Gross proceeds ☐ Gross proceeds less commissions and option premiums	
PAYER'S Federal identification number	RECIPIENT'S identification number	3 Bartering $	4 Federal income tax withheld $	**Copy B For Recipient**
RECIPIENT'S name		5 Description		This is important tax information and is being furnished to the Internal Revenue Service. If you are required to file a return, a negligence penalty or other sanction may be imposed on you if this income is taxable and the IRS determines that it has not been reported.
		Regulated Futures Contracts		
Street address (including apt. no.)		6 Profit or (loss) realized in 1996 $	7 Unrealized profit or (loss) on open contracts—12/31/95 $	
City, state, and ZIP code		8 Unrealized profit or (loss) on open contracts—12/31/96 $	9 Aggregate profit or (loss) $	
Account number (optional)				

Form **1099-B**   (Keep for your records.)   Department of the Treasury - Internal Revenue Service

Payers, Please Note—

Specific information needed to complete this form and other forms in the 1099 series is given in the **1996 Instructions for Forms 1099, 1098, 5498, and W-2G**. A chart in those instructions gives a quick guide to which form must be filed to report a particular payment. You can order those instructions and additional forms by calling 1-800-TAX-FORM (1-800-829-3676).

Furnish Copy B of this form to the recipient by January 31, 1997.

File Copy A of this form with the IRS by February 28, 1997.

Instructions for Recipient

Brokers and barter exchanges must report proceeds from transactions to the Internal Revenue Service. This form is used to report these proceeds.

Box 1a.—Shows the trade date of the transaction. For aggregate reporting, no entry will be present.

Box 1b.—For broker transactions, may show the CUSIP (Committee on Uniform Security Identification Procedures) number of the item reported.

Box 2.—Shows the proceeds from transactions involving stocks, bonds, other debt obligations, commodities, or forward contracts. Losses on forward contracts are shown in parentheses. This box does not include proceeds from regulated futures contracts. The broker must indicate whether gross proceeds or gross proceeds less commissions and option premiums were reported to the IRS. Report this amount on **Schedule D (Form 1040)**, Capital Gains and Losses.

Box 3.—Shows the fair market value of any trade credits or scrip credited to your account for exchanges of property or services as well as cash received through a barter exchange. Report bartering income in the proper part of Form 1040. See **Pub. 525**, Taxable and Nontaxable Income, for information on how to report this income.

Box 4.—Shows backup withholding. For example, persons not furnishing their taxpayer identification number to the payer become subject to backup withholding at a 31% rate on certain payments. See **Form W-9**, Request for Taxpayer Identification Number and Certification, for information on backup withholding. **Include this amount on your income tax return as tax withheld.**

Box 5.—Shows a brief description of the item or service for which the proceeds or bartering income is being reported. For regulated futures contracts and forward contracts, "RFC" or other appropriate description, and any amount subject to backup withholding, may be shown.

Box 6.—Shows the profit or (loss) realized on regulated futures or foreign currency contracts closed during 1996.

Box 7.—Shows any year-end adjustment to the profit or (loss) shown in box 6 due to open contracts on December 31, 1995.

Box 8.—Shows the unrealized profit or (loss) on open contracts held in your account on December 31, 1996. These are considered sold as of that date. This will become an adjustment reported in box 7 in 1997.

Box 9.—Boxes 6, 7, and 8 are used to figure the aggregate profit or (loss) on regulated futures or foreign currency contracts for the year. Include this figure on your 1996 **Form 6781**, Gains and Losses From Section 1256 Contracts and Straddles.

APPENDIX A

☐ CORRECTED (if checked)

CREDITOR'S name, street address, city, state, and ZIP code		OMB No. 1545-1424	**Cancellation of Debt**
		19**96** Form **1099-C**	
CREDITOR'S Federal identification number	DEBTOR'S identification number	1 Date canceled	2 Amount of debt canceled $	**Copy B** **For Debtor**
DEBTOR'S name		3 Interest included in box 2 $	4 Penalties, fines, admin. costs included in box 2 $	This is important tax information and is being furnished to the Internal Revenue Service. If you are required to file a return, a negligence penalty or other sanction may be imposed on you if taxable income results from this transaction and the IRS determines that it has not been reported.
Street address (including apt. no.) City, state, and ZIP code		5 Debt description		
Account number (optional)		6 Bankruptcy (if checked) ☐	7 Fair market value of property $	

Form **1099-C**   (Keep for your records.)   Department of the Treasury - Internal Revenue Service

Instructions for Debtor

If a Federal Government agency, financial institution, or credit union cancels or forgives a debt you owe of $600 or more, this form must be provided to you. Generally, if you are an individual, you must include the canceled amount on the "Other income" line of your tax return. If you are a corporation, partnership, or other entity, report the canceled debt on your tax return. See the instructions for your tax return.

However, some canceled debts, such as certain student loans (see Pub. 525), certain purchase money debt (see Pub. 334), qualified farm debt (see Pub. 225), qualified real property business debt (see Pub. 334), or debts canceled in bankruptcy (see Pub. 908), are not includible in your income. Do not report a canceled debt as income if you did not deduct it but would have been able to do so on your tax return if you had paid it. Also, do not include canceled debts in your income to the extent you were insolvent. If you exclude canceled debt from your income because it was canceled in a bankruptcy case or during insolvency, or because the debt is qualified farm debt or qualified real property business debt, file **Form 982,** Reduction of Tax Attributes Due to Discharge of Indebtedness (and Section 1082 Basis Adjustment).

Box 1.—Shows the date the debt was canceled.

Box 2.—Shows the amount of debt canceled.

Box 3.—Shows the amount of interest included in the canceled debt in box 2. See **Pub. 525,** Taxable and Nontaxable Income.

Box 4.—Shows penalties, fines, or adminstrative costs included in box 2 as part of the canceled debt.

Box 5.—Shows a description of the debt. If box 7 is completed, also shows a description of the property.

Box 6.—If the box is marked, the creditor has indicated the debt was canceled in a bankruptcy proceeding.

Box 7.—If, in the same calendar year, a foreclosure or abandonment of property occurred in connection with the cancellation of the debt, the fair market value of the property will be shown, or you will receive a separate **Form 1099-A,** Acquisition or Abandonment of Secured Property. You may have income or loss because of the acquisition or abandonment. See **Pub. 544,** Sales and Other Dispositions of Assets, for information about foreclosures and abandonments.

☐ **CORRECTED (if checked)**

PAYER'S name, street address, city, state, and ZIP code		**1a** Gross dividends and other distributions on stock (Total of 1b, 1c, 1d, and 1e) $	OMB No. 1545-0110	
		1b Ordinary dividends $	**19 96** Form **1099-DIV**	**Dividends and Distributions**
PAYER'S Federal identification number	RECIPIENT'S identification number	**1c** Capital gain distributions $	**2** Federal income tax withheld $	**Copy B**
RECIPIENT'S name		**1d** Nontaxable distributions $	**3** Foreign tax paid $	**For Recipient** This is important tax information and is being furnished to the Internal Revenue Service. If you are required to file a return, a negligence penalty or other sanction may be imposed on you if this income is taxable and the IRS determines that it has not been reported.
Street address (including apt. no.)		**1e** Investment expenses $	**4** Foreign country or U.S. possession	
City, state, and ZIP code		**Liquidation Distributions**		
Account number (optional)		**5** Cash $	**6** Noncash (Fair market value) $	

Form **1099-DIV**

(Keep for your records.)

Department of the Treasury - Internal Revenue Service

Instructions for Recipient

Box 1a.—Gross dividends include any amounts shown in boxes 1b, 1c, 1d, and 1e. If you file **Schedule B (Form 1040)** to report dividends, report the amount in box 1a. If you file **Form 1040** without **Schedule B**, report the sum of boxes 1b and 1e on the "Dividend income" line of **Form 1040**. Also report the amount in box 1c on **Schedule D (Form 1040)** or on the "Capital gain or (loss)" line of **Form 1040** (write "CGD" on the dotted line). If you do not file **Form 1040**, see the instructions for your income tax return.

The amount shown may be a distribution from an employee stock ownership plan (ESOP). Although you should report the ESOP distribution as a dividend on your income tax return, treat it as a plan distribution, not as investment income, for any other purpose.

Box 1b.—Ordinary dividends are fully taxable and are included in box 1a. This may include net short-term capital gains from a mutual fund.

Box 1c.—Capital gain distributions (long-term) are included in box 1a.

Box 1d.—This part of the distribution is nontaxable because it is a return of your cost (or other basis). You must reduce your cost (or other basis) by this amount for figuring gain or loss when you sell your stock. But if you get back all your cost (or other basis), you must report future nontaxable distributions as capital gains, even though this form shows them as nontaxable. This amount is included in box 1a. For more information, see **Pub. 550,** Investment Income and Expenses.

Box 1e.—Any amount shown is your share of the expenses of a nonpublicly offered regulated investment company, generally a nonpublicly offered mutual fund, which is included as a dividend in box 1a. The full amount shown in box 1a must be reported as income on your tax return. If you file **Form 1040,** you can deduct the expenses shown in box 1e on the "Other expenses" line on **Schedule A (Form 1040)** subject to the 2% limit. Generally, the actual amount you should have received or had credited to you is the amount in box 1a less the amount in box 1e.

Box 2.—Shows backup withholding. For example, persons not furnishing their taxpayer identification number to the payer become subject to backup withholding at a 31% rate on certain payments. See **Form W-9,** Request for Taxpayer Identification Number and Certification, for information on backup withholding. **Include this amount on your income tax return as tax withheld.**

Box 3.—You may elect to claim the amount shown as a deduction or a credit. See **Pub. 514,** Foreign Tax Credit for Individuals.

Nominees.—If your Federal identification number is shown on this form and the form includes amounts belonging to another person, you are considered a nominee recipient. You must file Form 1099-DIV for each of the other owners showing the income allocable to each, and you must furnish a Form 1099-DIV to each. File Form(s) 1099-DIV with **Form 1096,** Annual Summary and Transmittal of U.S. Information Returns, at the Internal Revenue Service Center for your area. On each Form 1099-DIV, list yourself as the "payer" and the other owner as the "recipient." On Form 1096, list yourself as the "filer." A husband or wife is not required to file a nominee return to show amounts owned by the other.

APPENDIX A

PAYER'S name, street address, city, state, and ZIP code		**1** Unemployment compensation $	OMB No. 1545-0120	**Certain Government Payments**
		2 State or local income tax refunds, credits, or offsets $	19**96** Form **1099-G**	
PAYER'S Federal identification number	RECIPIENT'S identification number	**3** Box 2 amount is for tax year	**4** Federal income tax withheld $	**Copy B** **For Recipient**
RECIPIENT'S name		**5**	**6** Taxable grants $	This is important tax information and is being furnished to the Internal Revenue Service. If you are required to file a return, a negligence penalty or other sanction may be imposed on you if this income is taxable and the IRS determines that it has not been reported.
Street address (including apt. no.)		**7** Agriculture payments $	**8** The amount in box 2 applies to income from a trade or business ▶ ☐	
City, state, and ZIP code				
Account number (optional)				

Form **1099-G**   (Keep for your records.)   Department of the Treasury - Internal Revenue Service

Instructions for Recipient

Box 1.—Shows the total unemployment compensation paid to you this year. This amount is taxable income to you. For details, see the instructions for your Federal income tax return. If you expect to receive these benefits in the future, you can request the payer to withhold Federal income tax from each payment. Or, you can make estimated tax payments using **Form 1040-ES,** Estimated Tax For Individuals.

Box 2.—Shows refunds, credits, or offsets of state or local income tax you received. If there is an entry in this box, it may be taxable to you if you deducted the tax paid as an itemized deduction on your Federal income tax return. Even if you did not receive the amount shown, for example, because it was credited to your estimated tax, it is still taxable if it was deducted. Any interest received on this must be included as interest income on your return. See the instructions for your tax return.

Box 3.—Identifies the tax year for which the refund, credit, or offset shown in box 2 was made. If there is no entry in this box, the refund is for 1995 taxes.

Box 4.—Shows backup withholding. For example, persons not furnishing their taxpayer identification number to the payer become subject to backup withholding at a 31% rate on certain payments. See **Form W-9,** Request for Taxpayer Identification Number and Certification, for information on backup withholding. **Include this on your income tax return as tax withheld.**

Box 6.—Shows the amount of taxable grants you received from the Federal, state, or local government.

Box 7.—Shows the amount of Department of Agriculture payments that are taxable to you. If the payer shown is anyone other than the Department of Agriculture, it means the payer has received a payment, as a nominee, that is taxable to you. This may represent the entire agricultural subsidy payment received on your behalf by the nominee, or it may be your pro rata share of the original payment. See **Pub. 225,** Farmer's Tax Guide, and the instructions for **Schedule F (Form 1040),** Profit or Loss From Farming, for information about where to report this income.

Box 8.—If this box is checked, the refund, credit, or offset in box 2 is attributable to an income tax that applies exclusively to income from a trade or business and is not a tax of general application. The amount, if taxable, should not be reported on page 1 of Form 1040, but should be reported on Schedule C, C-EZ, or F (Form 1040), as appropriate.

APPENDIX A

☐ CORRECTED (if checked)

PAYER'S name, street address, city, state, and ZIP code	Payer's RTN (optional)	OMB No. 1545-0112	
		19**96** Form **1099-INT**	**Interest Income**

PAYER'S Federal identification number	RECIPIENT'S identification number	1 Interest income not included in box 3 $	**Copy B**
RECIPIENT'S name		2 Early withdrawal penalty $	3 Interest on U.S. Savings Bonds and Treas. obligations $	**For Recipient** This is important tax information and is being furnished to the Internal Revenue Service. If you are required to file a return, a negligence penalty or other sanction may be imposed on you if this income is taxable and the IRS determines that it has not been reported.
Street address (including apt. no.)		4 Federal income tax withheld $	
City, state, and ZIP code		5 Foreign tax paid	6 Foreign country or U.S. possession
Account number (optional)		$	

Form **1099-INT**   (Keep for your records.)   Department of the Treasury - Internal Revenue Service

Instructions for Recipient

Box 1.—Shows interest paid to you during the calendar year by the payer. This does not include interest shown in box 3.

If you receive a Form 1099-INT for interest paid on a tax-exempt obligation, please see the instructions for your income tax return.

Box 2.—Shows interest or principal forfeited because of early withdrawal of time savings. You may deduct this on your Federal income tax return only on the specific line of Form 1040 under "Adjustments to Income."

Box 3.—Shows interest on U.S. Savings Bonds, Treasury bills, Treasury bonds, and Treasury notes. This may or may not be all taxable. See **Pub. 550,** Investment Income and Expenses. This interest is exempt from state and local income taxes. **This interest is not included in box 1.**

Box 4.—Shows backup withholding. For example, persons not furnishing their taxpayer identification number to the payer become subject to backup withholding at a 31% rate. See **Form W-9,** Request for Taxpayer Identification Number and Certification, for information on backup withholding. **Include this amount on your income tax return as tax withheld.**

Box 5.—Shows foreign tax paid. You may choose to claim this tax as a deduction or a credit on your Federal income tax return. See **Pub. 514,** Foreign Tax Credit for Individuals.

Nominees.—If your Federal identification number is shown on this form and the form includes amounts belonging to another person, you are considered a nominee recipient. You must file Form 1099-INT for each of the other owners showing the amounts allocable to each. You must also furnish a Form 1099-INT to each of the other owners. File Form(s) 1099-INT with **Form 1096,** Annual Summary and Transmittal of U.S. Information Returns, with the Internal Revenue Service Center for your area. On each Form 1099-INT, list yourself as the "payer" and the other owner as the "recipient." On Form 1096, list yourself as the "filer." A husband or wife is not required to file a nominee return to show amounts owned by the other.

☐ **CORRECTED (if checked)**

PAYER'S name, street address, city, state, and ZIP code	1 Rents $	OMB No. 1545-0115	
	2 Royalties $	19**96**	**Miscellaneous Income**
	3 Other income $	Form **1099-MISC**	

PAYER'S Federal identification number	RECIPIENT'S identification number	4 Federal income tax withheld $	5 Fishing boat proceeds $	**Copy B** **For Recipient**
RECIPIENT'S name		6 Medical and health care payments $	7 Nonemployee compensation $	This is important tax information and is being furnished to the Internal Revenue Service. If you are required to file a return, a negligence penalty or other sanction may be imposed on you if this income is taxable and the IRS determines that it has not been reported.
Street address (including apt. no.)		8 Substitute payments in lieu of dividends or interest $	9 Payer made direct sales of $5,000 or more of consumer products to a buyer (recipient) for resale ▶ ☐	
City, state, and ZIP code		10 Crop insurance proceeds $	11 State income tax withheld $	
Account number (optional)		12 State/Payer's state number		

Form **1099-MISC** (Keep for your records.) Department of the Treasury - Internal Revenue Service

Instructions for Recipient

Amounts shown on this form may be subject to self-employment tax computed on **Schedule SE (Form 1040)**. See **Pub. 533**, Self-Employment Tax, for information on self-employment income. If no income or social security and Medicare taxes were withheld by the payer, you may have to make estimated tax payments if you are still receiving these payments. See **Form 1040-ES**, Estimated Tax for Individuals.

If you are an individual, report the taxable amounts shown on this form on your tax return, as explained below. (Others, such as fiduciaries or partnerships, report the amounts on the corresponding lines of your tax return.)

Boxes 1 and 2.—Report rents from real estate on Schedule E (Form 1040). If you provided significant services to the tenant, sold real estate as a business, or rented personal property as a business, report on Schedule C or C-EZ (Form 1040). For royalties on timber, coal, and iron ore, see **Pub. 544**, Sales and Other Dispositions of Assets.

Box 3.—Report on the "Other income" line of your tax return and identify the payment. If it is trade or business income, report this amount on Schedule C, C-EZ, or F (Form 1040). The amount shown may be payments you received as the beneficiary of a deceased employee, prizes, awards, taxable damages, Indian gaming profits, or other taxable income.

Box 4.—Shows backup withholding or withholding on Indian gaming profits. Generally, a payer must backup withhold at a 31% rate if you did not furnish your taxpayer identification number to the payer. See **Form W-9**, Request for Taxpayer Identification Number and Certification, for information on backup withholding. **Include this on your income tax return as tax withheld.**

Box 5.—An amount in this box means the fishing boat operator considers you self-employed. Report this amount on Schedule C or C-EZ (Form 1040). See **Pub. 595**, Tax Guide for Commercial Fishermen.

Box 6.—Report on Schedule C or C-EZ (Form 1040).

Box 7.—Generally, payments for services reported in this box are income from self-employment. Since you received this form, rather than Form W-2, the payer may have considered you self-employed and did not withhold social security or Medicare taxes. Report self-employment income on Schedule C, C-EZ, or F (Form 1040), and **compute the self-employment tax on Schedule SE (Form 1040).** However, if you are not self-employed, report this amount on the "Wages, salaries, tips, etc." line of your tax return. Call the IRS for information about how to report any social security and Medicare taxes.

If "EPP" is shown, this is excess golden parachute payments subject to a 20% excise tax. See your Form 1040 instructions for the "Total Tax" line. The unlabeled amount is your total compensation.

Box 8.—Report on the "Other income" line of Form 1040. This amount is substitute payments in lieu of dividends or tax-exempt interest received by your broker on your behalf after transfer of your securities for use in a short sale.

Box 9.—An entry in the checkbox means sales to you of consumer products on a buy-sell, deposit-commission, or any other basis for resale have amounted to $5,000 or more. The person filing this return does not have to show a dollar amount in this box. Any income from your sale of these products should generally be reported on Schedule C or C-EZ (Form 1040).

Box 10.—Report on the "Crop insurance proceeds. . ." line on Schedule F (Form 1040).

☐ CORRECTED (if checked)

PAYER'S name, street address, city, state, and ZIP code	1 Original issue discount for 1996* $ 2 Other periodic interest $	OMB No. 1545-0117 19**96** Form **1099-OID**	**Original Issue Discount**
PAYER'S Federal identification number RECIPIENT'S identification number	3 Early withdrawal penalty $	4 Federal income tax withheld $	**Copy B** **For Recipient**
RECIPIENT'S name Street address (including apt. no.) City, state, and ZIP code	5 Description		This is important tax information and is being furnished to the Internal Revenue Service. If you are required to file a return, a negligence penalty or other sanction may be imposed on you if this income is taxable and the IRS determines that it has not been reported.
Account number (optional)	* This may not be the correct figure to report on your income tax return. See instructions on the back.		

Form **1099-OID**   (Keep for your records.)   Department of the Treasury - Internal Revenue Service

Instructions for Recipient

Original issue discount (OID) is the difference between the stated redemption price at maturity and the issue price of a bond, debenture, note, or other evidence of indebtedness, or the acquisition price of a stripped bond or coupon. OID rules also apply to **certificates of deposit (CDs)**, time deposits, bonus savings plans, and other deposit arrangements having a term of more than 1 year, provided the payment of interest is deferred until maturity.

OID is taxable as interest over the life of the obligation. If you are the holder of one of these obligations, you must include a part of the OID in your gross income each year you hold the obligation.

If, as the record holder, you receive Form 1099-OID showing amounts belonging to another person, you are considered a **nominee** recipient. You must file Form 1099-OID for each of the other owners showing the amounts allocable to each. Furnish a Form 1099-OID to each owner. File Form(s) 1099-OID with **Form 1096,** Annual Summary and Transmittal of U.S. Information Returns, with the Internal Revenue Service Center for your area. On each Form 1099-OID, list yourself as the "payer" and the other owner as the "recipient." On Form 1096, list yourself as the "filer." A husband or wife is not required to file a nominee return to show amounts owned by the other. If you bought or sold an obligation during the year and you are not a nominee, you are not required to issue or file Form 1099-OID showing the OID or stated interest allocable to the seller/buyer of the obligation.

Box 1.—Shows the OID on the obligation for the part of the year you owned it. Report the entire amount in box 1 as interest income on your income tax return. However, if you paid acquisition or bond premium,

or if the obligation is a stripped bond or stripped coupon, you must compute your proper amount of OID. If you must compute your proper OID, see **Pub. 1212,** List of Original Issue Discount Instruments, to figure the correct OID to report on your tax return.

Box 2.—Shows other interest on this obligation for the year, which is an amount separate from the OID. If you held the obligation the entire year, report this amount as interest income on your tax return. If you disposed of the obligation or acquired it from another holder during the year, see **Pub. 550,** Investment Income and Expenses, for reporting instructions. If you are a regular interest holder in a single-class REMIC (as defined in regulations under section 67(c)), this amount includes your share of the investment expenses of the REMIC, deductible as a "Miscellaneous Deduction" subject to the 2% limit.

Box 3.—Shows the interest or principal you forfeited if you withdrew the money before the maturity date of the obligation, such as from a CD. You may deduct this on your Federal income tax return only on the "Penalty on early withdrawal of savings" line of your tax return.

Box 4.—Shows backup withholding. For example, persons not furnishing their taxpayer identification number to the payer become subject to backup withholding at a 31% rate on certain payments shown on the form. See **Form W-9,** Request for Taxpayer Identification Number and Certification, for information on backup withholding. **Include this amount on your income tax return as tax withheld.**

Box 5.—Shows the identification number (CUSIP number) or description of the obligation. The description may include the stock exchange, issuer, coupon rate, and year of maturity.

☐ CORRECTED (if checked)

PAYER'S name, street address, city, state, and ZIP code	1 Patronage dividends $	OMB No. 1545-0118	Taxable Distributions Received From Cooperatives
	2 Nonpatronage distributions $	19**96**	
	3 Per-unit retain allocations $	Form **1099-PATR**	
PAYER'S Federal identification number	RECIPIENT'S identification number	4 **Federal income tax withheld** $	**Copy B For Recipient**
RECIPIENT'S name		5 Redemption of nonqualified notices and retain allocations $	This is important tax information and is being furnished to the Internal Revenue Service. If you are required to file a return, a negligence penalty or other sanction may be imposed on you if this income is taxable and the IRS determines that it has not been reported.
Street address (including apt. no.)		6 $	7 Energy investment credit $
City, state, and ZIP code		8 Jobs credit $	9 Patron's AMT adjustment $
Account number (optional)			

Form **1099-PATR**   (Keep for your records.)   Department of the Treasury - Internal Revenue Service

Instructions for Recipient

Distributions you received from a cooperative may be includible in your income. Generally, if you are an individual, report any amounts shown in boxes 1, 2, 3, and 5 as income, unless nontaxable, on **Schedule F (Form 1040)**, Profit or Loss From Farming; **Schedule C (Form 1040)**, Profit or Loss From Business; **Schedule C-EZ (Form 1040)**, Net Profit From Business; or **Form 4835**, Farm Rental Income and Expenses. See the instructions for Schedule F (Form 1040) and **Pub. 225**, Farmer's Tax Guide, for more information.

Box 1.—Shows patronage dividends paid to you during the year in cash, qualified written notices of allocation (at stated dollar value), or other property (not including nonqualified allocations). Any of the dividends that were paid on (1) property bought for personal use or (2) capital assets or depreciable property used in your business are not taxable. However, if (2) applies, reduce the basis of the assets by this amount.

Box 2.—Shows nonpatronage distributions paid to you during the year in cash, qualified written notices of allocation, or other property (not including nonqualified written notices of allocation).

Box 3.—Shows per-unit retain allocations paid to you during the year in cash, qualified per-unit retain certificates, or other property.

Box 4.—Shows backup withholding. For example, persons not furnishing their taxpayer identification number to the payer become subject to backup withholding at a 31% rate on certain payments. See **Form W-9**, Request for Taxpayer Identification Number and Certification, for information on backup withholding. **Include this amount on your income tax return as tax withheld.**

Box 5.—Shows amounts you received when you redeemed nonqualified written notices of allocation and nonqualified per-unit retain allocations. Because these were not taxable when issued to you, you must report the redemption as ordinary income to the extent of the stated dollar value.

Boxes 6, 7, and 8.—These boxes and the box under boxes 8 and 9 may show unused credits passed through to you by the cooperative. Report these credits on the following forms: 3468—energy credit; 5884—jobs credit; 8844—empowerment zone employment; 8845—Indian employment. See the instructions for your income tax return for information about where to report other credits.

Box 9.—Shows the Alternative Minimum Tax (AMT) adjustment passed through to you by the cooperative. Report this amount on Form 6251 on the "Patron's adjustment" line under "Other" in Part I, or on Form 4626 on the "Other adjustments" line, as applicable.

☐ CORRECTED (if checked)

PAYER'S name, street address, city, state, and ZIP code	**1** Gross distribution $	OMB No. 1545-0119 19**96** Form **1099-R**	**Distributions From Pensions, Annuities, Retirement or Profit-Sharing Plans, IRAs, Insurance Contracts, etc.**
	2a Taxable amount $		

		2b Taxable amount not determined ☐	Total distribution ☐	**Copy B**
PAYER'S Federal identification number	RECIPIENT'S identification number	**3** Capital gain (included in box 2a) $	**4** Federal income tax withheld $	**Report this income on your Federal tax return. If this form shows Federal income tax withheld in box 4, attach this copy to your return.**
RECIPIENT'S name		**5** Employee contributions or insurance premiums $	**6** Net unrealized appreciation in employer's securities $	
Street address (including apt. no.)		**7** Distribution code ☐	IRA/ SEP ☐	**8** Other $ %| **This information is being furnished to the Internal Revenue Service.**
City, state, and ZIP code		**9a** Your percentage of total distribution %	**9b** Total employee contributions $	
Account number (optional)		**10** State tax withheld $ $	**11** State/Payer's state no.	**12** State distribution $ $
		13 Local tax withheld $ $	**14** Name of locality	**15** Local distribution $ $

Form **1099-R**

Department of the Treasury - Internal Revenue Service

Instructions for Recipient

Generally, distributions from pensions, annuities, profit-sharing and retirement plans, IRAs, insurance contracts, etc., are reported to recipients on Form 1099-R.

IRAs.—For distributions from an individual retirement arrangement (IRA) or simplified employee pension (SEP), generally the payer is not required to compute the taxable amount. Therefore, the amounts in boxes 1 and 2a will be the same most of the time. See **Pub. 590**, Individual Retirement Arrangements (IRAs), and **Form 8606**, Nondeductible IRAs (Contributions, Distributions, and Basis), to determine the taxable amount. If you are at least age 70½, you must take minimum distributions from your IRA. If you don't, you may be subject to a 50% excise tax on the amount that should have been distributed. See Pub. 590.

Excess Distributions.—If your distribution from a qualified plan is more than $155,000, you may owe an excise tax. See **Form 5329**, Additional Taxes Attributable to Qualified Retirement Plans (Including IRAs), Annuities, and Modified Endowment Contracts. This does not apply to beneficiaries except a surviving spouse who elected not to have the estate pay the excess accumulation tax.

Beneficiaries.—If you receive a plan distribution as the beneficiary of a deceased employee, you may be entitled to a **death benefit exclusion** of up to $5,000. Only one $5,000 exclusion applies per decedent, and it must be divided among all beneficiaries. See **Pub. 575**, Pension and Annuity Income (Including Simplified General Rule).

Box 1.—Shows the total amount you received this year. The amount may have been a direct rollover or received as periodic payments, as nonperiodic payments, or as a total distribution. Report this amount on your tax return on the line for "Total IRA distributions" or "Total pensions and annuities" (or the line for "Taxable amount"), whichever applies, unless this is a lump-sum distribution and you are using **Form 4972**, Tax on Lump-Sum Distributions. However, if you have not reached minimum retirement age, report your disability payments on the line for "Wages, salaries, tips, etc." Also report on that line corrective

distributions of excess deferrals, excess contributions, or excess aggregate contributions.

If you received a death benefit payment made by an employer because you are the beneficiary of a deceased employee and the payment was not made from the employer's pension, profit-sharing, or retirement plan, report this amount, less any allowable death benefit exclusion, on your tax return on the line for "Other income." See **Pub. 525**, Taxable and Nontaxable Income.

If a life insurance, annuity, or endowment contract has been transferred tax free to another trustee or contract issuer, an amount will be shown in this box and Code 6 will be shown in box 7. You need not report this on your tax return.

Box 2a.—This part of the distribution is generally taxable. However, if there is no entry in this box, the payer may not have all the facts needed to figure the taxable amount. In that case, the first box in box 2b should be marked. You may want to get one of the following publications from the IRS to help you figure the taxable amount: **Pub. 571**, Tax-Sheltered Annuity Programs for Employees of Public Schools and Certain Tax-Exempt Organizations, **Pub. 575**, **Pub. 590**, **Pub. 721**, Tax Guide to U.S. Civil Service Retirement Benefits, or **Pub. 939**, Pension General Rule (Nonsimplified Method). For an IRA distribution, see **IRAs** on this page. For a direct rollover, zero should be shown, and you must enter zero on the "Taxable amount" line of your tax return.

If this is a total distribution from a qualified plan and you were at least age 59½ on the date of distribution (or you are the beneficiary of someone who had reached age 59½ or someone born before 1936), you may be eligible for the 5- or 10-year tax option. See Form 4972 for more information. The 5- or 10-year tax option does not apply to IRAs or tax-sheltered annuities.

Box 2b.—If the first checkbox is marked, the payer was unable to determine the taxable amount, and box 2a should be blank unless this is an IRA distribution. If the second checkbox is marked, the distribution was a total distribution that closed out your account.

(Continued on the back of Copy C.)

APPENDIX A

☐ **CORRECTED (if checked)**

FILER'S name, street address, city, state, and ZIP code	**1** Date of closing	OMB No. 1545-0997	
		19**96**	**Proceeds From Real Estate Transactions**
	2 Gross proceeds		
	$	Form **1099-S**	

FILER'S Federal identification number	TRANSFEROR'S identification number	**3** Address or legal description	**Copy B**
			For Transferor
TRANSFEROR'S name			This is important tax information and is being furnished to the Internal Revenue Service. If you are required to file a return, a negligence penalty or other sanction may be imposed on you if this item is required to be reported and the IRS determines that it has not been reported.
Street address (including apt. no.)			
City, state, and ZIP code		**4** Transferor received or will receive property or services as part of the consideration (if checked) . . ▶ ☐	
Account number (optional)		**5** Buyer's part of real estate tax	
		$	

Form **1099-S**   (Keep for your records.)   Department of the Treasury - Internal Revenue Service

Instructions for Transferor

Generally, persons responsible for closing a real estate transaction must report the real estate proceeds to the Internal Revenue Service and must furnish this statement to you. You must report the sale or exchange of real estate on your tax return even if you had a loss. If the real estate was your main home, file **Form 2119,** Sale of Your Home, with Form 1040 even if you had a loss or you did not replace your home. If the real estate was not your main home, report the transaction on **Form 4797,** Sales of Business Property, **Form 6252,** Installment Sale Income, and/or **Schedule D (Form 1040),** Capital Gains and Losses.

If you sold your home and (1) you did not own it for more than 9 years and (2) it was financed after 1990 under a Federally subsidized program (qualified mortgage bonds or mortgage credit certificates), you may have to recapture part of the subsidy. This will increase your tax. See **Form 8828,** Recapture of Federal Mortgage Subsidy, and **Pub. 523,** Selling Your Home.

Box 1.—Shows the date of closing.

Box 2.—Shows the gross proceeds from a real estate transaction, generally the sales price. Gross proceeds include cash and notes payable to you, notes assumed by the transferee (buyer), and any notes paid off at settlement. Box 2 does not include the value of other property or services you received or are to receive. See **Box 4.**

Box 3.—Shows the address of the property transferred or a legal description of the property.

Box 4.—If marked, shows that you received or will receive services or property (other than cash or notes) as part of the consideration for the property transferred. The value of any services or property (other than cash or notes) is not included in box 2.

Box 5.—Shows certain real estate tax on a residence charged to the buyer at settlement. If you have already paid the real estate tax for the period that includes the sale date, subtract the amount in box 5 from the amount already paid to determine your deductible real estate tax. But if you have already deducted the real estate tax in a prior year, generally report this amount as income on the "Other income" line of your tax return. For more information, see Pub. 523.

Form **1120**	**U.S. Corporation Income Tax Return**

Form **1120**

Department of the Treasury
Internal Revenue Service

U.S. Corporation Income Tax Return

For calendar year 1995 or tax year beginning .... , 1995, ending .... , 19 ...
▶ Instructions are separate. See page 1 for Paperwork Reduction Act Notice.

OMB No. 1545-0123

1995

A Check if a:
1 Consolidated return (attach Form 851) ☐
2 Personal holding co. (attach Sch. PH) ☐
3 Personal service corp. (as defined in Temporary Regs. sec. 1.441-4T— see instructions) ☐

Use IRS label. Otherwise, print or type.

Name

Number, street, and room or suite no. (If a P.O. box, see page 6 of instructions.)

City or town, state, and ZIP code

B Employer identification number

C Date incorporated

D Total assets (see page 6 of instructions)

E Check applicable boxes: (1) ☐ Initial return (2) ☐ Final return (3) ☐ Change of address $

Income

1a	Gross receipts or sales [ ] **b** Less returns and allowances [ ] **c** Bal ▶	1c
2	Cost of goods sold (Schedule A, line 8)	2
3	Gross profit. Subtract line 2 from line 1c	3
4	Dividends (Schedule C, line 19)	4
5	Interest	5
6	Gross rents	6
7	Gross royalties	7
8	Capital gain net income (attach Schedule D (Form 1120))	8
9	Net gain or (loss) from Form 4797, Part II, line 20 (attach Form 4797)	9
10	Other income (see page 7 of instructions—attach schedule)	10
11	**Total income.** Add lines 3 through 10 ▶	11

Deductions (See instructions for limitations on deductions.)

12	Compensation of officers (Schedule E, line 4)	12
13	Salaries and wages (less employment credits)	13
14	Repairs and maintenance	14
15	Bad debts	15
16	Rents	16
17	Taxes and licenses	17
18	Interest	18
19	Charitable contributions (see page 9 of instructions for 10% limitation)	19
20	Depreciation (attach Form 4562)	20	
21	Less depreciation claimed on Schedule A and elsewhere on return	21a	21b
22	Depletion	22
23	Advertising	23
24	Pension, profit-sharing, etc., plans	24
25	Employee benefit programs	25
26	Other deductions (attach schedule)	26
27	**Total deductions.** Add lines 12 through 26 ▶	27
28	Taxable income before net operating loss deduction and special deductions. Subtract line 27 from line 11	28
29	**Less:** **a** Net operating loss deduction (see page 11 of instructions)	29a	
	b Special deductions (Schedule C, line 20)	29b	29c

Tax and Payments

30	**Taxable income.** Subtract line 29c from line 28	30
31	**Total tax** (Schedule J, line 10)	31
32	**Payments: a** 1994 overpayment credited to 1995	32a	
b	1995 estimated tax payments	32b	
c	Less 1995 refund applied for on Form 4466	32c ( ) **d** Bal ▶	32d
e	Tax deposited with Form 7004	32e	
f	Credit from regulated investment companies (attach Form 2439)	32f	
g	Credit for Federal tax on fuels (attach Form 4136). See instructions	32g	32h
33	Estimated tax penalty (see page 12 of instructions). Check if Form 2220 is attached ▶ ☐	33
34	**Tax due.** If line 32h is smaller than the total of lines 31 and 33, enter amount owed	34
35	**Overpayment.** If line 32h is larger than the total of lines 31 and 33, enter amount overpaid	35
36	Enter amount of line 35 you want: **Credited to 1996 estimated tax** ▶ **Refunded** ▶	36

Sign Here

Under penalties of perjury, I declare that I have examined this return, including accompanying schedules and statements, and to the best of my knowledge and belief, it is true, correct, and complete. Declaration of preparer (other than taxpayer) is based on all information of which preparer has any knowledge.

▶ _____   ▶ _____
Signature of officer   Date   Title

Paid Preparer's Use Only

Preparer's signature ▶		Date	Check if self-employed ☐	Preparer's social security number
Firm's name (or yours if self-employed) and address ▶		EIN ▶	
		ZIP code ▶	

Cat. No. 11450Q

Form **1120-A**	**U.S. Corporation Short-Form Income Tax Return**	OMB No. 1545-0890
Department of the Treasury Internal Revenue Service	See separate instructions to make sure the corporation qualifies to file Form 1120-A. For calendar year 1995 or tax year beginning ...., 1995, ending................ , 19.....	**1995**

A Check this box if the corp. is a personal service corp. (as defined in Temporary Regs. section 1.441-4T—see instructions) ▶ ☐	Use IRS label. Other-wise, print or type.	Name	**B** Employer identification number
		Number, street, and room or suite no. (If a P.O. box, see page 6 of instructions.)	**C** Date incorporated
		City or town, state, and ZIP code	**D** Total assets (see page 6 of instructions) $

E Check applicable boxes: (1) ☐ Initial return (2) ☐ Change of address

F Check method of accounting: (1) ☐ Cash (2) ☐ Accrual (3) ☐ Other (specify) . . ▶

Income

1a	Gross receipts or sales	**b** Less returns and allowances	**c** Balance ▶	1c
2	Cost of goods sold (see page 12 of instructions).	2
3	Gross profit. Subtract line 2 from line 1c	3
4	Domestic corporation dividends subject to the 70% deduction	4
5	Interest	5
6	Gross rents	6
7	Gross royalties	7
8	Capital gain net income (attach Schedule D (Form 1120))	8
9	Net gain or (loss) from Form 4797, Part II, line 20 (attach Form 4797)	9
10	Other income (see page 7 of instructions).	10
11	**Total income.** Add lines 3 through 10 . . . . ▶	11

Deductions (See instructions for limitations on deductions.)

12	Compensation of officers (see page 8 of instructions)	12
13	Salaries and wages (less employment credits)	13
14	Repairs and maintenance	14
15	Bad debts	15
16	Rents	16
17	Taxes and licenses	17
18	Interest	18
19	Charitable contributions (see page 9 of instructions for 10% limitation)	19
20	Depreciation (attach Form 4562)	20	
21	Less depreciation claimed elsewhere on return	21a	21b
22	Other deductions (attach schedule)	22
23	**Total deductions.** Add lines 12 through 22 . . . . ▶	23
24	Taxable income before net operating loss deduction and special deductions. Subtract line 23 from line 11	24
25	**Less: a** Net operating loss deduction (see page 11 of instructions)	25a	
	b Special deductions (see page 11 of instructions)	25b	25c

Tax and Payments

26	**Taxable income.** Subtract line 25c from line 24	26
27	**Total tax** (from page 2, Part I, line 7)	27
28	**Payments:**	
	a 1994 overpayment credited to 1995	28a	
	b 1995 estimated tax payments	28b	
	c Less 1995 refund applied for on Form 4466	28c ( )	Bal ▶ 28d
	e Tax deposited with Form 7004	28e	
	f Credit from regulated investment companies (attach Form 2439) .	28f	
	g Credit for Federal tax on fuels (attach Form 4136). See instructions	28g	
	h Total payments. Add lines 28d through 28g	28h
29	Estimated tax penalty (see page 12 of instructions). Check if Form 2220 is attached . . ▶☐	29
30	**Tax due.** If 28h is smaller than the total of lines 27 and 29, enter amount owed	30
31	**Overpayment.** If line 28h is larger than the total of lines 27 and 29, enter amount overpaid . .	31
32	Enter amount of line 31 you want: **Credited to 1996 estimated tax** ▶ | **Refunded** ▶	32

Sign Here

Under penalties of perjury, I declare that I have examined this return, including accompanying schedules and statements, and to the best of my knowledge and belief, it is true, correct, and complete. Declaration of preparer (other than taxpayer) is based on all information of which preparer has any knowledge.

▶		
Signature of officer	Date	Title

Paid Preparer's Use Only

Preparer's signature ▶	Date	Check if self-employed ▶ ☐	Preparer's social security number
Firm's name (or yours if self-employed) and address ▶		EIN ▶ ZIP code ▶	

For Paperwork Reduction Act Notice, see page 1 of the instructions. Cat. No. 11456E Form **1120-A** (1995)

Form **1120S**		**U.S. Income Tax Return for an S Corporation**		OMB No. 1545-0130

Department of the Treasury
Internal Revenue Service

▶ Do not file this form unless the corporation has timely filed Form 2553 to elect to be an S corporation.
▶ See separate instructions.

1995

For calendar year 1995, or tax year beginning _____ , 1995, and ending _____ , 19 ___

A Date of election as an S corporation	Use IRS label. Otherwise, please print or type.	Name		**C** Employer identification number
		Number, street, and room or suite no. (If a P.O. box, see page 9 of the instructions.)		**D** Date incorporated
B Business code no. (see Specific Instructions)		City or town, state, and ZIP code		**E** Total assets (see Specific Instructions) $

F Check applicable boxes: (1) ☐ Initial return   (2) ☐ Final return   (3) ☐ Change in address   (4) ☐ Amended return

G Check this box if this S corporation is subject to the consolidated audit procedures of sections 6241 through 6245 (see instructions before checking this box) . ▶ ☐

H Enter number of shareholders in the corporation at end of the tax year . . . . ▶

Caution: Include only trade or business income and expenses on lines 1a through 21. See the instructions for more information.

Income

1a	Gross receipts or sales	**b** Less returns and allowances	**c** Bal ▶	**1c**
2	Cost of goods sold (Schedule A, line 8)	**2**
3	Gross profit. Subtract line 2 from line 1c	**3**
4	Net gain (loss) from Form 4797, Part II, line 20 *(attach Form 4797)*	**4**
5	Other income (loss) *(attach schedule)*	**5**
6	**Total income (loss).** Combine lines 3 through 5 . . . . . . ▶	**6**

Deductions *(see page 10 of the instructions for limitations)*

7	Compensation of officers	**7**
8	Salaries and wages (less employment credits)	**8**
9	Repairs and maintenance.	**9**
10	Bad debts	**10**
11	Rents	**11**
12	Taxes and licenses.	**12**
13	Interest	**13**
14a	Depreciation *(if required, attach Form 4562)* . . .	**14a**
b	Depreciation claimed on Schedule A and elsewhere on return .	**14b**
c	Subtract line 14b from line 14a.	**14c**
15	Depletion **(Do not deduct oil and gas depletion.)** . .	**15**
16	Advertising	**16**
17	Pension, profit-sharing, etc., plans	**17**
18	Employee benefit programs	**18**
19	Other deductions *(attach schedule)*	**19**
20	**Total deductions.** Add the amounts shown in the far right column for lines 7 through 19 . ▶	**20**
21	Ordinary income (loss) from trade or business activities. Subtract line 20 from line 6 . . .	**21**

Tax and Payments

22	**Tax: a** Excess net passive income tax *(attach schedule)*. . . .	**22a**	
	b Tax from Schedule D (Form 1120S)	**22b**	
	c Add lines 22a and 22b (see page 13 of the instructions for additional taxes)		**22c**
23	**Payments: a** 1995 estimated tax payments and amount applied from 1994 return	**23a**	
	b Tax deposited with Form 7004	**23b**	
	c Credit for Federal tax paid on fuels *(attach Form 4136)* . . .	**23c**	
	d Add lines 23a through 23c		**23d**
24	Estimated tax penalty. Check if Form 2220 is attached . . . . ▶ ☐		**24**
25	**Tax due.** If the total of lines 22c and 24 is larger than line 23d, enter amount owed. See page 3 of the instructions for depositary method of payment . . . . ▶		**25**
26	**Overpayment.** If line 23d is larger than the total of lines 22c and 24, enter amount overpaid ▶		**26**
27	Enter amount of line 26 you want: **Credited to 1996 estimated tax** ▶ _____ Refunded ▶		**27**

Please Sign Here

Under penalties of perjury, I declare that I have examined this return, including accompanying schedules and statements, and to the best of my knowledge and belief, it is true, correct, and complete. Declaration of preparer (other than taxpayer) is based on all information of which preparer has any knowledge.

▶ _____ _____ ▶ _____
Signature of officer   Date   Title

Paid Preparer's Use Only

Preparer's signature ▶		Date		Check if self-employed ▶ ☐	Preparer's social security number
Firm's name (or yours if self-employed) and address ▶				EIN ▶	
				ZIP code ▶	

For Paperwork Reduction Act Notice, see page 1 of separate instructions.   Cat. No. 11510H   Form **1120S** (1995)

Form 1120S (1995)   Page **4**

Schedule L	**Balance Sheets**	Beginning of tax year		End of tax year	
	Assets	(a)	(b)	(c)	(d)
1	Cash				
2a	Trade notes and accounts receivable . .				
b	Less allowance for bad debts				
3	Inventories				
4	U.S. Government obligations.				
5	Tax-exempt securities				
6	Other current assets (attach schedule). .				
7	Loans to shareholders				
8	Mortgage and real estate loans				
9	Other investments (attach schedule) . .				
10a	Buildings and other depreciable assets .				
b	Less accumulated depreciation				
11a	Depletable assets				
b	Less accumulated depletion				
12	Land (net of any amortization)				
13a	Intangible assets (amortizable only). . .				
b	Less accumulated amortization				
14	Other assets (attach schedule)				
15	Total assets				
	Liabilities and Shareholders' Equity				
16	Accounts payable				
17	Mortgages, notes, bonds payable in less than 1 year				
18	Other current liabilities (attach schedule)				
19	Loans from shareholders				
20	Mortgages, notes, bonds payable in 1 year or more				
21	Other liabilities (attach schedule) . . .				
22	Capital stock.				
23	Paid-in or capital surplus				
24	Retained earnings				
25	Less cost of treasury stock	(	)	(	)
26	Total liabilities and shareholders' equity . .				

Schedule M-1	**Reconciliation of Income (Loss) per Books With Income (Loss) per Return** (You are not required to complete this schedule if the total assets on line 15, column (d), of Schedule L are less than $25,000.)

1	Net income (loss) per books		5	Income recorded on books this year not included on Schedule K, lines 1 through 6 (itemize):	
2	Income included on Schedule K, lines 1 through 6, not recorded on books this year (itemize):		a	Tax-exempt interest $	
	....			....	
3	Expenses recorded on books this year not included on Schedule K, lines 1 through 11a, 15e, and 16b (itemize):		6	Deductions included on Schedule K, lines 1 through 11a, 15e, and 16b, not charged against book income this year (itemize):	
a	Depreciation $		a	Depreciation $	
b	Travel and entertainment $			....	
	....			....	
	....		7	Add lines 5 and 6	
4	Add lines 1 through 3		8	Income (loss) (Schedule K, line 23). Line 4 less line 7	

Schedule M-2	**Analysis of Accumulated Adjustments Account, Other Adjustments Account, and Shareholders' Undistributed Taxable Income Previously Taxed** (see page 22 of the instructions)

		(a) Accumulated adjustments account	(b) Other adjustments account	(c) Shareholders' undistributed taxable income previously taxed
1	Balance at beginning of tax year . . .			
2	Ordinary income from page 1, line 21 . .			
3	Other additions			
4	Loss from page 1, line 21	( )		
5	Other reductions	( )	( )	
6	Combine lines 1 through 5			
7	Distributions other than dividend distributions .			
8	Balance at end of tax year. Subtract line 7 from line 6			

*U.S. Government Printing Office: 1995 - 389-315

SCHEDULE K-1 (Form 1120S) Department of the Treasury Internal Revenue Service	**Shareholder's Share of Income, Credits, Deductions, etc.** ▶ See separate instructions. **For calendar year 1995 or tax year** beginning _____ , 1995, and ending _____ , 19 ____	OMB No. 1545-0130 **1995**

Shareholder's identifying number ▶	Corporation's identifying number ▶
Shareholder's name, address, and ZIP code	Corporation's name, address, and ZIP code

A Shareholder's percentage of stock ownership for tax year (see Instructions for Schedule K-1) . . . . ▶ .... %

B Internal Revenue Service Center where corporation filed its return ▶ --

C Tax shelter registration number (see Instructions for Schedule K-1) . . . . ▶ ---------------------------------

D Check applicable boxes: **(1)** ☐ Final K-1 **(2)** ☐ Amended K-1

	(a) Pro rata share items		(b) Amount	(c) Form 1040 filers enter the amount in column (b) on:
Income (Loss)	1 Ordinary income (loss) from trade or business activities	1		See pages 4 and 5 of the Shareholder's Instructions for Schedule K-1 (Form 1120S).
	2 Net income (loss) from rental real estate activities	2		
	3 Net income (loss) from other rental activities	3		
	4 Portfolio income (loss):			
	a Interest	4a		Sch. B, Part I, line 1
	b Dividends	4b		Sch. B, Part II, line 5
	c Royalties	4c		Sch. E, Part I, line 4
	d Net short-term capital gain (loss)	4d		Sch. D, line 5, col. (f) or (g)
	e Net long-term capital gain (loss)	4e		Sch. D, line 13, col. (f) or (g)
	f Other portfolio income (loss) *(attach schedule)*	4f		(Enter on applicable line of your return.)
	5 Net gain (loss) under section 1231 (other than due to casualty or theft)	5		See Shareholder's Instructions for Schedule K-1 (Form 1120S).
	6 Other income (loss) *(attach schedule)*	6		(Enter on applicable line of your return.)
Deductions	7 Charitable contributions *(attach schedule)*	7		Sch. A, line 15 or 16
	8 Section 179 expense deduction	8		See page 6 of the Shareholder's Instructions for Schedule K-1 (Form 1120S).
	9 Deductions related to portfolio income (loss) *(attach schedule)* .	9		
	10 Other deductions *(attach schedule)*	10		
Investment Interest	11a Interest expense on investment debts	11a		Form 4952, line 1
	b (1) Investment income included on lines 4a, 4b, 4c, and 4f above	b(1)		See Shareholder's Instructions for Schedule K-1 (Form 1120S).
	(2) Investment expenses included on line 9 above . . .	b(2)		
Credits	12a Credit for alcohol used as fuel	12a		Form 6478, line 10
	b Low-income housing credit:			
	(1) From section 42(j)(5) partnerships for property placed in service before 1990	b(1)		
	(2) Other than on line 12b(1) for property placed in service before 1990	b(2)		Form 8586, line 5
	(3) From section 42(j)(5) partnerships for property placed in service after 1989	b(3)		
	(4) Other than on line 12b(3) for property placed in service after 1989	b(4)		
	c Qualified rehabilitation expenditures related to rental real estate activities	12c		See page 7 of the Shareholder's Instructions for Schedule K-1 (Form 1120S).
	d Credits (other than credits shown on lines 12b and 12c) related to rental real estate activities	12d		
	e Credits related to other rental activities	12e		
	13 Other credits	13		
Adjustments and Tax Preference Items	14a Depreciation adjustment on property placed in service after 1986	14a		See page 7 of the Shareholder's Instructions for Schedule K-1 (Form 1120S) and Instructions for Form 6251.
	b Adjusted gain or loss	14b		
	c Depletion (other than oil and gas)	14c		
	d (1) Gross income from oil, gas, or geothermal properties . . .	d(1)		
	(2) Deductions allocable to oil, gas, or geothermal properties	d(2)		
	e Other adjustments and tax preference items *(attach schedule)*	14e		

For Paperwork Reduction Act Notice, see page 1 of Instructions for Form 1120S. Cat. No. 11520D **Schedule K-1 (Form 1120S) 1995**

APPENDIX A

(a) Pro rata share items		(b) Amount	(c) Form 1040 filers enter the amount in column (b) on:
Foreign Taxes	**15a** Type of income ▶		Form 1116, Check boxes
	b Name of foreign country or U.S. possession ▶		
	c Total gross income from sources outside the United States *(attach schedule)* 15c		Form 1116, Part I
	d Total applicable deductions and losses *(attach schedule)* . . 15d		
	e Total foreign taxes (check one): ▶ ☐ Paid ☐ Accrued 15e		Form 1116, Part II
	f Reduction in taxes available for credit *(attach schedule)* . . . 15f		Form 1116, Part III
	g Other foreign tax information *(attach schedule)* 15g		See Instructions for Form 1116
Other	**16** Section 59(e)(2) expenditures: **a** Type ▶		See Shareholder's Instructions for Schedule K-1 (Form 1120S)
	b Amount 16b		
	17 Tax-exempt interest income 17		Form 1040, line 8b
	18 Other tax-exempt income 18		
	19 Nondeductible expenses 19		See page 7 of the Shareholder's Instructions for Schedule K-1 (Form 1120S).
	20 Property distributions (including cash) other than dividend distributions reported to you on Form 1099-DIV 20		
	21 Amount of loan repayments for "Loans From Shareholders" . . 21		
	22 Recapture of low-income housing credit:		
	a From section 42(j)(5) partnerships 22a		Form 8611, line 8
	b Other than on line 22a 22b		

23 Supplemental information required to be reported separately to each shareholder *(attach additional schedules if more space is needed)*:

Supplemental Information

....

....

....

....

....

....

....

....

....

....

....

....

....

....

....

....

....

....

♻ *Printed on recycled paper*

U.S. Government Printing Office: 1995 - 389-319

Form 1127
(Rev. 11-93)
Department of the Treasury
Internal Revenue Service

APPLICATION FOR EXTENSION OF TIME FOR PAYMENT OF TAX

(ATTN: *This type of payment extension is rarely* <u>*granted*</u> *because the legal requirements are so strict. Please read the conditions on the back carefully before continuing.)*

Taxpayer's Name (include spouse if your extension request is for a joint return)	Social Security Number or Employer Identification Number
Present Address	
City, Town or Post Office, State, and Zip Code	Spouse's Social Security Number if this is for a joint return

District Director of Internal Revenue at _____
(Enter City and State where IRS Office is located)

I request an extension from _____ , 19 _____ , to _____ , 19 _____ .
(Enter Due Date of Return)

to pay tax of $ _____ for the year ended _____ , 19 _____ .

This extension is necessary because *(If more space is needed, please attach a separate sheet):* _____

_____

_____

_____

I can't borrow to pay the tax because: _____

_____

_____

To show the need for the extension. I am attaching: (1) a statement of my assets and liabilities at the end of last month (showing book and market values of assets and whether securities are listed or unlisted); and (2) an itemized list of money I received and spent for 3 months before the date the tax is due.

I propose to secure this liability as follows:

_____

_____

Under penalties of perjury, I declare that I have examined this application, including any accompanying schedules and statements, and to the best of my knowledge and belief it is true, correct, and complete.

_____   _____
SIGNATURE (BOTH SIGNATURES IF YOUR EXTENSION REQUEST IS FOR A JOINT RETURN)   *(DATE)*

The District Director will let you know whether the extension is approved or denied and will tell you if you need some form of security. However, the Director can't consider an application if it is filed after the due date of the return. We will send you a list of approved surety companies if you ask for it.

(The following will be filled in by the IRS.)

This application is ☐ approved   for the following reasons:
☐ denied

_____

_____

Interest _____ Date of assessment _____ Identifying no._____

Penalty _____   _____   _____
                    (SIGNATURE)   *(DATE)*

CAT. NO. 172380   *(over)*   Form **1127** (Rev. 11-93)

Form **2119**	**Sale of Your Home**	OMB No. 1545-0072

Department of the Treasury
Internal Revenue Service

▶ **Attach to Form 1040 for year of sale.**

▶ **See separate instructions.** ▶ **Please print or type.**

1995

Attachment
Sequence No. **20**

Your first name and initial. If a joint return, also give spouse's name and initial.   Last name

Your social security number

Fill in Your Address Only If You Are Filing This Form by Itself and Not With Your Tax Return

Present address (no., street, and apt. no., rural route, or P.O. box no. if mail is not delivered to street address)

City, town or post office, state, and ZIP code

Spouse's social security number

Part I   **Gain on Sale**

1.   Date your former main home was sold (month, day, year) . . . . ▶   **1**   /   /
2.   Have you bought or built a new main home? . . . . ☐ Yes ☐ No
3.   If any part of either main home was ever rented out or used for business, check here ▶ ☐ and see page 3.
4.   Selling price of home. Do not include personal property items you sold with your home . .   **4**
5.   Expense of sale (see page 3) **5**
6.   Subtract line 5 from line 4 . . . .   **6**
7.   Adjusted basis of home sold (see page 3) **7**
8.   **Gain on sale.** Subtract line 7 from line 6 . . . .   **8**

Is line 8 more than zero?	Yes ──▶	If line 2 is "Yes," you **must** go to Part II or Part III, whichever applies. If line 2 is "No," go to line 9.
	No ──▶	**Stop; see Loss on the Sale of Your Home** on page 1.

9.   If you haven't replaced your home, do you plan to do so within the **replacement period** (see page 1)? .   ☐ Yes ☐ No
   • If line 9 is "Yes," stop here, attach this form to your return, and see **Additional Filing Requirements** on page 1.
   • If line 9 is "No," you **must** go to Part II or Part III, whichever applies.

Part II   **One-Time Exclusion of Gain for People Age 55 or Older**—By completing this part, you are electing to take the one-time exclusion (see page 2). If you are not electing to take the exclusion, go to Part III now.

10.   Who was age 55 or older on the date of sale? . . . . ☐ You ☐ Your spouse ☐ Both of you
11.   Did the person who was 55 or older own and use the property as his or her main home for a total of at least 3 years of the 5-year period before the sale? See page 2 for exceptions. If "No," go to Part III now . . . ☐ Yes ☐ No
12.   At the time of sale, who owned the home? . . . . ☐ You ☐ Your spouse ☐ Both of you
13.   Social security number of spouse at the time of sale if you had a different spouse from the one above. If you were not married at the time of sale, enter "None" . . . . ▶   **13**
14.   **Exclusion.** Enter the **smaller** of line 8 or $125,000 ($62,500 if married filing separate return). Then, go to line 15 . . . .   **14**

Part III   **Adjusted Sales Price, Taxable Gain, and Adjusted Basis of New Home**

15.   If line 14 is blank, enter the amount from line 8. Otherwise, subtract line 14 from line 8 . .   **15**
   • If line 15 is zero, stop and attach this form to your return.
   • If line 15 is more than zero and line 2 is "Yes," go to line 16 now.
   • If you are reporting this sale on the installment method, stop and see page 4.
   • All others, stop and **enter the amount from line 15 on Schedule D, col. (g), line 4 or line 12.**
16.   Fixing-up expenses (see page 4 for time limits) **16**
17.   If line 14 is blank, enter amount from line 16. Otherwise, add lines 14 and 16 . .   **17**
18.   **Adjusted sales price.** Subtract line 17 from line 6 . . . .   **18**
19a   Date you moved into new home ▶   /   /   **b** Cost of new home (see page 4)   **19b**
20.   Subtract line 19b from line 18. If zero or less, enter -0- **20**
21.   **Taxable gain.** Enter the **smaller** of line 15 or line 20 . . . .   **21**
   • If line 21 is zero, go to line 22 and attach this form to your return.
   • If you are reporting this sale on the installment method, see the line 15 instructions and go to line 22.
   • All others, **enter the amount from line 21 on Schedule D, col. (g), line 4 or line 12,** and go to line 22.
22.   Postponed gain. Subtract line 21 from line 15 . . . .   **22**
23.   **Adjusted basis of new home.** Subtract line 22 from line 19b **23**

Sign Here Only If You Are Filing This Form by Itself and Not With Your Tax Return

Under penalties of perjury, I declare that I have examined this form, including attachments, and to the best of my knowledge and belief, it is true, correct, and complete.

Your signature   Date   Spouse's signature   Date

▶   ▶

If a joint return, both must sign.

For Paperwork Reduction Act Notice, see separate instructions.   Cat. No. 11710J   Form **2119** (1995)

✸ *Printed on recycled paper*   *U.S. Government Printing Office: 1995 - 389-???

Form **2553**
(Rev. September 1993)

Department of the Treasury
Internal Revenue Service

Election by a Small Business Corporation
(Under section 1362 of the Internal Revenue Code)
▶ **For Paperwork Reduction Act Notice, see page 1 of instructions.**
▶ **See separate instructions.**

OMB No. 1545-0146
Expires 8-31-96

Notes: 1. *This election, to be an "S corporation," can be accepted only if all the tests are met under **Who May Elect** on page 1 of the instructions; all signatures in Parts I and III are originals (no photocopies); and the exact name and address of the corporation and other required form information are provided.*

2. *Do not file **Form 1120S**, U.S. Income Tax Return for an S Corporation, until you are notified that your election is accepted.*

Part I   Election Information

Please Type or Print

Name of corporation (see instructions)	**A** Employer identification number (EIN)
Number, street, and room or suite no. (If a P.O. box, see instructions.)	**B** Date incorporated
City or town, state, and ZIP code	**C** State of incorporation

D   Election is to be effective for tax year beginning (month, day, year) . . . . ▶   /   /

E   Name and title of officer or legal representative who the IRS may call for more information

F Telephone number of officer or legal representative

(   )

G   If the corporation changed its name or address after applying for the EIN shown in **A**, check this box . . . . ▶ ☐

H   If this election takes effect for the first tax year the corporation exists, enter month, day, and year of the **earliest** of the following: (1) date the corporation first had shareholders, (2) date the corporation first had assets, or (3) date the corporation began doing business . . . . ▶   /   /

I   Selected tax year: Annual return will be filed for tax year ending (month and day) ▶ . . . .

If the tax year ends on any date other than December 31, except for an automatic 52-53-week tax year ending with reference to the month of December, you **must** complete Part II on the back. If the date you enter is the ending date of an automatic 52-53-week tax year, write "52-53-week year" to the right of the date. See Temporary Regulations section 1.441-2T(e)(3).

J Name and address of each shareholder, shareholder's spouse having a community property interest in the corporation's stock, and each tenant in common, joint tenant, and tenant by the entirety. (A husband and wife (and their estates) are counted as one shareholder in determining the number of shareholders without regard to the manner in which the stock is owned.)	**K** Shareholders' Consent Statement. Under penalties of perjury, we declare that we consent to the election of the above-named corporation to be an "S corporation" under section 1362(a) and that we have examined this consent statement, including accompanying schedules and statements, and to the best of our knowledge and belief, it is true, correct, and complete. (Shareholders sign and date below.)*		**L** Stock owned		**M** Social security number or employer identification number (see instructions)	**N** Shareholder's tax year ends (month and day)
	Signature	Date	Number of shares	Dates acquired		

*For this election to be valid, the consent of each shareholder, shareholder's spouse having a community property interest in the corporation's stock, and each tenant in common, joint tenant, and tenant by the entirety must either appear above or be attached to this form. (See instructions for Column K if a continuation sheet or a separate consent statement is needed.)

Under penalties of perjury, I declare that I have examined this election, including accompanying schedules and statements, and to the best of my knowledge and belief, it is true, correct, and complete.

Signature of officer ▶   Title ▶   Date ▶

See Parts II and III on back.   Cat. No. 18629R   Form **2553** (Rev. 9-93)

Form **4506**
(Rev. January 1987)
Department of the Treasury
Internal Revenue Service

Request for Copy of Tax Form

▶ **Please read instructions before completing this form.**

OMB No. 1545-0429

Expires 12-31-89

Important: Full payment must accompany your request.

1 Name of taxpayer(s) as shown on tax form (husband's and wife's, if joint return)	6 Social security number as shown on tax form (if joint return, show husband's number)
2 Current name and address	6a Wife's social security number as shown on tax form
	7 Employer identification number as shown on tax form
	8 Tax form number (Form 1040, 1040A, etc.)
3 If copy of form is to be mailed to someone else, show the third party's name and address.	9 Tax period(s) (1983, etc.) (No more than 4 per request)
3a If we cannot find a record of your return, check here if you want the payment refunded to the third party. ☐	10 Amount due for copy of tax form:
4 If name in third party's records differs from item 1 above, show name here. (See instructions for items 3, 3a, and 4.)	a Cost for each period . . . . . $ 4.25
	b Number of periods requested in item 9 . . . .
	c Total cost (multiply item 10a by item 10b) . . . . $
	Make check or money order payable to Internal Revenue Service

5 Check the box to show what you want:

☐ Copy of tax form and all attachments. The charge is $4.25 for each period requested.

Note: *If you need these copies for court or administrative proceedings, also check here.* ☐

☐ Copy of Form W-2 only. There is no charge for this.

Please ▶

Sign _____   Date _____

Here ▶

Signature

Title   (if item 1 above is a corporation, partnership, estate, or trust)

Telephone number of requester

(   )

Convenient time for us to call

Instructions

Privacy Act and Paperwork Reduction Act Notice.—We ask for this information to carry out the Internal Revenue laws of the United States. We need the information to gain access to your return in our files and properly respond to your request. If you do not furnish the information, we may not be able to fill your request.

Purpose of Form.—Use this form to request a copy of a tax return or Form W-2.

Note: *If you had your return filled out by a paid preparer, check first to see if you can get a copy from the preparer. This may save you both time and money.*

If you are not the taxpayer shown in item 1, you must send a copy of your authorization to receive the copy of the form. This will generally be a power of attorney, tax information authorization, or evidence of entitlement (for Title 11 Bankruptcy or Receivership Proceeding). If the taxpayer is deceased, you must send enough evidence to establish that you are authorized to act for the taxpayer's estate.

Copies of joint returns may be furnished to either the husband or the wife. Only one signature is required. If your name has changed, sign Form 4506 exactly as your name appeared on the return and also sign with your current name.

Please allow at least 45 days for delivery. Be sure to furnish all the information asked for on this form to avoid any delay in our sending your requested copies. (You must allow at least 6 weeks processing time after a return is filed before requesting a copy.)

Corporations, Partnerships, Estates, and Trusts.—For rules on who may obtain tax information on the entity, see Internal Revenue Code section 6103.

Items 3, 3a, and 4.—If you have named someone else to receive the tax form (such as a CPA, scholarship board, or mortgage lender), **you must include the name of an individual** with the address in item 3. Also, be sure to write the name of the client, student, or applicant in item 4 if it is different from the name shown in item 1. For example, item 1 may be the parents of a student applying for financial aid. Show the

student's name in item 4 so the scholarship board will know what file to associate the return with. If we cannot find a record of your return, we will notify the third party directly that we cannot fill the request. If you checked the box in 3a, we will refund the payment for the copies to the third party.

Item 5.—If you want a copy of your Form W-2 only and not a copy of your tax return, be sure to check the box for Copy of Form W-2 only and in item 8 show "Form W-2 only"; in item 10c show "no charge."

If you need only tax account information and not a copy of your tax return or Form W-2, do not complete this form. See the instructions on the back under "Tax Account Information Only."

Items 6 and 6a.—For individuals, enter the social security number as shown on the tax form. For joint returns, show the husband's social security number in item 6 and the wife's in item 6a. If you do not furnish this information, there may be a delay in processing your request.

(Continued on back)

Form **4506** (Rev. 1-87)

Form **4562**	**Depreciation and Amortization**	OMB No. 1545-0172
	(Including Information on Listed Property)	**19⁣95**
Department of the Treasury Internal Revenue Service (O)	▶ **See separate instructions.** ▶ **Attach this form to your return.**	Attachment Sequence No. **67**

Name(s) shown on return	Business or activity to which this form relates	Identifying number

Part I   **Election To Expense Certain Tangible Property (Section 179) (Note:** *If you have any "Listed Property,"*
complete Part V before you complete Part I.)

1	Maximum dollar limitation. If an enterprise zone business, see page 1 of the instructions	**1**	$17,500
2	Total cost of section 179 property placed in service during the tax year. See page 2 of the instructions	**2**	
3	Threshold cost of section 179 property before reduction in limitation	**3**	$200,000
4	Reduction in limitation. Subtract line 3 from line 2. If zero or less, enter -0-	**4**	
5	Dollar limitation for tax year. Subtract line 4 from line 1. If zero or less, enter -0-. If married filing separately, see page 2 of the instructions	**5**	

(a) Description of property	(b) Cost	(c) Elected cost
6		

7	Listed property. Enter amount from line 27.	**7**	
8	Total elected cost of section 179 property. Add amounts in column (c), lines 6 and 7	**8**	
9	Tentative deduction. Enter the smaller of line 5 or line 8	**9**	
10	Carryover of disallowed deduction from 1994. See page 2 of the instructions	**10**	
11	Taxable income limitation. Enter the smaller of taxable income (not less than zero) or line 5 (see instructions)	**11**	
12	Section 179 expense deduction. Add lines 9 and 10, but do not enter more than line 11	**12**	
13	Carryover of disallowed deduction to 1996. Add lines 9 and 10, less line 12 ▶	**13**	

Note: *Do not use Part II or Part III below for listed property (automobiles, certain other vehicles, cellular telephones,
certain computers, or property used for entertainment, recreation, or amusement). Instead, use Part V for listed property.*

Part II   **MACRS Depreciation For Assets Placed in Service ONLY During Your 1995 Tax Year (Do Not Include
Listed Property.)**

Section A—General Asset Account Election

14   If you are making the election under section 168(i)(4) to group any assets placed in service during the tax year into one or more
general asset accounts, check this box. See page 2 of the instructions   ▶ ☐

(a) Classification of property	(b) Month and year placed in service	(c) Basis for depreciation (business/investment use only—see instructions)	(d) Recovery period	(e) Convention	(f) Method	(g) Depreciation deduction
Section B—General Depreciation System (GDS) (See page 2 of the instructions.)						
15a 3-year property						
b 5-year property						
c 7-year property						
d 10-year property						
e 15-year property						
f 20-year property						
g Residential rental property			27.5 yrs.	MM	S/L	
			27.5 yrs.	MM	S/L	
h Nonresidential real property			39 yrs.	MM	S/L	
				MM	S/L	
Section C—Alternative Depreciation System (ADS) (See page 4 of the instructions.)						
16a Class life					S/L	
b 12-year			12 yrs.		S/L	
c 40-year			40 yrs.	MM	S/L	

Part III   **Other Depreciation (Do Not Include Listed Property.)** (See page 4 of the instructions.)

17	GDS and ADS deductions for assets placed in service in tax years beginning before 1995	**17**	
18	Property subject to section 168(f)(1) election	**18**	
19	ACRS and other depreciation	**19**	

Part IV   **Summary** (See page 4 of the instructions.)

20	Listed property. Enter amount from line 26.	**20**	
21	**Total.** Add deductions on line 12, lines 15 and 16 in column (g), and lines 17 through 20. Enter here and on the appropriate lines of your return. Partnerships and S corporations—see instructions	**21**	
22	For assets shown above and placed in service during the current year, enter the portion of the basis attributable to section 263A costs **22**		

For Paperwork Reduction Act Notice, see page 1 of the separate instructions.   Cat. No. 12906N   Form **4562** (1995)

Form **4822**
(Rev. 6-83)

Department of the Treasury - Internal Revenue Service

STATEMENT OF ANNUAL ESTIMATED PERSONAL AND FAMILY EXPENSES

TAXPAYER'S NAME AND ADDRESS

TAX YEAR ENDED

	ITEM	BY CASH	BY CHECK	TOTAL	REMARKS
1. PERSONAL EXPENSES	Groceries and outside meals				
	Clothing				
	Laundry and dry cleaning				
	Barber, beauty shop, and cosmetics				
	Education *(tuition, room, board, books, etc.)*				
	Recreation, entertainment, vacations				
	Dues *(clubs, lodge, etc.)*				
	Gifts and allowances				
	Life and accident insurance				
	Federal taxes *(income, FICA, etc.)*				
2. HOUSEHOLD EXPENSES	Rent				
	Mortgage payments *(including interest)*				
	Utilities *(electricity, gas, telephone, water, etc.)*				
	Domestic help				
	Home insurance				
	Repairs and improvements				
	Child care				
3. AUTO EXPENSES	Gasoline, oil, grease, wash				
	Tires, batteries, repairs, tags				
	Insurance				
	Auto payments *(including interest)*				
	Lease of auto				
4. DEDUCTIBLE ITEMS	Contributions				
	Medical Expenses — Insurance				
	Drugs				
	Doctors, hospitals, etc.				
	Taxes — Real estate *(not included in 2. above)*				
	Personal property				
	Income *(State and local)*				
	Interest *(not included in 2. and 3. above)*				
	Miscellaneous — Alimony				
	Union dues				
5. PERSONAL ASSETS, ETC.	Stocks and bonds				
	Furniture, appliances, jewelry				
	Loans to others				
	Boat				
	TOTALS ▶				

Cat. No. 23460C

*U.S. Government Printing Office: 1996 - 405-506/33726

Form 4822 (Rev. 6-83)

Form **4868** Department of the Treasury Internal Revenue Service	**Application for Automatic Extension of Time** **To File U.S. Individual Income Tax Return**	OMB No. 1545-0188 **1995**

1 Your name(s) (see instructions)		**2a Amount due—** Add lines 6c, d, and e ▶ $ _____
Address (see instructions)	**3 Your social security number**	
City, town or post office, state, and ZIP code	**4 Spouse's social security no.**	**b Amount you** **are paying** ▶ $

5 I request an automatic 4-month extension of time to August 15, 1996, to file my individual tax return for the calendar year 1995 or to _____ , 19 ____ , for the fiscal tax year ending _____ , 19 ____

6 **Individual Income Tax**—See instructions.

a Total tax liability for 1995 . . . . . $ _____
b Total payments for 1995 . . . . . $ _____
c **Balance due.** Subtract 6b from 6a . . $ _____

Gift or GST Tax Return(s)—See instructions.

Check here **ONLY** if filing a gift or GST
tax return . . . . } Yourself ▶ ☐
                                 Spouse ▶ ☐
d Amount of gift or GST tax **you** are paying $ _____
e **Your spouse's** gift/GST tax payment $ _____

Under penalties of perjury, I declare that I have examined this form, including accompanying schedules and statements, and to the best of my knowledge and belief, it is true, correct, and complete; and, if prepared by someone other than the taxpayer, that I am authorized to prepare this form.

▶ Your signature _____ Date _____   ▶ Spouse's signature, if filing jointly _____ Date _____

▶ Preparer's signature (other than taxpayer) _____ Date _____

Form **5213** (Rev. September 1994) Department of the Treasury Internal Revenue Service	**Election To Postpone Determination** **as To Whether the Presumption Applies That an** **Activity Is Engaged in for Profit** ▶ To be filed by individuals, estates, trusts, partnerships, and S corporations.	OMB No. 1545-0195

Name(s) as shown on tax return	Identifying number as shown on tax return

Address (number and street, apt. no., rural route) (or P.O. box number if mail is not delivered to street address)

City, town or post office, state, and ZIP code

The taxpayer named above elects to postpone a determination as to whether the presumption applies that the activity described below is engaged in for profit. The determination is postponed until the close of:
- The 6th tax year, for an activity that consists mainly of breeding, training, showing, or racing horses; or
- The 4th tax year for any other activity,

after the tax year in which the taxpayer first engaged in the activity.

1 Type of taxpayer engaged in the activity (check the box that applies):

☐ Individual   ☐ Partnership   ☐ S corporation   ☐ Estate or trust

2a Description of activity for which you elect to postpone a determination

2b First tax year you engaged in activity described in 2a

Under penalties of perjury, I declare that I have examined this election, including accompanying schedules, and to the best of my knowledge and belief, it is true, correct, and complete.

_____   _____
(Signature of taxpayer or fiduciary)   (Date)

_____   _____
(Signature of taxpayer's spouse, if joint return was filed)   (Date)

_____   _____
(Signature of general partner authorized to sign partnership return)   (Date)

_____   _____
(Signature and title of officer, if an S corporation)   (Date)

For Paperwork Reduction Act Notice, see instructions on back.   Cat. No. 42361U   Form **5213** (Rev. 9-94)

Form **6251**	**Alternative Minimum Tax—Individuals**	OMB No. 1545-0227
Department of the Treasury Internal Revenue Service (O)	▶ See separate instructions. ▶ Attach to Form 1040, Form 1040NR, or Form 1040-T.	**1995** Attachment Sequence No. **32**

Name(s) shown on Form 1040 — Your social security number

Part I Adjustments and Preferences

1　If you itemized deductions on Schedule A (Form 1040) (or you entered the amount from Form 1040-T, Section B, line t, on Form 1040-T, line 20), go to line 2. Otherwise, enter your standard deduction from Form 1040, line 34 (or Form 1040-T, line 20), and go to line 6 . . . . **1**

2　Medical and dental. Enter the smaller of Schedule A (Form 1040), line 4 **or** 2½% of Form 1040, line 32 (Form 1040-T filers, enter the smaller of Section B, line c **or** 2½% of Form 1040-T, line 16) . **2**

3　Taxes. Enter the amount from Schedule A (Form 1040), line 9 (or the total of lines d through g of Form 1040-T, Section B) . **3**

4　Certain interest on a home mortgage not used to buy, build, or improve your home **4**

5　Miscellaneous itemized deductions. Enter the amount from Schedule A (Form 1040), line 26 (or Form 1040-T, Section B, line r) **5**

6　Refund of taxes. Enter any tax refund from Form 1040, line 10 or line 21 (or Form 1040-T, line 4 or line 9) . **6** ( )

7　Investment interest. Enter difference between regular tax and AMT deduction **7**

8　Post-1986 depreciation. Enter difference between regular tax and AMT depreciation **8**

9　Adjusted gain or loss. Enter difference between AMT and regular tax gain or loss **9**

10　Incentive stock options. Enter excess of AMT income over regular tax income **10**

11　Passive activities. Enter difference between AMT and regular tax income or loss **11**

12　Beneficiaries of estates and trusts. Enter the amount from Schedule K-1 (Form 1041), line 8 . **12**

13　Tax-exempt interest from private activity bonds issued after 8/7/86 . . . . **13**

14　Other. Enter the amount, if any, for each item and enter the total on line 14.

a Charitable contributions .	h Loss limitations	
b Circulation expenditures .	i Mining costs	
c Depletion	j Patron's adjustment . .	
d Depreciation (pre-1987) .	k Pollution control facilities .	
e Installment sales . . .	l Research and experimental .	
f Intangible drilling costs .	m Tax shelter farm activities .	
g Long-term contracts . .	n Related adjustments . .	**14**

15　**Total Adjustments and Preferences.** Combine lines 1 through 14 . . . . ▶ **15**

Part II Alternative Minimum Taxable Income

16　Enter the amount from **Form 1040, line 35 (or Form 1040-T, line 21)**. If less than zero, enter as a (loss) . ▶ **16**

17　Net operating loss deduction, if any, from Form 1040, line 21. Enter as a positive amount **17**

18　If Form 1040, line 32 (or Form 1040-T, line 16), is over $114,700 (over $57,350 if married filing separately), and you itemized deductions, enter the amount, if any, from line 9 of the worksheet for Schedule A (Form 1040), line 28 (or line 9 of the worksheet for Section B, line t, of Form 1040-T). . . . . **18** ( )

19　Combine lines 15 through 18 . . . . ▶ **19**

20　Alternative tax net operating loss deduction. See page 5 of the instructions **20**

21　**Alternative Minimum Taxable Income.** Subtract line 20 from line 19. (If married filing separately and line 21 is more than $165,000, see page 5 of the instructions.) . . . . ▶ **21**

Part III Exemption Amount and Alternative Minimum Tax

22　**Exemption Amount.** (If this form is for a child under age 14, see page 6 of the instructions.)

　If your filing status is:　　　　　　**And line 21 is not over:**　　　　**Enter on line 22:**
　Single or head of household. . . . . $112,500 . . . . $33,750
　Married filing jointly or qualifying widow(er) . . 150,000 . . . . 45,000 } **22**
　Married filing separately 75,000 22,500

　If line 21 **is over** the amount shown above for your filing status, see page 6 of the instructions.

23　Subtract line 22 from line 21. If zero or less, enter -0- here and on lines 26 and 28 . . . . . . ▶ **23**

24　If line 23 is $175,000 or less ($87,500 or less if married filing separately), multiply line 23 by 26% (.26). Otherwise, multiply line 23 by 28% (.28) and subtract $3,500 ($1,750 if married filing separately) from the result . . . **24**

25　Alternative minimum tax foreign tax credit. See page 6 of the instructions **25**

26　Tentative minimum tax. Subtract line 25 from line 24 . . . . ▶ **26**

27　Enter your tax from Form 1040, line 38 (plus any amount from Form 4970 included on Form 1040, line 39), minus any foreign tax credit from Form 1040, line 43 (Form 1040-T filers, enter the amount from Form 1040-T, line 26) **27**

28　**Alternative Minimum Tax.** (If this form is for a child under age 14, see page 7 of the instructions.) Subtract line 27 from line 26. If zero or less, enter -0-. Enter here and on Form 1040, line 48 (or Form 1040-T, line 31) ▶ **28**

For Paperwork Reduction Act Notice, see separate instructions.　　✹ *Printed on recycled paper*　　Cat. No. 13600G　　Form **6251** (1995)
*U.S. Government Printing Office: 1995 - 389-414

Form 8275

(Rev. April 1995)

Department of the Treasury
Internal Revenue Service

Disclosure Statement

Do not use this form to disclose items or positions that are contrary to Treasury regulations. Instead, use Form 8275-R, Regulation Disclosure Statement.
See separate instructions.

▶ Attach to your tax return.

OMB No. 1545-0889

Attachment
Sequence No. **92**

Name(s) shown on return

Identifying number shown on return

Part I **General Information** (See instructions.)

(a) Rev. Rul., Rev. Proc., etc.	(b) Item or Group of Items	(c) Detailed Description of Items	(d) Form or Schedule	(e) Line No.	(f) Amount
1					
2					
3					

Part II **Detailed Explanation** (See instructions.)

1

2

3

Part III **Information About Pass-Through Entity.** To be completed by partners, shareholders, beneficiaries, or residual interest holders.

Complete this part only if you are making adequate disclosure with respect to a pass-through item.

Note: *A pass-through entity is a partnership, S corporation, estate, trust, regulated investment company, real estate investment trust, or real estate mortgage investment conduit (REMIC).*

1 Name, address, and ZIP code of pass-through entity	2 Identifying number of pass-through entity
	3 Tax year of pass-through entity / / to / /
	4 Internal Revenue Service Center where the pass-through entity filed its return

For Paperwork Reduction Act Notice, see separate instructions.   Cat. No. 61935M   Form **8275** (Rev. 4-95)

Form **8275-R**

(Rev. April 1995)

Department of the Treasury
Internal Revenue Service

Regulation Disclosure Statement

Use this form only to disclose items or positions that are contrary to Treasury regulations.
For other disclosures, use Form 8275, Disclosure Statement. See separate instructions.

▶ **Attach to your tax return.**

OMB No. 1545-0889

Attachment
Sequence No. **92A**

Name(s) shown on return

Identifying number shown on return

Part I   **General Information** (See instructions.)

	(a) Regulation Section	(b) Item or Group of Items	(c) Detailed Description of Items	(d) Form or Schedule	(e) Line No.	(f) Amount
1						
2						
3						

Part II   **Detailed Explanation** (See instructions.)

1

2

3

Part III   **Information About Pass-Through Entity.** To be completed by partners, shareholders, beneficiaries, or residual interest holders.

Complete this part only if you are making adequate disclosure for a pass-through item.

Note: *A pass-through entity is a partnership, S corporation, estate, trust, regulated investment company, real estate investment trust, or real estate mortgage investment conduit (REMIC).*

1 Name, address, and ZIP code of pass-through entity	2 Identifying number of pass-through entity
	3 Tax year of pass-through entity / / to / /
	4 Internal Revenue Service Center where the pass-through entity filed its return

For Paperwork Reduction Act Notice, see separate instructions.

Cat. No. 14594X

Form **8275-R** (Rev. 4-95)

Form **8283**
(Rev. October 1995)

Department of the Treasury
Internal Revenue Service

Noncash Charitable Contributions

▶ Attach to your tax return if you claimed a total deduction
of over $500 for all contributed property.

▶ See separate instructions.

OMB No. 1545-0908

Attachment
Sequence No. **55**

Name(s) shown on your income tax return

Identifying number

Note: *Figure the amount of your contribution deduction before completing this form. See your tax return instructions.*

Section A—List in this section **only** items (or groups of similar items) for which you claimed a deduction of $5,000 or less. Also, list certain publicly traded securities even if the deduction is over $5,000 (see instructions).

Part I Information on Donated Property—If you need more space, attach a statement.

1	(a) Name and address of the donee organization	(b) Description of donated property
A		
B		
C		
D		
E		

Note: *If the amount you claimed as a deduction for an item is $500 or less, you do not have to complete columns (d), (e), and (f).*

	(c) Date of the contribution	(d) Date acquired by donor (mo., yr.)	(e) How acquired by donor	(f) Donor's cost or adjusted basis	(g) Fair market value	(h) Method used to determine the fair market value
A						
B						
C						
D						
E						

Part II Other Information—Complete line 2 if you gave less than an entire interest in property listed in Part I. Complete line 3 if restrictions were attached to a contribution listed in Part I.

2 If, during the year, you contributed less than the entire interest in the property, complete lines a – e.

a Enter the letter from Part I that identifies the property ▶ _____ . If Part II applies to more than one property, attach a separate statement.

b Total amount claimed as a deduction for the property listed in Part I: **(1)** For this tax year ▶ _____
(2) For any prior tax years ▶ _____ .

c Name and address of each organization to which any such contribution was made in a prior year (complete only if different than the donee organization above):

Name of charitable organization (donee)

Address (number, street, and room or suite no.)

City or town, state, and ZIP code

d For tangible property, enter the place where the property is located or kept ▶ _____

e Name of any person, other than the donee organization, having actual possession of the property ▶ _____

3 If conditions were attached to any contribution listed in Part I, answer questions a – c and attach the required statement (see instructions).

		Yes	No
a	Is there a restriction, either temporary or permanent, on the donee's right to use or dispose of the donated property?		
b	Did you give to anyone (other than the donee organization or another organization participating with the donee organization in cooperative fundraising) the right to the income from the donated property or to the possession of the property, including the right to vote donated securities, to acquire the property by purchase or otherwise, or to designate the person having such income, possession, or right to acquire?		
c	Is there a restriction limiting the donated property for a particular use?		

For Paperwork Reduction Act Notice, see separate instructions. Cat. No. 62299J Form **8283** (Rev. 10-95)

Form 8300
(Rev. August 1994)
Department of the Treasury
Internal Revenue Service

Report of Cash Payments Over $10,000 Received in a Trade or Business

▶ See instructions for definition of cash.

Please type or print.

OMB No. 1545-0892

1 Check appropriate boxes if: **a** ☐ amends prior report;   **b** ☐ suspicious transaction.

Part I   Identity of Individual From Whom the Cash Was Received

2 If more than one individual is involved, see instructions and check here . . . . ▶ ☐

3 Last name	4 First name	5 M.I.	6 Social security number

7 Address (number, street, and apt. or suite no.)	8 Date of birth (see instructions)

9 City	10 State	11 ZIP code	12 Country (if not U.S.)	13 Occupation, profession, or business

14 Method used to verify identity: **a** Describe identification ▶ ....
   b Issued by .... **c** Number ....

Part II   Person (See Definitions) on Whose Behalf This Transaction Was Conducted

15 If this transaction was conducted on behalf of more than one person, see instructions and check here · · · · · · ▶ ☐

16 Individual's last name or Organization's name	17 First name	18 M.I.	19 Social security number

20 Doing business as (DBA) name (see instructions)	Employer identification number

21 Alien identification: **a** Describe identification ▶ ....
   b Issued by .... **c** Number ....

22 Address (number, street, and apt. or suite no.)	23 Occupation, profession, or business

24 City	25 State	26 ZIP code	27 Country (if not U.S.)

Part III   Description of Transaction and Method of Payment

28 Date cash received	29 Total cash received	30 If cash was received in more than one payment, check here . . . ▶ ☐	31 Total price if different from item 29
	$ .00		$ .00

32 Amount of cash received (in U.S. dollar equivalent) (see instructions):

   a U.S. currency $ _____ .00 (Amount in $100 bills or higher $ _____ .00)
   b Foreign currency _____ .00 (Country ▶ _____)
   c Cashier's check(s) _____ .00   Issuer's name(s) and serial number(s) of the monetary instrument(s) ▶ ....
   d Money order(s) _____ .00
   e Bank draft(s) _____ .00   ....
   f Traveler's check(s) _____ .00

33 Type of transaction

   a ☐ personal property purchased   **f** ☐ debt obligations paid
   b ☐ real property purchased   **g** ☐ exchange of cash
   c ☐ personal services provided   **h** ☐ escrow or trust funds
   d ☐ business services provided   **i** ☐ other (specify) ▶
   e ☐ intangible property purchased

34 Specific description of property or service shown in 33. (Give serial or registration number, address, etc.)

▶ ....
....
....

Part IV   Business That Received Cash

35 Name of business that received cash	36 Employer identification number

37 Address (number, street, and apt. or suite no.)	Social security number

38 City	39 State	40 ZIP code	41 Nature of your business

42 Under penalties of perjury, I declare that to the best of my knowledge the information I have furnished above is true, correct, and complete.

Sign Here

_____   _____   _____   ( )
(Authorized signature of business that received cash)   (Title)   (Date signed)   (Telephone number of business)

Cat. No. 62133S   Form **8300** (Rev. 8-94)

Form **8582**	**Passive Activity Loss Limitations**	OMB No. 1545-1008
Department of the Treasury Internal Revenue Service	▶ See separate instructions. ▶ Attach to Form 1040 or Form 1041.	**1995** Attachment Sequence No. **88**
Name(s) shown on return		Identifying number

Part I **1995 Passive Activity Loss**

Caution: *See the instructions for Worksheets 1 and 2 on page 8 before completing Part I.*

Rental Real Estate Activities With Active Participation (For the definition of active participation see **Active Participation in a Rental Real Estate Activity** on page 4 of the instructions.)

1a Activities with net income (from Worksheet 1, column (a)) . . .   **1a**

b Activities with net loss (from Worksheet 1, column (b))   . . .   **1b** ( )

c Prior year unallowed losses (from Worksheet 1, column (c)) . . **1c** ( )

d Combine lines 1a, 1b, and 1c **1d**

All Other Passive Activities

2a Activities with net income (from Worksheet 2, column (a)) . . .   **2a**

b Activities with net loss (from Worksheet 2, column (b))   . . .   **2b** ( )

c Prior year unallowed losses (from Worksheet 2, column (c)) . . **2c** ( )

d Combine lines 2a, 2b, and 2c **2d**

3 Combine lines 1d and 2d. If the result is net income or zero, see the instructions for line 3 on page 8. If this line and line 1d are losses, go to line 4. Otherwise, enter -0- on line 9 and go to line 10. **3**

Part II **Special Allowance for Rental Real Estate With Active Participation**

Note: *Enter all numbers in Part II as positive amounts. See page 8 of the instructions for examples.*

4 Enter the **smaller** of the loss on line 1d or the loss on line 3 . . . . **4**

5 Enter $150,000. If married filing separately, see page 8 of the instructions **5**

6 Enter modified adjusted gross income, but not less than zero (see page 8 of the instructions) **6**

Note: *If line 6 is equal to or greater than line 5, skip lines 7 and 8, enter -0- on line 9, and then go to line 10. Otherwise, go to line 7.*

7 Subtract line 6 from line 5 . . . . **7**

8 Multiply line 7 by 50% (.5). **Do not** enter more than $25,000. If married filing separately, see page 9 of the instructions **8**

9 Enter the **smaller** of line 4 or line 8 . . . . **9**

Part III **Total Losses Allowed**

10 Add the income, if any, on lines 1a and 2a and enter the total **10**

11 **Total losses allowed from all passive activities for 1995.** Add lines 9 and 10. See pages 10 and 11 of the instructions to find out how to report the losses on your tax return **11**

For Paperwork Reduction Act Notice, see separate instructions.   Cat. No. 63704F   Form **8582** (1995)

APPENDIX A

Form **8582-CR**

Department of the Treasury
Internal Revenue Service

Passive Activity Credit Limitations

▶ See separate instructions.

▶ Attach to Form 1040 or 1041.

OMB No. 1545-1034

1995

Attachment
Sequence No. **88a**

Name(s) shown on return

Identifying number

Part I   **1995 Passive Activity Credits**

Caution: *If you have credits from a publicly traded partnership, see **Publicly Traded Partnerships (PTPs)** on page 14 of the instructions.*

Credits From Rental Real Estate Activities With Active Participation (Other Than Rehabilitation Credits and Low-Income Housing Credits) (See **Lines 1a through 1c** on page 9 of the instructions.)

1a	Credits from Worksheet 1, column (a)	**1a**	
b	Prior year unallowed credits from Worksheet 1, column (b)	**1b**	
c	Add lines 1a and 1b.		**1c**

Rehabilitation Credits from Rental Real Estate Activities and Low-Income Housing Credits for Property Placed in Service Before 1990 (or From Pass-Through Interests Acquired Before 1990) (See **Lines 2a through 2c** on page 9 of the instructions.)

2a	Credits from Worksheet 2, column (a)	**2a**	
b	Prior year unallowed credits from Worksheet 2, column (b)	**2b**	
c	Add lines 2a and 2b.		**2c**

Low-Income Housing Credits for Property Placed in Service After 1989 (See **Lines 3a through 3c** on page 9 of the instructions.)

3a	Credits from Worksheet 3, column (a)	**3a**	
b	Prior year unallowed credits from Worksheet 3, column (b)	**3b**	
c	Add lines 3a and 3b.		**3c**

All Other Passive Activity Credits (See **Lines 4a through 4c** on page 9 of the instructions.)

4a	Credits from Worksheet 4, column (a)	**4a**	
b	Prior year unallowed credits from Worksheet 4, column (b)	**4b**	
c	Add lines 4a and 4b.		**4c**
5	Add lines 1c, 2c, 3c, and 4c		**5**
6	Enter the tax attributable to net passive income (see page 9 of the instructions).		**6**
7	Subtract line 6 from line 5. If line 6 is more than or equal to line 5, enter -0- and see page 9 of the instructions		**7**

Part II   **Special Allowance for Rental Real Estate Activities With Active Participation**

Note: *Complete Part II if you have an amount on line 1c. Otherwise, go to Part III.*

8	Enter the smaller of line 1c or line 7		**8**
9	Enter $150,000. If married filing separately, see page 9 of the instructions	**9**	
10	Enter modified adjusted gross income, but not less than zero (see page 9 of the instructions). If line 10 is equal to or greater than line 9, skip lines 11 through 15 and enter -0- on line 16	**10**	
11	Subtract line 10 from line 9	**11**	
12	Multiply line 11 by 50% (.50). Do not enter more than $25,000. If married filing separately, see page 10 of the instructions	**12**	
13	Enter the amount, if any, from line 9 of Form 8582	**13**	
14	Subtract line 13 from line 12	**14**	
15	Enter the tax attributable to the amount on line 14 (see page 10 of the instructions). . . .		**15**
16	Enter the smaller of line 8 or line 15		**16**

For Paperwork Reduction Act Notice, see separate instructions.

Cat. No. 64641R

Form **8582-CR** (1995)

Form **8586**

Department of the Treasury
Internal Revenue Service

Low-Income Housing Credit

▶ **Attach to your return.**

OMB No. 1545-0984

1995

Attachment
Sequence No. **36b**

Name(s) shown on return

Identifying number

Part I   Current Year Low-Income Housing Credit (See instructions.)

1 Number of Forms 8609 attached . . . . ▶ ....

2 Eligible basis of building(s) (total from attached Schedule(s) A (Form 8609), line 1) . . . . | **2**

3a Qualified basis of low-income building(s) (total from attached Schedule(s) A (Form 8609), line 3) . | **3a**

b Has there been a decrease in the qualified basis of any building(s) since the close of the preceding tax year? ☐ **Yes**   ☐ **No**   If "Yes," enter the building identification number (BIN) of the building(s) that had a decreased basis. If more space is needed, attach a schedule to list the BINs.

(i) ....   **(ii)** ....   **(iii)** ....   **(iv)** ....

4 Current year credit (total from attached Schedule(s) A (Form 8609), see instructions) . . . . | **4**

5 Credits from flow-through entities (if from more than one entity, see instructions):

If you are a—	Then enter total of current year housing credit(s) from—
a Shareholder	Schedule K-1 (Form 1120S), lines 12b(1) through (4)
b Partner	Schedule K-1 (Form 1065), lines 13a(1) through (4)
c Beneficiary	Schedule K-1 (Form 1041), line 13

–
....

EIN of flow-through entity

5

6 Add lines 4 and 5. (See instructions to find out if you complete Part II or file Form 3800.) . . . . . | **6**

7 **Passive activity credit** or **total current year credit** for 1995 (see instructions) . . . . . . | **7**

Part II   Tax Liability Limit

8a Individuals. Enter amount from Form 1040, line 40 . . . . }

b Corporations. Enter amount from Form 1120, Schedule J, line 3 (or Form 1120-A, Part I. line 1) } | **8**

c Other filers. Enter regular tax before credits from your return . . . . }

9a Credit for child and dependent care expenses (Form 2441, line 10) . . | **9a**

b Credit for the elderly or the disabled (Schedule R (Form 1040), line 20) | **9b**

c Mortgage interest credit (Form 8396, line 11) . . . . | **9c**

d Foreign tax credit (Form 1116, line 32, or Form 1118, Sch. B, line 12) | **9d**

e Possessions tax credit (Form 5735) . . . . | **9e**

f Orphan drug credit (Form 6765) . . . . | **9f**

g Credit for fuel from a nonconventional source . . . . | **9g**

h Qualified electric vehicle credit (Form 8834, line 19) . . . . . | **9h**

i Add lines 9a through 9h . . . . | **9i**

10 Net regular tax. Subtract line 9i from line 8 . . . . | **10**

11 Tentative minimum tax (see instructions):

a Individuals. Enter amount from Form 6251, line 26 . . . . }

b Corporations. Enter amount from Form 4626, line 13 . . . . . . } | **11**

c Estates and trusts. Enter amount from Form 1041, Schedule I, line 37 . }

12 Net income tax:

a Individuals. Add line 10 above and line 28 of Form 6251 . . . . . }

b Corporations. Add line 10 above and line 15 of Form 4626 . . . . } | **12**

c Estates and trusts. Add line 10 above and line 41 of Form 1041, Schedule I }

13 If line 10 is more than $25,000, enter 25% (.25) of excess (see instructions) . . . . . . | **13**

14 Subtract line 11 or line 13, whichever is greater, from line 12. If zero or less, enter -0- . . . . | **14**

15 **Low-income housing credit allowed for current year.** Enter the **smaller** of line 7 or line 14. This is your **General Business Credit** for 1995. Enter here and on Form 1040, line 44; Form 1120, Schedule J, line 4d; Form 1120-A, Part I, line 2a; or the appropriate line of other income tax returns | **15**

Paperwork Reduction Act Notice

We ask for the information on this form to carry out the Internal Revenue laws of the United States. You are required to give us the information. We need it to ensure that you are complying with these laws and to allow us to figure and collect the right amount of tax.

The time needed to complete and file this form will vary depending on individual circumstances. The estimated average time is:

Recordkeeping . . . . . 6 hr., 13 min.

Learning about the law
or the form . . . . . . 1 hr., 32 min.

Preparing and sending
the form to the IRS . . . . 4 hr., 6 min.

If you have comments concerning the accuracy of these time estimates or suggestions for making this form simpler, we would be happy to hear from you. You can write to the IRS at the address listed in the instructions for the tax return with which this form is filed.

General Instructions

Section references are to the Internal Revenue Code unless otherwise noted.

Purpose of Form

Owners of residential rental buildings providing low-income housing use Form 8586 to claim the low-income housing credit.

The low-income housing credit determined under section 42 is a credit of 70% of the qualified basis of each new low-income building placed in service after 1986 (30% in

Cat. No. 639871

Form **8586** (1995)

Form **8822**
(March 1990)
Department of the Treasury
Internal Revenue Service

Change of Address

▶ **Please type or print.**

OMB No. 1545-1163
Expires 3-31-93

You may use this form to notify the Internal Revenue Service if you change your mailing address. Mail it to the Internal Revenue Service Center for your old address. You can find the addresses of the Service Centers on the back of this form. If you are changing both your home and business addresses, please complete two separate forms. However, individuals who are also household employers and file Form 942 can use one form. They should be sure to check boxes 1 and 2 and complete lines 5b and 5c in addition to any other lines that apply.

Check **ALL** boxes that this change affects:

1 ☐ Individual income tax returns (Forms 1040, 1040A, 1040EZ, 1040NR, etc.)
   ▶ If your last return was a joint return and you are now establishing a residence
     separate from the spouse with whom you filed that return, check here . . . ▶ ☐
2 ☐ Employment, excise, and other business returns (Forms 720, 941, 942, 1041, 1065, 1120, etc.)
3 ☐ Gift, estate, or generation-skipping transfer tax returns (Forms 706, 709, etc.)
4 ☐ Employee plan returns (Forms 5500, 5500 C/R, and 5500EZ)

5a **Name** (first name, initial, and last name for individuals)	5b **Your Social Security Number**
	5c **Employer Identification Number**
6a **Spouse's Name** (first name, initial, and last name)	6b **Spouse's Social Security Number**

7 **Prior Name.** (Complete this item if you or your spouse changed last name due to marriage, divorce, etc.)

| 8a **Old Address:** Number, street, and apt. or suite no. | 8b **Spouse's Old Address:** Number, street, and apt. or suite no. (Complete only if different from address on line 8a.) |
| City, town or post office, state and ZIP code. (If a foreign address, enter city, province or state, postal code, and country.) | City, town or post office, state and ZIP code. (If a foreign address, enter city, province or state, postal code, and country.) |

9 **New Address:** Number, street, and apt. or suite no. (or P.O. box number if mail is not delivered to street address)

City, town or post office, state and ZIP code. (If a foreign address, enter city, province or state, postal code, and country.)

**Please
Sign
Here** ▶

Your signature _____ Date _____ ▶ Spouse's signature _____ Date _____

Paperwork Reduction Act Notice. — Use of this form is optional. It is provided for your convenience to notify IRS of a change of address.

The time needed to complete and file this form will vary depending on individual circumstances. The estimated average time is 10 minutes.

If you have comments concerning the accuracy of this time estimate or suggestions for making this form more simple, we would be happy to hear from you. You can write to the **Internal Revenue Service**, Washington, DC 20224, Attention: IRS Reports Clearance Officer, T:FP; and the **Office of**

Management and Budget, Paperwork Reduction Project (1545-1163), Washington, DC 20503.

Please **do not** send this form to either of the above addresses. Instead, mail it to the Internal Revenue Service Center address on the back of this form.

Form **8822** (3-90)

Form **8606**

Department of the Treasury
Internal Revenue Service

Nondeductible IRAs
(Contributions, Distributions, and Basis)
► Please see **What Records Must I Keep?** in the instructions.
► Attach to Form 1040, Form 1040A, Form 1040NR, or Form 1040-T.

OMB No. 1545-1007

1995

47

Name. If married, file a separate Form 8606 for each spouse who is required to file Form 8606.

Your Social Security Number

000-00-0000

Fill in your address only
if you are filing this
form by itself and not
with your tax return ►

Home address (number and street, or P.O. box if mail is not delivered to your home)

Apartment Number

City, town or post office

State   ZIP Code

Contributions, Nontaxable Distributions, and Basis

1	Enter your IRA contributions for 1995 that you choose to be nondeductible. Include those made during 1/1/96 - 4/15/96 that were for 1995	1
2	Enter your total IRA basis for 1994 and earlier years	2
3	Add lines 1 and 2	3

| **Did you receive any IRA distributions (withdrawals) in 1995?** | ── No ── | ► Enter the amount from line 3 on line 12. Then, stop and read **When and Where to File** in the instructions. |
| | ── Yes ── | ► Go to line 4. |

4	Enter only those contributions included on line 1 that were made during 1/1/96 - 4/15/96. This amount will be the same as line 1 if all of your nondeductible contributions for 1995 were made in 1996 by 4/15/96	4
5	Subtract line 4 from line 3	5
6	Enter the total value of **All** your IRAs as of 12/31/95 plus any outstanding rollovers	6
7	Enter the total IRA distributions received during 1995. Do not include amounts rolled over before 1/1/96	7
8	Add lines 6 and 7	8
9	Divide line 5 by line 8 and enter the result as a decimal (to at least two places). Do not enter more than '1.00'	9 X
10	Multiply line 7 by line 9. This is the amount of your **nontaxable distributions for 1995**	10
11	Subtract line 10 from line 5. This is the **basis in your IRA(s) as of 12/31/95**	11
12	Add lines 4 and 11. This is your **total IRA basis for 1995 and earlier years**	12

Taxable Distributions for 1995

13	Subtract line 10 from line 7. Enter the result here and on Form 1040, line 15b; Form 1040A, line 10b; Form 1040NR, line 16b; or Form 1040-T, line 5b, whichever applies	13

Sign here only if you
are filing this form
by itself and not with
your tax return

Under penalties of perjury, I declare that I have examined this form, including accompanying attachments, and to the best of my knowledge and belief, it is true, correct, and complete.

►   ►

Your signature   Date

BAA For Paperwork Reduction Act Notice, see instructions.

Form **8606** (1995)

Form **8615**	**Tax for Children Under Age 14**	OMB No. 1545-0998
	Who Have Investment Income of More Than $1,300	**1995**
Department of the Treasury Internal Revenue Service	▶ Attach Only to the child's Form 1040, Form 1040A, Form 1040NR, or Form 1040-T.	33

Child's Name Shown on Return	Child's Social Security Number

A Parent's Name (first, initial, and last). **Caution:** *See instructions before completing.* **B** Parent's Social Security Number

C Parent's filing status (check one):

☐ Single ☐ Married filing jointly ☐ Married filing separately ☐ Head of household ☐ Qualifying widow(er)

Step 1 Figure child's net investment income

1 Enter child's investment income, such as taxable interest and dividend income.
If this amount is $1,300 or less, **stop;** do not file this form **1**

2 If the child **did not** itemize deductions on Schedule A (Form 1040 or Form 1040NR) or Section B
(Form 1040-T), enter $1,300. If the child **itemized** deductions, see instructions **2**

3 Subtract line 2 from line 1. If the result is zero or less, **stop;** do not complete the rest of this form
but **attach** it to the child's return **3**

4 Enter the child's **taxable** income from Form 1040, line 37; Form 1040A, line 22; Form 1040NR, line 36; or Form 1040-T, line 25 . . . . **4**

5 Enter the **smaller** of line 3 or line 4 . . . . ▶ **5**

Step 2 Figure tentative tax based on the tax rate of the parent listed on line A

6 Enter parent's **taxable** income from Form 1040, line 37; Form 1040A, line 22; Form 1040EZ, line 6; Form
1040NR, line 36; Form 1040NR-EZ, line 13; or Form 1040-T, line 25. If the parent transferred property to a
trust, see instructions **6**

7 Enter the total net investment income, if any, from Forms 8615, line 5, of **all other** children of the parent
identified above. **Do not** include the amount from line 5 above **7**

8 Add lines 5, 6, and 7 . . . . **8**

9 Tax on line 8 based on the **parent's** filing status. If from Capital Gain Tax Worksheet, enter amount from
line 4 of that worksheet here . . . . ▶ **9**

10 Enter parent's tax from Form 1040, line 38; Form 1040A, line 23; Form 1040EZ, line 10; Form 1040NR,
line 37; Form 1040NR-EZ, line 14; or Form 1040-T, line 26. If from **Capital Gain Tax Worksheet,** enter
amount from line 4 of that worksheet here . . . . ▶ _____ **10**

11 Subtract line 10 from line 9. If line 7 is blank, enter on line 13 the amount from line 11; skip lines 12a & 12b . **11**

12 a Add lines 5 and 7 . . . . | **12a**

b Divide line 5 by line 12a. Enter the result as a decimal (rounded to two places) **12b**

13 Multiply line 11 by line 12b . . . . ▶ **13**

Step 3 Figure child's tax — If lines 4 and 5 above are the same, enter -0- on line 15 and go to line 16 .

14 Subtract line 5 from line 4 . . . . | **14**

15 Tax on line 14 based on the **child's** filing status. If from Capital Gain Tax Worksheet, enter amount from
line 4 of that worksheet here . . . . ▶ _____ **15**

16 Add lines 13 and 15 . . . . **16**

17 Tax on line 4 based on the **child's** filing status. If from Capital Gain Tax Worksheet, check here . . . . . ▶ ☐ **17**

18 Enter the **larger** of line 16 or line 17 here and on Form 1040, line 38; Form 1040A, line 23; Form 1040NR,
line 37; or Form 1040-T, line 26. Be sure to check the box (or, on Form 1040-T, fill in the space) for 'Form
8615' even if line 17 is more than line 16 . . . . ▶ **18**

BAA For Paperwork Reduction Act Notice, see instructions.   Form **8615** (1995)

Form **8829**	**Expenses for Business Use of Your Home**	OMB No. 1545-1266
	▶ **File only with Schedule C (Form 1040). Use a separate Form 8829 for each home you used for business during the year.**	**19 95**
Department of the Treasury Internal Revenue Service (O)	▶ **See separate instructions.**	Attachment Sequence No. **66**
Name(s) of proprietor(s)		Your social security number

Part I   Part of Your Home Used for Business

1	Area used regularly and exclusively for business, regularly for day care, or for inventory storage. See instructions	**1**	
2	Total area of home	**2**	
3	Divide line 1 by line 2. Enter the result as a percentage	**3**	%
	● **For day-care facilities not used exclusively for business, also complete lines 4–6.**		
	● **All others, skip lines 4–6 and enter the amount from line 3 on line 7.**		
4	Multiply days used for day care during year by hours used per day . [**4**] [hr.]		
5	Total hours available for use during the year (365 days × 24 hours). See instructions [**5**] [8,760 hr.]		
6	Divide line 4 by line 5. Enter the result as a decimal amount . . . [**6**]		
7	Business percentage. For day-care facilities not used exclusively for business, multiply line 6 by line 3 (enter the result as a percentage). All others, enter the amount from line 3 . . . . . ▶	**7**	%

Part II   Figure Your Allowable Deduction

8	Enter the amount from Schedule C, line 29, **plus** any net gain or (loss) derived from the business use of your home and shown on Schedule D or Form 4797. If more than one place of business, see instructions	**8**	

	See instructions for columns (a) and (b) before completing lines 9–20.	(a) Direct expenses	(b) Indirect expenses	
9	Casualty losses. See instructions	**9**		
10	Deductible mortgage interest. See instructions .	**10**		
11	Real estate taxes. See instructions	**11**		
12	Add lines 9, 10, and 11.	**12**		
13	Multiply line 12, column (b) by line 7		**13**	
14	Add line 12, column (a) and line 13.		**14**	
15	Subtract line 14 from line 8. If zero or less, enter -0-		**15**	
16	Excess mortgage interest. See instructions . .	**16**		
17	Insurance	**17**		
18	Repairs and maintenance	**18**		
19	Utilities	**19**		
20	Other expenses. See instructions	**20**		
21	Add lines 16 through 20	**21**		
22	Multiply line 21, column (b) by line 7	**22**		
23	Carryover of operating expenses from 1994 Form 8829, line 41 . .	**23**		
24	Add line 21 in column (a), line 22, and line 23		**24**	
25	Allowable operating expenses. Enter the **smaller** of line 15 or line 24		**25**	
26	Limit on excess casualty losses and depreciation. Subtract line 25 from line 15		**26**	
27	Excess casualty losses. See instructions	**27**		
28	Depreciation of your home from Part III below	**28**		
29	Carryover of excess casualty losses and depreciation from 1994 Form 8829, line 42	**29**		
30	Add lines 27 through 29		**30**	
31	Allowable excess casualty losses and depreciation. Enter the **smaller** of line 26 or line 30 . .		**31**	
32	Add lines 14, 25, and 31		**32**	
33	Casualty loss portion, if any, from lines 14 and 31. Carry amount to **Form 4684,** Section B .		**33**	
34	Allowable expenses for business use of your home. Subtract line 33 from line 32. Enter here and on Schedule C, line 30. If your home was used for more than one business, see instructions ▶		**34**	

Part III   Depreciation of Your Home

35	Enter the **smaller** of your home's adjusted basis or its fair market value. See instructions	**35**	
36	Value of land included on line 35	**36**	
37	Basis of building. Subtract line 36 from line 35	**37**	
38	Business basis of building. Multiply line 37 by line 7	**38**	
39	Depreciation percentage. See instructions	**39**	%
40	Depreciation allowable. Multiply line 38 by line 39. Enter here and on line 28 above. See instructions	**40**	

Part IV   Carryover of Unallowed Expenses to 1996

41	Operating expenses. Subtract line 25 from line 24. If less than zero, enter -0-	**41**	
42	Excess casualty losses and depreciation. Subtract line 31 from line 30. If less than zero, enter -0- .	**42**	

For Paperwork Reduction Act Notice, see page 1 of separate instructions.   ✪   *Printed on recycled paper*   Cat. No. 13232M   Form **8829** (1995)

*U.S. Government Printing Office: 1995 - 389-468

APPENDIX A

Form **9465**
(Rev. January 1996)
Department of the Treasury
Internal Revenue Service

Installment Agreement Request

▶ **See instructions below and on back.**

OMB No. 1545-1350

Note: *Do not file this form if you are currently making payments on an installment agreement. You must pay your other Federal tax liabilities in full or you will be in default on your agreement.*

If you can't pay the full amount you owe, you can ask to make monthly installment payments. If we approve your request, you will be charged a $43 fee. **Do not include the fee with this form.** We will deduct the fee from your first payment after we approve your request, unless you choose **Direct Debit** (see the line 13 instructions). We will usually let you know within 30 days after we receive your request whether it is approved or denied. But if this request is for tax due on a return you filed after March 31, it may take us longer than 30 days to reply.

To ask for an installment agreement, complete this form. Attach it to the front of your return when you file. If you have already filed your return or you are filing this form in response to a notice, see **How Do I File Form 9465?** on page 2. If you have any questions about this request, call 1-800-829-1040.

Caution: *A Notice of Federal Tax Lien may be filed to protect the government's interest until you pay in full.*

1	Your first name and initial	Last name	Your social security number
	If a joint return, spouse's first name and initial	Last name	Spouse's social security number
	Your current address (number and street). If you have a P.O. box and no home delivery, show box number.		Apt. number
	City, town or post office, state, and ZIP code. If a foreign address, show city, state or province, postal code, and full name of country.		

2   If this address is new since you filed your last tax return, check here . . . . ▶ ☐

3   ( )   4   ( )
    Your home phone number   Best time for us to call   Your work phone number   Ext.   Best time for us to call

5   Name of your bank or other financial institution: 6   Your employer's name:

Address   Address

City, state, and ZIP code   City, state, and ZIP code

7   Enter the tax return for which you are making this request (for example, Form 1040). But if you are filing this form in response to a notice, don't complete lines 7 through 9. Instead, attach the bottom section of the notice to this form and go to line 10 . . . . ▶ _____

8   Enter the tax year for which you are making this request (for example, 1995) . . . . ▶ _____

9   Enter the total amount you owe as shown on your tax return . . . . ▶ $ _____

10   Enter the amount of any payment you are making with your tax return (or notice). See instructions . ▶ $ _____

11   Enter the amount you can paym each month. **Make your payments as large as possible to limit interest and penalty charges.** The charges will continue until you pay in full . . . . ▶ $ _____

12   Enter the date you want to make your payment each month. Do not enter a date later than the 28th ▶ _____

13   If you would like to make your monthly payments using **Direct Debit** (automatic withdrawals from your bank account), check here. . . . . ▶ ☐

Your signature	Date	Spouse's signature. If a joint return, BOTH must sign.	Date

Privacy Act and Paperwork Reduction Act Notice.—Our legal right to ask for the information on this form is Internal Revenue Code sections 6001, 6011, 6012(a), 6109, and 6159 and their regulations. We will use the information to process your request for an installment agreement. The reason we need your name and social security number is to secure proper identification. We require this information to gain access to the tax information in our files and properly respond to your request. If you do not enter the information, we may not be able to process your request. We may give this information to the Department of Justice as provided by law. We may also give it to cities, states, and the District of Columbia to carry out their tax laws.

Cat. No. 14842Y

Form **9465** (Rev. 1-96)

APPENDIX B:
GUIDE TO FREE TAX SERVICES

Alternative Ways to File

The IRS offers alternatives to the traditional paper return filing method: electronic filing, telephone filing, on-line filing, and 1040PC return filing. These methods can make filing faster, easier, and more accurate. You may even be able to electronically file your state and federal income taxes together. (See Federal/State Electronic Tax Filing below.) For additional information on these alternative ways to file, call your local IRS Public Affairs Office or Electronic Filing Coordinator and ask for Publication 1857, *Alternative Ways of Filing*.

Electronic Tax Filing

Electronic filers (those who prepare tax returns and those who transmit them) can send your tax return over telephone lines directly to the IRS, where computers automatically check for errors and missing information. The IRS will notify your electronic filer that your return has been received and accepted within 48 hours after the transmission.

When expecting a refund, you can get it directly deposited into your checking or savings account. If you expect to owe taxes, you can go ahead and file electronically and then pay by April 15.

Many employers set up electronic filing sites in the workplace for employees, free or for a small fee. Your employer may have staff members or a contractor input, transmit, and even help prepare employees' tax data. Or, representatives from the IRS (Volunteer Income Tax Assistance (VITA) Program) may be able to come to your workplace and assist you for free. Similarly, many financial institutions set up these sites for employees and customers. Check with your employer or your financial institution to see if he/she will offer electronic filing this tax season. Also, electronic filing is available in most IRS walk-in offices for free.

Look in your local telephone directory for tax professionals who, for a fee, can transmit your return, whether they prepare the return or you do it yourself.

Federal/State Electronic Tax Filing

You may be able to electronically file your state income taxes together with your federal income taxes.

The IRS has teamed up with state tax agencies to offer this one-stop service. Many tax preparers who offer electronic tax filing offer joint federal/state electronic tax filing.

Call your local IRS office or your tax preparer to find out if your state participates in this program.

TeleFile

TeleFile is the first completely automated way to file federal income taxes using your telephone. You do not mail any forms to the IRS, not even W-2s. You simply complete the TeleFile worksheet before calling. Then dial the toll-free number listed in the special TeleFile tax package that the IRS mailed to you. (The IRS sends this tax package with the Tele-File worksheet and instructions along with Form 1040EZ to only those who qualify.) Follow recorded instructions. When you hang up, the TeleFile system has automatically calculated and filed your tax return.

If you filed taxes using Form 1040EZ last year, are single, have no dependents, and have the same address as last year, then you may be able to Tele-File.

TeleFile is also available in Spanish.

1040PC Tax Return Filing

The 1040PC Return is prepared on a personal computer using an IRS-accepted print option. This option is included in various tax preparation software packages, which are available at many computer software stores. The program automatically prints the return in a three-column "answer sheet" format. It prints only the line numbers, dollar amounts, and, when called for, brief descriptions of line entries. Since the format is condensed, an 11 page traditional paper return can be reduced to a two-to-three page 1040PC return. For easy understanding, a legend "description" paper, which explains each line entry made by the taxpayer, should accompany the return.

The 1040PC paper-return process allows direct deposit of a refund into a savings or checking account. You can expect your refund within weeks. If you owe taxes, you can file early and pay by April 15 using a payment voucher.

Business Owner Tax Information

The IRS has many publications containing information about the federal tax laws that apply to businesses. Publication 334, *Tax Guide for Small Business,* is a good place to start to learn more about sole proprietorships, partnerships, corporations, and S corporations. Look in section **Free Tax Publications** for other materials that can explain your business tax responsibilities.

Employee or Independent Contractor Status

A worker is either an employee or an independent contractor. The classification is determined by the facts and circumstances of his/her work relationship.

Generally, an employee is controlled by an employer in ways that a true independent contractor is not. If the employer sets the work hours, provides the tools needed to do the job, and can hire and fire, the worker is an employee, not an independent contractor.

An independent contractor will usually maintain an office and staff, advertise, and have a financial investment risk. Independent contractors will file a Schedule C and be able to deduct certain expenses that an employee would not.

Those who should be classified as employees, but aren't, may lose out on social security benefits, workers' compensation, unemployment benefits, and, in many cases, group insurance (including life and health), and retirement benefits. For details, get Publication 15-A, *Employer's Supplemental Tax Guide.*

Tax Tips Newsletter

The IRS publishes *Tax Tips,* a monthly newsletter for first-time small business owners. Written in simple terms, the newsletter covers basic business tax law, helpful bookkeeping and recordkeeping hints, explanations of how the IRS works, and where to go for additional help.

The twelve-month subscription is available free by sending a postcard with your name and address to:

Internal Revenue Service
Attn: *Tax Tips* Editor, M:C:DP
1111 Constitution Avenue NW
Washington, DC 20224

Tax Tips is also available on IRIS, an electronic bulletin board system located on FedWorld (via the Internet or through direct dial). See section **FedWorld** for dialing instructions.

> ▶ *Did You Know?*
>
> The IRS is responding to tax law, regulation, and policy concerns raised by small businesses through its Small Business Affairs Office. Read below for more information.

Small Business Affairs Office (SBAO)

One of the ways the IRS is listening and responding to concerns regarding tax laws, regulations, and policy raised by small businesses is through its Small Business Affairs Office (SBAO). Established in March 1994, this office is a national contact within IRS for small business owners to voice concerns.

The SBAO recommends changes to the federal tax system, such as recordkeeping requirements, payroll tax reporting, and simplifying tax forms. SBAO works with many other IRS offices and other government agencies (Small Business Administration) helping them understand small business owner needs and

concerns of reducing burden.

This office, however, does not handle small business owners' individual tax problems. If a problem has not been resolved after repeated attempts through normal IRS channels, small business owners should contact their local Problem Resolution Office for assistance. See section on *Problem Resolution Program (PRP)* under **Free Tax Services** for more information.

Write to the IRS Small Business Affairs office if you have questions.

Internal Revenue Service
Small Business Affairs
Office C:SB
ICC Building, Room 1211
1111 Constitution Avenue NW
Washington, DC, 20224

SSA/IRS (Social Security Administration/Internal Revenue Service) *Reporter* (Newsletter)

If you are an employer and have not been receiving a copy of the *SSA/IRS Reporter,* tell your local IRS Public Affairs Office.

The *SSA/IRS Reporter* is a quarterly newsletter that keeps you up-to-date on changes to taxes and employee wage obligations. This newsletter, produced jointly by the Social Security Administration and the IRS, is mailed to over six million employers along with quarterly Forms 941 and instructions.

Subjects You May Want to Know More About

The IRS has many programs and processes that can reduce anxieties of taxes. A description of some of the more popular ones follows. In most cases, the description lists free IRS publications for additional information.

Call 1-800-829-3676 to order IRS publications. You should receive your order within 7-15 workdays. If a publication is on backorder or discontinued, we will notify you.

Amending a Return

If you find that you made a mistake on your tax return, you can correct it by filing a Form 1040X, *Amended U.S. Individual Income Tax Return.* Generally, you must file this form within three years from the date you filed your original return or within two years from the date you paid your tax, whichever is later. File Form 1040X with the Internal Revenue Service Center for your area. (Your state tax liability may be affected by a change made on your federal income tax return. For more information on this, contact your state tax authority.)

Collection Process

The IRS checks tax returns for accuracy and to confirm that payment has been made. If there is an amount due, the IRS will send you a notice of tax due that you must pay within 10 days of the date of the bill.

If you believe a bill from the IRS is incorrect, contact the IRS immediately. You will need to provide information showing why you think the bill is wrong. If the IRS agrees with you, then your account will be corrected.

However, if the bill is correct and it is not paid within 10 days, interest and penalties will be charged on the amount you owe until the full amount due is paid. If the taxes, interest, and penalties are not paid, then a federal tax lien may also be filed on your property.

If you cannot pay the entire amount due, contact your local IRS office. Depending on your financial condition, an installment agreement or other payment arrangements may be approved. (See **Payment Methods** later in this section.)

If you ignore the notice of tax due, the IRS may enforce collection by taking your assets, including your income and other property.

The collection process can be stopped at any stage if the amount you owe is paid in full.

More information on the collection process and about your rights are found in Publication 594, *Understanding The Collection Process,* and Publication 1, *Your Rights as a Taxpayer* (both available in Spanish).

Copies of Prior Year Returns

There are occasions when you may need a copy of your prior year(s) Federal Tax Form 1040, 1040A, or 1040EZ, a transcript of return, or account information.

A transcript of return contains information from the original return. It does not contain information regarding amended returns or subsequent payments. If amended returns or subsequent payment summary is needed, account information can be secured.

Examples of when you may need a copy of a return or a return transcript include applying for a home mortgage loan or financial aid for education. While there is a fee for requesting a photocopy of a return, transcripts are free of charge. Ask the requester if a transcript will meet their needs.

- You can get a copy of a prior year(s) tax return by completing Form 4506, *Request for Copy or Transcript of Tax Form,* and mailing it to the IRS address where you filed your return. There is a fee of $14 for each return requested. Allow 60 days to receive your copy.
- For a transcript that reflects most items from your return, send a completed Form 4506 to the IRS address where the return was filed. There is no charge. You

should receive the transcript within 10 work days from the IRS office's receipt of your request.
- For tax account information, you can visit an IRS office or call the IRS toll-free number listed in your telephone directory. This list of basic tax data, like marital status, type of return filed, adjusted gross income, and taxable income, is available free of charge. Do not use Form 4506 to request this information. Please allow 30 days for delivery.

To obtain Form 4506, call the IRS at 1-800-829-3676.

Credits

The tax laws include a number of credits you may be entitled to take. The following are several of the more popular credits available.
- earned income tax credit
- child and dependent care credit
- mortgage interest credit
- foreign tax credit

Turn to the **Index of Topics and Related Publications** section and look under "Credits" for a list of the credits and the related publications for details.

Disasters

When property is damaged or lost in a hurricane, earthquake, fire, flood, or similar event that is sudden, unexpected, or unusual, it is called a casualty. Your unreimbursed loss from a casualty may be deductible on your tax return for the year the casualty occurred. If the loss happened in an area the President designated a disaster area, you may not have to wait until the end of the year to file a tax return and claim a loss. You may be able to file an amended return for last year right now and get a refund of taxes you have already paid. For details, get Publication 547, *Nonbusiness Disasters, Casualties, and Thefts.*

Estimated Tax

If you are self-employed or have other income not subject to income tax withholding, you may have to make estimated tax payments. For details on who must pay estimated taxes and how and when to make payments, get Publication 505, *Tax Withholding and Estimated Tax*.

Examination of Returns

If the IRS selects your return for examination, you may be asked to show records such as canceled checks, receipts, or other supporting documents to verify entries on your return. You can appeal if you disagree with the examination results. Your appeal rights will be explained to you.

You may act on your own behalf or have an attorney, a certified public accountant, or an individual enrolled to practice before the IRS represent or accompany you. Student Tax Clinics are available in some areas to help people during examination and appeal proceedings. Call your local IRS office and ask the Taxpayer Education Coordinator or the Public Affairs Officer about these clinics.

For more information, get Publication 556, *Examination of Returns, Appeal Rights, and Claims for Refund,* and Publication 1, *Your Rights as a Taxpayer* (available in Spanish). Also see Publication 947, *Practice Before the IRS and Power of Attorney*.

Form W-4, *Employee's Withholding Allowance Certificate*

Each time you start working for an employer, you should complete a Form W-4. This information will help your employer know how much federal tax to withhold from your wages. If your tax situation changes, complete a new Form W-4 so that the correct amount of tax will be withheld. For more information, get Publication 919, *Is My Withholding Correct for 1996?*

Form W-5, *Earned Income Credit Advance Payment Certificate*

You can file a Form W-5 with your employer if you are eligible for the earned income tax credit (EITC) and have a qualifying child. This will allow you to receive payment of the credit during the year instead of when you file your tax return. The amount of the advance EITC payment you receive will be shown on your Form W-2. For more information, get Publication 596, *Earned Income Credit* (available in Spanish).

> ### Did You Know?
> If you are not able to pay in full the taxes you owe, IRS staff will work with you to find the best way to meet your tax obligations. Read on for more information.

Late (Overdue) Returns

Sometimes people do not file their tax return(s) because of personal problems, no money to pay, lost records, or confusion over complex tax rules.

If you have not filed your federal income tax return for a year or so and should have filed, IRS staff will work with you to help you get back on track. Copies of missing documents like Form W-2, *Wage and Tax Statement,* can often be retrieved. If you owe taxes, the IRS will explain your payment options. And if you have a refund coming, they will explain the time limit on getting it.

Call your local IRS office or call toll-free 1-800-829-1040 for assistance. Remember, interest and penalties are adding up if you owe taxes, and time is running out if you are due a refund. For more information, get Publication 1715, *It's Never too Late* (available in Spanish).

Payment Methods

If you are not able to pay in full the taxes you owe, IRS staff will work with you to find the best way to meet your tax obligations. This may include an installment agreement or acceptance of an offer to settle the account for less than the amount owed. Call your local IRS office or call toll-free 1-800-829-1040 for assistance. More information is in Publication 594, *Understanding the Collection Process* (available in Spanish).

Social Security Number (SSN)

List the correct social security number for yourself, spouse, or dependent on your tax return. Other supporting forms and schedules you fill out for certain credits require SSNs, too. Be sure each SSN is complete and correct or processing of your return could be delayed. If you are getting a refund, that could be delayed also.

Name Change

If your name has changed for some reason, like marriage or divorce, notify the Social Security Administration (SSA) immediately.

If the name and social security number you show on your tax return does not match the one SSA has on record, there can be a processing delay, which could hold up your refund.

Dependent's SSN

If you claim an exemption for a dependent, you are required to show his or her social security number on your tax return. (You do not need to show a social security number for a child born in November or December of 1995.)

If you do not list a complete and correct social security number, any refund attributable to claiming the dependent may be held up.

To get a social security number, contact the nearest Social Security Administration Office to get Form SS-5, *Application for a Social Security Number Card.*

Tax Tips When Filing Your Return

Gathering forms, receipts, and other paperwork to file your taxes is your first step. Once you've completed your forms, it is equally important to double-check your figures, information, and packaging procedures (as applicable to your filing method).

Always review your filing entries for misprinted or overlooked data. And with a paper return, also review your forms for miscalculations. Any mistake can cause processing delays that may hold up your refund. When mailing a paper return, make sure you have enough postage and your complete return address on the IRS envelope to avoid mailing delays. If you owe taxes, remember any delay could result in penalty and interest charges.

The tips below can serve as your checklist to prevent filing mistakes.

Important Parts of Your Return

☐ **Age/Blindness Box Checked?** — If you are age 65 or older or blind, or your spouse is age 65 or older or blind, make sure you notate the appropriate box(es) on Form 1040 or Form 1040A.

☐ **Earned Income Credit Claimed, Figured Correctly?** — This is a special tax credit that can help some people who work and have incomes below a certain level. For more information on whether you qualify and how to figure the credit, get Publication 596, *Earned Income Credit*, or Publication 596SP, *Crédito por Ingreso del Trabajo* (Spanish version).

☐ **Federal Income Tax Withheld, not Social Security Tax, Entered on the Return?** — Form W-2 shows both the federal income tax and FICA (social security tax) withheld. Remember to use the amount for federal income tax on your return to calculate your total income tax withheld.

☐ **Entry for Standard Deduction Amount Correct?** — If you do not itemize deductions, use the correct standard deduction chart to find the right amount.

☐ **Refund or Balance Due Correct?** — Check your addition and subtraction. If your total payments are more than your total tax, you are due a refund. A balance due is figured when your taxes due are more than the amount you have already paid.

☐ **Tax from Tax Tables Entered Correctly?** — First, take the amount shown on the taxable income line of your Form 1040, 1040A, or 1040EZ and find the line in the tax table showing that amount. Next, find the column for your marital status (married filing joint, single, etc.) and read down the column. The amount shown where the income line and filing status column meet is your tax.

Important Double-Checks on Your Paper Return Before Mailing

☐ Check for math errors.

☐ Attach Copy B of all Forms W-2.

☐ Attach all required forms and related schedules.

☐ Place preprinted address label on your return and make any necessary changes on it.

☐ Check all SSNs for accuracy.

☐ Sign and date your return (both husband and wife must sign a joint return).

☐ If you owe tax, include your check or money order payable to "Internal Revenue Service," not the "IRS." You must write your social security number, daytime telephone number, tax form number, and tax year on your check or money order.

☐ Make a copy of the return for your records.

Important Mailing Procedures

☐ Use preprinted envelope that came in the tax package to mail your return. If you do not have one, address an envelope to the Internal Revenue Service Center for your state.

☐ Write your complete return address on the envelope.

☐ Attach the correct postage.

Toll-Free Tax Assistance Telephone Numbers

Call TeleTax to get Tax Information

TeleTax is recorded tax information and refund information available by dialing TeleTax from your telephone. The *Recorded Tax Information* includes about 140 recorded topics that provide basic tax information. You can listen to up-to-three topics on each call you make. *Automated Refund Information* allows you to check the status of your refund.

Choosing the Right Number

Use the toll-free number listed on this page for your area. Use a local city number if one is available.

Recorded Tax Information

A complete list of TeleTax topics is on the next page. This touch-tone service is available 24 hours a day, 7 days a week.

Select, by number, the topic you want to hear. Then, call the appropriate phone number listed on this page. **For the directory of topics, listen to Topic 123.** Have paper and pencil handy to take notes.

Automated Refund Information

Be sure to have a copy of your current tax return available since you will need to know the first social

security number shown on your return, the filing status, and the exact whole dollar amount of your refund. Then call the appropriate phone number listed on this page and follow the recorded instructions.

The IRS updates refund information every 7 days. If you call to find out about the status of your refund and do not receive a refund mailing date, please wait 7 days before calling back.

This touch-tone service is available Monday through Friday from 7:00 a.m. to 11:30 p.m. (Hours may vary in your area.)

TeleTax Telephone Numbers

Alabama
1-800-829-4477
Alaska
1-800-829-4477
Arizona
Phoenix, 640-3933
Elsewhere, 1-800-829-4477
Arkansas
1-800-829-4477
California
Oakland, 839-4245
Elsewhere, 1-800-829-4477
Colorado
Denver, 592-1118
Elsewhere, 1-800-829-4477
Connecticut
1-800-829-4477
Delaware
1-800-829-4477
District of Columbia
628-2929
Florida
1-800-829-4477
Georgia
Atlanta, 331-6572
Elsewhere, 1-800-829-4477
Hawaii
1-800-829-4477
Idaho
1-800-829-4477
Illinois
Chicago, 886-9614
In area code 708,
1-312-886-9614
Springfield, 789-0489
Elsewhere, 1-800-829-4477

Indiana
Indianapolis, 631-1010
Elsewhere, 1-800-829-4477
Iowa
Des Moines, 284-7454
Elsewhere, 1-800-829-4477
Kansas
1-800-829-4477
Kentucky
1-800-829-4477
Louisiana
1-800-829-4477
Maine
1-800-829-4477
Maryland
Baltimore, 244-7306
Elsewhere, 1-800-829-4477
Massachusetts
Boston, 536-0709
Elsewhere, 1-800-829-4477
Michigan
Detroit, 961-4282
Elsewhere, 1-800-829-4477
Minnesota
St Paul, 644-7748
Elsewhere, 1-800-829-4477
Mississippi
1-800-829-4477
Missouri
St Louis, 241-4700
Elsewhere, 1-800-829-4477
Montana
1-800-829-4477

Nebraska
Omaha, 221-3324
Elsewhere, 1-800-829-4477
Nevada
1-800-829-4477
New Hampshire
1-800-829-4477
New Jersey
1-800-829-4477
New Mexico
1-800-829-4477
New York
Buffalo, 685-5533
Elsewhere, 1-800-829-4477
North Carolina
1-800-829-4477
North Dakota
1-800-829-4477
Ohio
Cincinnati, 421-0329
Cleveland, 522-3037
Elsewhere, 1-800-829-4477
Oklahoma
1-800-829-4477
Oregon
Portland, 294-5363
Elsewhere, 1-800-829-4477
Pennsylvania
Philadelphia, 627-1040
Pittsburgh, 261-1040
Elsewhere, 1-800-829-4477
Puerto Rico
1-800-829-4477
Rhode Island
1-800-829-4477

South Carolina
1-800-829-4477
South Dakota
1-800-829-4477
Tennessee
Nashville, 781-5040
Elsewhere, 1-800-829-4477
Texas
Dallas, 767-1792
Houston, 541-3400
Elsewhere, 1-800-829-4477
Utah
1-800-829-4477
Vermont
1-800-829-4477
Virginia
Richmond, 783-1569
Elsewhere, 1-800-829-4477
Washington
Seattle, 343-7221
Elsewhere, 1-800-829-4477
West Virginia
1-800-829-4477
Wisconsin
Milwaukee, 273-8100
Elsewhere, 1-800-829-4477
Wyoming
1-800-829-4477

Call the IRS with Your Tax Questions

If you cannot answer your tax question by reading the tax form instructions or one of our free tax publications, please call us for assistance Monday through Friday from 7:30 a.m. to 5:30 p.m. Hours in Alaska and Hawaii may vary. If you want to check on the status of your refund, call TeleTax.

Choose The Right Number

Use the toll-free number listed on this page for your area. Use a local city number if one is available.

Before You Call

Your IRS representative can better provide you with accurate and complete answers to your tax questions if you have the following information available.
- The tax form, schedule, or notice to which your question relates.
- The facts about your particular situation (the answer to the same question often varies from one taxpayer to another because of differences in their age, income, whether they can be claimed as a dependent, etc.).
- The name of any IRS publication or other source of information that you used to look for the answer.

Before You Hang Up

If you do not fully understand the answer you receive, or you feel the IRS representative may not fully understand your question, the representative needs to know. The representative will be happy to take additional time to be sure he or she has answered your question fully.

By law, you are responsible for paying your fair share of federal income tax. If we should make an error in answering your question, you are still responsible for the payment of the correct tax. Should this occur, however, you will not be charged any penalty. To make sure that IRS representatives give accurate and courteous answers, a second IRS representative sometimes listens in on telephone calls. No record is kept of any taxpayer's identity.

Tax Help Telephone Numbers

Alabama
1-800-829-1040
Alaska
1-800-829-1040
Arizona
Phoenix, 640-3900
Elsewhere,
1-800-829-1040
Arkansas
1-800-829-1040
California
Oakland, 839-1040
Elsewhere,
1-800-829-1040
Colorado
Denver, 825-7041
Elsewhere,
1-800-829-1040
Connecticut
1-800-829-1040
Delaware
1-800-829-1040
District of Columbia
1-800-829-1040
Florida
Jacksonville, 354-1760
Elsewhere,
1-800-829-1040
Georgia
Atlanta, 522-0050
Elsewhere,
1-800-829-1040
Hawaii
1-800-829-1040
Idaho
1-800-829-1040
Illinois
1-800-829-1040
Indiana
Indianapolis, 226-5477
Elsewhere,
1-800-829-1040
Iowa
1-800-829-1040
Kansas
1-800-829-1040
Kentucky
1-800-829-1040
Louisiana
1-800-829-1040
Maine
1-800-829-1040
Maryland
Baltimore, 962-2590
Elsewhere,
1-800-829-1040
Massachusetts
Boston, 536-1040
Elsewhere,
1-800-829-1040

Michigan
Detroit, 237-0800
Elsewhere,
1-800-829-1040
Minnesota
Minneapolis, 644-7515
St Paul, 644-7515
Elsewhere,
1-800-829-1040
Mississippi
1-800-829-1040
Missouri
St Louis, 342-1040
Elsewhere,
1-800-829-1040
Montana
1-800-829-1040
Nebraska
1-800-829-1040
Nevada
1-800-829-1040
New Hampshire
1-800-829-1040
New Jersey
1-800-829-1040
New Mexico
1-800-829-1040
New York
Buffalo, 685-5432
Elsewhere,
1-800-829-1040
North Carolina
1-800-829-1040
North Dakota
1-800-829-1040
Ohio
Cincinnati, 621-6281
Cleveland, 522-3000
Elsewhere,
1-800-829-1040
Oklahoma
1-800-829-1040
Oregon
Portland, 221-3960
Elsewhere,
1-800-829-1040
Pennsylvania
Philadelphia, 574-9900
Pittsburgh, 281-0112
Elsewhere,
1-800-829-1040
Puerto Rico
San Juan Metro Area,
766-5040
Elsewhere,
1-800-829-1040
Rhode Island
1-800-829-1040
South Carolina
1-800-829-1040

South Dakota
1-800-829-1040
Tennessee
Nashville, 834-9005
Elsewhere,
1-800-829-1040
Texas
Dallas, 742-2440
Houston, 541-0440
Elsewhere,
1-800-829-1040
Utah
1-800-829-1040
Vermont
1-800-829-1040
Virginia
Richmond, 698-5000
Elsewhere,
1-800-829-1040
Washington
Seattle, 442-1040
Elsewhere,
1-800-829-1040
West Virginia
1-800-829-1040
Wisconsin
1-800-829-1040
Wyoming
1-800-829-1040

Phone Help for People With Impaired Hearing
All areas in U.S., including Alaska, Hawaii, Virgin Islands, and Puerto Rico:
1-800-829-4059.

Note: This number is answered by TDD equipment only.

Hours of TDD Operation:
8:00 a.m. to 6:30 p.m. EST
(Jan. 1 - April 6)
9:00 a.m. to 7:30 p.m. EST
(April 7 - April 15)
9:00 a.m. to 5:30 p.m. EST
(April 16 - Oct. 26)
8:00 a.m. to 4:30 p.m. EST
(Oct. 27 - Dec. 31)

APPENDIX B

Topic No.	Subject	Topic No.	Subject	Topic No.	Subject
	Tax Information for Puerto Rico Residents (in Spanish)		**Other TeleTax Topics in Spanish**	955	Who must file?
		951	IRS services–Volunteer tax assistance, toll-free telephone, walk-in assistance, and outreach programs	956	Which form to use?
901	Who must file a U.S. income tax return in Puerto Rico			957	What is your filing status?
902	Deductions and credits for Puerto Rico filers			958	Social security and equivalent railroad retirement benefits
903	Federal employment taxes in Puerto Rico	952	Refunds–How long they should take	959	Earned income tax credit (EITC)
904	Tax assistance for Puerto Rico residents	953	Forms and publications–How to order	960	Advance earned income tax credit
		954	Highlights of tax changes	961	Alien tax clearance

Mailing Addresses of Internal Revenue Service Centers

If an addressed envelope came with your return, and you are filing a paper return, please use it. If you do not have one, or if you moved during the year, mail your return to the Internal Revenue Service Center indicated for the state where you live. A street address is not needed.

Internal Revenue Service Centers

Alabama—Memphis, TN 37501
Alaska—Ogden, UT 84201
Arizona—Ogden, UT 84201
Arkansas—Memphis, TN 37501
California—*Counties of Alpine, Amador, Butte, Calaveras, Colusa, Contra Costa, Del Norte, El Dorado, Glenn, Humboldt, Lake Lassen, Marin, Mendocino, Modoc, Napa, Nevada, Placer, Plumas, Sacramento, San Joaquin, Shasta, Sierra, Siskiyou, Solano, Sonoma, Sutter, Tehama, Trinity, Yolo, and Yuba—*
Ogden, UT 84201
All other counties—
Fresno, CA 93888
Colorado—Ogden, UT 84201
Connecticut—Andover, MA 05501
Delaware—Philadelphia, PA 19255
District of Columbia—
Philadelphia, PA 19255
Florida—Atlanta, GA 39901
Georgia—Atlanta, GA 39901
Hawaii—Fresno, CA 93888
Idaho—Ogden, UT 84201
Illinois—Kansas City, MO 64999
Indiana—Cincinnati, OH 45999
Iowa—Kansas City, MO 64999
Kansas—Austin, TX 73301
Kentucky—Cincinnati, OH 45999
Louisiana—Memphis, TN 37501
Maine—Andover, MA 05501
Maryland—Philadelphia, PA 19255
Massachusetts—
Andover, MA 05501
Michigan—Cincinnati, OH 45999
Minnesota—Kansas City, MO 64999
Mississippi—Memphis, TN 37501
Missouri—Kansas City, MO 64999

Montana—Ogden, UT 84201
Nebraska—Ogden, UT 84201
Nevada—Ogden, UT 84201
New Hampshire—
Andover, MA 05501
New Jersey—Holtsville, NY 00501
New Mexico—Austin, TX 73301
New York—*New York City and Counties of Nassau, Rockland, Suffolk, and Westchester—*
Holtsville, NY 00501
All other counties—
Andover, MA 05501
North Carolina—
Memphis, TN 37501
North Dakota—Ogden, UT 84201
Ohio—Cincinnati, OH 45999
Oklahoma—Austin, TX 73301
Oregon—Ogden, UT 84201
Pennsylvania—
Philadelphia, PA 19255
Rhode Island—Andover, MA 05501
South Carolina—Atlanta, GA 39901
South Dakota—Ogden, UT 84201
Tennessee—Memphis, TN 37501
Texas—Austin, TX 73301
Utah—Ogden, UT 84201
Vermont— Andover, MA 05501
Virginia— Philadelphia, PA 19255
Washington—Ogden, UT 84201
West Virginia—
Cincinnati, OH 45999
Wisconsin—
Kansas City, MO 64999
Wyoming—Ogden, UT 84201
American Samoa—
Philadelphia, PA 19255

Guam: *Nonpermanent residents—*
Philadelphia, PA 19255
Guam: *Permanent residents—*
Department of Revenue
and Taxation
Government of Guam
Building 13-1 Mariner Avenue
Tiyjan Barrigada, GU 96913
Puerto Rico—
Philadelphia, PA 19255
Virgin Islands:
Nonpermanent residents—
Philadelphia, PA 19255
Virgin Islands:
Permanent residents—
V.I. Bureau of Internal Revenue
9601 Estate Thomas
Charlotte Amalie
St. Thomas, VI 00802
Foreign country: *U.S. citizens and those filing Form 2555, Form 2555-EZ, or Form 4563—*
Philadelphia, PA 19255
All A.P.O. and F.P.O. addresses—
Philadelphia, PA 19255

*U.S. G.P.O.:1996-397-774

APPENDIX B

STATE FILING AUTHORITY PHONE NUMBERS

Below is a listing of all the states and the telephone numbers for you to
order state forms and where your questions can be answered regarding
your state filing requirements. Most toll free numbers are for in–state
calls.

STATE FILING AUTHORITIES PHONE LISTING

STATE	FORMS NUMBERS	INFORMATION NUMBERS
Alabama	334/242–9681	334/242–1000
Alaska	907/465–2320	907/465–2320
Arizona	602/542–4260	602/255–3381
Arkansas	501/682–7255	501/682–7250
California	800/852–5711	800/338–0505
Colorado	303/534–1408	303/534–1209
Connecticut	203/297–4753	800/382–9463
Delaware	302/577–3310	302/577–3300
District of Columbia	202/727–6170	202/727–6104
Florida	904/488–6800	904/488–6800
Georgia	404/656–4293	404/656–4071
Hawaii	800/222–7572	800/222–3229
Idaho	208/334–7660	208/334–7660
Illinois	800/356–6302	800/732–8866
Indiana	317/486–5103	317/232–2240
Iowa	515/281–7239	515/281–3114
Kansas	913/296–4937	913/296–0222
Kentucky	502/564–3658	502/564–4580
Louisiana	504/925–7532	504/925–4611
Maine	207/624–7894	207/626–8475
Maryland	410/974–3981	800/638–2937
Massachusetts	617/727–4545	617/727–4545
Michigan	800/367–6263	517/373–3200
Minnesota	800/657–3676	800/652–9094
Mississippi	601/359–1142	601/359–1142
Missouri	314/751–4695	314/751–4450
Montana	406/444–0290	406/444–2837
Nebraska	800/742–7474	402/471–2971
Nevada	702/687–4820	702/687–4892
New Hampshire	603/271–2192	603/271–2186
New Jersey	609/588–2200	609/588–2200
New Mexico	505/827–2206	505/827–0700
New York	518/438–1073	518/438–8581
North Carolina	919/715–0397	919/733–4682
North Dakota	701/328–3017	701/328–2770
Ohio	614/846–6712	614/846–6712
Oklahoma	405/521–3108	405/521–3125
Oregon	503/378–4988	503/378–4988
Pennsylvania	800/362–2050	717/787–8201
Rhode Island	401/277–3934	401/277–2905
South Carolina	803/737–5085	803/737–4761
South Dakota	605/773–3311	605/773–3311
Tennessee	615/741–4466	615/741–2594
Texas	512/463–4600	512/463–4600
Utah	801/297–6700	801/297–2200
Vermont	802/828–2515	802/828–2501
Virginia	804/367–8205	804/367–2062
Washington	800/647–7706	800/647–7706
West Virginia	304/344–2068	304/558–3333
Wisconsin	608/266–1961	608/266–2486
Wyoming	307/777–7722	307/777–7722

APPENDIX C:
YOUR RIGHTS AS A TAXPAYER
(TAXPAYER BILL OF RIGHTS)

DECLARATION OF TAXPAYER RIGHTS

I. Protection of Your Rights

IRS employees will explain and protect your rights as a taxpayer throughout your contact with us.

II. Privacy and Confidentiality

The IRS will not disclose to anyone the information you give us, except as authorized by law. You have the right to know why we are asking you for information, how we will use it, and what happens if you do not provide requested information.

III. Professional and Courteous Service

If you believe that an IRS employee has not treated you in a professional manner, you should tell that employee's supervisor. If the supervisor's response is not satisfactory, you should write to your IRS District Director or Service Center Director.

IV. Representation

You may either represent yourself, or with proper written authorization, have someone else represent you in your place. You can have someone accompany you at an interview. You may make sound recordings of any meetings with our examination or collection personnel, provided you tell us in writing 10 days before the meeting.

V. Payment of Only the Correct Amount of Tax

You are responsible for paying only the correct amount of tax due under the law—no more, no less.

VI. Help from the Problem Resolution Office

Problem Resolution Officers can help you with unresolved tax problems and can offer you special help if you have a significant hardship as a result of a tax problem. For more information, write to the Problem Resolution Office at the District Office or Service Center where you have the problem, or call 1-800-829-1040 (1-800-829-4059 for TDD users).

VII. Appeals and Judicial Review

If you disagree with us about the amount of your tax liability or certain collection actions, you have the right to ask the IRS Appeals Office to review your case. You may also ask a court to review your case.

VIII. Relief from Certain Penalties

The IRS will waive penalties when allowed by law if you can show you acted reasonably and in good faith or relied on the incorrect advice of an IRS employee.

EXAMINATIONS, APPEALS, COLLECTIONS, AND REFUNDS

Examinations (Audits)

We accept most taxpayer's returns as filed. If we inquire about your return or select it for examination, it does not suggest that you are dishonest. The inquiry or examination may or may not result in more tax. We may close your case without change; or, you may receive a refund.

By Mail

We handle many examinations and inquiries by mail. We will send you a letter with either a request for more information or a reason why we believe a change to your return may be needed. If you give us the requested information or provide an explanation, we may or may not agree with you, and we will explain the reasons for any changes. Please do not hesitate to write to us about anything you do not understand. If you cannot resolve a question through the mail, you can request a personal interview with an examiner.

By Interview

If we notify you that we will conduct your examination through a personal interview, or you request such an interview, you have the right to ask that the examination take place at a reasonable time and place that is convenient for both you and the IRS. At the end of your examination, the examiner will give you a report if there are any proposed changes to your tax return. If you do not agree with the report, you may meet with the examiner's supervisor.

Repeat Examinations

If we examined your tax return for the same items in either of the two previous years and proposed no change to your tax liability, please contact us as soon as possible so we can determine if we should discontinue the repeat examination. Publication 556, *Examination of Returns, Appeal Rights, and Claims for Refund*, will give you more information about the rules and procedures of an IRS examination.

Appeals

If you do not agree with the examiner's findings, you can appeal them to our Appeals Office. Most differences can be settled without expensive and time-consuming court trials. Your appeal rights are explained in detail in Publication 5, *Appeal Rights and Preparation of Protests for Unagreed Cases*.

If you do not wish to use our Appeals Office or disagree with its findings, you can take your case to the U.S. Tax Court, U.S. Court of Federal Claims, or the U.S. District Court where you live. If the court agrees with you on most issues in your case, and finds that our position was largely unjustified, you may be able to recover some of your administrative and litigation costs. You will not be eligible to recover these costs unless you tried to resolve your case administratively, including going through our appeals system, and you gave us all the information necessary to resolve the case.

Collections

Publication 594, *Understanding The Collection Process*, explains your rights and responsibilities regarding payment of federal taxes. It is divided into several sections that explain the procedures in plain language. The sections include:

1. *When you have not paid enough tax.* This section describes tax bills and explains what to do if you think your bill is wrong.
2. *Making arrangements to pay your bill.* This covers making installment payments, delaying collection action, and submitting an offer in compromise.
3. *What happens when you take no action to pay.* This covers liens, releasing a lien, levies, releasing a levy, seizures and sales, and release of property. Publication 1660, *Collection Appeal Rights (for Liens, Levies and Seizures)*, explains your rights to appeal liens, levies, and seizures and how to request these appeals.

Refunds

You may file a claim for refund if you think you paid too much tax. You must generally file the claim within three years from the date you filed your return or two years from the date you paid the tax, whichever is later. The law generally provides for interest on your refund if it is not paid within 45 days of the date you filed your return or claim for refund. Publication 556, *Examination of Returns, Appeal Rights, and Claims for Refund,* has more information on refunds.

APPENDIX D:
PRACTITIONER HOT LINE
TELEPHONE NUMBERS
(FROM *OPERATION LINK*,
IRS PUBLICATION 1320)

Account-related inquiries on individual and business tax accounts will be accepted from tax practitioners when representing a client. A valid authorization must be on file with the IRS for the taxpayer, type of tax, and tax period involved.

MIDSTATES REGION

Dallas	214-767-1501
St. Louis	314-342-9325
Wichita	316-352-7171
Houston	713-541-3444
Chicago	312-886-1110
Springfield	217-527-6377
Aberdeen	605-226-7268
Fargo	701-239-5240
St. Paul	612-643-2424
Milwaukee	414-223-4428
Des Moines	515-243-4350
Omaha	402-221-3792
Austin	512-464-3337
Oklahoma City	405-297-4141
Little Rock	501-324-5141

NORTHEAST REGION

Manhattan	212-719-6045/46
Brooklyn	718-488-3595
Detroit	313-961-4690
Newark	908-417-4076
Boston	617-536-0739
Augusta	207-622-8468
Burlington	802-860-2093
Portsmouth	603-433-8981
Cincinnati	513-241-2929
Cleveland	216-623-1338
Philadelphia	215-440-1524
Pittsburgh	412-281-0281
Hartford	203-240-4101
Providence	401-528-4033
Albany	518-431-4491/92
Buffalo	716-846-5915

SOUTHEAST REGION

Atlanta	770-730-3123
Greensboro	910-378-2157
Columbia	803-253-3231/3107
New Orleans	504-558-3050

Birmingham	205-731-2237	Los Angeles	213-894-3706
Jackson	601-965-4131	Sacramento	916-974-5092
Nashville	615-781-4826	Seattle	206-220-5786
Louisville	502-582-5284	Anchorage	907-271-6210
Indianapolis	317-226-7698	Honolulu	808-541-3380
Baltimore	410-727-7965	Portland	503-326-2381
Wilmington	302-573-6421	Denver	303-820-3940
Jacksonville	904-358-3572	Boise	208-334-9673
Fort Lauderdale	305-982-5242/5423	Cheyenne	307-772-2609
	305-982-7763	Helena	406-449-5479
Richmond	804-771-8251	Salt Lake City	801-524-6959
Parkersburg	304-420-6842	Laguna Nigel	714-643-4206
		Phoenix	602-640-3935
WESTERN REGION		Albuquerque	505-837-5789
San Francisco	510-271-0781	Las Vegas	702-455-1201
San Jose	408-494-8113		

NOTES

All IRS publications are issued by the Department of the Treasury and published by the U.S. Government Printing Office in Washington, D.C. Please see the Bibliography, page 400, for further information on these publications.

2. THE IRS PERSONALITY: PLAYING IT TO YOUR ADVANTAGE

1. Kevin McCormally, "How a Dumb Idea Became a Law," *Kiplinger's Personal Finance*, July 1993, pp. 44–47.
2. Don Van Natta, Jr., "11 Officers Are Accused of Failure to Pay Taxes," *The New York Times*, July 17, 1996, Sec. B, 3:5.
3. Gerald Carson, *The Golden Egg: The Personal Income Tax—Where It Came From, How It Grew* (Boston: Houghton Mifflin, 1977), p. 129.
4. *IRS 1980 Annual Report*, pp. 10–11.
5. *IRS 1995 Data Book*, advance draft, Table 1.
6. Jerold L. Waltman, *Political Origins of the U.S. Income Tax* (Jackson, Miss.: University Press of Mississippi, 1985), p. 17.
7. *Ibid.*, p. 113.
8. Philip M. Stern, *The Best Congress Money Can Buy* (New York: Pantheon, 1988), pp. 43–44.
9. *The New York Times*, "Tax Breaks for the Few Hinge on Access to Power," July 19, 1976, Sec. A, 1:2.
10. *IRS 1995 Data Book*, advance draft, Table 1.
11. *IRS 1993–94 Data Book*, advance draft, Table 9.
12. *Journal of Accountancy*, "CPAs Recommend Simplifying Earned Income Tax Credit," July 1995, p. 36 ("Tax Matters").
13. *Tax Savings Report*, "IRS Fraud Efforts Were Successful," July/August 1995, p. 10 ("Economic Reality").
14. *IRS 1995 Data Book*, advance draft, Table 9.

15. *Ibid.*
16. Lillian Doris, ed., *The American Way in Taxation: Internal Revenue, 1862–1963* (Englewood Cliffs, N.J.: Prentice-Hall, 1963), p. 39.
17. Carson, *The Golden Egg*, p. 210.
18. Clayton Knowles, "Nunan Mentioned in Tax Cut Case," *The New York Times*, Feb. 15, 1952, 10:5.
19. Clayton Knowles, "Nunan Accused Before the Senate of Complicity in 4 New Tax Cases," *The New York Times*, Feb. 22, 1952, 1:2.
20. John C. Chommie, *The Internal Revenue Service* (New York: Praeger, 1970), p. 94.
21. *IRS 1995 Data Book*, advance draft, Table 22.
22. *Ibid.*, Table 18.
23. *IRS 1991 Annual Report*, p. 5; *IRS 1995 Data Book*, advance draft, Table 18.

3. WHO RUNS THE SHOW: WHAT YOU'RE UP AGAINST

1. IRS, *Tax Hints 1995*, p. 4.
2. IRS, *Guide to the Internal Revenue Service for Congressional Staff*, p. 29.
3. *IRS 1995 Data Book*, advance draft, Table 11.
4. IRS, *Guide*, p. 31.
5. Ibid., p. 33.
6. *IRS 1995 Data Book*, advance draft, Table 20.
7. IRS, *Internal Revenue Service Manual*, p. 4231–161.
8. *IRS 1992 Annual Report*, p. 47; *IRS 1993–94 Data Book*, advance draft, Table 28; *IRS 1995 Data Book*, advance draft, Table 28.
9. *IRS 1993–94 Data Book*, advance draft, Table 20; *IRS 1995 Data Book*, advance draft, Table 20.
10. Ibid.
11. IRS, *Guide*, p. 10.
12. *Ibid.*, pp. 10–11.
13. *IRS 1992 Annual Report*, p. 33.
14. *IRS 1993–94 Data Book*, advance draft, Table 10.

4. IRS PEOPLE

1. David Burnham, *A Law Unto Itself: Power, Politics and the IRS* (New York: Random House, 1989), p. 22.
2. *Ibid.*, p. 23.
3. Eugene C. Steuerle, *Who Should Pay for Collecting Taxes?* (Washington, D.C.: American Institute for Public Policy Research, 1986), p. 15.
4. *Ibid.*
5. IRS, *Guide to the IRS for Congressional Staff*, p. 8.

5. NEUTRALIZING THE IRS'S POWER

1. David Burnham, *A Law Unto Itself: Power, Politics and the IRS* (New York: Random House, 1989), p. 21.
2. Jeff A. Schnepper, *Inside IRS* (New York: Stein and Day, 1987), p. 57.
3. Burnham, *A Law Unto Itself*, p. 313.
4. IRS, *Guide to the IRS for Congressional Staff*, p. 38.

5. *IRS 1995 Data Book*, advance draft, Table 31.
6. *Ibid.*
7. IRS, *Guide*, p. 38.
8. *Ibid.*
9. *Ibid.*
10. *IRS 1995 Data Book*, advance draft, Table 31.
11. IRS, *Guide*, p. 38.
12. *Ibid.*
13. *IRS 1995 Data Book*, advance draft, Table 31.
14. As quoted in Burnham, *A Law Unto Itself*, p. 303.
15. John C. Chommie. *The Internal Revenue Service* (New York: Praeger, 1970), p. 177.
16. Seymour Hersh, "IRS Said to Balk Inquiry on Rebozo," *The New York Times*, April 21, 1974, 1:3; and "Ervin Unit to Get Rebozo Tax Data," *The New York Times*, April 24, 1974, 1:4.
17. U.S. Congress House Committee on Government Operations, fourth report, *A Citizen's Guide on Using the Freedom of Information Act and the Privacy Act of 1974 to Request Government Records*, House Report 102-146 (Washington, D.C.: GPO, 1991), p. 2.
18. *Ibid.*, pp. 5–6.
19. *Tax Loopholes* (Springfield, N.J.: Boardroom Classics, 1994), p. 34.
20. Randy Bruce Blaustein, *How to Do Business with the IRS—Taxpayer's Edition* (Englewood Cliffs, N.J.: Prentice-Hall, 1984), p. 13.
21. *The New York Times*, "Nuclear War Plan by IRS," March 28, 1989, Sec. D, 16:6.
22. *IRS 1995 Data Book*, advance draft, Tables 1, 11.
23. Joseph A. Pechman, *Federal Tax Policy*, 4th ed., Studies of Government Finance (Washington, D.C.: Brookings Institution, 1983), p. 61.
24. Burnham, *A Law Unto Itself*, p. 308.
25. Chommie, *Internal Revenue Service*, p. 11.

6. IRS TECHNOLOGY

1. *IRS 1991 Annual Report*, p. 10.
2. *IRS 1995 Data Book*, advance draft, Table 18.
3. *Ibid.*, Tables 1, 2.
4. *Ibid.*, Tables 18, 14, 19.
5. *NSPA Washington Reporter*, "IRS, NSPA Meet to Review '92 Tax Form Changes," August 1991, p. 3.
6. *Practical Accountant*, "Inside the IRS," June 1991, p. 22.
7. Albert B. Crenshaw, "Computer Problems Taxing IRS," *The Washington Post*, March 15, 1996, 1:5.
8. Robert D. Hershey, Jr., "A Technological Overhaul of IRS Is Called a Fiasco," *The New York Times*, April 15, 1996, 8:5.
9. National Society of Public Accountants, *The NSPA Practitioner*, "Internal Revenue Service Faces Significant Budget Cuts," vol. 38, no. 12, June 28, 1996, p. 1.
10. *Ibid.*, p. 5.
11. Hershey, "Technological Overhaul."
12. Crenshaw, "Computer Problems."

7. IRS TARGETS AND WHAT TO DO IF YOU'RE ONE OF THEM

1. Arthur Fredheim, "Audits Digging Deeper Beneath the Surface," *Practical Accountant*, March 1996, p. 20; taken from IRS commissioner Margaret Milner Richardson's speech to New York State Bar Association, Albany, N.Y., January 24, 1995.
2. Marguerite T. Smith, "Who Cheats on Their Income Taxes," *Money*, April 1991, pp. 101–102.
3. *Ibid.*, p. 104.
4. Jon Nordheimer, "You Work at Home: Does the Town Board Care?" *The New York Times*, July 14, 1996, Sec. B, 1:1.
5. Leonard Sloane, "Home Offices: Tough, Not Impossible," *The New York Times*, Feb. 28, 1993, Sec. F, 20:1.
6. Jan M. Rosen, "Trained on Home Offices: Secret Weapon 8829," *The New York Times*, March 1, 1992, Sec. F, 21:1.
7. Randall W. Roth and Andrew R. Biebl, "How to Avoid Getting Caught in the IRS Crackdown," *Journal of Accountancy*, May 1991, p. 35.
8. Kathy Krawczyk, Lorraine M. Wright, and Roby B. Sawyers, "Independent Contractor: The Consequences of Reclassification," *Journal of Accountancy*, Jan. 1996, p. 47.
9. Roth and Biebl, pp. 35–36.
10. Barry H. Frank, "What You Can Do About the IRS' All-Out Attack on Independent Contractors," *Practical Accountant*, April 1991, p. 34.
11. *Ibid.*, p. 35.
12. Smith, "Who Cheats," p. 108.
13. Roth and Biebl, "How to Avoid," p. 35.
14. Frank, "What You Can Do," p. 34.
15. *Standard Federal Tax Reporter*, CCH Comments (Chicago: Commerce Clearing House), March 21, 1996, Sec. 79,354 and Sec. 79,355, pp. 48,725–48,726.
16. Krawczyk, et al., p. 48.
17. *Ibid.*
18. *Standard Federal Tax Reporter*, CCH Comments, Feb. 29, 1996, Sec. 79,-340, p. 48,717.
19. Richard Byllott, "Compliance 2000 and Cash Transaction Reporting," *Nassau Chapter Newsletter* (published by New York State Society of Certified Public Accounts) vol. 36, no. 4 (Dec. 1992), p. 10.
20. Fredheim, p. 23.
21. *Ibid.*
22. *Standard Federal Tax Reporter*, CCH Comments, July 13, 1996, Sec. 79,-623, p. 48,860.
23. *Social Security Administration/IRS Reporter*, "Market Segment Specialization in the Examination Division," Summer 1995, p. 2.
24. *Practical Accountant*, "Latest IRS Audit Technique Guides," Jan. 1996, p. 52 ("Inside the IRS").
25. *Practical Accountant*, "MSSP Guides Issued on Architects and Cancellation of RTC Debt," April 1995, p. 16 ("Inside the IRS").
26. Materials handed out at IRS's Financial Status Audits Conference, presented by Donald Caterraccio, IRS Brooklyn District; Denis Bricker, IRS

Brooklyn District; Jack Angel, CPA, The Tax Institute, College of Management, Long Island University/C. W. Post Campus, July 11, 1996.

27. *Social Security Administration/IRS Reporter*, "Market Segment Understanding Program Provides Guidelines," Fall 1995, p. 2.
28. *Tax Wise Money*, June 1993, p. 8.
29. Gloversville-Johnstown (New York) *Leader-Herald*, "IRS Going After 10M Nonfilers," March 30, 1992, p. 5.
30. *IRS 1992 Annual Report*, p. 10.

8. HOW TO AVOID AN AUDIT COMPLETELY

1. *IRS 1980 Annual Report*, p. 52; *IRS 1991 Annual Report*, p. 26.
2. *IRS 1993 Annual Report*, advance draft, Table 11.
3. *Ibid.*, Tables 11, 13, 14, 16, and 17 (footnotes).
4. *Ibid.*, Table 11; *IRS 1993–94 Data Book*, advance draft, Table 11.
5. *IRS 1993–94 Data Book*, advance draft, Table 11.
6. *Practical Accountant*, "IRS Briefs," Oct. 1995, p. 13.
7. *IRS 1995 Data Book*, advance draft, Table 11.
8. *IRS 1976 Annual Report*, p. 99, Table 2.
9. *IRS 1993–94 Data Book*, advance draft, Table 11.
10. Alan E. Weiner, *All About Limited Liability Companies & Partnerships* (Melville, N.Y.: Holtz Rubenstein & Co., 1994), p. 4.

10. TEN GROUND RULES NEVER TO BREAK TO WIN WITH THE IRS

1. IRS, *Taxnotes*, 1993, p. 2 ("Procedure Changes for Granting Installment Agreements").
2. David Burnham, *A Law Unto Itself: Power, Politics and the IRS* (New York: Random House, 1989), p. 119.
3. *National Public Accountant*, "How to Communicate with Your Members of Congress," June–July 1995, p. 35 ("Client Report").

11. WHERE THE IRS IS (OR ISN'T) GOING

AND WHAT *TO* DO, OR *NOT* DO, ABOUT IT

1. Herbert J. Huff, "A Plan for Reinventing the IRS," paper read at Annual Tax Conference of the Nassau Chapter of the New York Society for CPA's, Foundation for Accounting Education, Woodbury, N.Y., Dec. 4, 1993.
2. *Ibid.*
3. *NSPA Washington Reporter*, "House Passes Budget for IRS," Aug. 6, 1993, p. 3 ("Federal Update").
4. *Ibid.*
5. Matthew L. Wald, "The Latest Pitch: 1040PC and the Promise of a Speedy Refund," *The New York Times*, Feb. 28, 1993, "Your Taxes," 17:1.
6. *Ibid.*
7. *IRS 1993 Annual Report*, advance draft, Table 8; *IRS 1993–94 Data Book*, advance draft, Table 8.
8. *Practical Accountant*, "GAO Says Future of Electronic Filing Isn't So Rosy," March 1996, p. 42.
9. IRS, *1994 Tax Hints*, p. 3.

10. IRS, *Tax Hints 1995*, p. 17.
11. *The New York Times*, "Happy New Tax Year," Jan. 3, 1994, editorial.
12. *Practical Accountant*, "Inside the IRS," Feb. 1996, p. 52.
13. Jan M. Rosen, "Caught in a Bind? IRS May Let You Pay Less," *The New York Times*, July 31, 1993, 34:1.
14. *Practical Accountant*, "Settlements with IRS Increase Dramatically," July 1993, p. 8 ("Practitioner's Update").
15. *NSPA Washington Reporter*, "Federal Tax Roundup," June 25, 1993, p. 4.
16. *Practical Accountant*, "Settlements with IRS Increase Dramatically," July 1993, p. 8 ("Practitioner's Update"); *Journal of Accountancy*, "Taxpayer Installment Agreements Are on the Rise," July 1995, p. 37 ("Tax Matters").
17. Robert D. Hershey, Jr., "A Technological Overhaul of IRS Is Called a Fiasco," *The New York Times*, April 15, 1996, 8:5.
18. *Practical Accountant*, "IRS Briefs," August 1995, p. 54 ("Inside the IRS").
19. "The Nasty Little Secret About the IRS's Do-It-Yourself Audits," *Money*, July 1991, p. 19 ("Money Update").
20. *Tax Hotline*, "Self-Audits," February 1992, p. 1.
21. *IRS 1995 Data Book*, advance draft, Table 10.
22. Robert D. Hershey, Jr., "IRS Staff Is Cited in Snoopings," *The New York Times*, July 19, 1994, Sec. D, 1:6.
23. Shirley D. Peterson, "The IRS: Today and Tomorrow," *National Public Accountant*, July 1992, p. 21.
24. Standard Federal Tax Reports, Commerce Clearing House Comments, August 1, 1996, p. 4.
25. Jeffrey A. Lear, "Electronic Payment Mandate Delayed," *NSPA Practitioner*, vol. 38, no. 15, August 9, 1996, p. 3.
26. *Ibid.*
27. *NSPA Practitioner*, "IRS Plans Downsizing," vol. 38, no. 15, p. 3.
28. Kelly D. Smith, "Why Private Tax Collectors May Be Going Begging," *Money*, September 1966, p. 23.
29. *Ibid.*
30. *Journal of Accountancy*, "IRS Announces Possible New Features for Web Site," August 1996, p. 32 ("Tax Matters").
31. Huff, "A Plan."
32. *IRS 1995 Data Book*, advance draft, Table 15.

BIBLIOGRAPHY

All IRS publications are listed under the Department of the Treasury.

Adams, Charles W. *Fight, Flight, Fraud: The Story of Taxation.* Curaçao, Netherlands Antilles: Euro-Dutch Publishers, 1982.

(American Institute of Certified Public Accountants). "IRS Financial-Status Audit Approach Spells Danger for CPAs, Clients; IRS Responds to AICPA's Concerns." *The CPA Letter,* August/September 1995, p. 6.

The Bar Examiner. "1993 Statistics." May 1994, pp. 63–65.

Blaustein, Randy Bruce. *How to Do Business with the IRS. Taxpayer's Edition.* Englewood Cliffs, N.J.: Prentice-Hall, 1984.

(Boardroom Classics). *Tax Loopholes.* Springfield, N.J.: Boardroom Classics, 1994.

Burnham, David. *A Law Unto Itself: Power, Politics and the IRS.* New York: Random House, 1989.

Bylott, Richard. "Compliance 2000 and Cash Transaction Reporting." *Nassau Chapter Newsletter.* Published by New York State Society of Certified Public Accountants. Vol. 36, no. 4 (December 1992).

Carlson, Robert C., ed. *Tax Wise Money,* vol. 2, no. 6 (June 1993).

Carson, Gerald. *The Golden Egg: The Personal Income Tax—Where It Came From, How It Grew.* Boston: Houghton Mifflin, 1977.

Chommie, John C. *The Internal Revenue Service.* New York: Praeger, 1970.

(Commerce Clearing House). *Standard Federal Tax Reporter,* Internal Revenue Code, "Historical Note." Chicago: Commerce Clearing House, Inc., 1994.

Cummins, H. J. "New Look for IRS." *Newsday,* Dec. 3, 1993, Business section, p. 63.

Daily, Frederick W. *Stand Up to the IRS: How to Handle Audits, Tax Bills and Tax Court.* Berkeley: Nolo Press, 1992.

Davis, Shelley, L. *IRS Historical Fact Book: A Chronology, 1646–1992*. Washington, D.C.: U.S. Government Printing Office, 1993.

Department of the Treasury, Internal Revenue Service. *1992 Tax Hints, 1993 Tax Hints, 1994 Tax Hints, Tax Hints 1995*. Brookhaven Service Center. Washington, D.C.: GPO, 1991, 1992, 1993.

———. *Guide to the Internal Revenue Service for Congressional Staff*. Legislative Affairs Division, Publication 1273. Washington, D.C.: GPO, 1991.

———. *Internal Revenue Service Manual*. Sections 912, 913, 940. Washington, D.C.: GPO, 1981.

———. *IRS 1993–94 Data Book* (advance report). Washington, D.C.: GPO, 1994.

———. *IRS 1995 Data Book* (advance report). Washington, D.C.: GPO, 1995.

———. *IRS 1976 Annual Report, IRS 1980 Annual Report, IRS 1990 Annual Report, IRS 1991 Annual Report, IRS 1992 Annual Report, IRS 1993 Annual Report* (advance draft). Washington, D.C.: GPO, 1977, 1981, 1991, 1992, 1993.

———. *IRS Service*. Washington, D.C.: GPO, 1990.

———. *Taxnotes*. A newsletter for practitioners. Brookhaven Service Center, Public Affairs Office. Washington, D.C.: GPO, 1993. See "Procedure Changes for Granting Installment Agreements." July 1994, see "Special Enrollment Exam Applications."

Doris, Lillian, ed. *The American Way in Taxation: Internal Revenue, 1862–1963*. Englewood Cliffs, N.J.: Prentice-Hall, 1963.

Frank, Barry H. "What You Can Do About the IRS' All-Out Attack on Independent Contractors." *Practical Accountant*, April 1991, pp. 33–37.

Gloversville-Johnstown (New York) *Leader-Herald*. "IRS Going After 10M Nonfilers." March 30, 1992, p. 5.

Hersh, Seymour M. "IRS Said to Balk Inquiry on Rebozo." *The New York Times*, April 21, 1974, 1:3.

———. "Ervin Unit to Get Rebozo Tax Data." *The New York Times*, April 24, 1974, 1:4.

Hershey, Robert D., Jr. "IRS Raises Its Estimate of Tax Cheating." *The New York Times*, Dec. 29, 1993, Sec. D, 1:1.

———. "IRS Staff Is Cited in Snooping." *The New York Times*, July 19, 1994, Sec. D, 1:6.

Horrock, Nicholas M. "IRS Trained Its Agents in Drinking." *The New York Times*, April 14, 1975, 1:3.

Huff, Herbert. "A Plan for Reinventing the IRS." Paper presented at the Annual Tax Conference of the Nassau Chapter of the New York Society for CPA's, Foundation for Accounting Education, Held at Woodbury, New York, Dec. 4, 1993.

Johnston, David Cay. "Detailed Audits Await Some Unlucky Taxpayers." *International Herald Tribune*, July 20, 1995, 3:2.

Journal of Accountancy. "CPAs Recommend Simplifying Earned Income Tax Credit ("Tax Matters"), July 1995, p. 36; "Taxpayer Installment Agreements Are on the Rise" ("Tax Matters"), July 1995, p. 37; "IRS Audits Focus on Market Segments" ("Tax Matters"), Aug. 1995, p. 21; "Independent Contractor: The Consequences of Reclassification," Jan. 1996, p. 47; "IRS Announces Possible New Features for Web Site" ("Tax Matters"), Aug. 1996, p.32.

Knowles, Clayton. "Nunan Accused Before the Senate of Complicity in 4 New Tax Cases." *The New York Times*, Feb. 22, 1952, 1:2.

———. "Nunan Mentioned in Tax Cut Case," *The New York Times*, Feb. 15, 1952, 10:5.

Lalli, Frank. "We're Cheating One Another." *Money*, April 1991, p. 5.

Lewis, Peter H. "In the Home Office, Equipment May Still Be Deductible." *The New York Times*, Jan. 24, 1993, Sec. F, 8:1.

Mansnerus, Laura. "Looking for an Attorney? Here's Counsel." *The New York Times*, June 11, 1995, Sec. 3, p. 1.

McCormally, Kevin. "How a Dumb Idea Became a Law." *Kiplinger's Personal Finance*, July 1993, pp. 44–47.

Money. "The Nasty Little Secret About the IRS' Do-It-Yourself Audits." July 1991, p. 19 ("Money Update").

Myerson, Allan R. "For Each Transgression the IRS Has a Penalty." *The New York Times*, Feb. 28, 1993, "Your Taxes," 24:1.

National Association of Enrolled Agents, Gaithersburg, Md., publications: "Career Option: Enrolled Agent, the Tax Professional," "Enrolled Agents: The Tax Professional."

(National Association of State Boards of Accountancy, CPA Examination Services Division). *CPA Candidate Performance on the Uniform CPA Examination*. New York: National Association of State Boards of Accountancy, 1995.

National Public Accountant. "How to Communicate with Your Members of Congress" ("Client Report"), June/July 1995, p. 35.

(New York State Bar Association). "Comparison of the Features of the Mandatory Continuing Legal Education Rules in Effect as of July 1994." New York: New York State Bar Association, 1994.

(New York State Society of Certified Public Accountants). "New IRS Audit Approach Sending Tremors Through the CPA Profession." *Tax and Regulatory Bulletin*, vol. 5, no. 2 (August/September 1995), p. 1.

The New York Times. "Tax Breaks for the Few Hinge on Access to Power," July 19, 1976, Sec. A, 1:2; "Nuclear War Plan by IRS," March 28, 1989, Sec. D, 16:6; "Happy New Tax Year," Jan. 3, 1994, Sec. A, 22:1; "11 Officers Are Accused of Failure to Pay Taxes," July 17, 1996, Sec. B, 3:5; "A Technological Overhaul of IRS Is Called a Fiasco," April 15, 1996, 8:5; "You Work at Home: Does the Town Board Care?," July 14, 1996, Sec. B, 1:1.

NSPA Practitioner. "Internal Revenue Faces Significant Budget Cuts," vol. 38, no. 12, June 28, 1996, p. 1; "Electronic Payment Mandate Delayed," vol. 38, no. 15, Aug. 9, 1996, p. 3.

NSPA Washington Reporter. Mary Beth Loutinsky, ed. Published by National Society of Public Accountants, Alexandria, Va. "IRS, NSPA Meet to Review '92 Tax Form Changes," August 1991; "Federal Tax Roundup," June 25, 1993; "Richardson Presides over First CAG [Commissioner's Advisory Group] Meeting Since Taking Office," July 9, 1993; "House Passes Budget for IRS" ("Federal Update," by Jeffrey A. Lear), Aug. 6, 1993; "TaxLink Foreshadows Future," Aug. 6, 1993; "Ways & Means Subcommittee Hears Testimony on IRS Troubles," Nov. 19, 1993.

Pechman, Joseph A. *Federal Tax Policy*. 4th ed. Studies of Government Finance. Washington, D.C.: Brookings Institution, 1983.

Peterson, Shirley D. "The IRS: Today and Tomorrow." *National Public Accountant*, July 1992, pp. 18–21.

Practical Accountant. "Alternative Filing Up This Year," April 1993, p. 20; "Inside the IRS," June 1991, p. 22; "Settlements with IRS Increase Dramatically" ("Practitioner's Update"), July 1993, p. 8; "IRS Briefs" ("Inside the IRS"), August 1995, p. 54; "Audits Digging Deeper Beneath the Surface," March 1996, p. 20; "Latest IRS Audit Technique Guides." Jan. 1996, p. 62; "MSSP Guides Issued on Architects and Cancellation of RTC Debt," April 1995, p. 16; "GAO Says Future of Electronic Filing Isn't So Rosy," March 1996, p. 42..

(Research Institute of America). *A Guide for Securing Independent Contractor Status for Workers.* New York: Research Institute of America, 1991.

Rosen, Jan M. "Caught in a Bind? IRS May Let You Pay Less." *The New York Times*, July 31, 1993, 34:1.

———. "Trained on Home Offices: Secret Weapon 8829." *The New York Times*, March 1, 1992, Sec. F, 21:1.

Roth, Randall W., and Andrew R. Biebl. "How to Avoid Getting Caught in the IRS Crackdown." *Journal of Accountancy*, May 1991, pp. 35–37.

Schmeckebier, Lawrence F., and Francis X. A. Eble. *The Bureau of Internal Revenue: Its History, Activities and Organization.* Baltimore: Johns Hopkins Press, 1923.

Schnepper, Jeff A. *Inside IRS.* New York: Stein and Day, 1987.

Shabecoff, Philip. "Misconduct in the IRS Is Termed Threat to the Collection of Taxes." *The New York Times*, Dec. 9, 1990, Sec. I, 36:5.

Sloane, Leonard. "Home Offices: Tough, Not Impossible." *The New York Times*, Feb. 28, 1993, Sec. F, 20:1.

Smith, Marguerite T. "Who Cheats on Their Income Taxes." *Money*, April 1991, pp. 101–108.

Social Security Administration/IRS Reporter. "Market Segment Specialization in the Examination Division," Summer 1995, p. 2; "Market Segment Understanding Program Provides Guidelines," Fall 1995, p. 2.

Standard Federal Tax Reporter, CCH Comments. March 21, 1996, Sec. 79.354 and Sec. 79.355, pp. 48,725–726; Feb. 29, 1996, Sec. 79.340, p. 48,717; July 13, 1996, Sec. 79.623, p. 48,810; Aug. 1, 1996, p. 4.

Stern, Philip M. *The Best Congress Money Can Buy.* New York: Pantheon, 1988.

———. *The Rape of the Taxpayer.* New York: Random House, 1972.

Steuerle, Eugene C. *Who Should Pay for Collecting Taxes?* Washington, D.C.: American Institute for Public Policy Research, 1986.

Strassels, Paul N., with Robert Wool. *All You Need to Know About the IRS: A Taxpayer's Guide.* New York: Random House, 1979.

Tax Hotline. David Ellis and James Glass, eds. Published by Boardroom Reports, Inc., New York, N.Y. February 1992. See "Self-audits."

Tax Savings Report. "IRS Fraud Efforts Were Successful" ("Economic Reality"), July/August 1995, p. 10.

Ueshiba, Kisshomaru. *The Spirit of Aikido.* Tokyo: Kodansha International, 1984.

U.S. Congress. House Committee on Government Operations. *A Citizen's Guide on Using the Freedom of Information Act and the Privacy Act of*

1974 to Request Government Records. Fourth Report. House Report 102-146. Washington, D.C.: GPO, 1991.

U.S. Congress. *The Public Statutes at Large of the United States of America from the Organization of the Government in 1789 to March 3, 1845*. Ed. Richard Peters. Vol. 1. Boston: Charles C. Little and James Brown, 1850.

Wald, Matthew L. "The Latest Pitch: 1040PC and the Promise of a Speedy Refund." *The New York Times*, Feb. 28, 1993, "Your Taxes," 17:1.

Walker, Jack L. *Mobilizing Interest Groups in America: Patrons, Professions, and Social Movements*. Ann Arbor: University of Michigan Press, 1991.

Waltman, Jerold L. *Political Origins of the U.S. Income Tax*. Jackson, Miss.: University Press of Mississippi, 1985.

The Washington Post. "Computer Problems Taxing IRS," March 15, 1996, 1:5.

Weiner, Alan E. *All About Limited Liability Companies & Partnerships*. Melville, N.Y.: Holtz Rubenstein & Co., 1994.

Wines, Michael. "A Plan to Catch Tax Cheats in a Blizzard of Paperwork." *The New York Times*, June 21, 1993, Sec. A, 4:1.

Witnah, Donald R., ed. *The Greenwood Encyclopedia of American Institutions*. S.V. "Government Agencies." Westport, Conn. and London: Greenwood Press, 1983.

Zorack, John L. *The Lobbying Handbook*. Washington, D.C.: Professional Lobbying and Consulting Center, 1990.

INDEX

INDEX

413

ABOUT THE AUTHORS

MARTIN KAPLAN has been a certified public accountant for over thirty years. For over twenty years, Mr. Kaplan has operated his own New York City public-accounting firm, whose clients include wholesalers, manufacturers, and service industries. The firm performs audit and accounting work but focuses its attention on the tax-planning opportunities available to its clients and on representation in IRS matters.

NAOMI WEISS writes fiction and nonfiction on a broad range of subjects. As president of her own firm, she also writes and produces marketing and communications materials for clients, from small businesses to multinationals. She has received awards from the National Council of Family Relations, the International Association of Business Communicators, and the Art Directors Club.